Oscar® Fever

OSCAR®
FEVER

*The History and Politics
of the Academy Awards*

EMANUEL LEVY

Continuum
New York   London

2001

The Continuum International Publishing Group Inc
370 Lexington Avenue, New York, NY 10017

The Continuum International Publishing Group Ltd
The Tower Building, 11 York Road, London SE1 7NX

Printed in the United States of America

Library of Congress Cataloging-in-Publication Data

Levy, Emanuel
    Oscar Fever: the history and politics of the Academy Awards / Emanuel Levy.
        p. cm.
    Rev. ed. of: And the winner is—.
    Includes index.
    ISBN 0-8264-1284-X (alk. paper)
        1. Academy Awards (Motion pictures) I. Levy, Emanuel-And the winner is—. II. Title.
    PN1993.92.L48 2001

    791.43'079—dc21   00-047427

Photographs are courtesy of The Museum of Modern Art/Film Stills Archive, 11 West 53rd Street, New York City, except *Shakespeare in Love, Titanic,* and *American Beauty,* courtesy Margaret Herrick Library, Academy Foundation.

For Rob Remley

And in memory of Nathan Waterman

Contents

Acknowledgments

My interest in studying the Oscar Awards in a systematic way began in 1977, when I was first asked to teach a course on popular culture at Hunter College in New York City. But my interest in the Oscar as a uniquely American spectacle goes back much further, to my childhood in Israel. Television was introduced to the Israeli public rather late, in 1967, and even then in limited dosage. There was one channel that broadcast only several hours per evening. Hence, movies were—and in many ways still are—the primary medium of entertainment.

My parents were both avid moviegoers. My father, a womanizer, loved beautiful women, on-screen and off; his favorites in the 1950s were Ava Gardner and Susan Hayward. But he also loved John Wayne and Gary Cooper Westerns, Hitchcock thrillers, screwball comedies, and crime-gangster pictures, so my movie education was pretty well-rounded.

As a research site and a symbol that captures the essence of the American Dream, I couldn't have found a more appropriate topic for my concerns than the Oscar Award, which was established by the Academy of Motion Picture Arts and Sciences in 1927. I have always been amazed by the immense popularity of the annual Oscar show and thought that exploring this subject from sociocultural and historical points of view would be of great interest—and tremendous fun too. It was.

Several of my books, *John Wayne: Prophet of the American Way of Life*, *Small-Town America in Film*, and *Cinema of Outsiders: The Rise of American Independent Film* deal with uniquely American phenomena. *Oscar Fever: The History and Politics of the Oscar Awards* adds another panel to what has emerged as a rather coherent research agenda, representing twenty-five years of teaching and writing about film. Singly and jointly, these books also indicate various phases of my assimilation into American culture, first as an outsider and then as an insider, particularly after I became a full-time film critic.

I began to collect data on the Oscars in 1981, which resulted in the first edition of this book in 1987, *And the Winner Is: The History and Politics of the Academy Awards*, a very different chronicle in both format and style from *Oscar Fever*. My determination to be thorough and comprehensive forced me to go back to the very beginnings, the establishment of the Academy of Motion Picture Arts and Sciences, also in 1927, the year in which the first talkie was released. I soon realized that due to limitations of time, budget, and space, the book would have to focus on the important award categories: Best Picture, Best Director, the four acting, and the two writing awards.

The present book, *Oscar Fever*, is not a chronological, year-by-year, history of the Oscars. Rather, it provides a view of the historical, cultural, and political contexts within which specific films and filmmakers have been nominated and have won the Award over the past seventy-two years.

Many friends and colleagues have read and commented on earlier drafts of this book or on papers presented in various conferences. I would like to thank Judith Blau, Herman Enzer, Gary Alan Fine, Wendy Griswold, Edward Johnson, Rob Remley, Pamela J. Riley, Yaffa Schlesinger, Bill Shepard, and Andrea Walsh for providing helpful comments. I have benefited immensely from conversations about film and popular culture with two of my professors and friends at Columbia University, Sigmund Diamond and Allan Silver. This book owes an intellectual debt to my teacher Harriet A. Zuckerman, whose excellent study of the Nobel Prize contributed to the way I formulated significant research problems about the Oscar. The application of the cumulative advantage theory to the film world is based on my teacher Robert K. Merton's influential ideas on the sociology of science.

During the past twenty-five years, I have shown numerous Oscar-winning and Oscar-nominated films to my students at City University of New York, Columbia University, Wellesley College, UCLA, and ASU. These students have contributed immeasurably to my evolution as a scholar-critic by incessantly challenging my ideas about the intricate links between film, popular culture, and society. Their sincere, often spontaneous remarks have continued to make the teaching of film a stimulating and rewarding enterprise.

The collection of data for the book took place in several libraries. I would like to thank the personnel of the Margaret Herrick Library of the Academy of Motion Picture Arts and Sciences, particularly Linda Mehr and Sondra Archer; the Lincoln Center Library for the Performing Arts, and the libraries of the AFI, the Museum of Modern Art, UCLA, and USC. My special thanks to Mr. Bruce Davis, the Executive Administrator of the Academy, for the useful information he provided, and to Mary Corliss and Terry Geesken of MoMA's Film Stills Archive for their patient guidance in selecting pictures for this book.

I am grateful to Dr. Thomas Keil, the Dean of Arts and Sciences at ASU West, for providing financial support for my film research. I would like to single out the work of two assistants, Lauren Caputo and particularly Beth A. Mooney, who helped in gathering information, library work, and typing appendixes and other materials for the book.

It gives me great pleasure to thank Evander Lomke of Continuum International for the interest he has shown in my film work and for improving the manuscript.

Finally, *Oscar Fever* could not have been written without the continuous support of two close friends, Nathan Waterman and particularly (again) Rob Remley. No writer could ever hope for a more inspirational and blissful encouragement than that provided by Rob. His meticulous criticism and high standards have contributed immeasurably to the depth, clarity, and quality of my writing over the past two decades.

Although I am trained as an academic, for *Oscar Fever*, I opted for a popular style that reduces scholarly jargon to a minimum. This book aims to reach educated people all over the world who go to the movies and are interested in knowing more about Hollywood and the Oscar Awards. It is my hope that *Oscar Fever* will increase an understanding of the various facets of the Oscar Awards and will also serve as a valuable guide for filmmakers, teachers, students, and viewers who want to know more about the history and politics of American movies.

EMANUEL LEVY
Los Angeles
November 2000

CHAPTER 1

The Greatest Show on Earth

Nothing denotes success so visibly and tangibly as the Oscars.
> —*British Observer*

The Oscar show is the most closely scrutinized and most widely watched entertainment event on global television.
> —*Andrew Sarris, film critic*

Aside from the campaign for President, the Oscar derby is America's most contentious horse race.
> —*Richard Corliss, film critic*

I watch it every year with my popcorn and my kids, but mostly I look at what people are wearing.
> —*Mare Winningham,*
> *Oscar-nominated actress*

When people see the label ACADEMY AWARD WINNER, they go to see that movie.
> —*Martin Scorsese,*
> *Oscar-nominated filmmaker*

The Oscar show is Hollywood's orgy of self-congratulation.
> —*anonymous executive*

The Oscar show is the Super Bowl of awards
> —*Louis J. Horvitz,*
> *director of the Oscarcast*

Why Do We Watch the Oscar Awards Show?

These quotes highlight different dimensions of the Oscar Awards and the Oscar show. Recently, there has been so much hoopla about the Oscars that between January and March, the whole country seems to be talking about Oscar-related scandals, issues, and controversies. In 2000, the deadline to turn in ballots to the Price/Waterhouse/Coopers offices was extended by two days when new ballots were mailed out to replace wayward ones that had been lost in the mail—about four thousand ballots were mistakenly diverted to another location.

There was another scandal: fifty-five Oscar statuettes were stolen. A few days later, fifty-two of them were rescued by Willie Fulger, who rebuilds car parts. Three were still missing. Fulger, who found the missing Oscars in a trash bin, was promised a fifty-thousand-dollar reward. Interestingly, Fulger called the media before notifying the police and, sure enough, he became an instant hero. Later, the police arrested two suspects (Anthony Keith Hart and Lawrence Edward Ledent) in connection with the theft; both men worked for Roadway Express, which had shipped the Oscars. Oscar host Billy Crystal was handed a ready-made issue that screamed for jokes, and he used the opportunity well.

Another potentially embarrassing disgrace almost occurred when the Academy confirmed that Robin Williams would croon "Blame Canada," the Best Song nominee from the rowdy and profane comedy, *South Park: Bigger, Longer & Uncut.* The tune's raunchy lyrics caused some consternation and gave the show's producers a workout. Without giving specifics, producers Richard and Lili Fini Zanuck gave assurances that audiences would be OK with the presentation. Earlier that evening, Trey Parker, who co-wrote the song with composer Marc Shaiman, arrived at the ceremonies dressed in a copy of Jennifer Lopez's green tropical-print, low-cut outfit that she had worn for the Emmys.

If you think the Oscar Award is mostly about prestige and symbolic value, you're wrong. The statuettes themselves have become a hot commercial item in public auctions and private transactions. In 1950, the Academy began to require recipients to offer the Oscar back to the Academy before selling it. Oscar Nominees are now required to sign a written agreement to this effect before the ceremonies take place.

It all began with the publicity for Vivien Leigh's 1939 Oscar (for *Gone With the Wind),* which was sold at Sotheby's for a then record-breaking $510,000. Since that time, dozens of Oscars have been sold, most of them in the 1990s. Producer Sid Luft was barred by a 1993 Academy-solicited court order from selling ex-wife Judy Garland's 1958 Oscar, which was a replacement for the one she had received as a juvenile at the 1940 ceremony, and subsequently lost.

Which takes us back to the Oscar show itself. The Oscars can be described as part variety show, part news event, part horse race, part fashion display—and all promotion. In 1999, *Premiere* magazine wrote: "Like everything else in Hollywood, the Oscar show is a big production surrounded by gushes of hype and hoopla, climaxing with a showbiz extravaganza, and ending with more bucks spent at the box-office."

A long production process begins in December and moves into high gear after the nominations are announced in early February. The countdown to Oscar night, known in the industry as Super Sunday, begins as soon as the nominations are made. The top candidates, from the frontrunners to the underdogs, begin to flood the airwaves with ads, tearing their opponents' campaign tactics to shreds.

One of the great qualities of the Oscar show is that each event reflects its era in its own fashion. "They reflect America," said Gilbert Cates, who has produced the show for years. "Look at the Oscar show from 1960, and you learn something about American society in 1960."

The challenge to produce a show that would combine the best of film and television is obviously not easy to meet. The producers feel that the spectacle should be much more than a tribute to film, that it should also be a thrilling television show in its own right, because the ceremonies are watched by people who are not moviegoers. Indeed, the Oscar *Show* is, ultimately, more important than the Oscar Awards.

The show is an important spectacle because, as John O'Connor observed in the *New York Times,* "The viewer gets not only the event, but also the overall television context." One can add to O'Connor's observation that the viewer gets not only the television context but also the overall cultural context. The Oscar show itself has become an integral part of American pop culture, functioning as an annual symbolic ritual with a long, seventy-two year tradition.

On a few occasions only, the Oscar ceremonies were postponed, though never canceled. The first disturbance occurred in 1938, when heavy floods delayed the show by one week. In 1967, a national network strike threatened the telecast, which, among other things, meant a substantial loss of money. However, the board of directors decided to keep the ceremonies on schedule, with or without television. Fortunately, the strike was settled a few hours before the April 10 show was to begin.

The second delay, by two days, occurred in 1968, when Martin Luther King Jr. was assassinated. Academy President Gregory Peck felt that "postponement was the only appropriate gesture of respect," a feeling that was embraced by the entire industry. In 1981, the ceremonies were delayed by twenty-four hours due to the assassination attempt on President Ronald Reagan the very day of the scheduled event, March 30. Ironically, the Oscar show was going to begin with a pre-taped greeting from the President. Emcee Johnny Carson commented on the occasion, "Because of the incredible events of yesterday, that old adage, the show must go on, seemed relatively unimportant." But the show did go on—only a day later—signaling the importance of the Oscar as a sacred ritual in American culture.

The unpredictability of the Oscar show is another critical quality. The show is live—"that's what makes it a white-knuckler," Stefan Kanter, one of the event's writers, noted. "You can't make people stick to the script. . . . You can't plan a thing like Jack Palance's one-armed push-ups, but you can take advantage of it in a series of running gags so perfect you might have thought the whole thing was rigged." The writers are sitting backstage with the host and they continue to write and modify jokes while the event is in progress, taking advantage of every gesture.

The unpredictability also extends to the choice of winners. Some feel that when it comes to Oscar, the only sure bet is that there are no sure bets. Surprises are the kind of events that keep the Oscar show quirky and exciting. A dark horse emerges almost every year in one of the major categories. In the 1976 race, the buzz focused on the two Best Picture contenders, *Network* and *All the President's Men,* but the Oscar winner was *Rocky.* In 1981, the talk was high on *Reds* and *On Golden Pond,* but the Oscar went to British import *Chariots of Fire.* In 1989, *My Left Foot,* another low-budget British import, about paraplegic artist-writer Christy Brown, became the dark horse after winning Best Picture from the New York Film Critics. In 1991, Jonathan Demme won the Directors Guild Award for *The Silence of the Lambs,* which, coming just before the Oscar, was a strong indicator for the Oscar's Best Director and Best Picture.

"You have to keep it interesting," said Miramax's Harvey Weinstein while campaigning for *The Piano* in 1993. "No one wants to be told by the media that the whole thing is wrapped up." Despite predictions that *Schindler's List* would sweep the Oscars, Miramax's point was to remind that "we're still here, that the race isn't over." In the same year, the Spanish entry, Fernando Trueba's comedy *La Belle Epoque* upset the expected winner, Chan Kaige's *Farewell, My Concubine,* submitted by Hong Kong. In 1995, too, the Best Picture race was wide-open, unlike years in which there were clear front-runners, such as *Schindler's List* in 1993, or *Forrest Gump* in 1994.

Year after year, the Oscar show is criticized on various grounds. Critics have long had a field day with the program. The usual rap on the Oscars is that it is too long and too boring, and that there are too many participants. Oscar winners are reproached for "wasting" too much time in thanking all of their families in their speeches. But every March, even Hollywood's biggest cynics fall for the annual glitter parade. As one critic noted: "We all tune in despite the grotesqueness of watching an entire industry congratulate itself on the pretenses that it's still an art form."

Some keep watching the show with condescension. No one has ever accused the Academy voters of displaying exquisite taste or radical sympathies—after all, Chaplin and Garbo never won a competitive Oscar. As Andrew Sarris noted: "The Oscars have fascinated me purely as a betting proposition. I enjoy matching my wits and presumed expertise against those of my colleagues, friends, students, and readers." But despite criticism, according to one study, 66 percent of the viewers enjoyed the show, 20 percent didn't, and 12 percent had no opinion. The two prime motives for watching the show were "to find out the winners," and "to see the celebrities."

The appearance of a celebrity who has been out of the public eye for a while has always elevated the show. In 1961, fans mobbed the entrance to the Santa Monica auditorium to catch a glimpse of the convalescing Liz Taylor, who was nominated for *Butterfield 8*. After accepting the Best Actress Oscar from Yul Brynner, Taylor walked to a backstage bathroom and fainted. The same show witnessed another emotional moment. Gary Cooper, dying of cancer in a hospital, received a special Oscar from his friend Jimmy Stewart. "We're all very proud of you," Stewart said with tears in his eyes. The beloved Cooper died on May 13, 1961, barely a month after the ceremony.

In 2000, Jane Fonda fit the bill of a celeb returning to the show. Recently estranged from Ted Turner, Fonda made a grand comeback to Hollywood after a decade of retirement, as presenter of the Honorary Oscar to Polish filmmaker Andrzej Wajda. It was Fonda's fourth time as participant since she was first nominated for *They Shoot Horses, Don't They?*, thirty-one years ago.

The Awards Ceremonies

The Oscar show is a truly global event, testified to by the extensive media coverage it generates. Indeed, no matter how one looks at it, the fact that once a year, the attention of the global community is focused on film and that people think and talk about the *same films* at the *same time* is an amazing achievement. Few media events can boast such an international dimension.

Most people relate to the Oscar Awards and to the Oscar show inter-changeably. For them, the Academy's raison d'etre is to bestow the Oscars. The Academy is deemed an organization that "comes to life" once a year for the "Oscar season." Few are aware of the Academy's other functions, such as preserving and restoring motion pictures, donating grants to vari-ous organizations, or providing fellowships to young screenwriters.

How did the Oscars become such a global media event?

When the Academy was founded in 1927, its purpose was to "establish the industry in the public mind as a respectable, legitimate institution, and its people as reputable individuals." The Oscars were originally designed as a local gesture by the Hollywood industry to honor film achievements. They were an afterthought on the Academy's agenda, barely mentioned in the 1927 statement of goals: "The Academy will encourage the improvement and advancement of the arts and sciences of the profession by the inter-change of constructive ideas and by awards of merit for distinctive achieve-ments." MGM's Louis B. Mayer, the Academy's chief architect, explained: "The awards have a dual purpose. To recognize fine achievements and to inspire others to give finer achievements tomorrow."

The initial idea was to bestow the awards in either an open meeting or a dinner. The board decided in favor of a dinner, a format that prevailed for the next seventeen years. Guests of the first Oscar ceremonies, on May 16, 1929, dined on jumbo squab perigeaux, lobster Eugenie, Los Angeles salad, terrapin, and fruit supreme at the Blossom Room of the Roosevelt Hotel. In 1944, due to the war situation, this practice seemed too conspic-uously luxurious and the banquet was discontinued; the Academy has always been sensitive to public opinion. But there was also a pragmatic rea-son: the membership had expanded so much that it was impossible to accommodate all members and their guests for dinner.

Veteran members are still shocked by the attention accorded to the Oscars. "It was just a small group getting together for a pat on the back," Janet Gaynor, the first Best Actress winner, recalled. In the first years, the banquet resembled an intimate "family affair," with not much radio or press coverage.

Sidney Kent, then Fox's President, was the one to propose the use of radio "to sell our pictures," an idea that was immediately and wholeheartedly accepted by the studios. Consequently, the third annual banquet, on April 3, 1931, was broadcast on radio over the KNX Station. However, for the next fifteen years, only a portion of the show was broadcast. The entire ceremonies were broadcast for the first time on March 15, 1945, over the ABC Network and the Armed Forces Radio Service. This signaled the beginning of what members would later describe as the Oscars' getting out of control.

The dramatic increase in the Oscar's public profile baffled the Academy. In 1940, the board of directors felt a need to issue the following statement: "Somewhat to the embarrassment of the traditional dignity of the Academy, the words 'Oscar' and 'Academy Awards' have slipped into the popular language like 'Sterling' and 'Nobel,' as recognized symbols of quality." The board was unaware that in a few years the Oscar would stand for something both more and less than "recognized symbols of quality."

The Oscars gradually received the endorsement and support of all segments of society, including the power elite. In 1941, Franklin D. Roosevelt became the first president to address the motion picture industry via radio. President Harry S. Truman followed in his footsteps, when in 1949 he sent a congratulatory message to the Academy. In 1981, President Ronald Reagan, a former Hollywood B-actor, participated actively in the proceedings via a pre-taped one-minute greeting.

The board continued to remind the public that the Academy was conceived as "an honorary association," whose "prime object is to advance the arts and sciences of motion pictures and to foster cooperation among the creative leadership of the industry for cultural, educational, and technological progress." The Academy would not let the public forget its many aims and purposes aside from "recognizing outstanding achievements." These functions included conducting cooperative research; providing common meeting grounds for the various film arts and crafts; serving as an impartial clearing house of records and statistics; cooperating in educational activities between the public and the film industry.

Needless to say, the Academy didn't fulfill all of these functions, and it is doubtful whether the awards have contributed "to raising the standard of production," as intended. But the Academy was successful in elevating the status of film among the arts, which was one of its goals, and in popularizing the Oscar Award, a function that was unintentional and unanticipated.

Over the years, the Academy has resisted the charge that it has become a commercial tool and a monetary spectacle. It has insisted that the Oscar was first and foremost "a merit award" designed to honor excellence, not to promote films' commerciality. However, in weak moments, members have conceded that "some awards have been given to commercial successes," but they also pointed out that "awards have also been given to commercial failures." For them, the winning films have always represented worthy attainments, regardless of how well they did at the box office. Nonetheless, once the Academy became aware of Oscar's influence, the tendency to shower mediocre films with multiple nominations and awards in order to boost their commercial standing became more prevalent.

The Academy actively promoted its self-image as a standard-setter that "reminds the public of worthy achievements," and "calls the attention of millions to the significance of motion pictures as a fine art as well as popular entertainment." The members wished to believe that the Academy functioned as "a constant incentive" for better work and as a stimulus "for hundreds of millions of people to think and to talk about the best in motion pictures."

In addition to bestowing awards, the Academy fulfills other, less publicized functions. It publishes "The Players Directory," a major casting tool with lists of actors and actresses. Another important publication is "The Screen Achievement Records Bulletin," which serves as a guide for individuals and organizations, and "Who Wrote the Movie," which enlists screenwriters and screenplays, and is prepared in collaboration with the Writers Guild. Affiliated with the Academy of Motion Pictures is the Academy Foundation, which sponsors educational and cultural activities, including scholarship programs, student film awards, and film preservation.

Funding for the ceremonies initially came from the studios which, for obvious reasons, had a vested interest in supporting the awards. In 1949, however, some of the major companies refused to underwrite the costs, even though the amount of money needed, about twenty thousand dollars, was shockingly minuscule. The decision to discontinue the support was conveyed to the Academy in December 1948, before the announcement of the year's nominations, which favored several British movies, *Hamlet* and *The Red Shoes,* over American ones.

Jean Hersholt, the Academy's president, explained that the moguls didn't want "Academy standards foisted upon them," and that they favor the making of "commercial pictures unhampered by consideration of artistic excellence." And while Hersholt saw in the studios' decision "the highest praise for our organization," he was upset that MGM, Paramount, Fox, and Warner each gave $12,500, whereas Universal, Columbia, and Republic didn't support at all.

In their statement, the studios claimed that their step was not based on commercial reasons, stressing that "the companies as companies were never members of the Academy," which was created as an organization to include only the most accomplished individual artists. Furthermore, they declared, though few believed, that they were "heartily in accord with the principle of individuals democratically selecting the best in artistic achievement," and that "it is in the interest of this principle," that they decided "to remove any suspicion of company influence."

However, *Hamlet*'s winning the 1948 Best Picture, and the multiple awards showered on *The Red Shoes* made it worse. Bosley Crowther wrote in the *New York Times:* "Prides had been wounded by the bombshell bestowal of the Academy upon *Hamlet,* making the timing of the studios' exposé sound like very sour grapes." The moguls were upset that the Academy favored British art films over what they considered superb American movies. In 1948, John Huston's *The Treasure of the Sierra Madre* was nominated in four categories; Jean Negulesco's *Johnny Belinda* in twelve; and Anatole Litvak's *The Snake Pit,* which was predicted to win Best Picture, received only one minor award (sound recording) out of six nominations. The studios denied—to no avail—any link between their decision and the prominence of British films. The British winners, by contrast, were bewildered, to say the least. "I can't believe American companies would do such a thing," said director Emeric Pressburger, and producer Alexander Korda noted, "I'm sure Americans are too generous for any ill-feeling to arise."

But the studios' withdrawal of support and the separation of the Oscar from the major production companies was seen by many as a positive move, hoping that the members would now be freer to vote. In the past, there was pressure by the studios on their employees to vote for their own pictures and personnel (see chapter 14). Emmet Lavery expressed that feeling in the *Saturday Review:*

> So we come now, in the twenty-first year of the Academy's existence, to the parting of the ways between the major Hollywood studios and the Academy as co-sponsors of the annual awards program. And a happy parting it is. The only cause for wonderment is that it did not happen sooner, preferably at the very beginning of the Academy's existence. This does not mean the end of the Academy. On the contrary, it means an expansion and development on a completely independent level. There can now be little question that the annual awards are the free choice of the 1800 members. This is the moment, and a very good moment, when Oscar comes into his own. At the ripe old age of 21, Oscar has shown that he is free to vote as he chooses.

For three years, from 1949 to 1951, radio commercials, increased annual dues, and a fund drive barely managed to finance the Oscar ceremonies. In 1952, a turning point occurred: television, Hollywood's and the studios' long-time enemy, came to the rescue in a move that was totally unexpected. In the past, the studios either prohibited or restricted the appearances of their movie stars on television, so intense was the animosity between the two media. But the new cooperation was mutually beneficial:

television needed stars, as it had not yet developed its own performers, and the Academy was desperate for funds to cover the show's rapidly escalating costs.

The Oscar Telecast

RCA Victor sponsored the 1952 awards ceremony and NBC televised it. The date was appropriate: Oscar was celebrating its twenty-fifth anniversary. A new era had begun.

Simultaneous ceremonies took place in New York and Los Angeles from 1953 to 1956, with the viewers switched back and forth, depending on the winners' location; this practice was discontinued in 1957. The ceremonies were televised in black and white, but in 1967, the show was telecast in color, which contributed even more to its popularity. American households that could not afford to buy a television set were not dropped. Simultaneous broadcasts on radio and TV prevailed as late as 1969, when the Academy realized that few people listened to the ceremonies on radio. By then, television had long become established as the dominant medium of entertainment in American culture.

The show's public grew rapidly: In 1948, an unprecedented audience of over fifty million listened to the proceedings, when ABC beamed the event to all its national affiliates and the Armed Forces Radio Service broadcast to American soldiers overseas. A decade later, in 1959, the audiences doubled: eighty million Americans watched the show on television or listened to it on the radio, and another hundred million people were reached overseas, also via radio.

The dramatic increase in audiences had a direct impact on the amount of money paid for the TV rights. In 1952, the rights were purchased for a hundred thousand dollars, and in 1964, they jumped to a million. No one could have predicted that in a few decades, the Oscar telecast would become the jewel in the Academy's crown. At present, the Academy's financial well-being rests on the Oscar. ABC is paying the Academy thirty-seven million dollars for broadcast rights to the Sunday-night event, under a new contract that runs through 2008. In 1999, after clearing all expenses, the Academy generated an Oscar-night profit of well above fifteen million dollars.

The Oscar ceremonies used to take place on a Monday night, with a dress rehearsal on the preceding Sunday. In 1999, they were moved to Sunday evening, which seemed to be a more satisfying format. The Academy produces its own telecast as a way of ensuring quality. "This way we can control our fortunes," President Robert Rehme told *Variety.* "We control everything, down to the number of commercials on the show. We look at every commercial and pass on the content. We want to protect the Oscar and the Academy as our brand."

ABC, which has the television contract for the show, takes advantage of this extraordinary exposure. Rates for ads during the 1997 Oscar telecast, which sold out last summer, climbed 5 percent over 1996, amounting to $835,000 per thirty seconds. In 1998, ABC charged a million dollars for each of the fifty-eight commercials spots slated to break up the four-hour-show adding up to a record-breaking dollar amount. In 2000, the Academy broke the seven-figure barrier for a thirty-second Oscar broadcast ad. Despite recurrent criticism of the show's format and length, most people realize that without television, which pays for all the preparations and work involved, the ceremonies would have been impossible.

Special attempts are made to produce an elegant show. The late Edith Head, Hollywood's best-known costume designer, herself a winner of numerous Oscars, served as the Academy's consultant for decades. The fashion aspect of the show has increased over the last decade: audiences now expect to see the latest trends in haute couture. For director Joel Schumacher, Oscar night draws millions of fans, because "it means glamour, glamour, glamour, just as the Super Bowl means fun, fun, fun."

Who can forget Cher's notorious appearance as a presenter in the 1986 show? Or her remark, "As you can see, I did receive my Academy booklet on how to dress like a serious actress"? People still talk about Angelina Jolie's appearance in the 2000 show, wearing a black Versace gown, looking like Morticia with her dyed-black long hair and skull ring, which *Entertainment Weekly* labeled "Oscar's latest glimpse of Gothic."

There are about forty slots available for presenters, who get no pay, but receive great publicity—when it comes to the Oscars, no adage is more appropriate than "you can't buy this kind of publicity." Political correctness is exercised, with producers trying to satisfy age, race, and sex quotas. Presenters must meet at least one requirement: they must be stars who can help generate good ratings. They must be newsworthy types who have won Oscars in the past and may win again that night. For the women, they must be celebs who are sure to make some kind of fashion statement, preferably like Cher's.

Using its old competitor, TV, the Academy tries to put on an entertaining show. The goal is to have exciting ceremonies, which depends on the intensity of the competition and potential winners, as well as on having a well-staged television show. It took several years for the show to evolve. In 1955, a reporter noted that, for the first time, "every word, every motion was designed for the camera. No more was the glittering festival a self-conscious performance with television's cameras guiltily watching what they could. Oscar has broken the twenty-five-year shroud of dignity, dullness, and routines for its sprightly marriage partner, television."

Popular figures such as movie star Will Rogers, humorist Irving S. Cobb, and comedian Jack Benny were among the show's hosts. But the emcee most closely identified with the ceremonies is comedian Bob Hope, serving as host twenty-two times, nine of which were solo performances. Hope was the perfect choice for the job: he was a popular movie-star, especially in his "Road Movies" with Bing Crosby. But Hope was much more than a star—he was an American *institution,* having entertained American soldiers in World War II, Korea, and Vietnam. Critic Walter Kerr once described Hope as "Oscar's Constant Uncle."

Johnny Carson, of NBC's "The Tonight Show," was a host for a few years. Unlike Bob Hope, Carson was uniquely a television creation, a genuine star of the small screen, though his popularity extends beyond television. Carson didn't last long as host: in 1984, the Oscar show changed into a multihost format. For the fifty-eighth ceremonies, there were three hosts, Jane Fonda, Alan Alda, and Robin Williams, all familiar faces on both film and television. The idea, of course, was to appeal to audiences of both screens.

The show continues to be popular—with an average rating of 35.0, and in many years even higher—regardless of its quality and production values. One of the most popular Oscar shows was in 1970, with an all-time record of 43.4 rating, attributable to the anticipation of John Wayne winning Best Actor, which he did. By contrast, the 1969 show had an average rating of 31.8, ranking as one of the least popular ceremonies. In the 1970s, the rating of the Oscar show ranged from 38.7 in 1972 to 34.6 in 1979.

Emcee Carson described the 1979 show as "two hours of sparkling entertainment spread over four hours." This was an understatement, compared to the dullness of the 1983 show, which the *New York Times's* Vincent Canby compared to "taking an extremely slow Seventh Avenue Local to heaven in a very long and over-crowded ride, and the arrival—by which time one is exhausted—is always a bit of an anticlimax." For Canby, the show's atmosphere is defined by "the solemnity of the annual Nobel ceremonies in Stockholm with the cheerful bad taste of the grand opening of a shopping center in Los Angeles."

The 1984 Oscar show, broadcast on April 9, captured an impressive audience with an average rating of 36.0. The other two networks did poorly that night: CBS got a 7.3 rating and NBC 7.2. The show itself was one of the longest, running three hours and forty-five minutes, which prompted Johnny Carson to depict is as a fund-raising gala on public television. "OK folks," Carson said, "we're into our fourth hour, let's check the tote boards and see how much money we've raised."

Nostalgia has become a key theme of Oscar shows. The 1985 show paid tribute to film achievements of 1934 and audiences were treated to clips of Shirley Temple, who later appeared in person, spectacular dancing by Fred Astaire and Ginger Rogers, and images from the 1934 Best Picture, Frank Capra's *It Happened One Night.* Director Capra later presented the Best Picture Oscar. The homage to Hollywood's glorious past came as a response to criticism that the show has become too much of a television spectacle. In the 1980s, many of the presenters were young performers who had little to do with movies, but whose popularity among television viewers was the reason for their standing on the Oscar platform.

In 1986, China, India, and France received a live telecast for the first time—emcee Robin Williams translated salutations to native languages. Choosing Williams as host proved to be fortuitous, as he provided the funniest moments with a quirky sense of humor. Appearing with two Price and Waterhouse representatives, carrying the winners' names in briefcases, he suggested to "open up the suckers right now." Rejected, the comedian told the public, "I'm afraid we have to do this show." Williams's one-liners were so fast that there was no time to be offended by them, as Jack Valenti could have been, when he was introduced as "the man you never heard of but you have to listen to anyway."

A tribute to MGM musicals, featuring its surviving female stars, Jane Powell, Cyd Charisse, June Allyson, Leslie Caron, Kathryn Grayson, Marge Champion, Anne Miller, and Esther Williams made up for the show's nostalgic highlight. Gene Kelly, Debbie Reynolds, and Donald O'Connor, who presented the music award, reprised their classic number from *Singin' in the Rain.*

There was another touching gesture when all the nominees were asked to stand up and were applauded as a group. Celebrating Old Hollywood was also the theme of "hymn to the losers," sung by Irene Cara and accompanied by clips from films which have been nominated for, but did not win, Best Picture, including *The Wizard of Oz, Citizen Kane, Sunset Boulevard,* and *Tootsie.* Stanley Donen, who produced the Oscar show, copped it by asking Billy Wilder, John Huston, and Akira Kurosawa to present the Best Picture.

In 1987, the Academy nominations were announced live on national television for the first time. Oscar winners Anjelica Huston and Don Ameche joined Academy president Robert Wise as hosts of the pre-dawn show, scheduled at 5:30 A.M. to accommodate the New York-based network morning shows.

In 1989, the phrase, "And the Oscar goes to," replaced "And the winner is," in an attempt to spare the feeling of the losers, or, as the Academy prefers to call them, "non-winners."

In the 1991 Oscar show, Billy Crystal made a colorful entrance with a horse, a plug for his upcoming summer movie, *City Slickers,* in which he played a New York yuppie who goes to a dude ranch. In the same show, Madonna's off-key, shake-your-bootie rendition of "Sooner or Later I Always Get My Man," Stephen Sondheim's Oscar-winning song from *Dick Tracy,* drew attention. "It's the NC-17 portion of our show," Crystal quipped. Another of the show's highlights was Michael Blake's acceptance speech for the script *Dances With Wolves.* Blake was accompanied By Doris Leader Charge, who translated his words into a Native American language.

This sixty-third Oscar show celebrated the centennial of motion pictures with an impressive kickoff. Actor Michael Caine, stationed in Paris at the Hotel Scribe, where the first films were exhibited, gave the order for the projector to start for an 1891 audience, which spilled out of the room (in a technological whizbang) onto the Shrine Auditorium stage for a classy opening production number choreographed by Debbie Allen.

In 1992, Crystal rode bareback on a twenty foot Oscar statuette that Oscar-winner Jack Palance dragged in by his teeth to open the show. Palance, who won supporting Oscar for *City Slickers,* then inexplicably dropped to the stage for one-armed push-ups, a gesture that became the most-remarked about Oscar bit for years to come.

Actress Whoopi Goldberg made her debut as host in 1994, replacing Billy Crystal, thus becoming the first female—and first black—solo host. Goldberg spiced up the show with some irreverent remarks and made good on her promise not to shy away from politics. People were nervous to see if Whoopi's ad libs would be proper for early evening network television. Buz Kohan, one of the show's writers, rationalized: "When you buy a Whoopi Goldberg, you buy the whole package and part of the package is that she is a free spirit who just might say anything that comes to mind at the moment."

For the 1994 show, film supervisor Douglas M. Stewart gathered clips from nominated pictures and assembled special presentations, one of which was dedicated to famous screen dogs (from Toto in *The Wizard of Oz* to Asta in *The Thin Man* series), and another to actors winking. In the same year, Tom Hanks delivered a lauded acceptance speech after winning Best Actor for *Philadelphia,* thanking his gay high school drama teacher,

Rawley Farnsworth. His remarks, which outed the teacher, would inspire Paul Rudnick to write the comedy *In & Out* with Kevin Kline.

In the 1995 show, the lead winners, Tom Hanks *(Forrest Gump)* and Jessica Lange *(Blue Sky)*, had their kids rooting for them up in the balcony. Before Spielberg announced the Best Director, he addressed a child in the public, "Alex, your father just won the Academy Award." Spielberg was talking to Robert Zemeckis's son, who was sitting on his mother's lap. Actor Christopher Reeve, paralyzed after a horse-riding accident, received a standing ovation when he hosted a segment on movies' power to deal with social issue.

The show has displayed good family values, as when Clint Eastwood brought his elderly mother to the show. When Mira Sorvino won a supporting Oscar for *Mighty Aphrodite,* TV viewers witnessed her father, actor Paul Sorvino, sobbing in the audience. Kirk Douglas's sons were also seen in the audience crying when he was accorded an Honorary Oscar, a compensation for never having won a competitive Oscar and a celebration for his survival of a helicopter accident and a severe stroke.

The 1996 show was dubbed the "year of the indies," because of the prominence of small-budget films made outside mainstream Hollywood, such as *Fargo, Secrets & Lies,* and *Shine.* In response to the indies' being nominated, director Joel Schumacher told the *Los Angeles Times:* "People get more excited when the contest seems to be between people they know and have invested in for years. They don't know who these people are. I hope they find out." Unfortunately, the ratings for the show were rather poor.

In 1996, Whoopi Goldberg was back after David Letterman's fiasco as host the year before. Her friend Quincy Jones, who had co-produced her feature debut, *The Color Purple,* was the show's producer. Nervous due to the mixed reviews for her first hosting, she made her displeasure known during the telecast over satirical skits comparing her to Billy Crystal. Though the Academy Awards were hosted and produced by African Americans, only one black person was nominated in this year. Indeed, there were external pressures on host Whoopi Goldberg. Reverend Jesse Jackson publicly urged African Americans attending the Oscars to wear a rainbow ribbon as a symbol of their opposition to Hollywood's "race exclusion and cultural violence." That year, there was not a single black performer among the twenty acting nominees. However, Jackson's threat to stage a grass-roots protest aimed at the Oscars backfired with the mainstream media.

As always, the most memorable Oscar moments were the small, personal ones, as in 1997, when Cuba Gooding Jr. won supporting Oscar for *Jerry Maguire,* unleashing a long aria of joy. Show director Louis J. Horvitz recalled: "We were standing up in the booth at that point, dreaming of a 40 share of the ratings."

The 1998 show saw the revenge of the majors against the indies, with big pictures like *Titanic* representing a return to Hollywood's tradition of grand cinema. The potential threat of a predictable *Titanic* sweep was not ideal for the show's producers, always hoping for the live, spontaneous moments, the surprises that come with the acceptance speeches. As Horvitz noted: "You hope they're meaty with meaningful words about filmmaking and its contribution to life, and have something more than a long list of thank yous." Nonetheless, for *Titanic*, the Oscar show delivered a 34.9 rating and a 55 share, the highest numbers in fifteen years, as some eighty-seven million Americans tuned in to see at least part of the show.

In 1999, Roberto Benigni stole the show in one of Oscar's indelible moments, akin to Jack Palance's one-armed push-ups, or Sally Field's nakedly vulnerable, "You like me. You really like me!" A bouncing ball of unselfconscious energy, Benigni made his way to the stage to accept Best Foreign-Language Picture for *Life Is Beautiful* by climbing over the backs of chairs and audience members, bunny-hoping up the stairs to stage. This was followed by his emotional "ocean of love" speech.

The first Oscar show of the millennium saw studios and indies, veterans and newcomers, blockbusters and upstarts. As always, the most treasured moments were the small, spontaneous ones, like the winner of the Best Documentary Short, *Defending Our Lives,* who blurted out: "Domestic violence is the leading cause of violence to women in the U.S. Please, we need all your help to stop this."

The 2000 Oscar show was not the condensed kudofest that producers Richard and Lili Zanuck promised. In fact, at four hours and nine minutes, it was one of the longest, exceeding last year's show's running time, four hours and two minutes. But it was also one of the best. Billy Crystal was introduced into a variety of classic scenes from *Taxi Driver, Spartacus, The Graduate, The Godfather,* and *Deliverance*, and another highlight was a medley of movie music that was orchestrated by Burt Bacharach.

In his introductory remarks, Academy president Robert Rehme referred to 1999 as "the least predictable year in Academy history," an apt remark since many Oscar races were wide open. There was head-to-head competition between *American Beauty* and *Cider House Rules*. DreamWorks refused to call *American Beauty* a shoo-in, lest history repeats itself. Last year, their studio's *Saving Private Ryan* was considered to be the easy front-runner, but it lost out to Miramax's *Shakespeare in Love*.

CHAPTER 2

The History of the Oscar Award

The Academy Award is universally nicknamed the Oscar. Various people have claimed credit for the name, though the issue has never been adequately resolved. Actress Bette Davis said that she labeled the Award "Oscar" since it looked like the backside of her then husband, Harmon Oscar Nelson.

Librarian Margaret Herrick, later the Academy's Executive Secretary, reported to her first day of work in 1931. After having been formally introduced to the gold statuette, she looked it over carefully and said it reminded her of her Uncle Oscar (Oscar Pierce was actually her second cousin, not uncle). Columnist Sidney Skolsky was apparently on the scene and he immediately seized on the name and used it in his byline: "Employees have affectionately dubbed their famous statuette 'Oscar.'"

But according to Skolsky, he was the first to use the word Oscar for the following reason: "I got tired of using statuette in my story. I wanted to give the guy a name, not only to make it easier to write about, but to give the thing an identity and a personality. I thought Oscar wouldn't be too dignified a name for a banquet that had so much dignity."

The statuette was designed by MGM's art director Cedric Gibbons and created by sculptor George Stanley. The Oscar Awards were first printed on scroll, then cast in gold. Gibbons sketched a knight standing on a reel of film holding a two-edged sword. Its base represented the Academy's five original branches: producers, writers, directors, actors, and technicians. A minor streamlining of the base is the only addition since the Oscar was created.

The Academy bestows various kinds of Oscars:

The Annual Merit Awards in twenty-three categories

The Scientific or Technical Achievement Awards

The Irving G. Thalberg Award "to a creative producer whose body of work reflects consistently high quality of motion picture productions."

The Jean Hersholt Humanitarian Award "to an individual in the motion picture industry whose humanitarian efforts have brought credit to the industry."

The Gordon E. Sawyer Award "to an individual in the motion picture industry whose technological contributions have brought credit to the industry."

The Honorary Awards "for outstanding achievements not strictly within the other categories, for exceptionally distinguished service in the making of the motion pictures or for outstanding service to the Academy."

The winners of Annual Awards, Class I Scientific or Technical Awards, Special Achievement Awards, and Jean Hersholt Humanitarian Awards receive the Oscar statuette. Class II Scientific winners receive a plaque, and Class III winners a certificate. The Irving G. Thalberg Award is a bronze head of the late distinguished producer. Honorary Awards may be a statuette, scroll, or any design approved by the Board of Governors.

The Oscar statuette is thirteen and a half inches tall and weighs eight and a half pounds. It is gold plated over a composition of 92.5 percent tin and 7.5 percent copper. During World War II, plaster statuettes were awarded as every piece of metal was needed for the war effort. After the war, the Academy went back to the original gold statuettes. The Oscars are awarded to winners without charge; the Academy, however, charges for the sale of duplicates in cases of loss, theft, or disposal.

Every year the Academy orders fifty statuettes from Southern California Trophy, which began producing them in 1930, to make sure there will be no shortage. While only twenty-three categories are honored, there have often been collaborations of two or three artists, particularly in the writing and technical areas, and there are also Honorary Oscars. Shortly after the nominees are announced, a count is made of the maximum number of awards that could conceivably be given.

In the first years, the statuettes were not numbered. In 1949, it was decided to number them, with 501 being chosen as a starting point, even though it is estimated that more than 500 statuettes were awarded in the first two decades.

The Idea for an Academy

The idea for an academy of film emerged under the leadership of Louis B. Mayer, the powerful head of Metro-Goldwyn-Mayer (MGM). On January 11, 1927, Mayer and a group of thirty-six directors and actors met at the Ambassador Hotel in Los Angeles and decided to establish an Academy of Motion Picture Arts and Sciences (AMPAS). On March 19, AMPAS was founded as a nonprofit association, set out to achieve the following goals:

> The Academy will take aggressive action in meeting outside attacks that are unjust.
>
> It will promote harmony and solidarity among the membership and among the different branches.
>
> It will reconcile internal differences that may exist or arise.
>
> It will adopt such ways and means as are proper to further the welfare and protect the honor and good repute of the profession.
>
> It will encourage the improvement and advancement of the arts and sciences of the profession by the interchange of constructive ideas and by awards of merit for distinctive achievements.
>
> It will take steps to develop greater power and influence of the screen.
>
> The Academy proposes to do for the motion picture profession in all its branches what other great national and international bodies have done for other arts and sciences and industries.

Note that in 1927, the bestowal of merit awards was only one, not the most important, goal of the Academy. A prime motive for AMPAS's foundation was the unionization of the industry, in 1926, when nine major studios and five unions signed the Studio Basic Agreement. But this Agreement applied only to technical workers; the creative groups, directors, writers, actors, still lacked standardized contracts. In its first years, the Academy regarded itself as a labor organization that represented the interests of all talent groups. As such, it was neither limited to the production studios nor to any particular creative group. Another goal was to create a forum in which artists of various expertise would exchange ideas. However, since the studios were instrumental in creating the Academy, film artists feared that the Academy would become the studios' stronghold and thus control and restrict the other talent groups.

That the functions of the Academy were not entirely clear to its founders is apparent from the power struggle between the Academy and the Actors Equity Association (founded in 1911) over the issue of which organization should represent actors. The matter was unclear, because many screen players came from the New York stage and thus were Equity members. The Academy won the battle in 1929, when it announced a contract for freelance actors, the first standardized contract arbitrating disagreements.

The Academy managed, as Larry Ceplair and Steven Englund have observed, "to forestall serious labor organizing among the Hollywood artists for five years," up to the creation of the various screen guilds, in 1933. AMPAS was a strange association: on the one hand, it lacked enforcement procedures for its labor code, but on the other, of all talent groups, it represented best the interests of the production companies. Even so, as a labor organization, the Academy was innovative in both structure and ambition, giving equal representation to both employers (studio executives) and employees (artists and craftsmen).

Academy membership has always been by invitation only. From the start, the idea was to create an association of Hollywood's creative elite. Artists are invited to join "when their services to the motion picture industry have been prominent enough to make the Academy members feel they would like to have them as brother members." Section I of the Constitution formalized the membership qualifications: "Any person who has accomplished distinguished work or acquired distinguished standing in or made valuable contributions to the production branches of the motion picture industry, directly or indirectly, and who is of good moral and personal standing may become an active member of the Academy by vote of the Board of Directors or recommendation of the Committee on Membership."

In 1931, the Academy distinguished between two classes of members: Academy Members, who "have all the privileges, are entitled to vote on all Academy matters, and may serve on the Board of Directors," and Associate Member, who "have voting privileges limited to branch policies and action." The new policy required for all invitees to be first admitted as associate members. And once a year, the Board of Directors, upon recommendation of the Branch Committee, would select from the associate members those entitled to "special distinction" of Academy membership. The rules allowed the membership to grow steadily, from the 270 artists who attended the second Academy banquet in 1929 to 1,200 members in 1932.

In 1933, AMPAS faced another crisis when President Roosevelt signed the National Industry Recovery Act, which suspended anti-trust laws and allowed industries to regulate themselves through "fair competition." The talent groups were concerned that the code would increase the studio's control over them, which it did. The studios used the Recovery Act as an excuse to reduce salaries. Attempting to mediate, the Academy intervened, but the resulting compromise, which stipulated that the reductions would be temporary, pleased no one. The studios withdrew their support from the Academy, and, as a counter-measure, the talent groups—writers, actors, directors—formed their own guilds. The Screen Actors Guild (SAG) was founded in October 1933, and within a year gained tremendous power for its 3,000 members.

Large numbers of the talent groups left the Academy in protest, including prominent actors such as James Cagney, Gary Cooper, Fredric March, and Paul Muni. The main issue was the dispute over the authority to represent talent groups in their labor negotiations with the studios. The SAG accused the AMPAS of trying to jeopardize the possibility of an organization representing the interests of actors. As a result, Academy membership was reduced dramatically, and its very existence threatened. Those remaining were described by Frank Capra, then AMPAS President, as "very staunch Academy-oriented visionaries, dedicated to the cultural recognition and preservation that has become the Academy's strong card."

On May 27, 1935, the Supreme Court declared Roosevelt's National Recovery Act unconstitutional. However, the SAG asked its members to boycott the eighth awards banquet, on March 5, 1936, and indeed, only a few members attended the ceremonies. Labor strikes continued, but under Capra's leadership, the Academy survived. In 1939, the Guilds won the battle, and Academy membership began to grow under a newly structured Constitution which was "non-economic and non-political in theory and in fact." From then on, the focus of the Academy became cultural and educational—not always by choice.

There has been a debate over AMPAS's historical significance. Some critics think it was a major force in industrial relations, because it helped artists to obtain standard contracts. They emphasize that, while AMPAS was not exactly a labor union (as some wished it to be), it introduced the principle of collective bargaining, which was later adopted by the Guilds.

During World War II, the political climate overrode industry concerns, and the strife between the Academy and the Guilds subsided. After the war, the membership increased dramatically: in 1939, there were 600 members; in 1947, 1433; in 1952, 1600; and in 1956, 1,770 members. In the 1960s, the Academy saw a further increase of its ranks from 2,084 members in 1959 to 3,030 in 1968. At present, there are 5,607 voting members in fourteen branches, of which the largest (24 percent) is the Acting branch, with 1,321 members.

The Academy's Structure and Membership

Originally, the Academy consisted of five branches, each representing a distinct talent group: producers, writers, directors, actors, and technicians. However, the increasing division of labor in the industry, based on specialized expertise, resulted in a more complex structure, composed at present of fourteen branches of film craftsmanship. They include four of the original ones (producers, writers, directors, actors), administrative units (executives, public relations), and subdivisions within the technical units (cinematography, editing, sound, art direction).

The Acting Branch has always been the largest, amounting to one-fourth of the membership. In 1928, there were 362 Academy members, of which 91 were actors, 78 directors, 70 writers, 69 technicians, and 54 producers.

In 1999, there were 6,209 members: 5,467 voting and 742 nonvoting (associate or retired members). Academy membership changes every year—annual net gain is estimated at about 150 members. In 1999, the voting membership was divided as follows: Actors 1,306, Art directors 342, Cinematographers 159, Directors 351, Executives 398, Film editors 209, Music 245, Producers 452, Public Relations 349, Shorts 308, Sound 388, Visual effects 183, Writers 393, Members at large 384.

Compared with the Screen Guilds, the Academy is small. The Acting branch amounts to two percent of the Screen Actors Guild's membership. The Academy's Writers and Directors branches are even smaller and more elitist in relation to their respective guilds. The Academy's small size and elitist nature accounts for its prestige and makes membership a desirable goal. Defenders of its size claim that democratizing its structure, by opening it to a larger number of industry workers, will defeat the original purpose of being an elite organization with the most accomplished film artists. The Academy was never meant to be an egalitarian organization representing all film artists.

Membership requirements differ from one branch to another. The easiest and fastest way to become a member is by gaining a nomination: All nominees are invited to become members. The Academy has seldom used its right to withhold an invitation to a nominee. Beyond that, each branch has its own criteria. In most branches, it is necessary to have several film credits, a few years of experience, and sponsorship by two established members.

The Actors Branch requires "a minimum of three feature film credits, in all of which the roles played were scripted roles, one of which was released in the past five years, and all of which are of a caliber that reflect the high standards of the Academy." But actors are also invited to join, if "in the judgment of the Actors Branch Executive Committee, (they) otherwise achieved unique distinction, earned special merit or made an outstanding contribution as a motion picture actor."

Academy membership is for life, though occasionally members are transferred from active to associate members, which means they cannot vote for Oscars. Needless to say, few members have relinquished their membership voluntarily. The Academy's prestige and the power to determine which films will win Oscars are two crucial rewards for maintaining membership. Composer David Raksin is the notable exception: Raksin resigned from the Music Branch "in disgust," after the theme from *Shaft* won the 1971 Best Song.

The membership composition is a controversial issue, about which the Academy is most sensitive. Critics feel that artists who have retired or have not been active in the industry should not vote. Others propose a distinction between members who have retired from their screen careers to pursue other lines of work and those who have retired as a result of old age. It's one thing to criticize the membership of actors like Susan Kohner or Pat Boone, who are no longer involved in film, but quite another to criticize veteran members who are old but have spent most of their lives making films.

Since Academy membership is for life, the average age of members is rather old, which poses some problems. The age difference between older members and those actively involved in filmmaking (writers, directors, players) suggests a generation gap with sociological and artistic implications. The members' older age makes them less competent and less up-to-date in evaluating current film work, thus impairing judgment of quality, which, after all, is the official purpose of the Oscars. Secondly, the increasingly younger age of frequent moviegoers in the United States contributes to a gap between them and Academy members. There is at least a one generation difference between Academy members and active filmmakers (those nominated for awards), and two generations between Academy members and average filmgoers. Age differences and generation gaps inevitably make the Academy vote more conservative, lagging behind the industry's aesthetic and technological innovations. This built-in conservative bias in the Academy vote is almost inescapable.

The average age of Academy members has decreased over the last decade, and younger filmmakers have been admitted. However, as critic Vincent Canby observed, younger members may be more sophisticated than their veteran counterparts, but they are still more conservative in their tastes and values than moviegoers. The teenage movie, a dominant genre in American cinema of the 1980s, was conspicuously missing from the Oscar race. None of the commercially popular or the more artistically acclaimed (John Hughes's *Sixteen Candles,* 1984; *The Breakfast Club,* 1985) movies received nomination. And no member of the younger performers, labeled by the media as "the brat pack" (Emilio Estevez, Ally Sheedy, Molly Ringwald) was nominated for an acting award during their prime.

A more severe criticism concerns the Academy's gender structure. With the exception of the Acting Branch, which consists of equal proportions of men and women, the other Branches are still male-dominated. In the Directors branch, only a few of the 351 members are women, including Martha Coolidge, Randa Haines, Elaine May, Joan Micklin Silver, and Claudia Weill. And there are only a few women among the 159 Academy cinematographers. Unfortunately, because of the secret balloting, it is impossible to assess the differences between male and female voting. One can assume that because the Acting Branch consists of both male and female members, the nominated performance are based on a more balanced vote. The disproportionately large size of the Acting Branch vis-a-vis the other branches means that the Best Picture nominees are often movies with strong acting. A movie like *The Dresser* would probably not have been nominated for Best Picture if one-fourth of the Academy members, all of whom nominate in this category, had not been players. It's not that *The Dresser* was not a high-quality film (it was), but that its subject matter (backstage life through the relationship between an aging, selfish actor and his dresser in World War II England) and extraordinary performances by Albert Finney and Tom Courtenay made it a likely candidate for Best Picture in the opinion of the Acting Branch. The Acting Branch's large size translates into greater impact over the films nominated for the top award.

This is the reason why many films about the entertainment world have been nominated for Best Picture: *The Great Ziegfeld, Stage Door, A Star Is Born, All About Eve, Sunset Boulevard, The Country Girl, Cabaret, Lenny, Nashville, The Turning Point, All That Jazz, Coal Miner's Daughter, Tootsie, Amadeus, Shine,* and most recently, *Shakespeare in Love.*

By contrast, because of the small size of other branches, it takes fewer votes to nominate achievements. Thus, 20 or 30 members of the Directors branch, which consists of only 351 filmmakers, can nominate a directorial achievement. The Directors Branch is not only small but cliquish as well, which explains why respected filmmakers such as David Lynch and Martin Scorsese can earn directing nominations for *Blue Velvet* and *The Last Temptation of Christ,* without their movies themselves being nominated. Amounting to only 6 percent of the entire membership, the directors have less clout than actors (who constitute about 25 percent), in determining which films are nominated for and win Best Picture.

Procedures for Nomination

In the first year, the Academy asked the entire membership to nominate achievements by the August 15, 1928 deadline. Five boards of judges, one from each branch, were appointed to consider the nominations. The ten nominees who received the highest number of votes were turned over to the board of judges, who narrowed them down to three in each category. A central board of judges, one from each branch, then examined the finalists and determined the winner and the two honorable mentions. The winners were announced immediately, though the ceremonies took place at the Academy's annual banquet.

For the next six years (1929–35), the selection process was broadened. The nominations were now made in primary elections by the branches, and the final voting by the entire membership. The regulations stated: "Each Branch will vote separately for nominations, like a primary election. The five highest persons, or achievements, for each award will be certified and placed on a ballot for submission to all members of the Academy. Academy members will then select from the submitted nominees, one for each award and those votes will govern the final selections."

However, these procedures came under severe attack in 1935, when Bette Davis's performance in *Of Human Bondage* failed to get a nomination. Consequently, in February 1935, the voting was thrown wide-open and write-ins were permitted; members were allowed to name anyone they chose and could substitute a write-in on request. The write-in votes were counted exactly as the votes for regular nominations. Hal Mohr, who won an Oscar for cinematography in *A Midsummer Night's Dream* (1935) became the first and last write-in winner. The confusion and technical problems involved in write-ins eventually brought about their demise.

In 1936, the nominations were made again by a committee of fifty members which represented all branches, but the final vote was retained by the entire membership. The labor problems and internal conflict, which resulted in the resignation of many members, led to other procedural changes. Frank Capra, then Academy President, decided on a novel strategy—to open up the Academy and extend voting privileges to the Screen Actors, Writers, and Directors Guilds. Getting the guilds' members to vote was not easy, for they accused the Academy of being against labor unions, but Capra succeeded.

For the acting nominations, only members of the Senior Screen Actors Guild took part, but final ballots were also sent to the Junior Screen Actors Guild and the Writers and Directors Guilds. Hence in 1936, the industry's participation was active: out of fifteen thousand ballots mailed,

80 percent came back. The Academy wanted to prove that it kept abreast of the times by making the awards representative of the entire industry. In 1938 again, the nominations for the acting awards were made by Class A of the Screen Actors Guild, and twelve thousand professionals of the guilds took part in the final balloting. The Academy publicized the fact that the Oscars "are awarded on the basis of ballots which receive industry-wide distribution," thus "representing the majority evaluation of those who work in the medium."

This practice continued into the 1940s. In 1943, 3,800 nomination ballots and 8,000 final ballots were sent out. In 1944, only Class A, Junior members of the Screen Actors Guild, and members of the Academy Actors Branch (a total of 4,500) were invited to take part in the nominations, but final ballots were sent to all members of the Academy and Class B members of the Screen Actors Guild (9,000 persons). In 1946, however, nomination ballots were sent to all 11,669 creative workers in the industry, but final ballots were mailed only to the 1,600 Academy members. And in 1956, nomination ballots were sent to the 16,721 industry workers, but final ballots to the 1,770 Academy members.

Voting was restricted for the first time to active Academy members in 1957; the guilds and unions no longer participated. Director George Seaton, then AMPAS President, was instrumental in bringing about this change, urging members "to exercise the privilege now reserved solely for Academy members." In a personal letter, Seaton wrote: "Since the number of eligible voters has been reduced, you can see how important it is that we get as nearly 100 percent return as possible, so that the nominations and final selections may truly reflect the majority choices of the Academy membership." The 1957 rules for nomination and final balloting are still in effect.

One of the few original practices still in effect is the reminder list. From the first year, a list of productions in the eligible year has been sent to all members to refresh their memories. The reminder list was first arranged according to studios; then according to movies, alphabetically. The list is not guaranteed to be complete or accurate, and each studio is asked to furnish its own inventory of movies. The Academy suggests, "if any film you wish to nominate is not included here, or if you need any further information please telephone the Academy office."

Rule six of the nominations states: "The Academy shall prepare reminder lists of all eligible pictures, but before distribution to voters, studios must check and assume full responsibility for errors and omissions." The list refers "only to the motion picture in which the achievement was made, and not to any individual responsible, except in the case of acting nominations which name both the individual and the one picture wherein the achievement occurred." The Academy assists members in coming to "intelligent decisions" in their voting by sending lists of booking dates of the nominated pictures, which they may see without admission charge.

Achievements are eligible for nomination if they have met the general rule of "The Awards Year":

> Academy Awards of Merit shall be bestowed for achievements in connection with feature-length motion pictures (defined as motion-pictures over 30 minutes in running time) first publicly exhibited by means of 35mm or 70mm film for paid admission (previews excluded) in a commercial motion picture theater in the Los Angeles Area, defined as Los Angeles, West Los Angeles or Beverly Hills, between January 1, 1999 and midnight of December 31, such exhibition being for a consecutive run of no less than a week after an opening prior to midnight of December 31st.

Several categories allow exception: Documentaries and short films are entered by their producers, and music awards require the creator to file official submission forms. Foreign films are submitted by each country's equivalent to the Academy; there is a limit of one picture per country. There are also exceptions to the location rule: documentaries need not play in the Los Angeles area, and foreign language films need not have opened in the United States, but must have English subtitles.

The first Oscars were presented on May 16, 1929, for 1927 and 1928. The period of eligibility was a specific twelve-month period, from August 1, 1927 to July 31, 1928. This eligibility period remained in effect for the next four years. In 1934, however, the time frame was changed to cover the calendar year, from January 1 to December 31, which required the addition of five months to the previous awards year: the 1932–33 awards covered the period from August 1, 1932, to December 31, 1933.

The voting timetable for the Annual Awards is as follows:

December 1, 1999	Deadline for receipt of official screen credit forms to qualify feature films for award consideration
December 31, 1999	Awards year ends at midnight
January 13, 2000	Nomination ballots mailed
January 30	Nominations polls close at 5 P.M.

February 15	Nominations announced at 5:30 A.M. at the Samuel Goldwyn Theater
March 1	Final ballots mailed
March 4	Scientific and Technical Awards presentations, at the Regent Beverly Wilshire Hotel
March 21	Final Ballots close 5:00 P.M.
March 26	Seventy-second Annual Academy Awards presentation at the Los Angeles Shrine Auditorium televised live on ABC at 5:30 P.M.

Price, Waterhouse and Company, a firm of certified public accountants, began counting the Oscar ballots in 1936. During the first twelve years, the results of the final balloting were released to the press prior to the presentation to accommodate newspaper deadlines. However, in 1940, when a newspaper printed the winners' names before the ceremonies, advance notice was discontinued. Consequently, in 1941 the Academy declined to give out any advance release, and the practice of sealed envelopes began. The winners' identity is unknown until they are actually called to the podium to be handed the award. The winners receive a blank Oscar; after the show their names are engraved on its base. This secrecy undoubtedly contributes to the tension and excitement of the awards ceremonies. The only exceptions to the rule of secrecy are the Honorary, Scientific-Technical, the Jean Hersholt, and the Irving Thalberg awards, which are announced in advance.

In this respect, the Oscars differ from other prestigious awards. The Nobel Prize Nomination Committees are silent about the names proposed for the awards, always abiding by the rule of secrecy. However, the winners' names are made public weeks before the actual ceremonies to accommodate their arrival in Stockholm from all over the world. By contrast, the Academy nominees are publicly disclosed six weeks before the ceremonies, but the winners' identity is kept in utmost secrecy up to the last moment. When the presenters say, "May I have the envelope please," the nominees, the voters, and the viewing public are in a state of genuine suspense.

Award Categories

The number of award categories has changed over the years, reflecting developments in the film industry, such as the advent of sound and color. All the nominees for the first Best Picture were silent films—the winner was *Wings*—and only one award was given to a "talkie."

In the first year, there were eleven categories: Actor, Actress, Director of Drama, Director of Comedy, Outstanding Picture (Producer),

Outstanding Quality (Production Company), Original Screenplay, Adaptation of Story, Cinematography, Art Direction, and Engineering Effects. The production awards distinguished between the Best Producer, "who produced the most outstanding motion picture, considering all elements that contribute to a picture's greatness," and Best Production Company, "which produced the most artistic, unique, and/or original motion picture without reference to cost or magnitude." Members were asked to choose the best performance, "with special reference to character portrayal and effectiveness of dramatic or comedy rendition."

In the second year (1928–29), awards were given in only seven categories. The distinction between the direction of a comedy and a drama was dropped as well as that between original and adapted screenplay. And there was no longer differentiation between Best Producer and Best Production Company—the top award was named Best Picture. In the third year, two new categories were added: Sound Recording and Scientific-Technical Achievement. In the fourth year (1930–31), the writing award was divided again into Original Story and Adaptation. By 1934, the number of categories had increased to thirteen, with new areas for Editing, Short Subjects, and Music. In the following year, due to the popularity of the musical films, a new category was created to honor Dance Direction.

For close to a decade, there were only two acting categories: Best Actor and Best Actress. In 1936, the Academy decided to create two more divisions: Best Supporting Actor and Best Supporting Actress, which required new rules to distinguish between lead and supporting performances (see chapter 4). In keeping abreast of the advent of color, the Cinematography and Art Direction Awards were subdivided in 1939 into black-and-white and color. The first winners in these areas were Gregg Toland for his distinguished black-and-white cinematography in *Wuthering Heights,* and Ernest Haller and Ray Rennahan for their color work in *Gone With the Wind.*

The largest number of awards bestowed by the Academy was in 1956, with twenty-seven categories including new fields such as documentaries. New categories were established and others dropped in accordance with industry developments. In 1957, the Academy eliminated Best Scoring of a Musical due to the genre's decline. The tendency was toward compressing categories, keeping the number of awards to a minimum. A major change occurred in 1967, when the duplicate awards in Art Direction, Set Decoration, and Cinematography, previously given for black-and-white and color, was discontinued. The feeling was that these awards would be more prestigious and meaningful if there would be one system, though it made the competition in these categories more intense.

One of the most recent categories is Makeup, given for the first time in 1982, after a lengthy battle by makeup artists. In previous years, honorary awards were given to makeup artists, such as William Tuttle for *Seven Faces of Dr. Lao* in 1964, and John Chambers for *Planet of the Apes* in 1968, but there was no regular award. A competitive category was established following the Academy's failure to honor the makeup achievement in David Lynch's *The Elephant Man*. For a few years, there was a distinction between Original Musical or Comedy Score and Original Dramatic Score, but it 1999 it was abolished.

At present, merit awards are conferred in twenty-three categories: Best Picture, Best Foreign Picture, Director, four acting awards (Actor, Actress, Supporting Actor, Supporting Actress), two writing (Original Screenplay and Adaptation), two documentary (Feature and Short Subject), two music (Original Score and Original Song), two short-film awards (Animated and Live Action), Art Direction, Cinematography, Costume Design, Editing, Sound, Sound Effects, Visual Effects, and Makeup.

In the first year, three actors were nominated for Best Actor: Richard Barthelmes, for two films, *The Noose* and *The Patent Leather Kid*; Emil Jannings, also for two films, *The Last Command* and *The Way of All Flesh*; and Charlie Chaplin, for *The Circus*. In the same year, three actresses were nominated for five performances: Janet Gaynor for three films, *Seventh Heaven, Street Angel,* and *Sunrise*; Louise Dressler for *A Ship Comes In*; and Gloria Swanson for *Sadie Thompson*.

Five nominees were singled out in each acting category in the second year. But in the third year, four actors were nominated for six roles (George Arliss and Maurice Chevalier were each nominated for two performances), and five actresses were nominated for seven roles (Greta Garbo was nominated for two, *Anna Christie* and *Romance*; and Norma Shearer also for two, *The Divorcee* and *Their Own Desire*). For three years (1932–34), the two acting categories contained three performers, each nominated for one role. But in 1935, there were four nominees in the Best Actor and six nominees in the Best Actress category. It wasn't until 1936 that the number of nominees was standardized to five in each group.

In the first year, there were two directing awards, for comedy and for drama, and three directors competed for each. The first directing winners were: Frank Borzage for the drama *Seventh Heaven,* and Lewis Milestone for the comedy *Two Arabian Nights*. This distinction was dropped in the following year. For two years (1929–30), five nominees competed for Best Director, but in 1932, the number of contestants was reduced again to three. From 1936 on, however, the number of directing nominations was standardized to five.

There have also been fluctuations in the number of films nominated for Best Picture. In the first four years, five movies were nominated, but in 1931–32, their number was increased to eight. In 1932–33, ten films were nominated, and in 1934 and 1935, twelve. In the next seven years (1936–1943), ten movies competed for Best Picture. The competition in these years was extremely fierce, as was evident in 1939, a watershed year in Hollywood's history, with so many excellent movies nominated for an Oscar: *Dark Victory, Gone With the Wind* (the winner), *Goodbye, Mr. Chips, Love Affair, Mr. Smith Goes to Washington, Ninotchka, Of Mice and Men, Stagecoach, The Wizard of Oz,* and *Wuthering Heights.*

But nominating ten movies for Best Picture made the competition intense, and also split the votes into too many subgroups. In 1944, the Academy standardized the Best Picture category to contain the same number of contestants—five—as in the other categories.

CHAPTER 3

Oscar's Preeminence in the Film World

The Oscar is the most popular and the most prestigious award in the film industry. But the Oscar goes beyond the film world—it enjoys an extraordinary preeminence in the entertainment world and in American pop culture at large. The Oscar's prestige and visibility surpass those of other showbiz awards, such as the Tony, the top award in the Broadway theater; the Emmy, which honors television achievements; and the Grammy, the most prestigious award in the recording industry. How did the Oscar Award and the Oscar telecast acquire such remarkable dimensions?

The Oscar is considered to be "the King of Awards" in the international film world, but it is not the only award honoring film achievements. Various awards are bestowed by film academies and institutes, international film festivals, and critics associations.

Film Institutes

Most countries with established film industries have national academies or institutes, which, among other activities, bestow merit awards. The Oscar is conferred by the Academy of Motion Picture Arts and Sciences, which is the oldest academy in the world (founded in 1927, as noted). That most people refer to it as *The Academy*, not the *American* Academy, attests to its status as the world's most famous film organization.

In England, the British Film Academy (BFA) was established in 1946 for the "advancement of film." In 1975, after a series of mergers and reorganizations, it became the British Academy of Film and Television Arts (BAFTA). BAFTA's annual awards honor achievements in film and television. In the United States, the separation between the Academy of Motion Picture and the Academy of Television Arts and Sciences underlines both functional and symbolic differences. The Academy and its Oscar Award have always been more prestigious than television and its Emmy Award. In the United States, unlike other countries, film and television are still considered to be different media that perform different functions in popular culture.

In France, the equivalent of the Oscars is the **César**, created in 1976 by publicist Georges Cravenne. It is voted on by the entire membership of the French Motion Picture Academy, consisting of about twenty-five hundred members of the film industry. The French Academy and its César are modeled after the Academy and its Oscar, honoring various film categories.

The top film award in Italy is the **David Di Donatello** Award, which is now administered by the Italian film industry. The bylaws of this award have changed, and its emphasis now is on European films. The Italian academy, like other national academies but unlike the Oscar, distinguishes between achievements by local and foreign artists, which increases the number of awards and decreases the intensity of competition.

Awards are also bestowed by the American Film Institute (AFI), which was established in 1967. Its Life Achievement Award, conferred since 1973, is highly respected, but it differs from most awards in its purpose, which is to honor "the total career contributions of a filmmaker, regardless of place of birth, whose talent has fundamentally advanced the art of film or television, whose accomplishments have been acknowledged by scholars, critics, professional peers, and the general public, and whose work has withstood the test of time." The award is based on the judgment of the AFI's board, but the entire membership is asked to suggest candidates. The annual ceremonies take place in February and are televised, but not live. Most of the winners have been directors (John Ford, Orson Welles, William Wyler, Alfred Hitchcock, Frank Capra, John Huston, Billy Wilder) or actors (James Cagney, Henry Fonda, James Stewart, Fred Astaire, Jack Nicholson, Dustin Hoffman). So far, only two actresses have been cited: Bette Davis and Lillian Gish.

In 1978, the John F. Kennedy Center for the Performing Arts began to honor five artists in the fields of theater, dance, film, and music, in ceremonies that are later broadcast. In 1983, three of the five winners were drawn from the film world: director Elia Kazan, Jimmy Stewart, and Frank Sinatra as a singer/actor. In 1999, two of the honorees were actors: Sean Connery and Jason Robards.

The Oscar is more internationally visible than these awards. Unlike the AFI or the Kennedy Center Awards, which honor *career* achievements (their recipients tend to be older), the Oscar honors, at least in theory, a single achievement in a single film. And as Oscar winners tend to be younger, the award has a stronger impact on their careers.

International Film Festivals

Most international film festivals bestow awards based on a competition of films from all over the world. Of the various festivals, four are of special importance: Venice, Cannes, Berlin, and New York.

Venice, the oldest international film festival, was first held in 1932 under the auspices of the Venice Biennial, but in 1934 it became an independent event. At its inception, the festival served as a vehicle for Fascist propaganda, receiving the sponsorship of Mussolini, who was highly aware of film's potential as a tool of political propaganda.

In the first years, no merit awards were conferred, but prizes based on public referendum were given to "the most touching," "the most amusing," and "the most original" film. The awards for "the favorite actor and actress" went to Fredric March *(Dr. Jekyll and Mr. Hyde)* and Helen Hayes *(The Sin of Madelon Claudet),* both of whom won Oscars for these films. The Venice festival is held in late August to early September and its chief prize is the Golden Lion. Its reputation was seriously damaged in the 1930s and 1940s, when political favoritism proved to be a crucial factor in the selection of winners. However, in the past two decades, the festival has restored its credibility, getting more Hollywood pictures for international premieres and honoring respected films, such as Krzystof Zanussi's *A Year of the Quiet Sun* in 1984, Agnes Varda's *Vagabond* in 1985, and Zhang Yimou's *Not One Less* in 1999.

The best-known of all international festivals, **Cannes** emerged in opposition to Venice. It was originally scheduled to open in 1939, but because of World War II, the first festival was held in September 1946. Cannes has always enjoyed tremendous publicity—and not just because of its cinematic functions. It has become over the years a highly commercial event, attended by celebs from all over the world. Cannes is also the biggest festival, screening hundreds of films, in and outside the official program. Until 1950, it took place in the fall, when it was decided to move it to May, mostly in order to precede Venice. The highest prize is the Golden Palm (Palme d'Or), which honors the best film from twenty to twenty-two entries in the official competition. The festival also honors juried achievements in acting, directing, and cinematography (or artistic contribution).

For two decades, Cannes was an important operation, presenting the latest developments in international cinema. However, as a result of the increasing number of festivals, Cannes has gradually lost its uniqueness. In fact, Toronto now performs this function more effectively. As in Venice, politics, in and outside the film world, have afflicted the Cannes's operation In 1968, political demonstrations forced the festival to close while in progress, but it recovered and even exceeded its former stature. The choice of competition films (and winners) is often motivated by political rather than artistic considerations.

Founded in 1951, the **Berlin Film Festival** has enjoyed immense publicity and official support due to the city's special political status. As a festival, it is less commercial than both Venice and Cannes, and more committed to the exhibition of documentaries and independent films. Until 1957, it was held in the summer, but at present, it takes place in February so that it will come well in advance of Cannes. In the first years, the bestowal of awards was democratic: a jury and the public participated in the process, but this practice was discontinued in 1957 due to growing criticism. The top prizes are the Golden Bear for best film and the Silver Bear for directing and acting achievements.

Established in 1963, under the auspices of the Lincoln Center Film Society (which also publishes the magazine *Film Comment*), the **New York Film Festival** was a prestigious forum. In its first twenty-five years, it was guided under the leadership of Richard Roud, a British cineaste and film critic. New York was the most important festival in the United States until the Sundance Film Festival was taken under the wing of Robert Redford, in 1985, thus emerging as the premiere festival in the country, second only to Cannes as far as the discovery of new hot talent is concerned.

During the New York festival's two-week duration (in late September to early October), about twenty-six features and some shorts are screened. The purpose of the festival is "to bring the most interesting films with the greatest artistic merit from all over the world to the attention of the New York film community." The films, selected by a five-member committee, tend to be either innovative or solid, well-made features.

New York is the only major festival that does not bestow awards, attempting to steer clear of the political favoritism and negative aspects of competitiveness. Appalled by "the shenanigans that go on at other festivals when there are prizes and pressures to win," Roud claimed that, "prizes are for the one who wins," and that for him, "all of the great filmmakers have won a prize by being in the festival." Indeed, competition to be included in the festival is fierce: the twenty-six selections are drawn from a pool of over four hundred films, though at least half of the films come from Cannes. In the 1990s, the New York festival has become a regional festival, mostly displaying programs from other festivals with few world premieres, which is what gives a modern festival the necessary cachet.

Most international festivals function as arenas in which lively (to say the least) aesthetic and political conflicts take place. Selections are often criticized as inadequate due to the operation of special-interest politics and other biases. On many occasions, prizes are given to those filmmakers and national cinemas the jury felt deserved recognition for political reasons. However, the politics of film festivals also have positive effects, since they call attention to the variety of yardsticks—aesthetic, moral, and ideological—that come into play when evaluating film as an art form. Another charge often raised against Cannes, New York, and others festivals, is that they consistently showcase the same favorite filmmakers—Truffaut, Godard, Fassbinder, and Wajda—while disregarding the work of younger, more innovative and experimental filmmakers.

Unlike the Academy, festivals depend on the good will of studios, producers, and directors to submit their films for competition. By contrast, every film released in the United States within a calendar year is eligible to compete for Oscars regardless of the studio or filmmaker's wishes. Availability of films through the studio machine is also a determining factor. Martin Scorsese's *After Hours* was not included in the 1985 New York festival because its producers demanded that it be shown on either opening or closing night. Moreover, some producers fear that displaying their films in festivals will label them as "arthouse" or "esoteric" films, and thus potentially damage their commercial prospects.

Critics Associations

The most influential critics associations in the United States are the New York Film Critics Circle, the Los Angeles Film Critics Association, and the National Society of Film Critics.

The New York Film Critics Circle was founded in 1935 with a twofold goal: to recognize the finest film achievements and to maintain high standards of film criticism. For three decades the circle recognized accomplishments in four categories: picture, actor, actress, and director. In 1969, it created additional categories for acting (supporting actor and actress), screenplay and cinematography. The Circle announces its winners at its annual meeting in December and certificates of honor are conferred in a dinner gathering, for many years held at Sardi's.

The National Society of Film Critics was founded in 1968 as a "highbrow" association to counter the "middle-brow" circles, whose tastes were considered to be too similar to the Academy's. In its first years, the Society was accused of being "too harsh and snobbish" toward Hollywood's commercial pictures and too "avant-garde" in its preference of European art films. One of the National Society's major purposes was "to give annual recognition to the best films without distinction of nationality." Unlike the other circles, in the first years, each critic's votes and the complete tabulations were published in an annual volume. In the 1980s, the Society broadened its base to include new members (it is composed of fifty-two critics), a democratic procedure that led to the departure of some of its more elitist founders.

The Los Angeles Film Critics Association, which consists of both print and television reviewers in the Los Angeles area, is one of the most recent circles, presenting its first awards in 1975. Its proximity to the film industry makes its influence on the Academy more direct and more pervasive than that of the other associations.

The National Society of Film Critics enjoys greater prestige than either the New York or the Los Angeles groups because it is small, elitist, and represents reviewers from all over the nation. In some circles, the choices of the New York Film Critics are considered to be less biased by commercial considerations than choices by their California counterparts. However, when *Brazil* was chosen as Best Picture by the Los Angeles Film Critics, it had tremendous influence on the conflict between director Terry Gilliam and his studio, Universal, over running time and ending. At the same time, there's no denying that the selection of *Brazil* by the Los Angeles Film Critics resulted in an earlier release, in December, so that it could be eligible for Oscar nominations—initially, the film wasn't scheduled for release until the following year.

Critics perform several roles in the film world. First, they confer prestige on the winning films and artists. Critics are considered to be "experts" who use more matter-of-fact yardsticks than the mass public in their evaluations. Critics also serve as tastemakers and guides for the public: As moviegoers can't possibly see all movies released in a given year, they often rely on critical judgments. But critics also exert influence on the Oscar Award. Most circles announce their choices in mid-December, about two months prior to the nominations (in mid-February), thus inevitably affecting the nominations. Like moviegoers, Academy members cannot possibly see all eligible films and critics' reviews and annual awards assist them in focusing their attention on a smaller number of films. "Ten Best" lists by influential critics, those writing for the *New York Times* or the *Los Angeles Times,* get a special consideration from the Academy.

With all their prestige, however, critical awards, unlike the Oscars, have little impact on films' standing at the box office. Furthermore, the critics' status is ambiguous, as Andrew Sarris once put it, "At best, movie reviewers are considered a necessary evil; at worst, a positive plague of locusts." If reviews are favorable, they are used for advertising the pictures, but if they are negative, critics are ignored and chastised for their "damaging impact on the industry."

Actors, too, attribute different meaning to the prizes given by the various critics groups. James Cagney was appreciative of the New York Film Critics, when he learned that it took nine ballots before he was cited Best Actor for *Angels With Dirty Faces* (1938). And after being honored for her role in *I Want to Live!* (1958), Susan Hayward said: "The big treat was winning the New York Film Critics Award. That's a tough one to win, not because they know so much, but because they're such rats and they don't like to give anyone a prize, especially anybody from Hollywood."

Other Awards

The National Board of Review is the country's oldest film association. Established in New York in 1909 by a voluntary group of film-oriented citizens, it was first called the National Board of Censorship of Motion Pictures, serving as a voluntary censorship agency and enjoying the industry's full support. In 1922, however, its powers were diminished when the industry established its own regulatory board under the leadership of Will H. Hays. Changing its name to the National Board of Review, it devoted its activities to the evaluation of films. In its first years, it honored the best films (American and foreign), but since 1930, it selects "Ten Best" films, best players, and other achievements.

Founded in 1940, the Hollywood Foreign Press Association consists of about eighty-five journalists who represent over a hundred million readers in more than fifty different countries. Its awards, the Golden Globes, were first presented in 1943. All members vote for the nominees, in December, and for the winners, in January. Due to its international nature, the occasion has enjoyed extensive media coverage. The Golden Globes were modeled on the Oscars, with several exceptions. They distinguish between achievements in drama and in comedy/musical, thus doubling the number of awards and diminishing their relative significance. The association honors achievements in television, not just in film, and it also celebrates impressive debuts and presents career achievement awards.

Critics often look down on the Golden Globes because they are selected by reporters, not reviewers, and because there are so many of them. The feeling is that if the Golden Globes took place after the Oscar nominations closed, nobody would go. But as far as box office is concerned, the Golden Globes are much more influential in foreign film markets than any of the critics' awards.

Popularity awards are also given by several associations and magazines. The oldest, most comprehensive, survey of America's "Top Box-Office

Stars" is the Quigley Publications Poll, first conducted in 1932, and known in the industry as "The Poll." Movie exhibitors in the United States are asked to name the year's Top Ten Box-Office Attractions, the ten players whose names on the marquees have drawn the largest number of customers to their theaters.

The disparity between the country's commercial stars and its acclaimed actors, reflected in Oscar nominations and awards, has widened considerably since the 1980s. In 1985, the ten box-office stars in America were: Sylvester Stallone, Eddie Murphy, Clint Eastwood, Michael J. Fox, Chevy Chase, Arnold Schwarzenegger, Chuck Norris, Harrison Ford, Michael Douglas, and Meryl Streep. Note that only one of the ten stars was a woman, and that most male stars specialized in action-adventures or comedy. Only a few of the stars have been nominated for an Oscar. By contrast, in 1932, seven of the nation's top stars were or would become Oscar winners: Marie Dressler, Janet Gaynor, Joan Crawford, Greta Garbo, Norma Shearer, Wallace Beery, and Clark Gable.

In recent years, there has been a proliferation of film awards. The People's Choice and the MTV awards honor the public's favorite performers in film, television, and music. The annual ceremony takes place in Santa Monica in March, a few weeks prior to the Oscar telecast, and there is live coverage of the event. Another contest is The American Movie Awards, which honor the best players and best films and are based on a national sample of moviegoers. Reaching large audiences, these awards cash in on the suspense and excitement that precede the Oscar ceremonies.

The Screen Actors Guild (SAG) began to honor acting achievements in 1994, immediately assuming power on the Oscar's operation. The reason is rather simple: actors represent about 24 percent of the Oscar vote, or 1,321 of the 5,607 ballot-casting members. Nominations for the SAG awards are based on poll results from 4,200 randomly selected SAG members, and the winners are determined via ballots sent to the entire 97,000 membership.

The SAG and the Golden Globes are good indicators of what might happen on Oscar night. About 80 to 90 percent of the SAG winners in the lead categories (Best Actor and Best Actress) have also won the Oscar. The few exceptions have been Jodie Foster, who won the SAG in 1994 for *Nell;* that year, the Oscar winner was Jessica Lange for *Blue Sky.* The SAG's supporting categories are less reliable. In 1998, the SAG awards went to Robert Duvall for *A Civil Action* and Kathy Bates for *Primary Colors,* but the supporting Oscars went to James Coburn for *Affliction* and Judi Dench for *Shakespeare in Love.* Highlights of the 2000 SAG Awards show, which is telecast live, included Roberto Benigni's (the previous year's Best Actor) appearance as a presenter of Best Actress to Hilary Swank, and Sidney Poitier receiving a Lifetime Achievement award from Denzel Washington.

Oscar—The King of Showbiz Awards?

For awards to have motivational significance, they have to fulfill at least three functions: They have to be known to every artist, they have to carry a high degree of prestige, and they have to be within reach. The Oscar Awards meet all of these conditions: They are visible, they are prestigious, and they are within reach.

The importance of the Oscar goes beyond the American film world. The Oscar is now universally embraced as a symbol of achievement in global entertainment. A combination of reasons account for that. First and foremost, the longevity of the award. Conferred for the first time in 1929 (for achievements in 1927–78), the Oscar is the oldest prize in history. A tradition of seventy-two years has made the Oscar a respectable symbol with historical heritage. The other entertainment awards are children and grandchildren of the Oscar. The Antoinette (Tony) Perry Awards, given by the League of New York Theaters and Producers and the American Theater Wing, were first presented in April 1947. The Emmys, awarded by the National Academy of Television Arts and Sciences, were presented for the first time in January 1949. The Grammys, the youngest showbiz awards, were first bestowed by the National Academy of Recording Arts and Sciences in May 1959.

Aside from longevity, there are differences in the scope of these awards. The Tony is essentially a local award, given for achievements in the Broadway theater—most people can't relate to the Tonys because they are confined to shows produced in New York. A growing criticism of the Tonys is that it excludes the Off Broadway and Off Off Broadway theater, where the more innovative work is done. Movies, by contrast, have the potential of reaching everyone. Even people who don't live in the United States and don't speak English can relate to the Oscar show and to the honored movies.

Much of Oscar's prestige stems from the Academy's status within the film industry. The Academy has always been elitist, with a membership that constitutes a very small percentage of the film industry. Yet despite elitism, the Academy's procedures are more democratic than those prevailing in other associations. The Academy, with its various branches, gives equal representation to all artists, regardless of specialty (writers, directors, players). Based on peer evaluation, the nomination process is democratic: The Acting branch selects nominees for acting awards, the Directors branch for directing awards, etc. However, each Academy member proposes nominees for the top award, Best Picture, and the entire membership participates in the final selection of winners in all the categories.

In contrast, the selection of nominees for the Tony Awards is done by a nomination committee. Final ballots are sent out to about seven hundred eligible Tony voters, members of the governing boards of the Actors Equity Association, the Dramatists Guild, the society of Stage Directors and Choreographers, the board of directors of the American Theater Wing, members of the League of the New York Theaters and Producers, and those on the first and second night press lists. Unlike the Oscar, which was always based on nominations, during the first decade of the Tonys, there were no nominations; the process began in 1956.

The Oscar is awarded by peers, not by the public. Film artists, like other professionals, attribute the utmost importance to peer recognition because they consider them the only experts with the necessary knowledge to make a competent evaluation of their work. For most filmmakers, the significant reference group, which sets standards to be emulated and also serves as a frame for judging one's performance, consists of fellow-workers. Film artists compare the rewards of their work (money, power, prestige) not with those of other professionals but with their peers.

The scarce number of awards also contributes to the Oscar's prestige. In the entire Academy history, only 608 players have been nominated for and only 188 have won an acting award. Every year, only 20 players are nominated in four categories, and only four win: Best Actor, Best Actress, Best Supporting Actor, and Best Supporting Actress. These performances are singled out of thousands of eligible performances.

Then, only five films compete for Best Picture. These five are selected from a large pool of over two hundred films eligible to compete for Oscars. Production in Hollywood has declined, though: In the past, the number of eligible films was twice as large because of the tremendous film output. In the 1940s, over four hundred films were released on an average year, and in the 1960s over three hundred.

The Oscar is much more competitive than the Tony Award. In some years, the Broadway theater is in such a dismal state that the Tony Committee has problems filling the categories with competent performers, particularly in the musical fields. But even in better times, no more than forty new plays and ten musicals open in a given season, in comparison to the hundreds of movies and performances, American and foreign, eligible for Oscars in a given year.

Superlative performances by foreign players are ignored or bypassed, but the Academy refuses to create an additional category for excellence in a foreign film. The suggestion to divide the categories by genre, say, best achievement in drama and comedy, has also been turned down. The Tonys have separate sets of categories for dramatic plays and for musicals. Those in favor of one prize, regardless of genre or artists' nationality, claim that increasing the number of awards will decrease their prestige; too many categories belittle the award. Grammys, for example, are awarded in no fewer than sixty or seventy categories, and singers can be nominated in three or four categories for the same song.

The Oscar is awarded to film artists of all nationalities: One fourth of the nominees have been foreign artists (see chapter 5). This international dimension has undoubtedly extended the Oscar's visibility and contributed to its prestige. And the Oscar's prestige in turn makes for intense international competition. No other award has matched the Oscar's international impact. The scarcity of awards, and the intense competition among filmmakers of all nationalities, have made the Oscar all the more desirable. Whereas other national industries distinguish between local and foreign achievements, the only Oscar category specifically designed to honor foreign achievements is the Best Foreign-Language Picture.

The Oscar's immense effects, both symbolic and pragmatic, on the winning films and artists, is another unique feature. Unlike the prestigious Nobel Prize, there is no financial honorarium, though the Oscar's economic worth is extraordinary: the winners' salaries skyrocket overnight! Winning an Oscar means hard cash at the box office: The Best Picture Award can add up to twenty to thirty million dollars in tickets sales. Winning the lead acting award can add four to six million dollars to a film's profitability—Hilary Swank's Best Actress Oscar for *Boys Don't Cry* (1999) almost doubled the film's grosses after her nomination was announced.

The Oscars are visible in both the domestic and global movie markets: foreign box-office receipts often amount to more than half of movies' overall grosses. In addition to prestige and money, the winners also gain negotiating power for better roles with better directors, and increased popularity outside the film industry and outside the United States.

No other entertainment award has such comparable effects. The Emmys are the least influential for the very reason that reruns of Emmy-winning programs, unlike rereleases of Oscar-winning films, cannot add more money. As for the Tonys, many of the winning productions are no longer running by the time of the ceremonies. However, winning a Tony for Best Play or Best Musical is more important for commercial appeal than winning the Pulitzer Prize for drama or the New York Drama Critics

Award. In 1978, *The Wiz,* the all-black musical which opened to lukewarm reception, became a long-running show after winning Best Musical. Plays that received favorable reviews, such as *The Elephant Man* and *Children of a Lesser God,* became more successful at the box office after winning Best Play in their respective years.

The Grammys do have an impact on record sales. Quincy Jones's 1982 album *The Dude* hit the top ten after winning five Grammys. The 1981 Grammy-winning album of songwriter-singer Christopher Cross leaped back up the charts and eventually sold more than four million copies, compared to the two million sale prior to winning. Still, these figures do not compare to the financial bonanza generated by Oscar-winning films.

The four showbiz awards divide the calendar year, with one big event every season: The Oscar show takes place in the spring, the Tonys in the early summer, the Emmys in the fall, and the Grammys in the winter. However, the Oscar telecast is the most popular event. The 1980 Oscar show, telecast by ABC on April 14, was the sixth most watched program in the 1979–80 television season. It received 33.7 of the ratings and 55 percent of the audience share, compared with the telecast of the Emmy Awards, on September 9, which occupied twenty-seventh place, with 27.3 of the rating and 45 percent of the audience share. The Grammy Awards, telecast on February 27, were the sixtieth most watched program, with 23.9 of the ratings and 30 points of the audience share. The five programs that exceeded the Oscar show in popularity were mostly sports events: Super Bowl XIV, NFC Football Conference Playoff, the screening of the adventure thriller *Jaws,* the World Series Game Seven, and the Super Bowl Post game Show.

In 1985, the thirty-seventh Emmy ceremonies captured an average rating of 21.2 percent, compared with the 33.2 of the Oscar show. The telecast of the 2000 Grammys, on CBS on February 23, was the kudocast's best Nielsen ratings since 1993, when Eric Clapton ruled the night with his album "Unplugged." Music's biggest night, which saw Santana walk away with eight of a possible nine Grammy statuettes, drew a smooth 27.78 million viewers and an adults 18–49 rating of 12.6/31, despite increased competition from "Who Wants to Be a Millionaire" and "NYPD Blue." The show's broad audience topped the night among all key demographics, with best scores coming from young adults between the ages eighteen and thirty-four and teens.

The Oscar's preeminence in the entertainment world is enhanced through extensive coverage in all the media: print and radio in the first two decades, and television in the last fifty years. This media blitz is not confined to the United States: the Oscar show is a popular TV program, watched live or on tape by over one billion people.

Every profession is stratified, though some more sharply than others. In acting, for example, the inequality between the elite and the rank-and-file in terms of rewards (money, prestige, popularity, power) is particularly sharp. There are three relevant audiences and three corresponding evaluations in the film world: evaluation by peers, evaluation by critics, and evaluation by the public. The first evaluation is internal, within the film world, whereas the other two are external, outside the industry. However, all three evaluations and audiences are important, because they operate at the same time, with each exerting some impact on the film world.

Most film artists, particularly actors, aim at achieving two distinct goals in their careers: professional attainment as defined by peers and critics, and a broader commercial popularity, as determined by the general public. Actors are aware of the potential conflicts in fulfilling these goals. They know that to be respected by peers and critics is one thing; to be popular, quite another. In film, more than in other arts, outsiders, namely moviegoers, exercise power over artists' careers. By choosing to see a particular film or a particular actor, the public determines not only their present status, but also their chances to work in the future.

What makes the Oscar such an influential award is its peculiar combination of the three evaluations—and audiences. Through the Oscar, the Academy functions as peers, critics, and tastemakers. No other award so well combines critical and popular judgment. The Oscar is the only award to exert a direct, pervasive influence on every element of the film world: the movies, their filmmakers, and their audiences.

CHAPTER 4

The Nomination

Earning an Oscar nomination means getting recognition by fellow artists, and getting the recognition early on can make or break careers. The first nomination serves as a predictor of future success, because it places the nominee in a different category of prestige and visibility.

The First Nomination

Actresses receive their first nomination at a much younger age than actors: 20 percent of all actresses, but only 5 percent of the actors, were younger than twenty-five when they were first nominated. About half of the actresses receive their first nomination prior to the age of thirty, compared with one-tenth of the actors. Supporting players earn their first nomination either at a very young or at a very old age, particularly among the women. Eleven percent of the supporting actresses earned their first nomination prior to the age of twenty, compared with only one percent of the lead actresses. And 10 percent of the supporting, but only 3 percent of the lead, were older than sixty when first nominated.

The youngest nominees in the Academy's history are in the supporting leagues. Justin Henry was only eight when first nominated for *Kramer vs. Kramer,* a remarkable achievement since he had never acted before. The youngest nominee among the supporting actresses is Quinn Cummings *(The Goodbye Girl)* who, at eleven, earned a nomination for her first picture, though she had previously appeared on TV.

Earning a nomination at an early age is more prevalent in the supporting categories because supporting players tend to be cast in younger screen roles. Furthermore, Academy voters have been less discriminating in appraising performances by children or teenagers; sentimentality has always played a considerable role in Hollywood.

The tendency to nominate children has prevailed since the supporting awards were created in 1936. Bonita Granville was the first child to earn a nomination in 1936, for *These Three,* based on Lillian Hellman's play *The Children's Hour.* In 1962, two young girls competed for the supporting award: Patty Duke *(The Miracle Worker)* and Mary Badham *(To Kill a Mockingbird);* Duke won. The same situation occurred in 1973, when Tatum O'Neal *(Paper Moon)* and Linda Blair *(The Exorcist)* were up for Best Supporting Actress; O'Neal won. 1977 saw the Quinn Cummings's nomination but the winner was Vanessa Redgrave for *Julia.*

By comparison, fewer child actors have been nominated: Brandon De Wilde *(Shane)* in 1953, Jack Wilde *(Oliver!)* in 1968, and Justin Henry in 1979. In 1999, at age eleven, child-actor Haley Joel Osment co-starred with Bruce Willis in *The Sixth Sense.* More than the other cast members, Osment was given credit for contributing to the most successful and most popular horror thriller in the genre's history.

No child actress has ever been nominated for Best Actress—the youngest nominee in this category is Kate Winslet, who was twenty-two when nominated for *Titanic.* Jackie Cooper, nominated at the age of ten for *Skippy,* is the only boy to compete for the Best Actor. But Cooper was a known quantity, a veteran of the Our Gang series.

The Academy has acknowledged the importance of star-children as money-makers with Special (Junior) Awards. In 1939, Deanna Durbin and Mickey Rooney were awarded miniature Oscar trophies. Durbin was honored for her performance in her first feature, *Three Smart Girls,* which made her a star and also saved Universal studio from bankruptcy. Rooney received the award in recognition of his Andy Hardy movies, "for significant contribution in bringing to the screen the spirit and personification of youth and as a juvenile player setting a high standard of ability and achievement."

In 1940, Judy Garland won a Special Oscar as "the year's best juvenile performer," for her appearance in the musical *The Wizard of Oz,* one of MGM's all-time smash hits. Other children were honored with a Special Oscar in the 1940s, but later, youthful performances qualified for nominations in the legitimate awards.

The youngest nominee among the Best Actresses is French Isabelle Adjani, for the title role in Francois Truffaut's *The Story of Adele H.* at the age of twenty-one. Adjani began her career in amateur productions at twelve, and made her film debut two years later. She rejected a tempting twenty-year contract with the noted Comédie-Française theater in order to appear in *The Story of Adele H.* It paid off: the movie, assisted by her nomination, put her at the forefront of international stars. In 1989, the Academy conferred on Adjani a second Best Actress nomination for another French film, *Camille Claudel*. That she played mentally disturbed women in both pictures was certainly a bonus, given the kinds of female roles the Academy has liked.

Consistent differences prevail between the careers of female and male nominees. Women receive their first nomination at a younger age than men: the median age at first nomination is thirty-one for the women, but forty for the men. The median age, which points to the age at which half of the group received their first nomination, is a more accurate measure than the average age because of the wide distribution of ages.

Of the four groups, the Best Actresses are the youngest at their first nomination. The median age at receiving the first nomination is twenty-nine for the Best Actresses, thirty-three for the Supporting Actresses, thirty-eight for the Best Actors, and forty-three for the Supporting Actors. Within each category, women have an advantage over men when it comes to getting early recognition.

Supporting players tend to be younger or older than the lead nominees, based on the kinds of screen roles they play. Character roles are typically younger or older than leading parts.

Very few Best Actresses have been older than forty at their first nomination. In the 1940s, Joan Crawford *(Mildred Pierce)* was the only actress in this age category, and in the 1950s, there were only two, Shirley Booth *(Come Back, Little Sheba)* and Anna Magnani *(The Rose Tattoo)*. Jessica Tandy, who at eighty-one became the oldest actress to be nominated and win Best Actress (for *Driving Miss Daisy)*, is the exception.

Actresses have rightly complained that once they reach the age of forty they either have to switch to supporting roles or to retire because of the dearth of scripts with middle-aged heroines. Leading ladies in American films are typically young and attractive. It's safe to predict that chances are slim to get Oscar recognition if actresses don't get a nomination by the age of thirty. Less than 10 percent of the Best Actresses, but 25 percent the Best Actors, were forty or older when first nominated.

The position of middle-aged actresses in the film industry began to change in the 1970s, and the Academy has slowly reflected these changes. Over the past two decades, there were more leading roles for middle-aged actresses than ever before. Gena Rowlands *(A Woman Under the Influence)*, Ellen Burstyn *(Same Time Next Year)*, and Mary Tyler Moore *(Ordinary People)*, were all mature actresses, nominated for playing mature women.

Another encouraging development is the nomination of elderly actresses for playing lead characters, such as Katharine Hepburn *(On Golden Pond)*, Geraldine Page *(The Trip to Bountiful)*, and Jessica Tandy *(Driving*

Miss Daisy). In the past, elderly actresses were mostly nominated in the supporting categories.

Nominating older players has also characterized the male categories over the last two decades. In the 1950s, only two supporting actors (Eric Von Stroheim in *Sunset Boulevard* and Sessue Hayakawa in *The Bridge on the River Kwai)* were in their sixties. But since the 1970s, a substantial cohort belongs to this age group, including: John Mills *(Ryan's Daughter)*, Lee Strasberg *(The Godfather, Part II)*, Burgess Meredith *(Rocky)*, Robert Preston *(Victor/Victoria)*, Denholm Elliott *(A Room With a View)*, and Armin Mueller-Stahl *(Shine)*.

Hollywood has finally caught up with the growing awareness of aging and ageism in American society. More screenplays and more movies about elderly protagonists are being produced. The Academy has expressed its concerns for elderly players with a larger number of nominations.

It's possible to win a Best Actor nomination at an old age. Take Richard Farnsworth, for example. More than half a century ago, Farnsworth swore off speaking roles after his first crack in a Roy Rogers Western. The director wanted the then stuntman to say a few lines, but every time he tried, he broke out in giggles. Eventually, the director gave up, and Farnsworth promised himself, Never again. But he was persuaded to give acting another shot by Alan J. Pakula, in his 1978 Western drama, *Comes a Horseman,* for which he was nominated for a supporting Oscar.

In the twilight of a career, which began with playing a Mongol horseman in 1938's *The Adventures of Marco Polo,* Farnsworth found himself nominated for a powerful performance in David Lynch's *The Straight Story,* playing the real-life, stubborn Alvin Straight, who insisted on driving a lawnmower hundreds of miles to visit his ailing brother. "I'm pretty limited in a lot of ways," Farnsworth told *Entertainment Weekly.* "But if I feel the character, it's damn easy to do." In truth, it hurt to connect with Straight: Bum hips were killing the actor during the driving scenes, and then there was the agony of recounting Straight's World War II memories—a vet himself, Farnsworth won't talk about his experience.

The oldest nominees in their respective categories are:

Richard Farnsworth *(The Straight Story)* 78, George Arliss *(Disraeli)* 63, and Art Carney *(Harry and Tonto)* 57, among the Best Actors;

George Burns *(The Sunshine Boys)* 80, and Don Ameche *(Cocoon)* 77, among the Supporting Actors;

Dame May Robson *(Lady for a Night)* 76, and Ida Kaminska *(The Shop on Main Street)* 68, among the Best Actresses;

Gloria Stuart *(Titanic)* 87, Jessica Tandy *(Fried Green Tomatoes)* 82, Eva Le Galienne *(Resurrection)* 80, and Dame Edith Evans *(Tom Jones)* 76, among the Supporting Actresses.

It's possible to win a nomination at any age, particularly in the supporting categories. The supporting nominees' age has ranged from eight (Justin Henry) to eighty (George Burns) among the men, and from ten (Quinn Cummings) to eighty-seven (Gloria Stuart) among the women. However, in each category, one age group is dominant, and the lead leagues are more rigid concerning age. Most Best Actresses were in their late twenties, and most Best Actors in their late thirties, at their first nomination. An age difference of a full decade, which is significant in performers' careers, reflects the double standards in American society regarding aged men and women.

Early and Late Oscar Recognition

At what phase of their careers do film artists receive their first nomination? How long does it take to get a nomination once a film career has been launched?

Surprisingly, a considerable proportion of players (16 percent) have received Academy nomination for their very first film, particularly among the supporting players. As expected, the time span between film debut and first nomination is shorter for the women than for the men: Half of the actresses, but only one-third of the actors, were nominated within a period of five years after their first movie. Women's talent is certified by the Academy much faster than men's. Indeed, the career "fate" of leading ladies is determined early on: Actresses failing to impress the Academy in their first five or six movies stand slim chances to get a nomination.

Supporting players tend to receive their first nomination either very early or very late in their careers: 18 percent of the supporting, but only 5 percent of the leads, had to wait two decades after their debuts to be nominated.

About one-tenth of the Best Actors have earned a nomination for their *first* film or for their first *major* film. They include: Paul Muni *(The Valiant)*, Montgomery Clift *(The Search)*, Anthony Franciosa *(A Hatful of Rain)*, Alan Arkin *(The Russians Are Coming, the Russians Are Coming)*, Ryan O'Neal *(Love Story)*, and Dexter Gordon *(Round Midnight)*.

A similar percentage of Best Actresses were nominated for their first film, some for re-creating successful stage roles. Among them: Julie Harris *(Member of the Wedding)*, Maggie McNamara *(The Moon Is Blue)*, Jane

Alexander *(The Great White Hope)*, Julie Walters *(Educating Rita)*. Other lucky actresses, singled out by the Academy for film debut, include Carrie Snodgress *(Diary of a Mad Housewife)*, Diana Ross *(Lady Sings the Blues)*, Bette Midler *(The Rose)*, Whoopi Goldberg *(The Color Purple)*, Emily Watson *(Breaking the Waves)*, and Janet McTeer *(Tumbleweeds)*.

Dustin Hoffman was fortunate to earn a nomination for his first major film, *The Graduate*, in 1967; his first film, *The Tiger Makes Out*, was made the same year. After graduating from the Pasadena Playhouse in Los Angeles, Hoffman moved to New York, where he was forced to make his living as a typist and moving man. For a while he could not get any acting job and, at one point, even considered quitting. Then, after working as an assistant director Off Broadway, Hoffman was cast in *Journey of the Fifth Horse*, which enjoyed a short life but won him an Obie Award. Director Mike Nichols was impressed with his performance and, looking for a young, unknown actor to play the lead in *The Graduate*, summoned Hoffman to Hollywood for a screen test. Hoffman became an instant star after this film.

Luck or "fate"—being the right player at the right time and place—plays a considerable role in earning early recognition. Take Martha Scott, who after a brief experience in stock scored a triumph in her first Broadway play, Thornton Wilder's *Our Town*. This success led to a Hollywood career, marked by a nomination for her movie debut. Accidents and coincidences have accounted for a considerable number of actors being cast in what later became their Oscar-nominated roles.

The Academy is more generous in conferring nominations for film debuts on supporting players. Actors who have immediately caught the Academy's attention include: John Garfield *(Four Daughters)*, Robert Morley *(Marie Antoinette)*, Sidney Greenstreet *(The Maltese Falcon)*, Richard Widmark *(Kiss of Death)*, Don Murray *(Bus Stop)*, Terence Stamp *(Billy Budd)*, Brad Dourif *(One Flew Over the Cuckoo's Nest)*, Howard Rollins Jr. *(Ragtime)*, John Malkovich *(Places in the Heart)*, Leonardo DiCaprio *(What's Eating Gilbert Grape?)*, Ralph Fiennes *(Schindler's List)*, and Edward Norton *(Primal Fear)*.

Among the supporting actresses nominated for their very first film are: Maria Ouspenskaya *(Dodsworth)*, Teresa Wright and Patricia Collinge (both for *Little Foxes)*, Angela Lansbury *(Gaslight)*, Lee Grant *(Detective Story)*, Diana Varsi *(Peyton Place)*, Maureen Stapleton *(Lonely Hearts)*, Shirley Knight *(Dark at the Top of the Stairs)*, Carol Channing *(Thoroughly Modern Millie)*, Cathy Burns *(Last Summer)*, Glenn Close *(The World According to Garp)*, Oprah Winfrey *(The Color Purple)*, and Julia Roberts *(Steel Magnolias)*.

Interestingly, some of the nominated performances were not delivered by professional actors. Harold Russell won two Oscars, a regular and a Special one, for re-creating on-screen *(The Best Years of Our Lives)* his real-life experience as a paratroop sergeant who lost both hands in World War II. It was Russell's first picture, and for many years his only one.

Born in Cambodia and trained as a doctor, Haing S. Ngor was captured and tortured by the Khmer Rouge after their takeover of the country. Ngor escaped to Thailand and finally settled in the United States, where he worked at various jobs. Ngor made his film debut in *The Killing Fields* (1984), for which he won a supporting Oscar. This was followed by a number of movies before he was murdered in 1996.

Several singers and dancers have received nominations for their debuts if their pictures were box-office hits. Miliza Korjus, a Polish opera singer, was nominated for her first and only movie, *The Great Waltz*. Mikhail Baryshnikov and Leslie Browne, both dancers of the American Ballet Theater, earned supporting nods for playing dancers in *The Turning Point*.

Some noted writers were singled out for acting debuts. Jason Miller, a successful Broadway playwright *(That Championship Season)* was nominated for portraying a priest in *The Exorcist*. Michael V. Gazzo, who wrote *A Hatful of Rain*, earned a nomination for his first movie, *The Godfather, Part II*. Both Miller and Gazzo earned nominations not so much for distinguished acting, but for performances contained in blockbuster movies. Deservedly or not, commercial hits tend to earn nominations in a disproportionately large number of categories.

Receiving a nomination for a first film, thus reaching a professional height with only one credit, is unique to acting careers. In most professions, a lengthy period of formal training and working experience are required before praise and promotion are granted. But in the performing arts, neither formal education nor training are prerequisites for entry into the profession or for climbing to the top. One film, especially if it is a commercial hit, can make or break a career. Besides, many factors, not just acting talent, are responsible for making a particular performance (or a particular film) worthy of Oscar recognition.

In contrast to those recognized early for their work, some artists had to wait for a long time (over two decades) to earn a nomination. This is particularly the case of foreign actors, who began to perform at a young age, but were much older by the time they received their first nomination since it took a long time until they were cast in American movies, or made foreign movies that were visible in the American market.

Anna Magnani received her first nomination and Oscar for *The Rose Tattoo,* twenty-one years after her Italian film debut. Had it not been for

Tennessee Williams's demand that she play the title role, Magnani would never have been nominated for an Oscar, despite her being one of the world's greatest screen actresses.

The crucial factor in the foreign players' careers is the age at which they were brought to Hollywood. Many actors showed promise in their own countries, but for a variety of reasons didn't get international recognition. Maximilian Schell did not establish a reputation as a movie star in Europe, despite good work early on in his career. He arrived in Hollywood as Maria Schell's younger brother, but it took only one American film, *The Young Lions,* in which he was cast at the suggestion of Marlon Brando, to make him a player of international caliber. Three years later, Stanley Kramer assigned him the role of the German counselor in *Judgment at Nuremberg,* for which he received the 1961 Best Actor Award.

Several British players became movie stars only after their relocation to Hollywood. Rex Harrison began his film career in England when he was twenty-two, but his first American movie *(Anna and the King of Siam)* occurred sixteen years later, and he received his first nomination (for *Cleopatra*) thirty-three years after his film debut, at the age of fifty-five. Peter Finch, another excellent actor, began his career in Australia in his late teens, and established himself as a prominent actor in the British industry in the 1950s. However, he too received his first nomination *(Sunday, Bloody Sunday)* thirty-six years after his first movie.

Richard Burton's first five pictures in England failed to launch him as a major international star, despite acclaim for his acting. In America, however, it took one Broadway play, Christopher Frye's *The Lady's Not for Burning,* and one movie, *My Cousin Rachel,* which earned him a supporting nomination, to make Burton a big star.

While movies are seemingly dominated by young up-and-comers, Hollywood discovered Dame Judi Dench when she was in her sixties. In 1997, Dench became a star with her Oscar-nominated performance as Queen Victoria in *Mrs. Brown,* for which she won a Golden Globe. The next year, she played another royal figure, Queen Elizabeth, in *Shakespeare in Love,* for which she won a supporting Oscar. Dench followed her record with a Tony Award for *Amy's View,* her first Broadway play in forty years, though she's a staple of the London stage.

Dench was nominated in 1998 for the same figure that Cate Blanchett played in *Elizabeth,* as a younger queen. She has only eight minutes of screen time in *Shakespeare in Love,* and yet she is unforgettable. "I just played her like I imagined she would be," Dench told *Premiere.* "She was a fierce woman. People didn't like messing with her. I was in all those clothes and I couldn't do much but stay very still and pray I didn't have to go to the loo in the middle."

In contrast to the British, American players who received tardy recognition were box-office stars who developed as *actors* later in their careers. John Wayne made his film debut in his early twenties, but received his first nomination *(Sands of Iwo Jima)* twenty-one years later, at the age of forty-two. Wayne became a movie star after his breakthrough role as the Ringo Kid in John Ford's *Stagecoach,* and he matured as a screen actor a decade later, when Howard Hawks cast him in an epic character part in *Red River.* This performance and the Oscar nomination a year later certified Wayne's talent.

Late recognition also characterizes popular performers who appeared in commercially successful films but failed to gain peer esteem. Later on, for a reasonably good performance, preferably in a successful film, they were honored with a nomination, which served as both acknowledgment of their skills and as tribute to their endurance. Doris Day made her film debut in 1948, after which she appeared in musicals and romantic comedies. As a tribute to her popularity, the Academy conferred on her a nomination for the popular romantic comedy *Pillow Talk.*

Harrison Ford, too, was a box-office champion before earning recognition as a "serious" actor. Ford has appeared in more box-office hits than any other contemporary star; his pictures have grossed collectively more than two billion dollars at the box office. Among others, Ford's screen credits include Han Solo in George Lucas's *Star Wars* trilogy (1977–83) and the archeological soldier of fortune in Spielberg's *Raiders of the Lost Ark* and its sequels. Some of these films were nominated in several categories, including Best Picture, but their special effects overshadowed Ford the actor. In 1985, when Ford played a more substantial dramatic character, in Peter Weir's *Witness,* the Academy rewarded him with a Best Actor nomination at the age of forty-three.

Actresses who managed smooth transition from being child performers to ingenues and leading ladies have also been rewarded. This group includes Carole Lombard, Mary Astor, Loretta Young, Natalie Wood, and Tuesday Weld. A striking beauty, Elizabeth Taylor made her first film at the age of ten in *There's One Born Every Minute.* In 1942, she was signed by MGM to a long-term contract. In the decade that followed, Taylor matured into one of the most beautiful and most popular screen personalities. She somehow skipped adolescence, moving almost directly from child roles to romantic leads. Taylor received her first nomination for playing a troubled Southern belle in *Raintree County,* fifteen years after her debut.

A small group of Academy players began their careers in the silent era, long before the Oscars existed, then made the transition to the talkies. These actresses, usually nominated for featured roles, include Alice Brady,

Jane Darwell, Ethel Barrymore, Marjorie Rambeau, and Billie Burke. The most distinguished among them is Lillian Gish, a pioneer of the American cinema, joining D. W. Griffith in 1912, when she was sixteen. In the 1930s, Gish retired from the screen, but a decade later she returned, this time as a character actress. In 1946, Gish received a supporting nomination for playing a wife driven to drink by her brutal cattle baron husband in the Western *Duel in the Sun,* a sweeping box-office success. This nomination was as much a symbolic tribute to Gish's comeback and lengthy career as a legitimate honor to a particular role.

The Academy, and Hollywood in general, have shown tremendous respect for comeback performances by distinguished players who, after years of absence from the screen, or after years of mediocre work, can still surprise with effective acting. A major silent star who began performing in her early teens, Gloria Swanson was nominated for the silent movie *Sadie Thompson,* and for her first talkie, *The Trespasser.* However, her subsequent movies were unsuccessful, and in 1934 she retired. Swanson did make an abortive comeback in the comedy *Father Takes a Wife* (1941), and then, after a decade, made a memorable comeback in *Sunset Boulevard,* in which she played a neurotic fading movie queen. Hollywood couldn't deny Swanson a nomination for her comeback as well as for her indelible portrayal.

The Academy history is replete with comeback stories, some successful, others less so. Rosalind Russell was a popular star in the 1940s with three Best Actress nominations to her credit, but in the 1950s, her career declined. Instead of despairing, or waiting for the right role, Russell went back to the stage and bounced back with a triumphant performance in *Auntie Mame,* which she first played on Broadway, then repeated on screen. The Academy honored her with a fourth nomination, eleven years after her third one *(Mourning Becomes Electra).*

In nominating comeback performances, Hollywood shows loyalty to its champions, based on the belief that they should get a second chance. Several of these comeback nominations have proved instrumental in providing second chapters to previously faltering careers. Since *Easy Rider* (1969), for which he received a writing nomination, Peter Fonda has made peace with both mainstream Hollywood and his late father, Henry, whom he credits for inspiring his characterization in *Ulee's Gold* (1997), a strong comeback role, for which he received his first Best Actor nomination.

The first Oscar nomination of Peter's sister, Lynn Redgrave, came in 1966 for her role in *Georgy Girl.* In the 1970s, Lynn's film career stagnated, but she worked consistently in TV, until her 1996 career-reviving role in *Shine.* Two years later, and thirty-two years after her first nomination, Lynn received a second, this time supporting nod, for *Gods and Monsters,* in which she played James Whale's housekeeper, speaking in a thick Hungarian accent.

Nominated at the age of eighty-seven for a supporting role in *Titanic,* Gloria Stuart also qualifies as an Oscar "comeback kid." A founding member of SAG, it had been ten years since Stuart made a film and decades since she starred in one.

Lead versus Supporting Oscars

For eight years, there were two acting awards: Best Actor and Best Actress. In 1936, the Academy created two additional categories: Best Supporting Actor and Best Supporting Actress. New rules were required to clarify the distinction between lead and supporting roles. At first, the Academy asked the studios to designate lead and supporting roles in their annual reminder lists, which gave them power. For instance, Luise Rainer's role in *The Great Ziegfeld,* as the showman's first wife, was so small that by today's standards she would have been nominated for a feature role. Nonetheless, with the backing of MGM's publicity machine, Rainer was nominated (and won) the lead award.

The criteria designating lead and supporting roles were often controversial. In 1942, Agnes Moorehead was nominated for a supporting role in Orson Welles's *The Magnificent Ambersons* because the studio (RKO) believed she had no chance to win the lead. The competition that year was particularly fierce, and Greer Garson *(Mrs. Miniver)* was considered to be the favorite. But Moorehead's role as the neurotic spinster aunt was of considerable size, which convinced many she deserved Best Actress nomination; she was cited as Best Actress by the New York Film Critics Circle.

The Academy instructed its members: "Actors marked in the Reminder List by a star are considered Leads and can be nominated only for the Best Acting Awards." But members were given the option "to nominate any supporting player for both the Supporting Award and the Best Performance Award." Hence, in 1944, Barry Fitzgerald became the first (and last) player to be nominated for the same role *(Going My Way)* in both the lead and supporting leagues. A compromise was reached when Bing Crosby, also nominated for that film, won Best Actor and Fitzgerald the Supporting Award. Many were disappointed, because they believed Fitzgerald's role was clearly a major one; once again, the New York Film Critics cited Fitzgerald's work as Best Actor.

To avoid unclarities, in the following year, the Academy changed its rules. It determined that "performance by an actor or actress in any leading role shall be eligible for nomination only for the General Awards for acting achievements." But performance by an actor or actress in a supporting role may be nominated for either the lead or the supporting category. The rules still allowed players to be nominated in both the lead and supporting categories, but for different screen roles.

Not surprisingly, nomination in both categories in the same year has occurred only a few times in the Academy's history. In 1938, Fay Bainter was nominated for Best Actress in *White Banners* and for supporting Actress in *Jezebel*. In 1942, Teresa Wright became the second actress to be nominated twice in the same year, for a lead role in *The Pride of the Yankees* and for a featured role in *Mrs. Miniver*.

In 1982, Jessica Lange won two nominations, both for portraying an actress: the fiery and doomed Frances Farmer in *Frances,* and a supporting role, as the soft and submissive TV actress, in *Tootsie*. In 1988, Sigourney Weaver was nominated for a lead in *Gorillas in the Mist* and for a supporting role in the comedy *Working Girl*. In 1993, for the first and last time, two actresses were nominated in both categories: Holly Hunter for a lead in *The Piano* and supporting in *The Firm*, and Emma Thompson for a lead in *The Remains of the Day* and supporting turn in the Irish drama, *In the Name of the Father*.

Three of these actresses lost the major but won the supporting Oscar: Fay Bainter, Teresa Wright, and Jessica Lange. The Best Actress winners in those years were: Bette Davis for *Jezebel,* Greer Garson for *Mrs. Miniver,* and Meryl Streep for *Sophie's Choice,* respectively. Holly Hunter won the lead Oscar for *The Piano,* but Thompson (who had won an Oscar the year before for *Howards End)* and Sigourney failed to win in either category.

In 1950, a further clarification was introduced: "If a performance by an actor or actress should receive sufficient votes to be nominated for both the Best Actress and Supporting Award, only the achievement which, in the preferential tabulation process, first received the quota shall be placed on the ballot. The votes for the second achievement shall there upon be redistributed."

Classifications of nominations continued to be made by the studios, regardless of the role's size and billing considerations. In 1950, Anne Baxter persuaded Fox to campaign for her for a lead nomination in *All About Eve,* thereby running against Bette Davis, who was the film's star. Had Baxter been nominated for a featured role, as many believed she should have, Davis would have won Best Actress. Baxter had already earned a supporting Oscar in 1946 for *The Razor's Edge,* which was her reason for competing in the Best Actress league. The industry's feeling was that Davis and Baxter canceled each other out, leaving the award to the least expected nominee that year, Judy Holliday in *Born Yesterday*.

By contrast, Betsy Blair's 1955 performance in *Marty,* as the shy and lonely schoolteacher, was nominated for a supporting Oscar despite the fact that some considered it to be a lead role; earlier, Blair was honored with the Best Actress Award at the Cannes Festival. However, the competition for the Best Actress that year, headed by Anna Magnani *(The Rose Tattoo),* was intense, and Blair had no chance of winning.

A serious dispute erupted the following year, when Dorothy Malone volunteered, under her studio's "suggestion," to lower her standing in *Written on the Wind* to qualify for a supporting nomination. Malone received co-star billing, but Universal designated her performance as supporting because her chances to win were better in this league, which turned out to be true. However, Malone's switch was seen as "grossly unjust" to performers who deserved recognition as supporting players.

This resulted in a new rule in 1957, according to which the Academy, not the studios, would make final determination as to the appropriate classification of screen roles. The Academy would consider the information provided by the studios, but should any screen credit be questioned, the matter would be submitted to a special committee for final decision.

Unexpected nominations continued to be made. In 1961, Piper Laurie was nominated for Best Actress, as Paul Newman's alcoholic girlfriend in *The Hustler,* in which she received co-star billing with George C. Scott and Jackie Gleason. It was a pleasant surprise as Scott and Gleason were nominated for featured roles.

A major change in the rules occurred in 1964, when the Academy decided that "the determination as to whether a role was a lead or supporting is made individually by members of the Acting Branch at the time of the balloting." Branch members could nominate any player in either lead or supporting league, regardless of studio billings and publicity. The Academy felt that each member should have the right to exercise his/her judgment—without interference from other sources.

Nonetheless, politicking through ad campaigns have prevailed. At times, chances to win determine the specific designation. This became clear in 1966, when Walter Matthau was nominated for a supporting role in Billy Wilder's *The Fortune Cookie,* despite the fact that his role was major and the whole film was based on team acting by him and co-star Jack Lemmon (who was not nominated). But Matthau's prospects were better in the supporting classification, because there were two strong lead performances that year: Paul Scofield *A Man for All Seasons,* and Richard Burton in *Who's Afraid of Virginia Woolf?* When the results were announced, these political considerations turned out to be true: Scofield won Best Actor and Matthau Supporting Actor.

In 1980, Columbia campaigned for Meryl Streep for a supporting nomination in *Kramer vs. Kramer*. Streep's role, as the confused wife-mother, was small but constituted the center of the movie. The studio's decision, however, had nothing to do with the role's size but with the realization that she had no chance beating Sally Field's performance in *Norma Rae*, particularly after Field had been honored with all the critics awards: the New York, Los Angeles, and National Society of Film Critics.

That players attribute greater importance to star billing and lead roles is self-evident. Winning lead nominations and awards is more prestigious and has far more influence on their careers. Shelley Winters has not forgotten to this day that her two Oscars were for supporting roles. Peter Finch was upset at his publicists' suggestion that they try for the supporting award in *Network*, which the actor felt represented his best work. Finch was determined "to go for the top award or be out of the competition altogether."

The new rules sometimes lead to surprising results. Marlon Brando's role in *The Godfather* was considered to be suitable for a supporting nomination, but he was nominated for (and won) Best Actor. Valerie Perrine would have had better chances to win, for playing Lenny Bruce's sluttish wife in *Lenny*, had she been nominated for a featured role. Perrine was cited as Supporting Actress by both the New York Film Critics and the National Board of Review, but the Acting Branch nominated her for a lead because it was a weak year for actresses. In 1982, the biggest surprise of the acting branch was placing Susan Sarandon for Best Actress in *Atlantic City*. Paramount had been pushing for a supporting nomination, and Sarandon herself admitted that she had voted for herself in the supporting category.

The criteria used to distinguish lead from supporting roles are not clear, a confusion that also prevails in other groups. In 1985, Peggy Ashcroft's role as Mrs. Moore, the bright elderly lady in David Lean's *A Passage to India*, received rave reviews and won a number of critical citations. But even the critics circles were divided as to the appropriate category for her role. The New York Film Critics cited Ashcroft as Best Actress, but the Los Angeles Film Critics singled her out as supporting actress. The Academy followed the Los Angeles group and honored her with Supporting Actress. Judy Davis, her co-star, playing the mysterious young woman, was nominated for Best Actress. The feeling was that had Ashcroft been nominated for the lead, neither she nor Davis would have won, because they would have canceled each other.

In recent years, Samuel Jackson was upset by Miramax's decision to campaign for him in the supporting league in Quentin Tarantino's *Pulp Fiction*, despite the fact that he played a co-starring role with John Travolta, who was pushed by the studio and then nominated for the lead Oscar. A few years later, Miramax's Harvey Weinstein held that Michael Caine had a better chance to receive a supporting nod for *Little Voice*, but the actor disagreed.

Single and Multiple Nominations

How democratic is the nomination process? Is earning a nomination a once-in-a-lifetime achievement? Apparently not, judging by the high percentage (one-third) of actors and directors who have received multiple nominations.

There are differences between the lead and supporting players. The vast majority (over 80 percent) of supporting players have received a single nomination, but a considerable proportion (about 50 percent) of the lead nominees have been cited more than once. Since the pool of leading players is smaller than that of supporting players, the competition for lead roles is tougher, though it increases the chances of those who get them to earn a second nomination.

Winning an Oscar almost ensures another nomination in the very near future. The average number of nominations is 3.5 for the women and 2.9 for the men. However, women tend to receive multiple nominations *after* their first Oscar, whereas men tend to get them *prior* to winning. This difference stems from the fact that women tend to win the Oscar at their first nomination, whereas men win at their second or third nomination (see chapter 6).

The vast majority (85 percent) of the Best Actresses have received two or more nominations. In Oscar's entire history, only nine of the sixty female winners have received a single nomination: Mary Pickford, Ginger Rogers, Judy Holliday, Shirley Booth, Louise Fletcher, Marlee Matlin, and the three past winners, Helen Hunt, Gwyneth Paltrow, and Hilary Swank. Obviously it is premature to assess their Oscar prospects since all three are very young and just beginning their careers.

By contrast, about one-third (or twenty-one) of the Best Actors have received one nomination: Emil Jannings, Warner Baxter, George Arliss, Lionel Barrymore, Paul Lukas, Ray Milland, Broderick Crawford, Ernest Borgnine, Yul Brynner, David Niven, Charlton Heston, Lee Marvin, Paul Scofield, Cliff Robertson, Art Carney, Ben Kingsley, F. Murray Abraham, Michael Douglas,

Jeremy Irons, Nicolas Cage, and Roberto Benigni. Some of these actors, like Scofield and Kingsley, have received a second, supporting nomination.

The elite of film actresses has been much smaller than that of actors. In every decade, a smaller number of women have dominated Hollywood, that is, were popular with the public, sought by the studios, and in control of their careers. Not surprisingly, in each era, the best screen roles circulate among a small group of women.

Multiple nominations take two forms: in one category (either lead *or* supporting) or in two categories (lead *and* supporting). Most of the multiple nominations have been within the same category, either in the lead or in the supporting. For better or worse, once players are labeled by agents, producers, and directors as leading or character players, these labels are hard to change, a phenomenon known in Hollywood as "the curse of typecasting."

In the last two decades, however, it has become easier to cross over from one category to another. In the past, the direction was usually one-sided, from leading to supporting roles. One of the positive developments within the film industry is that the rigid concepts of leading and character players are not as clearly defined and observed as they used to be.

About one-tenth of all players have been nominated in both lead and supporting categories. Most of the men began in character roles, then earned nominations in the lead categories. For years, this was considered to be the natural evolution of acting careers. John Garfield's first nomination *(Four Daughters)* was for a featured role, but his second *(Body and Soul)* was for a lead. And Rod Steiger's three nominations include one in the supporting *(On the Waterfront)*, and two in the lead *(The Pawnbroker* and *In the Heat of the Night)* categories. The other direction, from lead to character roles, marks the careers of elderly actors. James Mason's first nomination *(A Star Is Born)* was for a lead, but his two subsequent nominations *(Georgy Girl* and *The Verdict)* were for supporting roles.

By contrast, few of the actresses who began in supporting roles were able to make the transition to leading ladies. Women are much more limited than men by cultural restrictions concerning the range of their screen roles. Indeed, several actresses who began as leading ladies found themselves relegated to playing character roles. British actress Wendy Hiller, who won her first nomination for playing Eliza Doolittle in *Pygmalion,* always commanded leading roles on stage, but in Hollywood she was classified as a supporting actress, earning second *(Separate Tables)* and third *(A Man for All Seasons)* nominations for featured roles.

Shelley Winters also played leads early on in her career, earning a Best Actress nomination for her portrayal of the pregnant factory girl in *A Place in the Sun.* However, shortly after this nomination, producers and casting directors relegated her to supporting roles, and she remained in this league for the rest of her career, winning three supporting nominations (*The Diary of Anne Frank, A Patch of Blue,* and *The Poseidon Adventure*).

Recently though, women in Hollywood have been more flexible in their choice of roles, often beginning in one category and moving to another, or switching back and forth between lead and supporting roles. Ellen Burstyn, Meryl Streep, Glenn Close, and Frances McDormand have all begun their careers by playing supporting roles but later succeeded in becoming leading ladies. At the same time, for a good role in an interesting film, these women are still willing to play secondary roles. The "stigma" of being a supporting, and therefore "second-class" player, is less evident and has less impact on acting careers than it has had in the past.

Academy nominations have been concentrated within a small group of players: one-fifth of the Best Actors and Best Actresses have earned more than four nominations. Among those nominated four times were: Barbara Stanwyck, Rosalind Russell, Jane Wyman, Charles Boyer, Mickey Rooney, Anthony Quinn, and Anthony Hopkins. A smaller group of actors, including Irene Dunne, Audrey Hepburn, Glenn Close, Fredric March, Paul Muni, Arthur Kennedy, earned five nominations.

The top of the pyramid is composed of players with six or more nominations. This distinguished elite is small, eighteen players, or 2 percent of all the nominees.

6 nominations:	Thelma Ritter, Deborah Kerr, Robert Duvall
7 nominations:	Richard Burton, Peter O'Toole, Jane Fonda, Dustin Hoffman
8 nominations:	Marlon Brando, Jack Lemmon, Geraldine Page, Paul Newman, Al Pacino
9 nominations:	Spencer Tracy
10 nominations:	Bette Davis, Laurence Olivier
11 nominations:	Jack Nicholson
12 nominations:	Katharine Hepburn, Meryl Streep

The time span between the first and last nominations attests to the degree of viability of acting careers as perceived by the Academy. Along with providing peer recognition, Oscar nominations reflect the standing (and popularity) of the nominees in the movie colony.

Surprisingly, the viability of players' careers, as measured by the number of years between first and last nomination, is rather short. For half of the players, the time span between first and last nomination is about a decade, indicating that most players receive multiple nominations within a short period of time. For one-third of the multiple nominees, two decades elapsed between first and last nominations, and only one-sixth received their multiple nominations in a period extending over two decades.

The span between first and last nominations is much shorter for actresses. For two-thirds of the women, it is less than a decade. With few exceptions, the viability of actresses' screen careers tend to be short (fifteen to twenty years), because they cannot find rewarding or suitable screen roles when they reach middle-age. By contrast, the durability of men's careers can last three or four decades since aging has less of an impact on the range of roles they can play.

Hence, it is possible to describe most actresses' careers in terms of the *one decade* (or at most two decades) in which they were popular and in demand. Greta Garbo and Irene Dunne were stars of the 1930s, and Olivia de Havilland, Rosalind Russell, and Greer Garson of the 1940s. Audrey Hepburn, Susan Hayward, and Deborah Kerr did their best work in the 1950s, and Anne Bancroft, Patricia Neal, and Shirley MacLaine in the 1960s. The 1970s were dominated by Ellen Burstyn, Faye Dunaway, and Diane Keaton, and the 1980s saw the rise of a new cohort headed by Sally Field, Sissy Spacek, Meryl Streep, Jessica Lange, and Glenn Close. The 1990s have been good for Susan Sarandon (a late bloomer), Holly Hunter, Jodie Foster, Emma Thompson, Michelle Pfeiffer, and Winona Ryder.

In contrast, male careers tend to be viable for a prolonged period of time, spanning three, four, and even five decades. Men who do good work consistently are rewarded with multiple nominations. Laurence Olivier's film career began in 1930 and continued to be viable for half a century. His ten nominations spanned thirty-nine years, from *Wuthering Heights* in 1939 to *The Boys from Brazil* in 1978. Olivier's brilliant career was rewarded with one nomination in the 1930s, three in the 1940s, one in the 1950s, two in the 1960s, and three in the 1970s.

Spencer Tracy, another Hollywood giant, began his career in 1930 and went on to make movies up to is death, in 1967. His thirty-seven-year-career brought him nine nominations: three in the 1930s, three in the 1950s, and three in the 1960s, the first of which was for *San Francisco* in 1936 and the last for *Guess Who's Coming to Dinner,* which was released posthumously.

Of the current generation of actors, Jack Lemmon and Jack Nicholson continue to enjoy spectacular screen careers. Lemmon has earned seven nominations (so far), from *Mister Roberts* in 1955 to *Missing* in 1982. And Nicholson has received eleven nominations, including three Oscars: two Best Actor *(One Flew Over the Cuckoo's Nest, 1975; As Good As It Gets,* 1997) and one supporting *(Terms of Endearment, 1983).*

For the supporting players, the time span between first and last nomination is shorter, because most were older when gaining Academy recognition in the first place. Distinguished character players, such as Walter Brennan, Charles Coburn, Charles Bickford, and Gladys Cooper, won multiple nominations, usually within a short period of time because they weren't young at their first nomination.

Claude Rains, who made his stage debut as a choirboy in London at the age of eleven, went on to hold every possible position in the theater world, from call boy and prompter to leading actor and stage manager. However, Rains's impressive debut, *The Invisible Man,* in which he appeared faceless, occurred when he was forty-four. He won his first nomination in 1939, at the age of fifty, for playing the corrupt senator in *Mr. Smith Goes to Washington.* Rains soon established himself as one of Hollywood's finest character actors, winning four supporting nominations within seven years; his second nomination was for *Casablanca,* and his third for *Mr. Skeffington.* Perhaps most memorable was his role in Hitchcock's *Notorious,* as the mother-ridden Nazi betrayed by the woman (Ingrid Bergman) he loves, for which he received his fourth and last nomination. Rains, who distinguished himself in numerous films, worked up to his death in 1967, but never won an Oscar.

As Rains's career attests, the Academy has not hesitated to nominate the same players year after year. Over one-third of all the nominees have won consecutive nominations at one time or another in their careers. As expected, their numbers are much higher among the lead players.

The peak of Bette Davis's career occurred between 1938 and 1942, during which she received five successive nominations. And in the 1940s, Greer Garson and Gary Cooper were perennial nominees; Garson was nominated four times from 1941 to 1944, and Cooper three times between 1941 and 1943. Marlon Brando won his first Oscar *(On the Waterfront)* in 1954, which was followed by three consecutive nominations. Of Elizabeth Taylor's five nominations, four were in successive years, from 1957 to 1960. Jessica Lange was a perennial Academy nominee in the 1980s, earning nominations in 1982, 1984, and 1985, and Susan Sarandon in the 1990s, with Best Actress nominations in 1991, 1992, 1994, and 1995. Not all of these citations were justified: critics raised their eyebrows when Sarandon received a nomination for *The Client.*

Meryl Streep is the ultimate Academy nominee, holding a tie with Oscar favorite Katharine Hepburn with twelve nominations. Streep was nominated in 1978, 1979, 1981, 1982, 1983, 1985, 1987, 1988, 1990, 1995, 1998, and 1999. Since Streep has just celebrated her fiftieth birthday, chances are she will surpass Hepburn's record and become the Academy's most celebrated actress.

The Nomination's Effects

The very nomination for an Oscar has pervasive impact on artists' careers, contributing to their visibility in the film industry through the exposure that follows the nomination. Once artists are nominated, their careers are watched more carefully by producers, directors, and critics. The nomination places artists on a different level, one that carries with it greater status and popularity.

Many artists were unknown prior to their nomination, but leaped into stardom afterwards, particularly if their performances were in commercially successful pictures. Gregory Peck's first nomination in *The Keys of Kingdom,* which was his second movie, made him a star. Kirk Douglas did not make much impression in Hollywood until he earned a nomination for *Champion.* Joan Fontaine played small, undistinguished parts in several movies *(The Women,* for example) until she won a nomination for *Rebecca.*

In 1969, *Midnight Cowboy* brought to Jon Voight the kind of instant stardom that *The Graduate* had brought to Dustin Hoffman in 1967. Voight and Hoffman would have become international stars without getting nominations for their respective debuts, but the nomination expedited the process by making them more visible.

Ann-Margret's career not only benefitted from her first nomination, but also got a tremendous boost when she appeared at the 1962 Oscar show, in which she sang "Bachelor in Paradise," one of the nominated songs. In the space of three minutes, she became "the Hottest Name in Town." This got her work, but no recognition as a serious actress, having begun her career in night clubs. It took an imaginative director, Mike Nichols, and a good supporting part, as Bobbie Templeton, Jack Nicholson's love-starved actress-girlfriend in *Carnal Knowledge* (1971) to change her screen image of a teenage sex kitten *(Bye Bye Birdie, Viva Las Vegas).* The nomination brought critical acclaim and bolstered Ann-Margret's self-confidence, forcing her to mature as an actress.

Several foreign players became international stars only after their movies had been Oscar-nominated. Brit Laurence Harvey established himself as a screen actor after *Room at the Top,* which earned him a nomination, was released in the United States. The nomination of fellow Brit Albert Finney in *Tom Jones* and the commercial success of that movie made him a household name in America. Richard Harris's first starring role in *This Sporting Life* established him as an actor of the first rank with the help of a nomination; it was the kind of movie that would have received limited release had it not been for the Academy's recognition. *Alfie* performed the same function for Michael Caine, and *Georgy Girl* for Lynn Redgrave—both Caine and Redgrave became international stars after their Oscar nominations.

Perhaps equally important is the effect of the first nomination on artists' status and power in Hollywood. Most artists are anxious to receive a nomination at a young age, because they know that it will bring them not only work but further nominations. In some cases, only the first nod was deserved, but subsequent nominations were conferred because of increased visibility and prestige *after* the first nomination.

Of Marsha Mason's four nominations, only the first *(Cinderella Liberty)* and possibly the fourth *(Only When I Laugh)* were justified. Mason received her second *(The Goodbye Girl)* and third *(Chapter Two)* nominations for lukewarm performances because by that time she had established herself as an Oscar-caliber performer. Her new status meant that more attention was paid to each of her new movies.

Glenn Close's meteoric rise to stardom also owes a debt to her first nomination. Close earned a supporting nomination for her screen debut, *The World According to Garp,* in which she played the plum role of Robin Williams's eccentric, liberated mother. In the following year, Close was the only actress from *The Big Chill's* gifted ensemble to be singled out by the Academy. The success of *The Big Chill* was based on ensemble acting by Kevin Kline, William Hurt, JoBeth Williams, and others. Yet only Close's performance was nominated, indicating that it wasn't just the high-quality of her acting, but also her newly gained status as an Oscar-caliber actress.

In 1984, Close earned her third consecutive nomination for *The Natural,* as Robert Redford's naive girlfriend. Neither the role nor her acting were extraordinary, and had the same role been played by another actress it would probably not have been recognized. Yet while watching *The Natural,* her fellow-actors focused their attention on her acting *because* of her Academy status. Close became a perennial nominee in the 1980s, making an effective transition from secondary to lead roles.

Ironically, it took a villainess role, the "Other Woman" in the suspenseful blockbuster *Fatal Attraction,* to put Close at the forefront of leading ladies, for which she was rewarded with a fourth (and first Best Actress) nomination. "I wanted to break out of the kinds of roles I used to do, because I was boring myself," Close said about her typecasting as an earth mother. Close's new, more sexual look convinced producers of her versatile talent and wide range. In 1988, she was cast by Stephen Frears in the sumptuous costume picture, *Dangerous Liaisons,* playing another unsympathetic role, a manipulative French aristocrat, for which she received her fifth nomination. The cumulative effect of all that is that Close became a bankable star and one of Hollywood's busiest actresses.

Wings, the first film ever to win Best Picture (1927/28), receiving a second Oscar for engineering effects. Its spectacular aerial sequences and running time (136 minutes) set a trend favoring grand-scale, epic films. (Courtesy of The Museum of Modern Art/Film Stills Archive)

The Broadway Melody, MGM's first musical and the Academy's first winning musical (1928/29). (Courtesy of The Museum of Modern Art/Film Stills Archive)

Cimarron, the only Western ever to win Best Picture (1930/31). (Courtesy of The Museum of Modern Art/Film Stills Archive)

Greta Garbo and John Barrymore in *Grand Hotel,* the 1931/32 Best Picture and the only Oscar winner to be nominated in one category. The two legendary players never won an Oscar Award. (Courtesy of The Museum of Modern Art/Film Stills Archive)

Clark Gable and Claudette Colbert in Frank Capra's *It Happened One Night* (1934), the first comedy to win Best Picture and the first film to sweep all five major awards. (Courtesy of The Museum of Modern Art/Film Stills Archive)

Charles Laughton and Clark Gable in *Mutiny on the Bounty* (1935), the only film to contain three Best Actor nominations; the third was Franchot Tone. (Courtesy of The Museum of Modern Art/Film Stills Archive)

Vivien Leigh and Hattie McDaniel in *Gone With the Wind*, the 1939 Best Picture, sweeping eight competitive and one Special award. McDaniel became the first black actress to be honored with an Oscar. (Courtesy of The Museum of Modern Art/Film Stills Archive)

Rebecca (1940), the only suspense-thriller to win Best Picture. Its famous director, Alfred Hitchcock, was nominated five times, but never won a regular Oscar. (Courtesy of The Museum of Modern Art/Film Stills Archive)

Mrs. Miniver (1942), the first film to be nominated for 12 awards, winning 6, including Best Picture. One of William Wyler's less impressive features, it won for ideological rather than artistic considerations. The Best Actress for Greer Garson (left) typecast her for the rest of her career as a gentle, civilized lady. (Courtesy of The Museum of Modern Art/Film Stills Archive)

Casablanca, the 1943 Best Picture, features Humphrey Bogart (right) in his best-known role, as Rick Blain, the most famous cafe owner in film history. Bogart should have won an acting award, but did not. (Courtesy of The Museum of Modern Art/Film Stills Archive)

Ray Milland in *The Lost Weekend* (1945), Billy Wilder's first Oscar-winner and Hollywood's first major film about alcoholism; Milland won Best Actor for playing an alcoholic writer. (Courtesy of The Museum of Modern Art/Film Stills Archive)

Fredric March (right), Harold Russell (left), and Dana Andrews (back) in *The Best Years of Our Lives,* the 1946 Best Picture and one of the greatest social-problem films. March won his second Best Actor Oscar, and Russell received two awards, Supporting Actor and a Special Oscar. (Courtesy of The Museum of Modern Art/Film Stills Archive)

Gregory Peck at his best, a liberal crusading journalist in Elia Kazan's 1947 Oscar-winning *Gentleman's Agreement*. It was Peck's third nominated performance. (Courtesy of The Museum of Modern Art/Film Stills Archive)

Broderick Crawford (left), Mercedes McCambridge, and John Ireland in the 1949 Best Picture, *All the King's Men*, a serious warning against political corruption and demagogery. Its director, Robert Rossen, was blacklisted during the McCarthy era. (Courtesy of The Museum of Modern Art/Film Stills Archive)

A "meaningful" look between Bette Davis (left) and Anne Baxter (right), as the "aging" and "rising" actresses, watched by George Sanders (right) and Gary Merrill in *All About Eve*, the 1950 Best Picture, the most nominated (fourteen) film in the Academy's history, and the first to feature two Best Actress nominations. (Courtesy of The Museum of Modern Art/Film Stills Archive)

Marlon Brando (center) finally won an Oscar at his fourth nomination for *On the Waterfront* (1954), which was also named Best Picture and honored Eva Marie Saint with a supporting award. It was the first film to feature three supporting actor nominations, all of whom lost. (Courtesy of The Museum of Modern Art/Film Stills Archive)

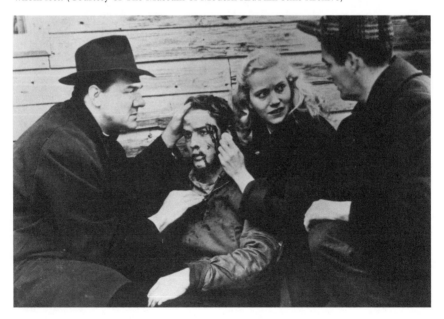

The chariot race in the blockbuster *Ben-Hur* (1959), the only remake to win Best Picture and the only film to win eleven awards. (Courtesy of The Museum of Modern Art/Film Stills Archive)

Rita Moreno, the only Hispanic player to win an Oscar (Supporting Actress), in a production number from the musical *West Side Story* (1961), which won Best Picture and nine other awards. Her award typecast her as a "Latin spitfire" for over a decade. (Courtesy of The Museum of Modern Art/Film Stills Archive)

Peter O'Toole should have won an Oscar for his performance in David Lean's historical epic *Lawrence of Arabia,* the 1962 Best Picture, but did not. With seven nominations, all in the lead category, O'Toole is the greatest loser of the Academy. (Courtesy of The Museum of Modern Art/Film Stills Archive)

My Fair Lady, the 1964 Best Picture: Rex Harrison (right) received the Best Actor award, Wilfrid Hyde-White (left) a supporting nomination. Audrey Hepburn was ignored by the Academy, which resented the fact that Julie Andrews, who created the role on stage, was not cast by Warners. (Courtesy of The Museum of Modern Art/Film Stills Archive)

Paul Scofield (right) was honored as Best Actor for his noble portrayal of Sir Thomas More in *A Man for All Seasons,* the 1966 Oscar winner. Robert Shaw was nominated as supporting actor for his eccentric interpretation of King Henry VIII. (Courtesy of The Museum of Modern Art/Film Stills Archive)

In the Heat of the Night (1967), one of the least distinguished Oscar winners, nevertheless, featured good performances by Rod Steiger (right), who won Best Actor and Sidney Poitier (left), and set a trend for films celebrating male friendship. (Courtesy of The Museum of Modern Art/Film Stills Archive)

Dustin Hoffman (right) and Jon Voight (left) canceled each other out as Best Actor nominees in John Schlesinger's *Midnight Cowboy*, the 1969 Best Picture about friendship in sleazy and impersonal New York City. (Courtesy of The Museum of Modern Art/Film Stills Archive)

George C. Scott shocked the film world when he refused his nomination for *Patton* (1970), but his colleagues honored him as Best Actor and the film as Best Picture. One thing was beyond doubt: the brilliance of Scott's acting. (Courtesy of The Museum of Modern Art/Film Archive)

Francis Ford Coppola's crime saga, *The Godfather* and *The Godfather, Part II,* won Best Picture of 1972 and 1974, respectively. Marlon Brando (Best Actor, 1972) and Robert De Niro (Supporting Actor, 1974) won the award for playing the same character, Don Vito Corleone in different ages. (Courtesy of The Museum of Modern Art/Film Stills Archive)

Films about mental illness and asylums were never big box office until Milos Forman's *One Flew Over the Cuckoo's Nest* (1975), winning Best Picture, Best Actor (Jack Nicholson), and Best Actress (Louise Fletcher). (Courtesy of The Museum of Modern Art/Film Stills Archive)

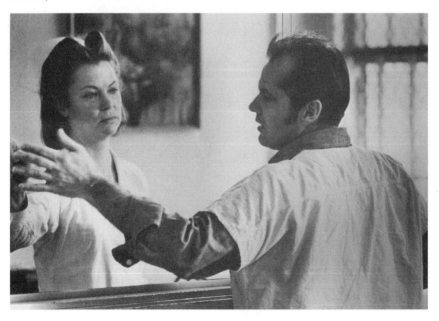

Annie Hall, the 1977 Oscar-winning comedy, established its heroine, Diane Keaton, as a household word and its director, Woody Allen, as one of America's foremost directors. (Courtesy of The Museum of Modern Art/Film Stills Archive)

Robert Benton's *Kramer vs. Kramer,* the 1979 Oscar winner, summed up the changes in gender roles, male and female, of the decade. Dustin Hoffman won Best Actor, and Justin Henry's supporting nomination made him the youngest nominee in the Academy's history. (Courtesy of The Museum of Modern Art/Film Stills Archive)

Terms of Endearment (1983), the last comedy to win Best Picture, was popular with the public because of its honest treatment of sexuality among the middle-aged and relationship between mother and daughter. The acting of Shirley MacLaine (Best Actress) and Jack Nicholson (Supporting Actor) was superb. (Courtesy of The Museum of Modern Art/Film Stills Archive)

CHAPTER 5

The Oscar as a Global Award

Most countries with established film industries bestow film awards, usually through their film academies. However, none of these awards is nearly as visible or prestigious as the Oscar Award.

The Oscar has always been regarded as much more than an American prize. Compared with other countries that have two systems of awards, one for local and one for foreign achievements, the Oscar disregards nationality. In theory, foreign-born artists can compete in any of the categories. The only exception is the Best Picture Oscar, which differentiates between films in English and in foreign languages.

From the very beginning, the rules stated that "No national or Academy membership distinctions are to be considered." The awards were going to be conferred with no regard to nationality. The Academy was very proud that the first Best Actor, German Emil Jannings, "was not even a citizen of our country," and that the first Best Actress, Janet Gaynor, "was not even a member of the Academy." As merit awards, the Oscars were based on the philosophy that true art knows no boundaries. But philosophy is one thing and practice another, and the question to what extent the Oscars are truly global awards that ignore national borders is still very much relevant.

Oscar's International Dimension

By and large, Americans have dominated the Oscar-acting race. The vast majority (over 70 percent) of Oscar nominees have been American, about one-fifth British, and about one-tenth of other nationalities. The proportion of foreign players in the lead categories is bigger than that in the supporting, mostly because lead players are more visible and hence attract greater attention to their films. There's a difference between the male and female winners in the lead category: women represent a larger number of nationalities than the men, who have mostly been British.

Do foreign players have better chances to get a nomination and not win the award? A clear case of favoritism, of preferential treatment based on nationality, would prevail if there were significant differences between the nominees and the winners. In actuality, there are no such differences. The same proportion of foreign winners and foreign nominees exists in all four acting categories. Despite accusations of favoring American over foreign artists, the nominees' nationality has had little impact on their chance to win.

The fact that over one-fourth of all winners and nominees have come from other countries attests to Oscar's internationalism, extending its visibility beyond the borders of the United States. In Oscar's seventy-two-year-history, there have only been twenty years in which all four acting awards were conferred on Americans. In most other years, at least one of the four winners was of a foreign origin.

Overall, despite historical fluctuations in British representation, one out of every three foreign players has been British, indicating the English dominance in the Oscar contest. But is it the high quality of British films and British acting that accounts for their preeminence in the Oscar race? Or is it the simple fact that they appear in English-speaking movies?

The British Dominance

The British representation in the Oscar race has ranged from 11 percent in the 1950s to an all-time high of 31 percent in the 1960s. The 1960s were the most hospitable decade to all foreign artists, not just the British: two-fifths (40 percent) of the acting nominees were foreign actors. British players also made a strong showing in the 1940s, commanding one-fifth of the acting nominations. In other decades, the British contingent is estimated at 15 percent of all acting nominees. The poorest British representation was in the 1950s, the most conservative and most patriotically American decade in Oscar's history.

Compared with the British representation, the share of other foreign artists in the Oscar contest has been more or less stable, ranging from 6 to 10 percent of all acting nominees, with one notable exception: in the early 1980s, only 2 percent of the acting nominees were drawn from foreign countries. The 1980s resemble the 1950s in more senses than one.

In the 1930s, the American movie market was accused by the British of being insular, of denying support to their products. Alexander Korda's *The Private Life of Henry VIII* (1933) was considered to be an exception—it was the first British commercial hit in the United States since the advent of sound.

Not many British films were nominated for major awards in the 1930s. One notable exception was Anthony Asquith's *Pygmalion* (1938), which brought acting nominations to its stars, Leslie Howard and Wendy Hiller, and two writing awards for Best Writing Adaptation and Best Screenplay to playwright Bernard Shaw. It was one of the high "literary" moments in Oscar's history, though the notably acerbic writer greeted the award with a bemused irony: "It's an insult for them to offer me any honor, as if they had never heard of me before—and it's very likely they never have."

In 1939, the two lead acting awards went to British players for the first time, though both Robert Donat *(Goodbye, Mr. Chips)* and Vivien Leigh *(Gone With the Wind)* were honored for American movies. Ironically, Vivien Leigh won two Best Actress Oscars (the second was for *A Streetcar Named Desire)* for portraying two of the most famous Southern belles in American literature. The casting of *Gone With the Wind* received such extensive coverage in the press, that apparently some Southern women threatened to boycott the movie if Vivien Leigh did not measure up to their expectations of how Scarlett O'Hara should be portrayed.

This generosity to English performers was used by the Academy for public relations, promoting the notion of a matter-of-fact voting that disregards political considerations. At the same time, it prompted many speculations as to "whether England would have done the same to us," to which patriotic columnist Louella Parsons answered unequivocally, "I doubt it."

In the early 1940s, two British movies were nominated for Best Picture, both dealing with the war. Michael Powell's *The Invaders* (1942), about the survival attempts of a group of Nazis, also earned Emeric Pressburger an Oscar for best original story. The second, *In Which We Serve* (also 1942), co-directed by David Lean and Noel Coward, won the latter a Special Award for his outstanding production. Coward also wrote the music and starred in the film.

Prior to that, British movies had won a few technical awards. In 1940, *The Thief of Bagdad,* also directed by Michael Powell, won Oscars for cinematography, color art direction, and special effects. Alexander Korda's *That Hamilton Woman,* a huge success in America, starring Laurence Olivier and Vivien Leigh, won for its sound recordings.

It wasn't until the late 1940s that British films began to make a real impact on the Academy and the American movie market. The nominations for Laurence Olivier's screen version of *Henry V* (1946) for Best Picture and Actor annoyed the major Hollywood studios, which regarded the nominations as acts of treason. *Henry V* was such a box-office hit in New York that it ran for forty-six consecutive weeks.

As if that were not enough, three other British pictures were nominated for important awards in 1946. David Lean's exquisite tale of an unconsummated adulterous affair, *Brief Encounter,* won acting and other nominations. Compton Bennett's *The Seventh Veil,* the film that made James Mason an international star, won Best Screenplay. Gabriel Pascal's *Caesar and Cleopatra,* the most expensive English film to date, was nominated but didn't win any awards.

The resentment against the Academy's seemingly preferential treatment of British movies increased in the following year, when David Lean's version of Charles Dickens's *Great Expectations* was nominated for Best Picture and Director, and most deservedly earned the best black-and-white cinematography and art direction. One journalist, who took the matter seriously, wrote that the United States helped the British win the war, but shouldn't help them win "our Oscars."

The British were disappointed, because they believed that *Great Expectations* should have won the 1947 Best Picture; the winner was *Gentleman's Agreement.* "Certain amount of bias influences Hollywood's Oscar Awards," said J. Arthur Rank, the powerful British producer, in response to the 1947 awards. But at the same time, he expressed hopes that the number of bookings for British films in the United States would double from six to twelve thousand a year, which was the number that American films received in Britain. Curiously, Rank reported that exhibitors complained to him about difficulties some American audiences experienced in understanding the speech of British players and that "efforts are being made to correct this."

A turning point in the American-British relationship occurred in 1948, when, against all expectations, *Hamlet* was named Best Picture and Laurence Olivier won Best Actor. The film also won black-and-white art direction and costume design. It was the first time that a British movie won the top award, an act which reinforced the moguls' earlier decision to withdraw their financial support from the awards ceremonies. In the same year, another British film, Michael Powell's *The Red Shoes,* a romantic drama set in the ballet world, was also nominated for Best Picture and went on to become the top money-maker of the year, grossing five million dollars.

The "*Hamlet* incident" was recalled in 1956, when Mike Todd's *Around the World in 80 Days* won Best Picture. Its British director, Michael Anderson, received a nomination but not the directorial award; the winner was George Stevens for *Giant.* It was one of the few occasions in which the Academy split its vote for Best Picture and Best Director. In most years, there's strong correlation between the two categories.

In the 1950s, few British movies were nominated for or won important awards. Carol Reed's masterpiece, *The Third Man* (1950), based on Graham Greene's mystery novel, was singled out for its evocative black-and-white cinematography of postwar Vienna. And Charles Crichton's *The Lavender Hill Mob* (1952), which made Alec Guinness a star in the United States, won best story and screenplay Oscars. Most of the nominations for British films in this decade were in the writing categories. In 1953, two British screenplays competed in the same category: *The Cruel Sea*, based on Nicholas Monsarrat's best-seller, and the comedy *The Ladykillers*, featuring Alec Guinness as a sinister lodger plotting to kill his old landlady. Neither won.

David Lean became the first British filmmaker to ever win Best Director in 1957 for the war epic *The Bridge on the River Kwai*, which was named Best Picture and also won Best Actor (Alec Guinness), screenplay, editing, cinematography, and music scoring. Financed and distributed by Columbia, *The Bridge on the River Kwai* used a mostly British cast and crew.

The British representation in the Oscar contest improved dramatically in the 1960s, undoubtedly the best decade for British movies. A considerable number of movies were nominated for Best Picture: Jack Clayton's *Room at the Top* (1959), John Schlesinger's *Darling* (1965), Lewis Gilbert's sex farce *Alfie* (1966), and Anthony Harvey's historical melodrama *The Lion in Winter* (1968). Moreover, four British-made films won the top award: *Lawrence of Arabia* (1962), *Tom Jones* (1963), *A Man for All Seasons* (1966), and *Oliver!* (1968). The directors of these movies (David Lean, Tony Richardson, Fred Zinnemann, and Carol Reed, respectively) were singled out by the Academy for their achievements.

A fifth British filmmaker, John Schlesinger, won the directing Oscar for *Midnight Cowboy* (1969), made with American stars Dustin Hoffman and Jon Voight. The victory of *Midnight Cowboy* was symptomatic of Hollywood's tendency to co-opt young British talent at the time. *Midnight*'s director John Schlesinger was soon brought to America. This helped cause a brain drain from which British cinema would not recover, at least for a decade, until 1981 and 1982, with the back-to-back wins of *Chariots of Fire* and *Gandhi*.

In the 1970s, few British films were nominated for important awards, perhaps reflecting the depression of the British industry. Two movies, *A Clockwork Orange* (1971) and *Barry Lyndon* (1975), both financed with American money but made in England by expatriate director Stanley Kubrick, were nominated for Best Picture; neither won. *Midnight Express* (1978), a thriller about Billy Hayes, the American student arrested in Turkey for carrying hashish, was directed by Brit Alan Parker, and nominated for Best Picture. The poor British representation in the Oscars was reflected in other film forums. In 1980, for the first time in thirty-three years, not even one British movie competed in the Cannes Film Festival.

But in the early 1980s several movies about distinctly British subjects made their mark, artistically and commercially. *The Elephant Man* (1980) was not a British film. It was financed by Paramount, produced by Mel Brooks, and directed by David Lynch, but it had a distinctly British flavor in its tale of John Merrick—the grossly deformed man victimized and exploited by Victorian society—and was cast with mostly British actors, headed by John Hurt in the title role (who won a nomination) and Anthony Hopkins, as his caring doctor. The Academy showed its appreciation with eight nominations, including Best Picture, though the film lost in every category. Roman Polanski's romantic historical epic, *Tess* (1980), beautifully made in England, was also nominated for six awards.

After *Oliver!*, it took thirteen years for another British-made film, *Chariots of Fire* (1981), to win Best Picture. Directed by Hugh Hudson and based on the true tale of two British runners in the 1924 Olympics, it was the upset winner, competing against such big-scale movies as Steven Spielberg's *Raiders of the Lost Ark* and Warren Beatty's *Reds*. Made in England for the modest budget of six million dollars, *Chariots of Fire* was turned down by every major Hollywood studio. Its success—it won four Oscars—was attributed to its emotionally compelling tale about the courage and passion of its two characters (played by unknown actors), who triumphed against great odds. Despite the fact that the movie was considered "too British" and "too specialized" (dealing with sports), it became a commercial hit, though *after* winning the Oscar. Many filmmakers resented the fact that American money (Fox helped to finance it) was used to help a British product in a year in which *Reds,* an ambitious historical epic, failed at the box office despite critical acclaim.

The British had even better reasons to celebrate the following year, when Richard Attenborough's *Gandhi,* financed by Columbia, was nominated for eleven awards and swept most of them, including Best Picture, Director, and Actor. British movies continued to fare well throughout the decade. In 1983, Peter Yates's screen adaptation of *The Dresser* was nominated for five awards, including the top one. And in 1984, two British films were recognized by the Academy with multiple nominations. Roland Joffe's *The Killing Fields,* which was based on Sydney Schanberg's 1980 *New York Times Magazine* article, "The Death and Life of Dith Pran," and recounted the political situation in Cambodia during its civil war, was nominated for seven awards and won three, including a citation for Chris Menges's exhilarating cinematography. David Lean's epic *A Passage to India,* based on E. M. Forster's famous novel, was nominated for eleven awards, though won only two. The big winner was *Amadeus,* which swept most of the awards.

Trevor Nunn's 1982 Tony Award acceptance speech (for his adaptation of Charles Dickens's *Nicholas Nickleby),* in which he exclaimed, "The British Are Coming, the British Are Coming," turned out to be true in 1986, when two Best Picture nominees were British. The production team of *Killing Fields* returned to the Oscar arena with the high-minded but dull epic *The Mission,* which received seven nominations and one award (for Menges's cinematography).

The other nominee, *A Room With a View,* Ismail Merchant and James Ivory's adaptation of E. M. Forster's novel, won in three out of its eight categories: writing, art direction-set decoration, and costume design. John Boorman's charming autobiographical saga, *Hope and Glory* (1987), which reconstructed his adolescence in war-time London, was acclaimed by the critics and received five nominations, but no awards. Another foreign-directed film, Bertolucci's *The Last Emperor,* won most of them.

The one category in which the British have always excelled and fared even better than their movies is acting. British acting continues to enjoy great prestige in the United States—it is a most revered institution. British players are admired for their versatility and technical skills. Meryl Streep expressed the opinion of many American actors when she observed: "I am vastly intimidated by English actors. We American actors think we're just a bunch of slobs compared to them, and that they can quote all of Shakespeare by heart."

The prestige of English players is reflected in both the nomination and winning processes. Eighteen of the sixty-six Best Actors (27 percent), sixteen of the sixty Best Actresses (also 27 percent), eight of the Supporting Actors (18 percent), and five of the Supporting Actresses (11 percent) have been British.

The first British player to win Best Actor was George Arliss, but he won for two American films *(Disraeli* and *The Green Goddess).* Charles Laughton was actually the first Brit to win for a British film *(The Private Life of Henry VIII).* Other British-born winners include: Victor McLaglen, Robert Donat, Ray Milland, Ronald Colman, Laurence Olivier, Alec Guinness, David Niven, Rex Harrison, Paul Scofield, Peter Finch, and Ben Kingsley.

The British dominated the Best Actor category for three consecutive years: Daniel Day Lewis *(My Left Foot)* in 1989, Jeremy Irons *(Reversal of Fortune)* in 1990, and Anthony Hopkins *(The Silence of the Lambs)* in 1991, elevating the visibility of British players to an unparalleled level. Note that, with the exception of Olivier *(Hamlet),* Day-Lewis, and a few others, most British actors, such as Irons and Hopkins, have won for American-made pictures.

There's little doubt that it is much easier for the British to win the Oscar if they appear in American movies. Most of the British-born Best Actresses, including Vivien Leigh, Greer Garson, Audrey Hepburn, Julie Andrews, Maggie Smith, Glenda Jackson, and Emma Thompson have won for American movies. The two exceptions are Julie Christie *(Darling)* and Glenda Jackson in her first Oscar-winning film *(Women in Love)*; the second Oscar was for an American picture *(A Touch of Class)*.

A similar trend prevails among the British players who won supporting awards, like Donald Crisp *(How Green Was My Valley)*, Edmund Gwenn *(Miracle on 34th Street)*, Hugh Griffith *(Ben-Hur)*, Peter Ustinov *(Spartacus* and *Topkapi)*, John Gielgud *(Arthur)*, Michael Caine *(Hannah and Her Sisters, Cider House Rules)* and Sean Connery *(The Untouchables)*. The only supporting winner in a British-made film was John Mills in David Lean's *Ryan's Daughter*.

Among the Supporting Actresses too, Dame Peggy Ashcroft and Dublin-born Brenda Fricker were the only ones to win for a British or Irish-made movie, *A Passage to India* and *My Left Foot,* respectively. The other British actresses won for American films: Wendy Hiller *(Separate Tables)*, Margaret Rutherford *(The V.I.P.'s)*, Vanessa Redgrave *(Julia)*, Maggie Smith *(California Suite)*, and Judi Dench *(Shakespeare in Love)*.

The illustrious list of Oscar-nominated British players reads like the "Who's Who" register of performers honored with titles of "Sirs" and "Dames." Sir Michael Redgrave, Sir Ralph Richardson, Sir John Gielgud, Sir Ian McKellen, Sir Anthony Hopkins, and most recently, Sir Michael Caine, have all been nominated and several have won. The same applies to Dame Edith Evans, Dame May Whitty, Dame Judith Anderson, Dame Gladys Cooper, Dame Flora Robson, Dame Peggy Ashcroft, and Dame Judi Dench. Both the Academy and the British benefitted from the Oscar game. The Academy has made some of these players into international movie stars, and the British players in turn have contributed to the prestige of the Academy, making it a more reputable institution.

The largest number of British players were nominated in the 1960s, marking that decade's high quality of British films. It included Peter O'Toole, Michael Caine, Albert Finney, Ron Moody, Tom Courtenay, Alan Bates, Rachel Roberts, Deborah Kerr, Jean Simmons, and Janet Suzman. These players' prestige goes beyond the film world because of the different structure of the arts in Britain, where there's mutual fertilization among the theater, film, and TV industries. By contrast, American players tend to specialize in one medium, often to the exclusion of the other two, but British players continue to commute successfully between theater and film, or film and TV, to the appreciation of all three arts and their respective audiences.

Along with high-quality acting, there were other reasons for the favorable reception of British movies in the 1960s, not a particularly good decade for American movies. American films, still suffering from fierce competition with television, had not yet adjusted to their new status as the second cultural medium, having been for half a century the dominant form of entertainment.

The decline in American films was quantitative as well as qualitative. In 1963, the industry reached an all-time production low, with only 141 American movies released. Compare this poor figure with over 400 movies released in a typical year in the 1940s, and over 300 films in the 1950s. For years, American films ruled the market, but in the 1960s, their dominance was shattered. In 1960, of the 320 movies distributed in the United States, 208 were American and 112 were foreign, but in 1968, of the 380 new pictures, only 176 were American.

By contrast, in the 1960s, the British cinema witnessed a renaissance. Shortly after 1956, which saw the premiere of John Osborne's *Look Back in Anger,* considered to be a turning point in the history of British theater, a new generation of filmmakers that included Tony Richardson and Lindsay Anderson began to leave their mark on British culture. The flowering of British cinema in the 1960s, led by Lindsay Anderson, Tony Richardson, Karel Reisz, and others, was a cross-fertilization of documentaries and works by playwrights and novelists, such as John Osborne and Shelah Delaney. The prevailing mood of their movies was bitter—they dealt with what critic David Denby called "declining-empire anguish." Chillingly bleak, they had a bitter flavor, a humiliating familiarity with poverty and rage.

As members of an innovative cultural movement, "The Free Cinema," they were the British equivalent of the French New Wave. Among their best works were: Jack Clayton's *Room at the Top* (1959), Karel Reisz's *Saturday Night and Sunday Morning* (1960), Jack Cardiff's *The Loneliness of the Long Distance Runner* (1962), and Lindsay Anderson's *This Sporting Life* (1963). Each of these movies received important nominations.

Pauline Kael once noted that "Heaven seems to have sent English moviemakers the upper class so that they would have something to justify their malice." True, the 1960s saw the nasty Harold Pinter-Joseph Losey exposés of decadence in the wealthy and educated classes: *The Servant* (1963), *Accident* (1967). Frederic Raphael's acidulous lampoon of social climbing was captured in *Nothing But the Best* (1964), and in the Oscar-nominated *Darling* (1965).

The popularity of British films and actors in the 1960s also indicated that the previous provincialism and parochialism of American culture had subsided. This decade saw ideological changes that affected American culture and movies, specifically the repudiation of the conservative and isolationist trends of the 1950s, represented by Senator Joseph McCarthy and the hearings of the House UnAmerican Activities Committee.

Furthermore, the melting-pot ideology which had prevailed in American society for decades, ignoring racial and class differences, began to disintegrate. In the 1960s, the youth and ethnic segments of society became more vocal in their demands for cultural representation. For the first time, youth not only required films specifically dealing with their problems, but could also determine which movies would become box-office hits. Both younger and more sophisticated, these viewers greeted with enthusiasm the new European films, not just British, but also Italian, French, Swedish, and Japanese.

The number of foreign-made films, particularly British, among the top money-makers was the highest in the 1960s. In the 1940s and 1950s, only five of the hundred most commercial movies were foreign-made, but in the 1960s, their proportion increased dramatically, amounting to sixteen movies. The most successful British films, nominated for Oscars and ranking among their year's top money-grossers were David Lean's *Lawrence of Arabia,* Tony Richardson's *Tom Jones,* Richard Lester's Beatles movie *Hard Day's Night* (1964), Lewis Gilbert's *Alfie* (1966), Silvio Narizzano's *Georgy Girl* (1966), Carol Reed's *Oliver!* (1968), and, of course, the James Bond movies starring Sean Connery.

The Oscar race reflected the popularity of British films. In 1963, four of the five supporting actresses were British: Diane Cilento, Dame Edith Evans, Joyce Redman (all for *Tom Jones),* and Dame Margaret Rutherford *(The V.I.P.'s),* who won. In 1964, all five Best Actor nominees were born outside the United States, and four of them were British: Richard Burton, Peter O'Toole (both for *Becket),* Peter Sellers *(Dr. Strangelove),* and Rex Harrison *(My Fair Lady),* the winner. The fifth nominee was Mexican-born Anthony Quinn, who gave the performance of a lifetime in *Zorba the Greek.*

Indeed, 1964 was probably the most "international" year in the history of the Academy. In addition to Harrison, the other winners in the acting categories were all foreign-born: Brits Julie Andrews *(Mary Poppins),* Peter Ustinov *(Topkapi),* and French-Russian Lila Kedrova *(Zorba the Greek).* "This will be an unusual night," emcee Bob Hope predicted at the beginning of the ceremonies; "Tonight Hollywood is handing out foreign aid." Indeed, Julie Andrews, overwhelmed by her win, said in her acceptance speech: "You Americans are famous for your hospitality, but this is ridiculous."

The *Hollywood Reporter* noted that the show was "a reminder that Hollywood has never been chauvinistic and that its great days are those when artists from throughout the world flocked here or were imported. The winners are reminders that the movies are the true international medium." This feeling was reaffirmed in 1965, when, once again, only one of the Best Actress nominees was American, Elizabeth Hartman, as the blind girl in *A Patch of Blue*. That year, three of the nominees were British: Julie Christie who won for *Darling*, Julie Andrews for *The Sound of Music,* and Samantha Eggar for *The Collector;* the fifth actress was French Simone Signoret, for the American production *Ship of Fools*.

In 1983, when British actors again dominated the race, various explanations were offered. Critics found it strange that four of the five Best Actors were English: Michael Caine *(Educating Rita),* Albert Finney and Tom Courtenay (both for *The Dresser),* and Tom Conti *(Reuben, Reuben,* an American film). The fifth nominee was American, Robert Duvall *(Tender Mercies),* who turned out to be the winner. One voice of reason, who understood the roots of the problem, was the *New York Times*'s critic Vincent Canby. Canby observed that the Academy's "customary respect" for English players was no greater in 1983 than in previous years, and that "Hollywood today is no more or less Anglophile than it's ever been."

However, he stated that "If you are a good American actor and you want to make it big in contemporary American movies, you've got to be able to upstage special effects and futuristic hardware, with very little or no help from the screenwriters." Hence Roy Scheider was engaged in an unfair competition with a marvelous space-age helicopter in *Blue Thunder*. Indeed, despite being a box-office champion, Harrison Ford failed to get nominations for either Han Solo in *Star Wars* or Indiana Jones in *Raiders of the Lost Ark*. In addition to competing with technology, American actors were stereotyped as machos and/or psychopaths (Al Pacino in *Scarface,* Robert De Niro in *The King of Comedy),* roles that usually don't get Academy recognition. At the same time, it was no accident that the British dominated the Best Actor—but not the Best Actress—categories. As Canby noted, for the first time in years, the American cinema offered richer parts for women than for men.

In the 1980s, the new British pictures concerned feminism, racism against Third World populations (Indian, Pakistani) in England, the strange multiculturalism in London, as expressed in Stephen Frears's *My Beautiful Laundrette* (1985), which received a writing nomination. These movies professed an anti-Thatcher message, spelling out their political position explicably and didactically in the work of Ken Loach *(Riff-Raff),* Mike Leigh *(High Hopes)* and others. They enacted the British working class's revenge against years of Thatcherite callousness.

For David Denby, the one emotion that always comes through and links the different styles of serious English cinema of the last twenty-five years is disgust. It takes various forms: disgust at an empire maintained by force and then precipitously lost, disgust at mean industrial cities, disgust at the exploitation and destruction of the working class, disgust at social hypocrisy, and even disgust at squalid sex

But bleak British films, such as *Dance With a Stranger, Wetherby, Mona Lisa, Wish You Were Here, The Good Father, Letter to Brezhnev,* don't win Academy recognition. What wins is a safer fare, like the comedy *Four Weddings and a Funeral,* which was nominated for the 1994 Best Picture, a movie celebrating the Oxford complacency of a circle of British yuppies. As John Powers noted, it is easier for Americans to digest the stereotypes of *Four Weddings*—stuttering vicars, idiot Yanks who think Oscar Wilde is still alive, clumsy aristocrats who step into every available cow pie—than face the harsh realities of the working class.

In some years, an entire category is dominated by British players. In 1992, three of the Supporting Actresses were British: Joan Plowright *(Enchanted April),* Miranda Richardson *(Damage),* and Vanessa Redgrave *(Howards End);* one was Australian, Judy Davis *(Husbands and Wives);* and one, the winner, was American, Marisa Tomei *(My Cousin Vinny).* Jack Palance, who presented the Oscar in this category, quipped: "This is the first time in the history of the Academy Awards that five foreign actress are up for the same award: four from England and one from Brooklyn."

Variety labeled 1992 as "Year of the Visa," because, in addition to the nods to British and Irish artists, the Academy also acknowledged French and Japanese achievements. Foreign nominees won in ten different categories, the most international cross-section in decades. *Howards End,* which won three Oscars, embodied the international flavor of contemporary filmmaking. Based on a classic of English literature, it was technically a British production, except it was made by an Indian producer, Ismail Merchant, American director James Ivory, and written by a Polish-born writer, Ruth Prawer Jhabvala, who received the best adapted screenplay Oscar.

The following year, 1993, showed again that British industry may be dead, but the U.K. certainly made its impact felt when acting nominations were concerned. Half of the Best Actor and Supporting Actor nominations went to individuals from Britain. Daniel Day-Lewis was nominated for his portrayal of the wrongly accused Gerry Conlon in *In the Name of the Father,* and Pete Postlethwaite earned a supporting nod for playing his father. Welsh man Anthony Hopkins played a repressed butler in the Oscar-nominated *The Remains of the Day,* which also earned a nomination for Emma Thompson. In the same year, Northern Ireland native Liam Neeson was nominated for the title role in *Schindler's List,* and Ralph Fiennes became a star after winning a supporting nomination for playing a Nazi commandant in the same film.

In a *Los Angeles Times* interview, producer Ismail Merchant attributed the British rule to strong theatrical training and solid technique, noting that "British actors have an extraordinary training and are very disciplined. They have a profound knowledge of the characters they are playing and exceptional acting ability." But for Judi Dench, there's no difference between American and British acting styles. "Good acting is good acting," she told *Premiere*, "Sometimes people say it's the Method. The other day I heard Rod Steiger talking about the Method, and it didn't make any sense to me. He said that no longer do you come in, say, in mourning for your daughter. It's mourning for *your* daughter, not the character's. It's self-indulgent, and you can see self-indulgent acting all over the world. Good acting is not the things you say, it's the things you don't say. It's like in watercolor—it's what you leave out that's most important."

Who's right? Merchant or Dench? No matter. The trend continues. On the occasion of Mike Leigh's powerful family drama, *Secrets & Lies,* which was nominated for the 1996 Best Picture Oscar, *Los Angeles Times* critic Kenneth Turan observed that "Britain's supposedly moribund film industry is turning into cinema's most celebrated invalid. Though economic difficulties have seriously curtailed output, the British films that do get made are invariably models of strength and compassion. The ensemble riches of British acting help explain why a country with no financially viable film industry keeps turning out such good movies—and performances.

Four of the 1997 Best Actress nominees were British: Helena Bonham Carter for *The Wings of the Dove,* Julie Christie for *Afterglow,* Judi Dench for *Mrs. Brown,* and Kate Winslet for *Titanic.* The winner was all-American nominee Helen Hunt for James Brooks's comedy *As Good As It Gets.* Most critics attribute a lack of good women roles in American cinema to a brand of filmmaking typified by Hollywood studios that calls for big stars and high concepts heavy on special effects and fast-paced action. "A lot of our studio movies are boys' flicks and testosterone events," casting director Mali Finn told *USA Today,* "and the women get shoved into the background."

"The British are coming!" screamed Brit writer Colin Welland in 1981, after winning for *Chariots of Fire,* a proclamation that showed how the British measured the success of their own film industry—in terms of how well they are doing "over there" in the United States.

"Nothing denotes success so visibly and tangibly as the Oscars," wrote Brit Peter Whittle in the *Los Angeles Times.* "There's a feeling that being big in Britain is not quite enough, that you haven't really made it until you've made it in Hollywood."

Ambiguity prevails: "On the one hand, there is a superior disdain for the whole circus, and on the other a keenly patriotic desire to see Brits beating Americans at their own game." This ambiguity is not new. At their prime, Kenneth Branagh and Emma Thompson were chronic irritants to the British media, because they have achieved success at an early age—and in America—and because they showed every sign of relishing it. In 1989, when Branagh received two nominations, as Actor and Director for *Henry V*, his audacious and brilliant film debut at the very young age of twenty-nine, comparisons were made to the young Olivier, whose own version of *Henry V*, in 1946, also earned Best Picture and Best Actor nominations.

In 1999, Sam Mendes, the much-praised London theater director, won a directing Oscar for *American Beauty*, and four British were nominated for their acting: Samantha Morton for *Sweet and Lowdown*, Janet McTeer for *Tumbleweeds*, Jude Law for *The Talented Mr. Ripley*, and Michael Caine, "that quintessence of a certain kind of Britishness," for *Cider House Rules*. There was extensive coverage in the London media, and not just in the tabloids but in quality press like *The Times*, which hailed an outstanding lineup of British talent "on course for Oscar glory." When there is a big Oscar triumph featuring prominent British talent or British theme, as with *The English Patient*, *Shakespeare in Love*, or *American Beauty*, British media can even cheat a bit and "forget" to mention that it was American money and American executives that got these movies made.

Best Foreign-Language Picture Nominees

In the Academy's history, a few foreign-language movies have been nominated for Best Picture. Jean Renoir's antiwar masterpiece, *Grand Illusion* (1938) competed for the top award, but that was before the creation of a distinct category for foreign pictures. Officially, the first winner in this category was Fellini's *La Strada* (1956), in which Anthony Quinn and Giulietta Masina gave probably their most memorable performances as traveling performers in postwar Italy.

Prior to the creation of a separate category, the Academy recognized several foreign films with an Honorary Oscar, beginning with Vittorio De Sica's neorealistic movie *Shoeshine*, in 1947, and the French film *Monsieur Vincent*, in 1948. The citation for De Sica read: "The high quality of this motion picture, brought to eloquent life in a country scarred by war, is proof to the world that the creative spirit can triumph over adversity."

Since the creation of Best Foreign-Language Picture, only five foreign movies have been nominated for Best Picture. Costa-Gavras's political thriller *Z* (1969), a French-Algerian co-production starring Yves Montand and Jean-Louis Trintignant, enjoyed a special position in 1969: it was nominated for and won the Best Foreign Picture and it was also nominated in the competitive category of Best Picture. According to Academy rules, foreign pictures that have opened in the United States are eligible to compete in the at large categories. To qualify for Foreign Picture, however, a film must be sent by its country of origin to the Academy, where a committee selects the five nominees. *Z* qualified on both grounds: It was nominated by Algeria, and it opened in the United States in December.

Jan Troell's *The Emigrants* (1972), which deals with the emigration of Swedish peasants to America in the nineteenth century, starred Liv Ullmann and Max von Sydow. Another Swedish entry, Ingmar Bergman's *Cries and Whispers* (1973), a haunting film about death and dying, featuring unforgettable performances by Liv Ullmann, Ingrid Thulin, and Harriet Andersson, was nominated for Best Picture.

Two Italian movies were nominated for Best Picture in the 1990s, both distributed by Miramax: *Il Postino (The Postman)* in 1995, and *Life Is Beautiful* in 1998. *Il Postino* told the story of an Italian postman who bonds with a legendary poet, Pablo Neruda, and wins the affections of a local girl through heartfelt poetry. Massimo Troisi, who played the poetic postman, suffered from heart problems and died only one day after the final take. Troisi headed an international cast, with French actor Philippe Noiret, New Delhi-born English director Michael Radford, and the film was based on "The Postman of Pablo Neruda," a novel by Chilean author Antonio Skarmeta. The film, in trying to re-create Southern Italy in the 1950s, was shot on two islands off the coast of Sicily.

Life Is Beautiful became the second film after *Z* to have been nominated for Best Foreign and Best Picture in the same year. A comedy-drama about the Holocaust, the film carried with it gravity and importance. It received seven nominations, including Best Actor and Best Director, a record for a foreign-language film.

The story concerns an accident-prone Italian bookshop owner (Benigni), who is imprisoned with his family in a World War II concentration camp. He bravely attempts to protect his son (Giorgio Cantarini) by making a game out of their tragic predicament. Benigni, known in the United States for his performances in *Down by Law* and *Johnny Stecchino,* came under fire when word got out that he was making a comedy about the Holocaust. Though not Jewish, the Italian director and co-writer had personal roots in the saga: his father served time in a German labor camp. Benigni recalled how "each evening my father was telling me a story, some awful and revolting tragedy things, always in a very light way. Maybe he was scared to make a trauma on me."

Citing Benigni's success at the European Film Awards (Best Actor) and at Cannes (winning the Grand Jury Prize), industry experts felt that Benigni had a strong shot at a lead performance award. Harvey Weinstein remarked that, "Miramax has gotten nominations in the past for Max von Sydow in *Pelle the Conqueror* and Massimo Troisi for *Il Postino*," a testament that the actor category has been foreign-actor friendly. "But it's the film's popularity with audiences that is the real ace up its sleeve. Benigni's work pushes all the right emotional buttons."

Even before its American release, *Life Is Beautiful* showed the same trademarks as *Il Postino*. Indeed, Benigni received high praise from Weinstein, who hyped the film as the next *Il Postino*. Ultimately, *Life Is Beautiful* shattered box office records for foreign films, eventually outdoing *Il Postino*'s commercial success by far.

Most of the foreign (non-British) nominees have come from countries with major film industries, such as France, Italy, Germany, Scandinavia, and Japan. Smaller countries, such as Greece, Israel, Egypt, and Hungary, had representation in the Oscar race only if their players appeared in American-made movies. One of the few exceptions is Polish actress Ida Kaminska, who was nominated for the Czech film, *The Shop on Main Street*, which was voted as 1965's Best Foreign-Language Picture.

Most foreign male winners received the award for American movies. Emil Jannings was German, but he earned Best Actor for two American films *(The Last Command* and *The Way of All Flesh)*. Born in Switzerland, Maximilian Schell worked in Germany and Austria prior to winning the 1961 Best Actor for *Judgment at Nuremberg*. The same is true for the other foreign nominees, such as French Charles Boyer *(Conquest)*, Austrian Oskar Werner *(Ship of Fools)*, and Israeli Topol *(Fiddler on the Roof)*.

The only actors nominated for performances in foreign-language pictures were Italians: Marcello Mastroianni in *Divorce—Italian Style* and *A Special Day*, Giancarlo Giannini in *Seven Beauties*, Massimo Troisi in *Il Postino*, and Roberto Benigni in *Life Is Beautiful*, who won.

In the Best Actress category too, most foreign women have won for American movies. Austrian actress Luise Rainer won two Oscars for American films, *The Great Ziegfeld* and *The Good Earth*, and Italian actress Anna Magnani won for the movie based on Tennessee Williams's *The Rose Tattoo*. The one exception in this category has been Sophia Loren, the only foreign actress to have won for a foreign-language film, *Two Women* (1961), directed by Vittorio De Sica.

None of the foreign actors (male or female) in the supporting categories has ever won for a role in a foreign-language movie, though several foreign actresses earned awards for an American film: Greek actress Katina

Paxinou in *For Whom the Bell Tolls,* Japanese Miyoshi Umeki in *Sayonara,* Russian-French Lila Kedrova in *Zorba the Greek,* French Juliette Binoche in *The English Patient.*

To get the Academy recognition, foreign players have to appear in commercially successful movies; a good performance has no impact if it is contained in a small art film. Similarly, most foreign pictures nominated for writing or technical awards have been box-office hits.

Never on Sunday (1960), produced, written, and directed by Jules Dassin, who starred in it with his wife-actress Melina Mercouri, would not have been nominated in major categories (Director, Best Actress) had it not been a commercial success. A kind of contemporary version of *Pygmalion,* focusing on the relationship between a serious American writer and a joyous Greek prostitute, the movie is credited with stimulating the tourism trade to Greece. *Never on Sunday* won one award, Best Song (written by Manos Hadjidakis), thus becoming the first song in a foreign picture to win an Oscar since the Academy began to recognize achievements in this category in 1934.

Fellini's satirical view of Italian high society, *La Dolce Vita* (1960), would not have been nominated for screenplay, Director, and other awards had it not created a world sensation with its view of Italian decadence. Praised by critics, it became one of the most popular foreign films in America, grossing in domestic rentals over eight million dollars. By the time *La Dolce Vita* was shown in the United States, it had already received recognition in Cannes and had achieved immense popularity in Europe. The movie won, however, only best costume design, with the Academy failing to recognize the great acting of Marcello Mastroianni as the journalist whose experiences are the center of the movie.

In 1976, Marie Christine Barrault won a Best Actress nomination for the French comedy *Cousin, Cousine,* written and directed by Jean-Charles Tacchella, whose script was also nominated. She was nominated because the movie proved to be a commercial hit in New York and Los Angeles. The screenplay deserved recognition for being funny, witty, and original, recounting an open adulterous affair between two cousins.

In the same year, Giancarlo Giannini won Academy recognition for his performance in Lina Wertmuller's controversial movie *Seven Beauties*. This film put Wertmuller, nominated as writer and director, at the front rank of international filmmakers. Giannini excelled as the contemptible Neapolitan macho, driven to self-degradation in his attempts to survive, but his performance would not have been singled out if the movie had not been a box-office hit.

It's always encouraging when a foreign movie gets recognition in major categories, as did Wolfgang Peterson's *Das Boot* (1982), a German film that chronicled the physical and psychological hardships endured by a Nazi crew of a U-Boat. This fascinating movie occupied the fifth place among 1982's most nominated pictures, receiving six citations, some in major categories (writing, directing). Unanimously acclaimed by critics, *Das Boot* also proved popular with the public, grossing $4.5 million, which made it the most popular German film ever to be shown in the United States.

Distinguished performances by foreign players in arthouse films that were not commercial have been consistently overlooked by the Academy. This list is too long to document, but two recent examples demonstrate the point. Ettore Scola's *La Nuit de Varenne* (1983), which opened to acclaim but did poor business, featured a great performance by Marcello Mastroianni as the aging Casanova in a story set during the French Revolution.

One of Europe's best and busiest actors, Gerard Depardieu didn't receive any nomination, despite excellent appearances in numerous films, including the frustrated husband in Bertrand Blier's *Get Out Your Handkerchiefs*, and the title role in Andrzej Wajda's *Danton*. Depardieu finally received a nomination for the lead in the new, French version of *Cyrano de Bergerac* (1990); José Ferrer had won Best Actor in the 1950 American version.

Of all award categories, the best chances for foreigners to get nominations is in the writing categories: Best Original Screenplay and Best Adaptation from another medium. The 1945 Swiss film, *Marie-Louise,* about a group of French children during World War II, was the first European movie to win Original Screenplay. Some of the best Italian neorealistic movies were also nominated for writing awards: Roberto Rossellini's *Open City* (1946) and Vittorio De Sica's *Umberto D* (1952).

In 1959, two of the five nominated original scripts were foreign-language: Francois Truffaut's stunning debut, *The 400 Blows,* which launched the French New Wave, and Ingmar Bergman's arthouse hit, *Wild Strawberries,* which boasted a legendary performance. Neither won—the winner was *Pillow Talk*.

Over the last two decades, the writers of the French *Day for Night* (1974), the Italian *Seven Beauties* (1976), the French *Mon Oncle d'Amerique* (1980), the West-German *Das Boot* (1982), the Swedish *Fanny and Alexander* (1983), the Argentinean *The Official Story* (1985), Louis Malle's *Au Revoir, Les Enfants* (1987), and Agnieszka Holland's *Europa, Europa* (1991), have all received writing nominations, if not awards.

It takes longer for foreign filmmakers to get recognition in the United States, particularly if they don't make American movies. Many good "art" films are not widely shown if they don't boast an internationally known star or are not made by a prestigious director, such as Fellini, Truffaut, or Bergman. To a large extent, the distribution of these movies depends on favorable review by major critics in New York and Los Angeles.

This is one reason why foreign players, particularly men, tend to be older than their American counterparts by the time they earn nominations. Marcello Mastroianni was not only one of the most distinguished actors in the world, but one who was extremely popular outside of Italy. Mastroianni made his screen debut in 1949, at the age of twenty-five, after studying acting and acquiring stage experience with Luchino Visconti's theatrical troupe. In the 1950s, he achieved stature in Italy, but he attained international stardom in 1960, as a result of his starring role in Fellini's *La Dolce Vita*. A year later, he appeared in another Fellini masterpiece, *8 1/2,* which was even more commercially successful than *La Dolce Vita*.

The Academy failed to nominate him for either of these performances, though the movies themselves were nominated for a number of awards. Mastroianni earned his first Best Actor nomination in 1962, at age thirty-eight, for the Italian comedy, *Divorce—Italian Style,* in which he excelled as the bored Sicilian baron who plans to get rid of his nagging wife. Mastroianni would probably not have received the nomination were it not for the publicity and awards that *Divorce—Italian Style* received from the Cannes Festival and from Hollywood's Golden Globes.

Foreign players who work in the United States tend to be older than their American colleagues, because they first have to excel in their own countries before they are brought to Hollywood. Anna Magnani and Maggie Smith were older than American actresses when they first won their Oscars. American and foreign actors make their debuts at more or less the same age, with women (both foreign and American) being younger than men both when they are first nominated and first win the Oscar. The gap between American and foreign players is wider in the men's careers: American actors tend to win the Oscar at the median age of thirty-six, the foreigners at forty-three.

The foreign directors made their debuts at a younger age than their American peers, but the latter are younger (in their thirties) when they get their first nomination. This difference increases by the time they win directorial Oscars: the American at the median age of forty, the foreign at forty-four.

British director Carol Reed's international reputation reached a peak with *The Fallen Idol* (1949), earning him his first nomination, and *The Third Man* (1950), his second. Nonetheless, Reed won the award many years later for a musical, *Oliver!* (1968). The long overdue Oscar was received by an aging director (sixty-nine) who was then in decline.

Most foreign filmmakers have done their best work by the time they earn first nominations. Jean Renoir received his one and only nomination for *The Southerner* (1945), a film he made in the United States at fifty-two, but he didn't receive nominations for his French masterpieces, *Grand Illusion* (1937) and *The Rules of the Game* (1939). Fellini, another film master, never won a directorial Oscar despite four nominations: *La Dolce Vita, 8 1/2, Satyricon* (1970), and *Amarcord* (1975). Fellini was older (forty-two) than his American peers at his first nomination and, like other foreigners, had not been nominated for his earlier masterworks, *La Strada* and *Nights of Cabiria,* though both won Best Foreign Picture Oscar in 1956 and 1957, respectively. Fellini later received an Honorary Oscar, which was basically a compensatory gesture.

That the Academy tends to ignore the work of first-rate foreign film-makers is clear from the career of Ingmar Bergman. It is difficult to believe, but Bergman received his first nomination as late as 1973, for *Cries and Whispers,* when he was fifty-six. None of his earlier landmarks, *The Seventh Seal* (1957), *The Virgin Spring* (1960), or *Persona* (1966) was rec-ognized, though *The Virgin Spring* and *Through a Glass Darkly* won the Best Foreign Picture Oscar of 1960 and 1961. Bergman, like Fellini, has not won a Best Director Oscar, though he earned a second nomination for *Face to Face* (1976) and a third for *Fanny and Alexander,* which also won Best Foreign Picture. In all likelihood, Bergman, like Fellini, will win an Honorary Oscar for his career, but the opportunity to confer the award on a unique artist while at his peak was missed. Bergman's story is by no means unique: the foreign directors have all had established reputations in international film forums before earning Oscar nominations.

Yet every once in a while foreign filmmakers feature prominently in the competition. In 1987, all five of the nominated directors were born outside of the United States: Italian Bertolucci (who won) for *The Last Emperor,* Brit John Boorman for *Hope and Glory,* Swedish Lasse Hallstrom for *My Life as a Dog,* Canadian Norman Jewison for *Moonstruck,* and Brit Adrian Lyne for *Fatal Attraction.*

The revered Indian director, Satyajit Ray, who made such classics as *Pather Panchali* and *The World of Apu,* was awarded the 1991 Honorary Oscar. Too ill to attend the ceremonies, he appeared on videotape from his hospital bed in Calcutta, clutching the Oscar statuette in his arms.

In 1995, the noted Polish filmmaker Krzysztof Kieslowski received two Oscar nominations, Best Director and Original Screenplay for *Red,* the Swiss-made picture and last entry in his acclaimed *Three Colors* trilogy that won almost every critics group award for best foreign film. Nonetheless, a furor erupted when the film was disqualified to compete in the best foreign language category due to rigid bureaucratic rules.

Another Polish filmmaker, Andrzej Wajda, made history in 1999, when he became the first ever East European director to be given an honorary Oscar. That he received the award from a politically oriented actress like Jane Fonda made his moment in the limelight all the more memorable. "I think to create film in a foreign language and yet to be known and recognized by everyone is the best kind of success one can expect," Wajda said in his eloquent speech.

In 1997, James Cameron became the first Canadian to win Best Director, for *Titanic*. Born in Ontario, Cameron remains a Canuck by citizenship. Another Canadian, Atom Egoyan, was nominated in the same year for directing and adapting *The Sweet Hereafter*.

Nationalism versus Globalism

There's another dimension to Oscar's growing globalism. In 1995, four out of the five Best Picture nominees were filmed outside of the United States, highlighting the globalization of film production and blurring the definition of Hollywood studio product. The smorgasbord of locations, directors, casts, and crews gave that year's picks an international flavor usually seen only in the foreign-language film category. The trend continued into the late 1990s. In a subtle statement about the state of the film industry, every one of the 1998 Best Picture nominees did all or most of its shooting overseas. In 1999, *American Beauty* became the first Best Picture in twenty-three years—since *Rocky* in 1976—to be lensed in Hollywood.

The production of foreign-language films have also reflected the internationalism of the movie industry. The UK entry, *Solomon & Gaenor,* was directed by a Brit (Paul Morrison), set in Wales, with actors speaking Yiddish, English, and Welsh. Nepal's first-ever nomination, *Caravan,* was a French/British/Swiss/Nepalese co-production, set in the highest reaches of the Himalayas, with a French crew and cast, and Tibetans speaking their native language.

Despite a strong international dimension, periodically, the Academy is accused of "chauvinism," of favoring American over foreign artists. Just how distinctly American, or nationalistic, is the Oscar, compared with other prestigious prizes, such as the New York Film Critics Awards?

Not surprisingly, American players have dominated both forums. The Oscar is more of an "American" award (about 80 percent of all winners) than the New York Film Critics Award (60 percent). British players have occupied the second place in both contests, but their representation is greater in the New York Film Critics competition than in the Oscar race.

In both venues, there is more national diversity among the female winners. Among the women cited by the New York Film Critics were two Italians (Anna Magnani and Sophia Loren), two French (two-time nominee Isabelle Adjani and Catherine Deneuve, for *Indochine*). In 1988, Norma Aleandro became the first South American actress to be nominated for an Oscar for *Gaby—A True Story,* an Argentinean movie. By that time, Aleandro was a known quantity, having starred in *The Official Story,* which won the 1985 Best Foreign-Language Picture.

Some of Oscar's "greatest losers" are foreign-born actresses who have won multiple awards from the New York Film Critics. British actress Deborah Kerr, a six-time Oscar nominee, won three New York Film Critics Awards for *Black Narcissus, Heaven Knows, Mr. Allison,* and *The Sundowners.* Swedish Greta Garbo, a three-time Oscar nominee, was cited twice by the New York Film Critics for *Anna Karenina* and *Camille.* Liv Ullmann, the quintessential Bergman actress, has earned two Oscar nominations but three New York Film Critics citations, for *Cries and Whispers, Scenes from a Marriage,* and *Face to Face.*

No such striking cases exist among the men, though two British winners of the New York Film Critics Award were not even nominated for their performances: Ralph Richardson, singled out for his performance in *Breaking the Sound Barrier,* and John Gielgud for *Providence.* Both actors were nominated by the Academy for other performances, and Gielgud won a supporting Oscar for *Arthur.*

Nationalistic considerations do play a role beyond the quality of the competing performances. In 1980, a furor arose in Cannes, when Peter Sellers's brilliant performance in *Being There* was overlooked by the jury for reasons that apparently had nothing to do with its merits. Kirk Douglas, the jury's president, was furious when his colleagues chose Michel Piccoli and Anouk Aimee (both in Marco Bellocchio's *Leap Into the Void),* because they felt it was time for French performers to win. This incident was not isolated. In other years too, political considerations have played a crucial role in determining the winners. Critics felt that the motive for awarding the 1975 Palm d'Or to an Algerian film, *Chronicle of the Burning Years,* was based on political reasons: Algeria and other Third World cinemas had been underrepresented and overlooked.

The greater number of ties at Cannes also attests to the prevalence of compromises in making the final choices. In 1979, the Cannes Jury conferred the Palm d'Or on both the German picture *The Tin Drum* and the American *Apocalypse Now.* In 1980, a tie was declared between the Japanese film *Kagemusha* by Akira Kurosawa, and the American entry, Bob Fosse's *All That Jazz.* By contrast, there has never been a tie in the

Best Picture Oscar, and only one tie in the history of the New York Film Critics Circle—in 1960, when *The Apartment* and *Sons and Lovers* were both cited.

All film forums are biased in their choices—that's the nature of awards determined by majority vote. Yet the disagreements within each group, and among the various groups, fulfill an important function: They call attention to the operation of multiple criteria—artistic, ideological, political—in evaluating the quality of film art.

CHAPTER 6

Winning the Oscar

If winning the Oscar is the ultimate achievement in the film world, and the epitome of professional success, it is important to know at what age and at what career phase film artists win the award?

The Winners' Age

In theory, it is possible to win the Oscar at any age, and, indeed, there have been winners in practically every age group. In practice, however, the best chances to win the Oscar are between the ages of thirty and forty-nine, with two-thirds of all winners in these age brackets.

As with first nomination, actresses are much younger when receiving their first Oscar. About two-fifths of the women, compared with a minority (5 percent) of the men, have won the Oscar prior to the age of thirty. And two-thirds of the women, but only one-third of the men, won the Oscar by the time they reached forty. The gap in winning age is particularly large in the lead categories: half of the Best Actresses, but only 2 percent of the Best Actors, are younger than thirty at their first win.

Within each category, there's a concentration of winners in one or two age groups. Among the Best Actresses, the largest concentration is of winners who are in their late twenties. By contrast, the dominant group of Best Actors is in their early forties. There's no dominant norm in the two supporting categories, in which the age range is wide, with winners in every age from the early teens to the late seventies.

The likelihood of winning at a particular age is determined by the range of screen roles allotted to men and women, and to leading and supporting players. Cultural norms have prescribed these roles, and these prescriptions are more rigid and confining for the lead players. The variability of supporting roles in age and appearance explains why the age distribution among supporting winners is wide. Compared with leading roles, there are no specific requirements that character roles be played by young and attractive players.

The impact of gender on the winning age is paramount: the median age at first win is thirty-four for actresses (lead and supporting) and forty-four for actors (in both leagues). The median age at winning is thirty-one for the Best Actresses, thirty-eight for the Supporting Actresses, forty-one for the Best Actors, and forty-six for the Supporting Actors.

Thus, in response to the question, "is the Oscar a young artists' game?" the answer is no, but it is a qualified no. Only one-fifth of all winners have received the award prior to the age of thirty. Even so, the Oscar is more of a young women's than young men's game: 15 percent of the Best Actresses, but no Best Actors, are in their twenties. Middle-age is the norm for the male winners, with most Best Actors between the ages of thirty-five and fifty when they first win the Oscar.

Some actors have been particularly lucky to win the Oscar at a young age. The youngest winner in each category is:

Tatum O'Neal	10	Supp. Actress	*Paper Moon*
Timothy Hutton	19	Supp. Actor	*Ordinary People*
Janet Gaynor	22	Best Actress	*Sunrise, Street Angel, Seventh Heaven*
Richard Dreyfuss	29	Best Actor	*The Goodbye Girl*

Among directors, the youngest winners are: William Friedkin, at thirty-two, for *The French Connection* in 1971; Norman Taurog, also thirty-two, for *Skippy* in 1930–31; and Lewis Milestone, at thirty-three, for *Two Arabian Nights* in 1927–28, the only year in which the Academy separated between comedic and dramatic direction. Most directors are in their late thirties and early forties when first winning the Oscar.

Other players have had to wait until old age to win. The oldest winners are:

Jessica Tandy	81	Best Actress	*Driving Miss Daisy*
Henry Fonda	77	Best Actor	*On Golden Pond*
Peggy Ashcroft	77	Supp. Actress	*A Passage To India*
George Burns	79	Supp. Actor	*The Sunshine Boys*

Older actresses have been more prominent over the last two decades: Ellen Burstyn *(Alice Doesn't Live Here Anymore)* was forty-three, Shirley

MacLaine *(Terms of Endearment)* fifty, and Geraldine Page *(The Trip to Bountiful)* sixty-one. But Jessica Tandy and Marie Dressler (who was sixty-two) are the exceptions: few women have received their first Oscar after the age of sixty.

By contrast, elderly supporting winners have prevailed in each decade: Helen Hayes *(Airport)*, John Houseman *(The Paper Chase)*, Don Ameche *(Cocoon)*, Jack Palance *(City Slickers)*, and James Coburn *(Affliction)* were all over seventy at their winning.

Ruth Gordon's winning age, seventy-two, demonstrates the career opportunities available to supporting players at an older age. Though a late bloomer on-screen, Gordon was an accomplished stage actress. After a few appearances in silent movies and one substantial role, as Mary Todd Lincoln in *Abe Lincoln in Illinois* (1940), she dedicated herself almost exclusively to the theater. In 1966, however, Gordon made an impressive comeback, as Natalie Wood's demented mother in *Inside Daisy Clover*, for which she earned her first supporting nomination. Two years later, she won the supporting Oscar for playing a modern witch in *Rosemary's Baby*. "Well, I can't tell you how encouragin' a thing like that is!" said Gordon whole-heartedly in her acceptance speech. "The first money I ever earned was as an extra in 1915, and here it is 1969. I don't know what took me so long."

Husband-writer Garson Kanin, with whom she collaborated on many screenplays, responded similarly, "Suddenly Hollywood discovered Ruth; it's only taken them fifty years." Among the many congratulatory cables Gordon received was one from her colleague Mary Pickford: "Dear Ruth, why did you take so long?" Gordon saw in her Oscar not only a tribute to past achievements, but also a prelude to a new career. And it was. For the next fifteen years, up to her death at the age of eighty-eight, she worked nonstop, delivering some of her best performances, including the one in the cult film, *Harold and Maude*.

The Oscar as an Instant Reward

How long does it take to win the Oscar once actors make their film debut? Once again, women tend to receive faster recognition for their talent: About one-fifth of the actresses, but only 5 percent of the actors, won the Oscar during the first year of their careers. Over half of the actresses received the Oscar within a decade of their debut, compared with one-third of the actors.

As with nomination, the Oscar functions as an instant reward for the women, but not for the men. Actresses experience a shorter period of time between their debuts and their winning. The median number of years between first film and the first Oscar is seven for the women and fourteen for the men. Consistent with other career patterns, of all groups, the Best Actresses are the ones to receive immediate recognition by the Academy. The median number of years between debut and winning is six for the Best Actresses, eight for the Supporting Actresses, twelve for the Best Actors, and fifteen for the Supporting Actors.

Six Best Actresses have received the Oscar for their film debuts or during the first year of their careers: Katharine Hepburn *(Morning Glory)*, Shirley Booth *(Come Back, Little Sheba)*, Julie Andrews *(Mary Poppins)*, Barbra Streisand *(Funny Girl)*, Louise Fletcher *(One Flew Over the Cuckoo's Nest)*, and Marlee Matlin *(Children of a Lesser God)*. By contrast, only two Best Actors, Ben Kingsley *(Gandhi)* and Geoffrey Rush *(Shine)* have received the Oscar for their first major film.

Supporting players have displayed one of two extremes patterns, winning either at a very early or at a very late phase. Twice as many supporting as lead players have won the Oscar during the first year of their careers, and more supporting players have had to wait longer before winning.

The Academy is more likely to bestow the Oscar for a debut, or during the first year of one's career, on the female supporting players. Of the winners in this group, more than half are women, including: Gale Sondergaard *(Anthony Adverse)*, Mercedes McCambridge *(All the King's Men)*, Eva Marie Saint *(On the Waterfront)*, Jo Van Fleet *(East of Eden)*, Goldie Hawn *(Cactus Flower)*, Meryl Streep *(The Deer Hunter)*, and Anna Paquin *(The Piano)*.

Instant recognition through an Oscar is often gained by players who repeated on screen previously successful stage roles. At times, several members of the original stage cast were rehired for the film version. When Lillian Hellman's 1941 stage hit, *Watch on the Rhine,* an antifascist play, was made into a movie two years later, two of its cast members, Paul Lukas, as the freedom fighter, and Lucille Watson, as the benevolent matriarch, were recast; Lukas won Best Actor, and Watson received a supporting nomination.

Three of the four principals in Tennessee Williams's prize-winning play, *A Streetcar Named Desire,* Marlon Brando, Karl Malden, and Kim Hunter, were cast in the 1951 film version, directed by Elia Kazan, who has staged the Broadway production with great mastery. Jessica Tandy, who had originated the role of Blanche DuBois, was not cast in the movie, because Warner wanted a major star. Instead, they chose Vivien Leigh, an Oscar winner who had played the part in London under the direction of her husband-actor Laurence Olivier. Brando earned his first Best Actor nomination, and Vivien Leigh, Karl Malden, Kim Hunter, and director Kazan all won Oscars.

Other stage players recruited for the screen versions of their work, for which they received nominations or awards, include: Nancy Kelly and Patty McCormack in *The Bad Seed* (1956), Paul Newman and Burl Ives in *Cat on a Hot Tin Roof* (1958), Rosalind Russell and Peggy Cass in *Auntie Mame* (1959), Anne Bancroft and Patty Duke in *The Miracle Worker* (1962), James Earl Jones and Jane Alexander in *The Great White Hope* (1970), and Richard Burton and Peter Firth in *Equus* (1977).

Four Best Actresses have won the Oscar for an acclaimed stage role with which they were intimately connected: Judy Holliday *(Born Yesterday)*, Shirley Booth *(Come Back, Little Sheba)*, Anne Bancroft *(The Miracle Worker)*, and Barbra Streisand *(Funny Girl)*. Streisand established herself as a Broadway musical star in *Funny Girl*, won for it a Tony nomination, and went on to become a movie star after the film version. Director Herbert Ross held that Streisand was extremely lucky to make her film debut in *Funny Girl,* holding that, "Having had the advantages of playing Fanny Brice for two years on Broadway, Streisand knew her part inside out." It was the perfect part for Streisand, ideally suited to her range as an actress and as a singer.

The proportion of women nominated for re-creating stage roles is considerable, about 10 percent of all Best Actresses. Despite the fact that they have appeared in other pictures, some are still identified with these memorable roles. This group includes: Lynn Fontanne in *The Guardsman,* Katharine Hepburn in *The Philadelphia Story,* Julie Harris in *The Member of the Wedding,* Maggie McNamara in *The Moon Is Blue,* and Geraldine Page in *Sweet Bird of Youth.* Most recently, Stockard Channing, best known for her New York theater career, was nominated for an Oscar for *Six Degrees of Separation* (1993), for the same role that had earned her a Tony nomination.

Of the Best Actors too, no fewer than seven have received the award for re-creating a famous stage role, beginning with George Arliss, who played the British statesman in *Disraeli* on stage, then in both the silent and sound film versions. Yul Brynner made the part of the King of Siam, in the Rodgers and Hammerstein's *The King and I,* so much his own that it was unthinkable for anyone else to play it when the film was made. Brynner won for it a supporting Tony Award, an Oscar, and a lifetime lease on this role, playing it on Broadway and on the road in several subsequent revivals. Brynner also starred as the monarch in the short-lived CBS series, *Anna and the King,* in 1972. It became Brynner's very last role, which he played in New York just weeks before his death in 1985.

Rex Harrison scored such a triumph in the Lerner and Lowe's musical, *My Fair Lady,* on both sides of the Atlantic, that when the movie was made he was the natural choice for it. Like Brynner, Harrison became intimately identified with the role, arguably his best, in a long and distinguished career. The Academy could not deny the award to other actors who excelled in transferring a stage role to the big screen, like José Ferrer in *Cyrano de Bergerac* and Paul Scofield in *A Man for All Seasons.*

A large number of Best Actor nominees received recognition for playing a popular role in both theater and film: Walter Huston in *Dodsworth,* Raymond Massey in *Abe Lincoln in Illinois,* Anthony Franciosa in *A Hatful of Rain,* Ron Moody in *Oliver!,* Israeli Topol in *Fiddler on the Roof,* James Whitmore in his one-man show, *Give 'Em Hell, Harry,* Tom Courtenay in *The Dresser,* Kenneth Branagh in *Henry V,* Nigel Hawthorne in *The Madness of King George.*

Getting instant recognition is often a result of luck or circumstances over which actors have little control. Fluke and happenstance are often-used terms in showbiz because they describe accurately how careers can be made—from getting a "break," to being cast in an important film, to being nominated and winning an Oscar. Being "the right person at the right time in the right place," may be a more crucial factor in determining the shape of screen careers than acting talent and skills.

Many players gave their Oscar-winning performances not at their home studios, but when they were loaned out to other studios. Producer Samuel Goldwyn let Warner Brothers borrow Gary Cooper for the title role of *Sergeant York* (his first Oscar) in exchange for Warner's contract player, Bette Davis, whom they cast in *The Little Foxes,* which became one of her best-known roles and earned her a nomination.

Clark Gable and Claudette Colbert scored a great victory in Columbia's *It Happened One Night,* despite the fact that both were at first reluctant to appear in Frank Capra's comedy. Colbert, in fact, was about to sail for Europe, and Gable was loaned out to Columbia by Louis B. Mayer as a disciplinary measure, having rejected scripts which the studio had created for him. MGM considered *It Happened One Night* a minor project at a minor studio. Film history proved otherwise: *It Happened* won Best Picture, Director, and acting awards and also changed the previously low status of Columbia in Hollywood. The movie's unanticipated critical and commercial success shows again that once a movie is made, it assumes an independent life of its own. There are always elements of unpredictability and adventurism in filmmaking because the audiences' response cannot always be accurately predicted.

The Oscar's history is replete with such stories. Warner Baxter was assigned the role of the Cisco Kid in the Western *In Old Arizona* by default;

the intended actor was Raoul Walsh, who had a car accident in which he lost an eye. Mercedes McCambridge believed that she might have never "stumbled onto an Oscar," for *All the King's Men,* "if it hadn't been for a pushy friend of mine who took me to a 'cattle call' in New York. This part launched a vital screen career after McCambrdige won a supporting Oscar.

Many players have won their Oscars for parts for which they had not been the first or second choice. Cary Grant was given the choice between the two male leads in *The Philadelphia Story:* Tracy Lord's ex-husband or the canny journalist. He chose the former and Jimmy Stewart, cast as the reporter, went home with an Oscar. In retrospect, Grant committed another error, when he turned down the part of Judy Garland's down-and-out husband-actor in *A Star Is Born,* later played with great distinction by James Mason, who received a Best Actor nomination for it.

One can't guarantee, of course, that if the original actors play the roles intended for them, they would have been singled out by the Academy, but chances are they would at least have been nominated. In the absence of her husband, the producer Irving Thalberg (who died in 1938), Norma Shearer made what turned out to be major errors of judgment. Shearer turned down the title role in *Mrs. Miniver,* which then went to Greer Garson, bringing her an Oscar and her best-remembered role.

Joan Crawford is best known for *Mildred Pierce,* but few people know that her role was first offered to Bette Davis, who turned it down. And Davis herself delivered the finest performance of her career, Margo Channing in *All About Eve,* by accident. Claudette Colbert was initially cast, but a back injury prevented her from doing it. Producer Darryl Zanuck's replacement choice was Ingrid Bergman, who was then in Italy. Bette Davis was his "last minute" choice; in retrospect, it is hard to imagine any actress but Davis in that role.

Director Anatole Litvak wanted Ingrid Bergman to play the mentally disturbed woman in *The Snake Pit,* but she declined, based on her feeling that "it all takes place in an insane asylum and I couldn't bear that." Instead, the role went to Olivia de Havilland, who scored a great victory, winning a nomination and a citation from the New York Film Critics. After the film's success, Litvak confronted Bergman, "look what you turned down!" "It was a very good part," she humorously replied, "but if I had played it, I wouldn't have got an Oscar for it." Bergman also turned down the part of the Swedish maid in *The Farmer's Daughter,* because, as she noted, "for me to play my own part as a Swedish girl was not what I wanted." Loretta Young was cast in this comedy and received an Oscar for her first and only nomination. But Bergman never regretted refusing either of those roles.

Marlon Brando's stunning role in *On the Waterfront,* as the none-too-bright ex-prizefighter Terry Malloy, was first offered to Frank Sinatra, on the strength of his 1953 Oscar for *From Here To Eternity.* However, when director Kazan learned that Brando was available, he broke his promise to Sinatra and cast Brando. And in 1962, Brando himself turned down the title role in David Lean's epic, *Lawrence of Arabia,* which went to a then unknown actor named Peter O'Toole. Though physically wrong for the role, O'Toole became an international star overnight, receiving for it the first of his seven nominations.

Rod Steiger scored critical acclaim in Paddy Chayefsky's television drama *Marty,* but when it was transferred to the big screen, he refused to do it again. Instead, a relatively obscure Ernest Borgnine, until then cast in villainous roles *(From Here to Eternity),* was chosen. *Marty,* which won Best Picture, Best Actor, and other awards, broadened Borgnine's range and placed him on a higher prestige level of acting.

Sophia Loren's part in *Two Women* was first intended for Anna Magnani, under George Cukor's direction. The idea was to cast Magnani in the mother's role and Loren as her daughter. Magnani, however, rejected this proposition, because Loren was taller than her, claiming that she could not perform with a daughter "I have to look up to." Loren was excited about the prospects of performing with Magnani, who at the time was the doyenne of Italian actresses. She tried to convince Magnani, but to no avail. As it turned out, this part was singlehandedly responsible for breaking Loren's image as a sex symbol, establishing her as a dramatic actress, which she had always wanted to be.

Fate also played a major factor in Peter Finch's best screen roles. Ian Bannen was originally cast as the Jewish homosexual doctor in *Sunday, Bloody Sunday,* but after a month of shooting, he became sick and had to be replaced. Finch's first reaction when the role was offered to him was, "I'm not queer," but, on a second thought, he was persuaded that "it was a fabulous script and a fabulous part." Director John Schlesinger later said that he "can't think of anyone who could have done it better," and that Finch was "definitive." Finch won for this role international recognition, including his first Best Actor nomination.

Nor was Finch the top choice to play the demented television commentator in Sidney Lumet's *Network.* The role had been previously offered to—and rejected by—George C. Scott, Glenn Ford, and Henry Fonda. It was screenwriter Paddy Chayefsky who suggested Finch for the juicy part. According to Finch's biographer, the arrival of the script in Jamaica, where Finch was a the time, "absolutely galvanized" him, his major concern being that someone else would take it before he could stake his claim. As soon as he finished reading the screenplay, "Finch was frantic to let them know he was more than interested."

Finch knew that *Network* was not only a plum role, but "Oscar material," and subsequently did not want to miss the opportunity. However, it is not always easy for actors to assess the quality of screen roles before, or even after, shooting begins. *Coming Home,* one of Hollywood's first anti–Vietnam War movies, was in various phases of preparation for six years, until Jane Fonda's production company, IPC, brought it to the screen. Its casting, which earned Jane Fonda and Jon Voight acting laurels, is now considered to be perfect, but Voight's role, as the paraplegic war veteran, was first offered to Jack Nicholson and Sylvster Stallone, the latter fresh from the glory of *Rocky.* United Artists wanted a bankable star, though producer Jerome Hellman and director Hal Ashby persuaded the studio that Voight was the right actor for the part.

Nomination and Winning

The Academy claims that the number of nomination does not affect the candidates' chances to win the Oscar. Indeed, two-thirds of all winners have earned the Oscar at their first nomination. At the same time, those charging that the number of nominations *do* count point out that 22 percent of the winners have been nominated twice, and 12 percent three or more times prior to winning. It's a matter of interpretation, depending on how statistics are read.

Overall, it is been much easier for supporting players to win the Oscar at their first nomination: 80 percent, compared with 50 percent of the lead winners. The competition for supporting awards is usually less intense. Besides, the Academy has been more discriminating in evaluating lead performances; the lead Oscars are, after all, much more prestigious and influential.

But once again, of the four groups, the Best Actors are the least likely to get the award at first nomination. Two thirds of the Best Actresses, compared with less than half of the Best Actors, have won the Oscar at first nomination. The disadvantage of the Best Actors derives from the fact that until the late 1970s American films have provided better roles for men, thus making the competition within this category much fiercer.

In the Oscar's first decade, all Best Actresses won at their first nomination. Joan Fontaine was the first actress to win the award at her second nomination, for *Rebecca,* in 1941. Until the 1970s, at least half of the Best Actresses won for their first nominated roles. In the last two decades, however, Faye

Dunaway *(Network)* won at her third nomination, Shirley MacLaine *(Terms of Endearment)* at her fifth, and Geraldine Page *(The Trip to Bountiful)* broke all records by winning the Oscar at her eighth nomination.

By contrast, except for the first decade, it has been almost a rarity for men to win at their first or even second nomination. In the 1970s, only two winners, Art Carney for *Harry and Tonto* and Richard Dreyfuss for *The Goodbye Girl*, received the award for their first nomination. The other actors were nominated three or four times before winning. However, in the 1980s, the trend has reversed itself, with many actors winning at their first nomination. This group includes: Ben Kingsley *(Gandhi)*, F. Murray Abraham *(Amadeus)*, William Hurt *(Kiss of the Spider Woman)*, Michael Douglas *(Wall Street)*, Jeremy Irons *(Reversal of Fortune)*, Nicolas Cage *(Leaving Las Vegas)*, Geoffrey Rush *(Shine)*, and Roberto Benigni *(Life Is Beautiful)*.

Fourteen players had to wait for a while before winning the Oscar:

4th nomination:	Lawrence Olivier, Marlon Brando, Elizabeth Taylor, Dustin Hoffman, Maureen Stapleton, Robert Duvall, Robin Williams
5th nomination:	Susan Hayward, Gregory Peck, Jack Nicholson, Shirley MacLaine
6th nomination:	Paul Newman, Al Pacino
8th Nomination:	Geraldine Page

If chances to win an Oscar increase with the number of nominations, the following actors are likely candidates for the award: Peter O'Toole (seven nominations), Glenn Close (five), Albert Finney, Jane Alexander, Marsha Mason, and Warren Beatty (each four), Jeff Bridges, Morgan Freeman, Sigourney Weaver, Michelle Pfeiffer, and Tom Cruise (each three). The late Richard Burton was also nominated seven times, six in the lead and one in the supporting category.

The careers of the Oscar Directors resembles those of the women: about half have won the Oscar at their first nomination, one-fourth at their second, and one-fourth at their later nominations.

3rd nomination:	Michael Curtiz, Fred Zinnemann, Carol Reed, Sydney Pollack
4th nomination:	David Lean, Steven Spielberg
5th nomination:	William Wyler, George Cukor

The greatest losers in the directing category are: King Vidor, Clarence Brown, and Hitchcock (each with five nominations), Sidney Lumet,

Federico Fellini, and Stanley Kubrick (each with four), and Ernst Lubitsch, William A. Wellman, Sam Wood, Richard Brooks, Stanley Kramer, Ingmar Bergman, Robert Altman, Martin Scorsese, Peter Weir, and James Ivory (each with three). Of these, judging by their current work, Altman, Scorsese, Weir, and Ivory are likely to win an Oscar in the future.

Ties and Multiple Oscars

Ties have been a rare occurrence: neither the Academy nor the filmmakers like the idea of sharing the coveted award. There have never been ties in the Best Picture category and only two in the acting awards. The first tie was declared in 1932, when Wallace Beery *(The Champ)* and Fredric March *(Dr. Jekyll and Mr. Hyde)* split the Best Actor award. Beery came within one vote of March, and in those years, when a nominee came within three votes of another, a tie was declared. The second tie occurred in the 1968 Best Actress award, which was shared by Katharine Hepburn *(The Lion in Winter)* and Barbra Streisand *(Funny Girl)*. This time, however, the number of votes for each candidate was not disclosed.

In other awards too, ties have been rare. In its sixty-five years of existence, the New York Film Critics Circle has declared a tie only a few times. In 1960, two films were cited as Best Pictures, *The Apartment* and *Sons and Lovers;* both films were nominated for Oscars, but the winner was *The Apartment*. And in 1966, Elizabeth Taylor *(Who's Afraid of Virginia Woolf?)* and Lynn Redgrave *(Georgy Girl)* were singled out as Best Actresses; the Oscar winner was Taylor.

The Los Angeles Film Critics Association has also refrained from splitting its awards, though in 1976, Sidney lumet's *Network* and John Avildsen's *Rocky* were named Best Picture; the Oscar winner was *Rocky*. In 1984, the Los Angeles group honored two male performances: Albert Finney in *Under the Volcano* and F. Murray Abraham in *Amadeus;* the Oscar winner was Abraham. In 1998, Ally Sheedy *(High Art)* and Brazilian actress Fernanda Montenegro *(Central Station)* were both cited by the Los Angeles Film Critics; Sheedy wasn't even nominated, and the Oscar winner was Gwyneth Paltrow *(Shakespeare in Love)*.

For most actors, winning an Oscar has been a once-in-a-lifetime achievement. Yet considering the intensity of competition, the proportion of players winning multiple awards is quite impressive: about 20 percent. As could be expected, lead players have better chances than supporting to win a second Oscar. Quite consistently, the Best Actresses have the best prospects of winning a second Oscar: 30 percent, compared with 13 percent of the Best Actors.

The following players won two Oscars in the same category:

Best Actor	Fredric March, Spencer Tracy, Gary Cooper, Marlon Brando, Jack Nicholson, Tom Hanks
Best Actress	Bette Davis, Luise Rainer, Vivien Leigh, Ingrid Bergman, Olivia de Havilland, Elizabeth Taylor, Glenda Jackson, Jane Fonda, Sally Field, Jodie Foster
Supp. Actor	Anthony Quinn, Peter Ustinov, Melvyn Douglas, Jason Robards, Michael Caine
Supp. Actress	Shelley Winters, Diane Wiest

Two players stand out in their Oscar achievements. Katharine Hepburn, Hollywood's most respected screen actress, ties the record of the most nominations with Meryl Streep (each twelve), and holds the record for winning the most awards (four). Hepburn's Oscars have been won over period of half a century, from *Morning Glory* in 1932, to *Guess Who's Coming to Dinner* in 1967, to *The Lion in Winter* in 1968, and *On Golden Pond* in 1981. Walter Brennan holds another kind of a record, having won three supporting Oscars within a short period of time (five years): *Come and Get It* in 1936, *Kentucky* in 1938, and *The Westerner* in 1940.

Ten players won Oscars in both the leading and supporting categories: five actors (Jack Lemmon, Robert De Niro, Jack Nicholson, Gene Hackman, and Kevin Spacey) and five actresses (Helen Hayes, Ingrid Bergman, Maggie Smith, Meryl Streep, and Jessica Lange). With the exception of Nicholson and Hackman, the men first won a supporting, then a lead Oscar. The first two-time male winner was Jack Lemmon, first cited for a featured role in *Mister Roberts* in 1955, then twenty-eight years later for the lead in *Save the Tiger*.

Three of the women first won Best Actress, then Supporting Actress. Helen Hayes was the first multiple winner, receiving Best Actress for *The Sin of Madelon Claudet* in 1932, and a second, supporting Oscar for *Airport* in 1970. This different career pattern stems in part from the rigid specifications for women's roles, demanding that leading ladies be young and attractive. Nonetheless, the careers of Meryl Streep and Jessica Lange, two actresses who first won a supporting (*Kramer vs. Kramer, Tootsie,* respectively) then a leading Oscar (*Sophie's Choice, Blue Sky),* is seen as an encouraging development in increasing flexibility for women in Hollywood.

Multiple wins have been more prevalent among filmmakers, reflecting a different ratio of supply and demand of directing talent. The concentration of awards and nominations within a small group of talented filmmakers has been a consistent trend in Hollywood. Of the fifty-three Oscar-winning directors, sixteen (30 percent) have been multiple recipients. The all-time record is still held by John Ford, who won four Oscars, followed by Frank Capra and William Wyler, each with three Oscars. Only fourteen of the fifty-three winning directors have received one nomination. Ten directors have been nominated five or more times, including Capra, Billy Wilder, Kazan, Huston, and Zinnemann.

Only five players have won two Oscars in a row: Luise Rainer in 1936 and 1937, Spencer Tracy in 1937 and 1938, Katharine Hepburn in 1967 and 1968, Jason Robards in 1976 and 1977, and Tom Hanks in 1993 and 1994. Of the Oscar directors, only two have achieved that: John Ford for *The Grapes of Wrath* in 1940 and *How Green Was My Valley* in 1941, and Joseph L. Mankiewicz for *A Letter to Three Wives* in 1949 and *All About Eve* in 1950.

The Academy is reluctant to bestow the Oscar posthumously: Peter Finch is the only player to have won the award after his death, for *Network*. Some suspect that the Academy has avoided posthumous awards because of its realization that they have much less impact on the commercial appeal of the winning films. Others claim that the Academy's reluctance stems from its belief that the awards should affect the careers of practicing artists. In some categories, such as the Irving G. Thalberg Memorial Award for distinguished producers and the Honorary Oscars, the rules state explicitly that the awards "shall not be voted posthumously."

The Academy is pretty much a rule-abiding organization. In 1972, Raymond Rasch, Larry Russell, and Charlie Chaplin earned the best original score for *Limelight,* a film made twenty years earlier. Released in Los Angeles in 1972 for the first time, *Limelight* was eligible for nominations. Both Rasch and Russell were dead, but Chaplin accepted the award for a film which had been banned in the United States for many years, though it was shown in Europe.

Posthumous nominations have been only slightly more frequent. James Dean is one of few exceptions, earning two Best Actor nominations posthumously, for *East of Eden* in 1955, and for *Giant* in 1956. Dean was killed in a highway car crash while driving his Porsche to Salinas to compete in a race. *East of Eden* was released a few weeks after his death, on September 30, 1955, and *Giant,* which he did not complete, about a year later. When the 1956 awards were presented, on March 27, 1957, Dean had been dead for eighteen months. The consensus was that Dean's second nomination was based on sentimentality, though his performances in both pictures were outstanding. Dean's Oscar nominations not only contributed to the box-office success of *East of Eden* and *Giant,* but also helped to elevate his status to legendary.

Spencer Tracy was also nominated posthumously for *Guess Who's Coming to Dinner,* a film that provided a grand acting reunion with Katharine Hepburn—it was their ninth film together. Were it not for Hepburn, Tracy would not have made the film. Frightened that he might not get through with picture, a sickly Tracy told director Stanley Kramer four days before shooting ended: "You know, I read the script again last night, and if I were to die on the way home tonight, you can still release the picture with what you've got." Had Tracy lived, he would probably have won an award, both for his acting and for sentimental reasons. Hepburn's Oscar was probably based on personal reasons too: she selflessly nursed Tracy throughout the demanding shoot. Aware of this, Hepburn said upon winning the award for Best Actress: "I'm sure mine is for the two of us."

Sir Ralph Richardson received posthumous supporting nomination for his bravura performance in *Greystoke: The Legend of Tarzan* (1984), in which he played the eccentric Lord Greystoke. Undeterred by his death, the New York Film Critics Circle cited Richardson. The Academy's Acting Branch, too, acknowledged Richardson's genius and the fact that it was his last film; the winner was Haing S. Ngor for *The Killing Fields.*

In 1994, Italian actor Massimo Troisi *(Il Postino)* received the first posthumous Best Actor nod since Peter Finch, in 1976. Troisi died just twelve hours after completing the shoot, a factor no doubt contributing to the film's immense popularity.

The Oscar—A White Man's Award?

Spike Lee, the dean of African American filmmakers, has never been nominated for the Best Director Oscar, despite impressive achievements in such films as *Do the Right Thing* (1989), one of the past decade's most important movies, and *Malcolm X* (1992). Lee's documentary, *4 Little Girls,* was nominated in that category in 1997, but didn't win. In the Oscar's seventy-two years, the only African American to have won a directing nomination is John Singleton, for the 1991 urban family drama, *Boyz N the Hood.*

Black actors have fared slightly better than black filmmakers. In the Academy's entire history, only six performers have won the Oscar, five in the supporting categories, and only one, Sidney Poitier, in the lead. They are, chronologically:

Hattie McDaniel, *Gone With the Wind* (1939)
Sidney Poitier, *Lilies of the Field* (1963)
Lou Gossett Jr., *An Officer and a Gentleman* (1982)
Denzel Washington, *Glory* (1988)
Whoopi Goldberg, *Ghost* (1990)
Cuba Gooding Jr., *Jerry Maguire* (1996)

No black woman has ever won Best Actress, and only six have been nominated: Dorothy Dandridge for *Carmen Jones* in 1954, Diana Ross for *Lady Sings the Blues* in 1972, Cicely Tyson for *Sounder* also in 1972, Diahann Carroll for *Claudine* in 1974, Whoopi Goldberg for *The Color Purple* in 1985, and Angela Bassett for *What's Love Got to Do With It* in 1993.

The two black female winners, Hattie McDaniel and Whoopi Goldberg, amount to 3 percent of all Oscar winners, a vast underrepresenation considering the proportion of blacks in American society. In 1990, when Goldberg won the supporting Oscar for *Ghost,* she became the first black actress to win an Oscar since McDaniel in *Gone With the Wind,* back in 1939. So much for progress. Goldberg told the press rather revealingly: "I never say I'm black when I'm looking for work. I just don't admit it, because as soon as you say it, they tell you there's no work for you. You wouldn't say to a doctor that he couldn't operate on your kneecap because he is black. In the same way, art should have no color and no sex."

The black actresses nominated for supporting Oscars are: Ethel Waters for *Pinky* (1949), Juanita Moore for *Imitation of Life* (1959), Bea Richards for *Guess Who's Coming to Dinner* (1967), Alfre Woodard for *Cross Creek* (1983), Margaret Avery and Oprah Winfrey for *The Color Purple* (1985), Marianne Jean-Baptiste, a British black actress, for *Secrets & Lies* (1996). They amount to 7 out of 189 supporting nominees, which is also about 3 percent.

Black actor James Baskett received a Special Oscar in 1947 for *Song of the South* in recognition of his "able and heartwarming characterization of Uncle Remus, friend and storyteller to the children of the world." But Sidney Poitier is the only black to have won a competitive Oscar, representing one out of sixty-six Best Actors (1.5 percent).

The number of African American men nominated for Best Actor is slightly larger, 6 out of 116 nominees (5.2 percent). They are: James Earl Jones for *The Great White Hope* (1970), Paul Winfield for *Sounder* (1972),

Dexter Gordon for *Round Midnight* (1986), Morgan Freeman with two lead nominations, for *Driving Miss Daisy* (1989) and *The Shawshank Redemption* (1994), Denzel Washington also with two nominations, for *Malcolm X* (1992) and *The Hurricane* (1999), and Lawrence Fishburn for *What's Love Got to Do With It* (1993).

Only two black men have won supporting Oscars: Denzel Washington for *Glory* (1989) and Cuba Gooding Jr. for *Jerry Maguire* (1996). The 7 black supporting nominees, who amount to 3.6 percent of all 195 nominees, are: Rupert Crosse for *The Reivers* (1969), Howard E. Rollins for *Ragtime* (1981), Adolph Caesar for *A Soldier's Story* (1984), Morgan Freeman for *Street Smart* (1989), Jaye Davidson for *The Crying Game* (1992), Samuel Jackson for *Pulp Fiction* (1994), and Michael Clarke Duncan for *The Green Mile* (1999).

In 1995, the live-action short contender, Dianne Houston, the producer-director of *Tuesday Morning Ride*, was the only African American among the 166 Oscar-nominated artists, a low that precipitated cover stories in various news magazines and the ire of politician Jesse Jackson, who asked black performers to boycott the Oscar ceremonies.

Black-themed movies, whether helmed by white or black directors, have seldom won recognition for their creators, though the films themselves have been nominated. Steven Spielberg's *The Color Purple* (1985), adapted to the screen from Alice Walker's best-selling novel, is one of the greatest losers in the Oscar annals. Though denying Spielberg a Best Director nomination, *The Color Purple* received a record of eleven nominations, but when it came to the actual voting, the film lost out in each and every category; the big winner was *Out of Africa*.

Similarly, *In the Heat of the Night* won the 1967 Best Picture, but the directing Oscar that year went to Mike Nichols for *The Graduate* rather than Norman Jewison. In 1984, *A Soldier's Story* was nominated for Best Picture, but helmer Jewison failed to receive a directing nod. The Academy finally compensated Jewison for his three nominations (the other two were for *Fiddler on the Roof* in 1971 and *Moonstruck* in 1987) with an Honorary Oscar.

The women's record with the Oscars is not much better than that of African Americans. In its entire history, the Academy has had only two female presidents: Bette Davis and Fay Kanin. It may be indicative that when the Oscar announcer, Hank Sims, introduced Fay he mistakenly referred to her as Mr. Fay Kanin.

In seventy-two years, only two women have received Best Director nominations. In 1993, *The Piano*'s Jane Campion became the first woman director to be nominated since Lina Wertmuller had received the nod for *Seven Beauties,* in 1976. Several women-directed films were nominated for

Best Picture, but their helmers were not. *Children of a Lesser God* was nominated in 1986, but its director, Randa Haines, was not, and *Awakenings* was Oscar-nominated in 1990, but helmer Penny Marshall was totally ignored.

Barbra Streisand, the driving force behind *The Prince of Tides,* which grossed over seventy million dollars, also was denied a Best Director nomination. The omission of Streisand was interpreted as a slight against women directors. Producer Lynda Obst *(The Fisher King),* said: "When you're celebrating a woman behind the camera, that's a woman in power, and people are still uncomfortable with that." "Streisand's snub by the Academy may be less sexism than Barbarism," wrote *Newsweek's* Jack Kroll; "Many in Hollywood consider her self-absorbed, difficult and controlling."

Streisand did receive a Best Director nomination from the Directors Guild, which usually portends Oscar nomination. However, in 1991, John Singleton, the twenty-three-year-old black director, "took" Streisand's place. To some, this suggested the industry's political correctness at the moment, as though saying: blacks, yes, women, no. But Streisand refused to let the Academy rain on her parade. She told the *Los Angeles Times:* "I can't honestly say that I was wronged in any way, since there are a lot of good movies in contention." At the same time, she allowed that sexism is still a problem: "It's as if a man were allowed to have passion and commitment to his work, but a woman is allowed that feeling for a man, but not her work."

Women's track record in other branches is also far from impressive. Lyricist Dorothy Fields became the first woman to win the Best Song Oscar, "The Way You Look Tonight," from *Swing Time,* in 1936, though she collaborated on it with Jerome Kern.

Between 1980 and 1999, of the two hundred nominated films for writing awards (both original and adapted), only 2.5 percent of the winners have been women. For solo winners, not husband and wife teams, it took forty years between Clemence Dane, who had won for *Perfect Strangers,* in 1947, and Ruth P. Jhabvala, who won for *A Room With a View,* in 1986. Jhabvala, who won a second writing Oscar for *Howards End* in 1992, was joined by three other women: Callie Khouri for *Thelma & Louise* in 1991, Jane Campion for *The Piano* in 1993, and Emma Thompson for *Sense and Sensibility* in 1995. Thompson thus became the only individual, male or female, to have won competitive Oscars for acting *(Howards End)* and writing.

The Nominees as a Social Community

The Oscar winners and nominees function as members of a closely knit artistic community. To begin with, they form a small group comprised of the most distinguished players. The Oscar-nominated players amount to a small percentage of the membership of the Screen Actors Guild. The Oscar directors have also been a select group, 53 winners and 130 nominees, amounting to about 10 percent of the Directors Guild membership.

Intensely stratified, the filmmaking professions are marked by sharp inequality between the elite and the rank-and-file. According to the Screen Actors Guild, on any randomly chosen day, over 80 percent of its members are unemployed, and only a minority makes more than twenty thousand dollars a year from acting. By contrast, Oscar-winning players make millions of dollars per picture and work nonstop, moving from one project to another.

The Oscar contest reflects this acute inequality: nominations are concentrated within an extremely small group. The median number of nominations is 3.7 among the Best Actresses, 3.2 among the Best Directors, and 2.9 among the Best Actors.

The winners and nominees form a social community in other ways. Many players were under contract to the same studio for the duration of their careers, thus appearing opposite the same players and working under the same directors in film after film. Bette Davis, Humphrey Bogart, and James Cagney were Warner's stars. Clark Gable, Spencer Tracy, Joan Crawford, and Norma Shearer defined the signature of MGM as much as the studio shaped their careers. Lengthy studio affiliations meant, among other things, that performers appeared in similar films and specialized in similar kinds of screen roles, which helped audiences to distinguish a "Bette Davis" from a "Joan Crawford" film, a "Clark Gable" from a "James Cagney" movie.

To increase audience interest in their stars, the studios went out of their way to create on-screen romantic couples. Janet Gaynor appeared so often with Charles Farrell that they became known as "America's lovebirds." Other famous romantic teams include: Olivia de Havilland and Errol Flynn (*Captain Blood*), Katharine Hepburn and Spencer Tracy (who made nine pictures together, beginning with *Woman of the Year*), Margaret Sullavan and James Stewart (*The Shop Around the Corner*), Greer Garson and Walter Pidgeon (*Mrs. Miniver*), Humphrey Bogart and Lauren Bacall (*To Have and Have Not*), Doris Day and Rock Hudson (*Pillow Talk*). With the demise of the old studio system, this distinctive aspect of American cinema is completely gone.

Then there is a high percentage of direct occupational inheritance, that is, children stepping into their parents' occupations. This dimension is more prevalent in acting than in other professions, resulting in an even smaller and more intimate community. About 10 percent of the Oscar players had one parent in the acting profession, and 5 percent had both. If related professions (writing, producing, directing) are taken into account, the proportion is even higher (15 percent), particularly among women (20 percent). In some cases, occupational inheritance has prevailed for three or more generations. Consider the acting dynasties of the Barrymores, the Powers, the Fondas, the Robards, and the Bridges in the United States, and the Redgraves in England.

Many performers were literally born into showbiz. Paul Muni was reared in a theater trunk. His parents were strolling players who toured all over Europe and America with him and his two brothers. Shunning the financial hazards of acting, Muni's parents hoped that he would pursue a career as a violinist. But he was stagestruck, and at thirteen, became a regular member of his parents' troupe. Muni never studied acting; there was no need for it.

Another Academy nominee, Mickey Rooney, spent his infancy and childhood on tour with his parents, who were both entertainers. Rooney made his stage debut at fifteen months, appearing as a midget in a vaudeville act, for which he wore a tuxedo and smoked a big rubber cigar. The parents of Oscar-winner Jennifer Jones were the owners-stars of the Isley Stock Company, a tent show which toured the Midwest. After working as a ticket and soda seller, Jones made her stage debut at the young age of ten.

A high rate of endogamy—that is, marriages within the same profession—is another distinctive attribute of acting. These marriages contribute to the integration of its members into a social group that has its own lifestyle and subculture. At least two-thirds of the nominated artists have married within the film colony; most, more than once. The only difference between the genders is that actors usually marry actresses, whereas actresses tend to marry producers and directors in addition to actors. Academy nominees could almost be accused of "incest," based on the fact that 20 percent of all nominated actors and directors have been married to other members of the profession at one time or another in their careers. Furthermore, many have met their prospective spouses at work, while appearing in a play or shooting a movie. Some have fallen in love and subsequently married their leading men or leading ladies.

The Oscar ceremonies themselves have functioned as dating grounds. In 1994, Oscar-winning actress Holly Hunter *(The Piano)* and Oscar-winning cinematographer Janusz Kaminski *(Schindler's List)* met backstage during the ceremonies. Several months later they were married.

Three of Merle Oberon's *(The Dark Angel)* four spouses were drawn from show business. Oberon's first husband was British film producer Alexander Korda, and her second, cinematographer Lucien Ballard. Oberon's third, and longest, marriage, was the exception, to an Italian industrialist. However, in 1973, Oberon wed her co-star, Robert Walders, many years her junior, in her comeback film *Interval,* a film in which Walders was cast as a young man falling in love with an aging woman.

Oberon is by no means unique. Oscar-nominee James Earl Jones met his prospective wife, Julienne Marie, when she played Desdemona to his Othello in the New York Shakespeare's production in Central Park.

Marital and familial bonds are reflected in the Oscar contest with inter-generational nominations of parents and children, marital nominations of husbands and wives, and nominations of siblings.

Take the Huston family. In 1948, John Huston won two Oscars, for writing and directing *The Treasure of the Sierra Madre,* a film which pro-vided his father, Walter Huston, with one of his best roles, as the shrewd old gold prospector, for which he won a supporting Oscar. This double win was the emotional highlight of the evening, after which Walter Huston jok-ingly remarked: "I always told my boy that if he ever became a director, to find a part for the old man." Thirty seven years later, John Huston's daugh-ter, Anjelica Huston, accepted a supporting Oscar for her stunning perfor-mance as the don's wild and wronged granddaughter in *Prizzi's Honor,* directed by none other than her father.

Polls predicted that John Huston would win a second directorial Oscar for *Prizzi's Honor,* and people were excited at the prospects of seeing father and daughter sharing the spotlight. However, the winner was Sydney Pollack for *Out of Africa.* In her acceptance speech, Anjelica, who had made her debut in one of her father's pictures, acknowledged her family debt: "This means a lot to me, especially since it comes for a role in which I was directed by my father, and I know it means a lot to him." John Huston thus became the only director to have directed both his father and his daughter for Oscar victories.

The 1975 awards ceremonies were described as "The Francis Ford Coppola Family Hour," because *The Godfather, Part II* won six Oscars, including Best Director (Coppola) and Best Dramatic Score for the direc-tor's father, Carmine Coppola, shared with Nino Rotta. "I want to thank my son for my being up here," said Carmine, "Without him, I wouldn't be here. However, if I wasn't here, he wouldn't be here either, right?" Talia Shire, Coppola's sister, was nominated for a supporting award, as Connie Corleone, Al Pacino's sluttish sister, but did not win.

A family reunion imbued with symbolic meanings on and offscreen, took place at the 1982 Oscar show, when Henry Fonda won for *On Golden Pond.* Jane Fonda purchased the screen rights to Ernest Thompson's stage play as a vehicle for her father. Though Jane had made her acting debut opposite her father at the Omaha Community House Theater, *On Golden Pond* was the first and only movie they made togeth-er, with Jane cast as Chelsea, a daughter at odds with her father over some childhood misunderstandings.

The film's reconciliation scene, under the sturdy guidance of Katharine Hepburn, who plays Fonda's wife, in which Chelsea finally comes to terms with her past, was autobiographical. Jane's unhappy childhood and later radical politics created tension with her dad. Jane agreed to play a thankless role in *On Golden Pond* for familial reasons. The Academy respectfully honored Henry Fonda and Katharine Hepburn with Oscars, and Jane with her sixth (and first supporting) nomination. In an emotional speech, Jane accepted the Oscar for her father, who was unable to attend the ceremonies due to poor health. After the show, the cameras followed the dutiful daughter as she drove to her father's house to present him the statuette. Fonda died a few months later.

Jane Fonda also proved dutiful sister, when she accompanied her brother Peter Fonda to several awards ceremonies upon his first Best Actor nomination for *Ulee's Gold*. Since *Easy Rider*, for which Peter was nominated for a writing Oscar, he has made peace with Hollywood and with his father Henry, whom he credited for inspiring his performance in *Ulee's Gold*.

Angelina Jolie and Jon Voight joined Henry Fonda and Jane Fonda as the second father-daughter team to win acting Oscars; he for *Coming Home* in 1978, she for *Girl, Interrupted* in 1999. An awards darling—with three Golden Globes to her credit—Jolie's bad girl reputation and the film's lukewarm box office obviously didn't hurt her.

Famous Hollywood families have become an integral part of Oscar's history. In 1978, Vincente Minnelli was named Best Director for the musical *Gigi*. His ex-wife, Judy Garland, was not nominated for any of their collaborations, but she was nominated twice for other films: Best Actress for the musical *A Star Is Born*, and supporting actress for the court drama *Judgment at Nuremberg*. Their daughter, Liza Minnelli, who at the age of two made her film debut in a walk-on part in her mother's musical *In the Good Old Summertime*, was also nominated twice: for *The Sterile Cuckoo*, and for *Cabaret*, for which she won Best Actress.

The Redgrave clan is one of England's most renowned acting dynasties, so far consisting of five generations of players. Sir Michael Redgrave's grandfather and both of his parents were actors, and he was married to Rachel Kempson, known for her stage and TV work. All of their children, Vanessa, Lynn, and Corin pursued acting careers. On the evening of Vanessa's birth, Michael was playing opposite Olivier in *Hamlet* at the Old Vic. Olivier was so excited by the event that in his curtain speech he announced: "Tonight a lovely new actress has been born. Laertes (played by Redgrave) has a daughter." Olivier's prophecy became self-fulfilling, when Vanessa made her first screen appearance in *Behind the Mask*, in which she played the daughter of her real-life father.

Talent has been in abundance in the Redgrave dynasty, and some of which was certified by the Academy. Three family members have been nominated, beginning with Sir Michael, as Best Actor for the 1947 film version of Eugene O'Neill's *Mourning Becomes Electra*. Vanessa and Lynn received their first Best Actress nomination in the same year, 1966, the former for *Morgan*, the latter for *Georgy Girl*. For the part of Georgy, a young woman who just missed being beautiful, the producers tried to get every girl in London, including Vanessa, who turned it down because of other commitments.

The nomination of Vanessa and Lynn in the same year was taken in stride by the sisters, with both making sure to publicly dispel any feelings of rivalry or animosity. Lynn told reporters: "We like each other's work and each other as people. Vanessa takes the spotlight one week, I get it the next." In the next decade, however, it was Vanessa who distinguished herself as a performer. Considered to be the best actress in the English-speaking world, Vanessa has been nominated five times, winning a supporting Oscar for *Julia*. As for Lynn, after a long dry period, she bounced back with a comeback performance in *Gods and Monsters* (1998), as Ian McKellen's Hungarian housekeeper, for which she received a second, supporting nomination.

The Redgrave acting torch is passing down from generation to generation: All three of Vanessa's children have appeared on stage and/or in film. Daughter Joely Richardson played Vanessa's character as an adolescent in David Hare's *Wetherby*. Vanessa's daughter, Natasha Richardson, played Nina to her mother's Irina in a British production of Chekhov's *The Sea Gull*, which had been one of her mother's earlier roles, in Sidney Lumet's 1968 screen version.

The Redgrave sisters' amicable sportsmanship didn't prevail when another pair of ambitious sisters was nominated in the same year, 1941: Joan Fontaine for *Suspicion* and Olivia de Havilland for *Hold Back the Dawn*. Rumors of the "feuding sisters," who were close in age, circulated in the movie colony. De Havilland's beginning was more auspicious than her sister's, having made a number of popular films opposite Errol Flynn.

Fontaine's life as the Cinderella sister of De Havilland was well covered by the press. Until 1939, life seemed to give Olivia all the good breaks and all the bad ones to Joan. Fontaine's stage debut was in an English domestic comedy, *Call It a Day* (1935), but when Warner bought the picture rights, the role she had played was given to her sister. Fontaine was then determined to make her way independent of the famous Olivia. She tested for *Gone With the Wind,* and lost. The childhood taunt, "Livva can, Joan can't," continued to haunt Fontaine for years.

The rivalry of the two sisters for the Oscar was more than a Hollywood publicity story. In 1941, the New York Film Critics had cast five ballots before getting the majority necessary decision. During four of the ballots, De Havilland had vied with Fontaine for the Best Actress honor. It was the first time in the history of the Oscar and the New York Film Critics that they had selected the same actress for the award.

When Fontaine won Best Actress for *Suspicion*, De Havilland, nominated that year for *Hold Back the Dawn*, clapped the loudest of all, exclaiming, "We've won." Fontaine told the press: "If *Suspicion* had been delayed just a little it wouldn't have got under the wire for this year's award. I've been runner-up so often it isn't funny anymore. If it happens again, I'm likely to break something." Fontaine recalled in her memoirs that when she won Best Actress for *Suspicion*, "Olivia took the situation very graciously. I am sure it was not a pleasant moment for her, as she'd lost the previous year for Melanie in *Gone With the Wind* in the supporting actress category."

Magazines of the time tell in great detail how De Havilland backed off and gave her sister the cold shoulder when Fontaine tried to shake her hand upon winning an Oscar for *To Have and Have Not*. Recalled Fontaine: "In later years, Olivia made it up with two Oscars, for *To Each His Own* and for *The Heiress*, so the evening of *Suspicion* was only a temporary setback."

Oscar anxieties and frustrations have also dominated the Barrymore family. Two of the Barrymore siblings have won Oscars. Lionel Barrymore earned the 1930–31 Best Actor, as Norma Shearer's alcoholic lawyer-father, in *A Free Soul*. His sister, Ethel Barrymore, was nominated four times for supporting actress within five years, finally winning for *None But the Lonely Heart*, as Cary Grant's poor mother. Nonetheless, John Barrymore, the most famous sibling, was never nominated. The Barrymores, like the Redgraves, have been an acting clan, extending over five generations. Drew Barrymore is the most recent family member to have graced the screen, beginning with *E.T.* in 1982.

The Oscar race has included several marital nominations. Three husband-and-wife teams have been nominated for the same film. Alfred Lunt and Lynn Fontanne were nominated for re-creating on screen their famous Broadway roles, as the jealous husband-actor and his flirtatious wife-actress, in the Hungarian comedy *The Guardsman*. The second team, Charles Laughton and Elsa Lanchester, who made a number of films together, were both nominated for Billy Wilder's *Witness for the Prosecution*, in which Laughton played Sir Wilfred Robards, the eccentric Queen's Defense Counsel, and Lanchester his maidenly owlish nurse. In one memorable scene, Lanchester tells Laughton, "It's time for our nap," to which he replies, "You go ahead, start it without me." Neither Laughton nor Lanchetser won, as 1957 was a year of intense competition, with Alec

Guinness winning for *The Bridge on the River Kwai,* and Miyoshiu Umeki as Supporting Actress for *Sayonara.*

Elizabeth Taylor and Richard Burton, one of Hollywood's most glamorous couples, were the third team to be nominated for the same film, also playing husband and wife. Taylor, as the earthy Martha, and Burton, as her husband-professor George, probably gave their finest performances in Mike Nichols's adaptation of Edward Albee's prize-winning *Who's Afraid of Virginia Woolf?* Taylor won a second Oscar, but Burton lost to Paul Scofield in *A Man for All Seasons.*

British couple Rex Harrison and Rachel Roberts were also nominated in the same year, 1963, but for different films, he for *Cleopatra,* she for *This Sporting Life.* Paul Newman and wife-actress Joanne Woodward met while they were performing on Broadway in *Picnic.* They went on to appear in many films together, *From the Terrace, Paris Blues, A New Kind of Love,* among them. But none of their acting collaborations was as critically acclaimed as their team work as director-actress. *Rachel, Rachel* (1968) earned Woodward her second Best Actress nomination and, though Newman was not nominated as director, the film was nominated for Best Picture.

Amy Madigan was nominated for a supporting Oscar in *Twice in a Lifetime* in 1985, and her husband Ed Harris was nominated twice for supporting roles, for *Apollo 13* in 1995 and for *The Truman Show* in 1998.

In 1991, Diane Ladd and Laura Dern became the first real-life mother-daughter team to be nominated for the same film, *Rambling Rose,* though they didn't play mother-daughter in the story. Father-and-son teams have included Raymond Massey, as Best Actor nominee for playing the president in *Abe Lincoln in Illinois* in 1940, and son Daniel Massey, as supporting actor for impersonating Noel Coward in the musical *Star!* in 1968.

A bizarre mood prevailed on the set of *Ransom* in 1996, a thriller directed by Ron Howard and starring Mel Gibson, both of whom had made a splash that year as directors: Howard with *Apollo 13,* and Gibson with *Braveheart.* In one of the Academy's shameful omissions, *Apollo 13* was nominated in many categories except for direction, which made Gibson's Best Director win a sure thing.

When Kevin Spacey and Mare Winningham were both nominated for supporting roles in 1995—he for *The Usual Suspects* and she for *Georgia*—no one suspected any link between them, but there was. Spacey fondly recalled a happy time in his twelfth grade at Chatsworth High, when he and Winningham co-starred in *The Sound of Music,* as Baron and Maria Von Trapp. This is yet another example of how small the film world is.

CHAPTER 7

Oscar-Winning Films—Biopictures

Every year, about 250 to 280 movies are eligible for Oscar nominations, but only five are selected for the top award, the Best Picture. How are these five films chosen out of hundreds released in the United States? What are the criteria for selection? Are there any patterns? To what extent has the Academy displayed consistent biases in favor of—or against—particular kinds of films. How crucial is the films' genre in the nomination and in the winning processes?

To answer these questions, all 422 films nominated for Best Picture from 1927 to 1999 were considered with respect to the sociopolitical contexts in which they were made.

Real to Reel—Biopictures

The Academy has displayed a clear bias in favor of biopictures, i.e., films inspired by actual events and/or real-life personalities. Twenty two (30 percent) of the seventy-two Oscar-winning films have been based on real-life events or actual individuals. Diverse in both theme and locale, these movies have depicted showbiz personalities *(The Great Ziegfeld)*, scientists *(The Story of Louis Pasteur)*, writers *(The Life of Emil Zola)*, historical figures *(Lawrence of Arabia, A Man for All Seasons),* and even gangsters *(Bugsy).*

The degree of accuracy of biopictures to their source materials is variable, as demonstrated by last year's discussions of *The Hurricane*—based on the black boxer Rubin "Hurricane" Carter (played by Denzel Washington) who was wrongly accused of murder—and *Boys Don't Cry,* which re-created the life of Brandon Teena (Teena Brandon, a girl who passed as a boy). A claim could be made that, in the final account, every film is fictional, even if it attempts to re-create the life of a particular individual or of a specific historical era.

Biopictures have featured more prominently in the last two decades: Five of the ten winning films of the 1980s were inspired by real-life figures. In 1981, *Chariots of Fire,* the inspirational tale of two British runners, Harold Abrahams and Eric Liddell in the 1924 Paris Olympics, won Best Picture. *Gandhi,* an earnestly noble biopicture about the venerable Indian politician, was the 1982 Oscar winner. In 1984, *Amadeus* offered an intriguing view of the musical genius Wolfgang Amadeus Mozart in eighteenth-century Vienna. *Out of Africa,* based on the life of Karen Blixen, the Danish writer who published under the name of Isak Dinesen, won in 1985, and *The Last Emperor,* an expansive epic about Pu Yi, China's last Manchu emperor, was the 1987 winner.

In the 1990s, too, *Schindler's List,* an epic film about Oskar Schindler (Liam Neeson), the Catholic war profiteer who initially flourished by collaborating with the Nazis but eventually saved more than a thousand Polish Jews, won the 1993 Best Picture. Mel Gibson's *Braveheart,* an epic tale of the thirteenth century Scottish rebel warrior William Wallace (played by the star himself), won the 1995 prize. James Cameron's bombastic *Titanic,* a fictionalized account of the 1912 ship disaster, won the 1997 award.

Biopictures have used the narrative conventions of various genres: musicals *(Yankee Doodle Dandy),* war films *(Patton, Saving Private Ryan),* Westerns *(Butch Cassidy and the Sundance Kid),* historical epics *(Mutiny on the Bounty, Ben-Hur, Schindler's List, Braveheart),* political exposes (Oliver Stone's *JFK*) action-adventures *(The French Connection, The Right Stuff)* and even disaster movies *(Titanic).*

In the 1930s, the studio most associated with the production of biopictures was Warner. A biopicture cycle began with *Disraeli* (1929), starring George Arliss as the wily British statesman, and it became more prominent later in the decade with the release of two notable Warner movies, both starring Paul Muni. In 1936, *The Story of Louis Pasteur* recounted the life of the French chemist who discovered the anthrax vaccine, which saved French cattle from the black plague. The Oscar winner of 1937 was *The Life of Emil Zola,* which dealt with the exposure of anti-Semitism in the French government. These films, as historian Lewis Jacobs suggested, were social in outlook, realistic in interpretation, and imbued with strong messages about democratic values. As such, they drew parallels between the past and the present, particularly in their condemnation of the rampant Fascism and Nazism in Europe.

The percentage of biopictures in the 1940s (23 percent of all nominees) was much larger than that in the 1950s (7 percent). The American involvement in World War II had a strong impact on Hollywood, which produced many war films inspired by actual military figures. Of these, perhaps the best-known was *Sergeant York* (1941), which celebrated the courage of the World War I hero. By contrast, the few 1950 films drawing on actual events or figures dealt with biblical *(The Ten Commandments)* and Christian heroes *(Quo Vadis?, The Robe)*. Unlike 1940s biopictures, 1950s historical epics didn't even attempt to be realistic.

Biopictures nominated in the 1960s either concerned showbiz personae *(Funny Girl),* or royalty intrigues and affairs *(Cleopatra, Becket, The Lion in Winter, Anne of the Thousand Days, Nicholas and Alexandra).* However, from the mid-1970s on the range of nominated biopictures became wider. They included, of course, the perennial topic of entertainment, such as *Lenny* and *All That Jazz,* both directed by Bob Fosse, with the latter film drawing on his own life.

But there were also movies about working-class protagonists, which in the past were neglected by mainstream American cinema. Sidney Lumet's *Dog Day Afternoon,* based on a Brooklyn bank robbery, depicted the life of marginal people, centering on Sonny (Al Pacino), the doomed bisexual whose motive for the robbery was to provide money for his lover's sex-change operation. *Norma Rae*'s protagonist would have been an unlikely heroine for a Hollywood film of yesteryear, but Martin Ritt made an uplifting movie, inspired by the life of a Southern hillbilly (Sally Field) who undergoes a major transformation after gaining political consciousness.

Biopictures reached an apogee in the 1980 Oscar contest, in which three of the nominated films were based to varying degrees of authenticity on real-life figures. *Coal Miner's Daughter* re-created the life of country and Western singer Loretta Lynn (Sissy Spacek), from her backwoods childhood to her national success. Martin Scorsese's *Raging Bull* offered an uncompromisingly tough look at the disintegrating life of the brutish and abusive middleweight champion Jake La Motta (Robert De Niro). *The Elephant Man* probed the life of John Merrick (John Hurt), the grossly deformed victim of neurofibromatosis, in the context of nineteenth century Victorian society. It was also the first year in which both lead acting awards, to De Niro and Spacek, honored contemporary personalities, with Jake La Motta and Loretta Lynn present as guests of honor in the ceremonies.

In 1989, *My Left Foot,* a low-budget British import about the paraplegic artist-writer Christy Brown, became a dark horse after winning the New York Film Critics Award for Best Picture and Best Actor for Daniel Day-Lewis. In 1990, Jeremy Irons won a well-deserved Oscar for playing millionaire Claus von Bulow, who was accused of trying to kill his wife, in *Reversal of Fortune.* "I'd love to meet him and tell him what he's all about," Irons told the press. "But the man's had enough invasion of his privacy without my calling him."

The glamorous gangster Benjamin (Bugsy) Siegel (played by glamorous star Warren Beatty) in *Bugsy,* and the mythic politician, John F. Kennedy in Oliver Stone's *JFK,* dominated the 1991 Best Picture and acting nominations, though neither picture won the top prize; the winner was *The Silence of the Lambs.*

Year after year, biopictures have been nominated for the top award. In 1994 *Quiz Show,* Robert Redford's gracefully intelligent and engrossing story of the late-1950s' TV quiz show scandal, was a top Oscar contender. Using the show as a metaphor for a nation newly hypnotized by the artifice of TV, the story focused on a hotheaded loser (John Turturro) and his successor on "Twenty-One," instant hero Charles Van Doren (Ralph Fiennes), a scion of a socially prominent and intellectual family. *Quiz Show* brought the 1950s to life as no other movie has since the Barry Levinson directed *Diner,* who had a cameo in the 1994 picture.

In 1995, Ron Howard's *Apollo 13* provided an exhilarating chronicle of the ill-fated Apollo 13 mission to the moon, and how the heroic work of astronaut Jim Lovell and his crew, combined with the dogged persistence of the NASA team in Houston, averted tragedy. The 1996 Australian art-house hit, *Shine,* recounted how the piano prodigy, David Helfgott (Oscar-winning Geoffrey Rush) was pushed to the breaking point by his domineering father (Oscar-nominated Armin Mueller-Stahl).

Of the five pictures nominated in 1998, two featured the British monarchy *(Elizabeth* and *Shakespeare in Love),* and three dealt with different aspects of World War II. *Saving Private Ryan* and *The Thin Red Line* re-created actual combats, and *Life Is Beautiful* was a fable set in a concentration camp.

Aside from favoring biographical over fictional features, the Academy has endorsed some specific genres, while overlooking others. The two most dominant genres among Oscar-winning movies are the social-problem drama (about 40 percent) and the historical epic (about 20 percent). Comedies, musicals, war films, action-adventures, suspense-thrillers, and Westerns have been much less successful in the Oscar contest.

The Serious-Problem Picture

The most respected and honored genre in the Best Picture competition is the serious-problem film. About half of all Oscar-winning or nominated pictures have dealt with "important" social or political issues. The greatest representation of this genre in the Oscar contest was in the 1930s and 1940s, and the weakest in the 1960s.

What distinguishes the serious-problem film is its reliance on other literary sources, such as best-selling novels and Broadway hits. With one major exception, in the 1950s, the primary source for the Hollywood problem picture was the Broadway theater. Three of Tennessee Williams's stage hits were nominated for Best Picture: *A Streetcar Named Desire* in 1951, *The Rose Tattoo* in 1955, and *Cat on a Hot Tin Roof* in 1958. The impact of Broadway on Hollywood was apparent in every film genre. Most film musicals in the 1950s, such as *The King and I* in 1956 and *Gigi* in 1958, had originated on the New York stage. Along with stage plays, some TV dramas were transferred to the big screen: *Marty* in 1955, *Twelve Angry Men* in 1957, *Judgment at Nuremberg* in 1961.

Reflecting relevant issues, serious-problem films are intimately linked with the socio-political contexts in which they are made. As such, they tend to appear in cycles whose duration is about three to five years. In the late 1940s, Hollywood produced a cycle of films dealing with racial prejudice and discrimination. Two of these films were nominated for Best Picture: *Crossfire* and *Gentleman's Agreement*, both in 1947. In the late 1960s and early 1970s, there was a cycle of films about the position of blacks in American society, such as *In the Heat of the Night* in 1967 and *Sounder* in 1972. In 1979, *Kramer vs. Kramer* launched a cycle of high-profile family dramas, which included *Ordinary People, On Golden Pond,* and *Terms of Endearment.*

Problem films have often centered on the public domain— professions, careers and the workplace—or on the political arena, dealing with racial hatred, discrimination, and violence. But many films are hybrids, dealing with both public and private lives, conflicts between work and family, career and marriage, the impact of war and politics on individual behavior. Few movies have dealt exclusively with strictly public or political issues.

This is characteristic of the American cinema in general, not just of the nominated pictures. Even a committed political filmmaker like Costa-Gavras understands that to attract the mass public to serious "message" films, they must deal with issues in a more intimate and emotional way. Hence the two Costa-Gavras Oscar-nominated pictures, *Z* in 1969 and *Missing* in 1982, are political films that convey their ideological messages through emotionally engaging personal stories.

The Woman's Film

Problem pictures that feature mostly male roles have differed from those focusing on women. Most female-nominated roles are contained in what is known as "the woman's film." These films, which feature female protagonists, revolve around romantic issues and are specifically designed for female audiences. The woman's film—the weepie—doesn't exist anymore as a pure form, but it was quite popular in the 1930s and 1940s.

Bette Davis distinguished herself in such melodramatic vehicles. In William Wyler's *Jezebel* (1938), a romantic melodrama of the Old South, advertised by Warner as "Half-angel, half-siren, all-woman," Davis won an Oscar for playing a Southern belle. Edmund Goulding's *Dark Victory* (1939), with a screenplay by Casey Robinson about a society girl who discovers she is dying of a brain tumor, was one of 1939's most popular films, earning Best Picture and Actress nominations.

All This and Heaven Too (1940), based on Rachel Field's book about the love of a nineteenth-century married French nobleman (Charles Boyer) for his governess (Davis), was also nominated for Best Picture, but did not win any awards. In the same year, William Wyler's *The Letter,* a remake of the 1929 film based on Somerset Maugham's tale of an adulterous wife (Davis) who shoots her lover in a jealous rage, was marked by a distinctive visual style, and was nominated for Best Picture and five other awards. The role of Leslie Crosbie was played on stage by Katharine Cornell and by Jeanne Eagels in the first film version; both Eagels and Davis were nominated, though neither won. Director Wyler cast Davis again as the conniving and greedy Regina Giddens, in Lillian Hellman's *The Little Foxes* (1941), which was nominated for nine awards, but did not win any.

None of the so called "woman's pictures" has ever won an Oscar, and after the 1940s few were even nominated. The only two Oscar-winning films that come close to approximate this genre, featuring strong women and dealing specifically with women's problems were *Grand Hotel* and *All About Eve.*

Based on Vicki Baum's novel, adapted to the screen by William A. Drake, *Grand Hotel* was an MGM prestige production which won the 1931–32 Best Picture. *Grand Hotel* featured an all-star cast, showing that MGM did indeed live up to its claim, "more stars than in heaven." There were *five* star performances, each exhibiting his/her particular screen persona, though best of all were Greta Garbo, as the fading dancer, and John Barrymore, as the declining nobleman. Their scenes together were the strongest in the film, and Garbo's line, "I want to be alone," became forever associated with her screen image. Also good were Joan Crawford, as a determined secretary; Wallace Beery, as her brutish tycoon-employer; and Lionel Barrymore, as a pathetic dying man. The movie, as a whole, lacks coherence; it is too much of a patchwork—each star has a "big scene"—but obviously audiences didn't mind as they turned it into the year's top-grossing movie. Seen from today's perspective, *Grand Hotel* serves up an example of a type of film that "Hollywood does not make anymore."

Grand Hotel competed against seven movies, including John Ford's *Arrowsmith,* King Vidor's *The Champ, One Hour with You,* (co-directed by George Cukor and Ernst Lubitsch), and Josef Von Sternberg's *Shanghai Express.* Strangely enough, none of *Grand Hotel*'s star players or director, Edmund Goulding, was nominated. It is one of three Oscar-winning films to have received only one Oscar; the other two films are *The Broadway Melody* and *Mutiny on the Bounty.* At present, the tendency is for a few films to get multiple nominations and awards, but in the 1930s and 1940s, Academy votes were spread among a larger number of pictures.

In contrast to *Grand Hotel,* the 1950 Oscar-winning *All About Eve* was the first movie to be nominated in fourteen categories (the largest number of nomination up until *Titanic* in 1997), winning six Oscars. Joseph L. Mankiewicz won two Oscars, as writer (original screenplay) and director. George Sanders won supporting Oscar, as the acerbic drama critic. Edith Head and Charles LeMaire won black-and-white costume design, and W. D. Flick and Roger Herman won best sound. Its two leading ladies, Bette Davis and Anne Baxter, were nominated in the same category but cancelled each other out.

All About Eve's major competitor that year was Billy Wilder's *Sunset Boulevard,* a darkly humorous probing of the movie industry that contrasted the old and the new Hollywood through the relationship of a fading, demented silent queen, played by Gloria Swanson, and a young gigolo-writer, played by William Holden. Neither film was very successful at the box office when initially released; each grossed less than three million dollars. However, both have acquired cult status over the years and for the same reasons: the star performances of Davis in *Eve* and Swanson in *Sunset.* Their wittily campy dialogue entered movie lore, with such lines as Davis exclaiming, "fasten your seat belts, it's going to be a bumpy night," or Swanson telling Holden, "They don't make faces like that anymore," or "I'm still big. It's the pictures that got small."

Nominated features with strong female protagonists have usually dealt with showbiz, like *Stage Door* and *A Star Is Born,* both in 1937. Gregory La Cava's *Stage Door,* nominated for four Oscars, focused on a clique of would-be actresses living in a theatrical boarding house, all anxious to get their "big break." Katharine Hepburn, playing one of her many rich girls, and Ginger Rogers have the best parts in an all-female cast that included Eve Arden, Lucille Ball, and Ann Miller. Andrea Leeds was the only actress to be nominated for playing an ingenue who, after waiting for a whole year for "the one role," commits suicide. Like *All About Eve* and *Sunset Boulevard, Stage Door* has become a cult item, with such memorable lines as Hepburn declaring: "If I can act I want the world to know it, but if I can't act, *I* want to know it."

Along with Bette Davis and Katharine Hepburn, Greer Garson was the third female star to appear in prestige, Oscar-nominated films. Indeed, until 1950, only one of the other Oscar-winning films featured a female heroine, Greer Garson in *Mrs. Miniver*. Garson was MGM's most respected star and Louis B. Mayer's favorite actress, for whom he chose the studio's best vehicles. No other MGM actress has ever enjoyed as complete a support of MGM's top brass as Garson.

From 1939 to 1943, five of Garson's serious dramas were nominated for Best Picture. Garson was introduced to the American public in Sam Woods's 1939 *Goodbye, Mr. Chips,* as the actress who humanizes a public school teacher (Oscar-winning Robert Donat), rescuing him from being a failure. In Mervyn LeRoy's 1941 *Blossoms in the Dust,* based on Anita Loos's script, playing the child welfare crusader Edna Gladney, Garson exclaimed: "There are no illegitimate children; there are only illegitimate parents!" And in 1943, Garson re-created the life of the noted French scientist in *Madame Curie,* arguably one of the era's more distorted biopictures.

Except for the three aforementioned women, few of the leading female stars made films that were nominated for Best Picture. Rosalind Russell and Barbara Stanwyck received their nominations for films that for one reason or another weren't considered "Oscar stuff." Stanwyck was first nominated for her portrait of the self-sacrificing mother in King Vidor's *Stella Dallas* (1937), a prototype of the woman's film, and her second nomination was for playing the striptease queen in Howard Hawks's *Ball of Fire* (1941). Neither film was Oscar-nominated. Russell first received the Academy recognition for the comedy *My Sister Eileen* (1942), then for the biopicture *Sister Kenny* (1946), as the woman who devoted her life to getting the medical profession's approval of her unorthodox method of treating infantile paralysis.

What could be more revealing—and condemning—about the status of the woman's film, and the screen roles allotted to women than the weak correlation between the Best Picture and the Best Actress awards? Twenty-six (36 percent) of the seventy-three female-winning roles were contained in films that were *not* nominated for Best Picture, compared with thirteen (18 percent) of the seventy-two male-winning roles. (The number of winning roles is not the same, because there was a tie in the 1968 Best Actress category)

Hence movies that featured strong female roles weren't considered vigorous or "important" enough to compete for Best Picture. And films nominated for Best Picture featured no—or few—leading roles for women. Femme-themed films weren't taken as seriously by the Academy: Up to the late 1970s, there was a strong correlation between the Best Picture and Best Actor, but not Actress, awards.

This was particularly the case during the heyday of the studio system. Mary Pickford *(Coquette)*, Marie Dressler *(Min and Bill)*, Helen Hayes *(The Sin of Madelon Claudet)*, Katharine Hepburn *(Morning Glory)*, Bette Davis *(Dangerous)*, Olivia de Havilland *(To Each His Own)*, Loretta Young *(The Farmer's Daughter)*, all won Oscars for roles that were *not* contained in Oscar-nominated films. In the last decade too, the winning roles of Kathy Bates *(Misery)*, Jessica Lange *(Blue Sky)*, and Hilary Swank *(Boys Don't Cry)* were in films that failed to earn Best Picture nominations.

Message Movies: Race, Politics, and Crime

More male than female-winning roles were contained in the serious-problem film, attesting to the prestigious status of both films and male performances. The overwhelming majority of the Best Actors' roles were featured in message films that dealt with important social or political issues.

Warner's *The Life of Emil Zola* was nominated for the largest number of awards (ten) in 1937, and won three: Best Picture, Screenplay, and Supporting Actor to Joseph Schildkraut, as the wrongly accused Captain Alfred Dreyfus. Had Paul Muni not won the previous year for another biopicture, *The Story of Louis Pasteur,* he would have received it for portraying the French writer who exposed anti-Semitism in the French government. Reviewing *Emil Zola*, critic Otis Fergusson suggested that "Along with *Louis Pasteur,* it ought to start a new category—the Warner crusading films, costume division."

Nine other movies competed with *Emil Zola* in 1937, including Leo McCarey's marital comedy *The Awful Truth* with six nominations, and Gregory La Cava's *Stage Door,* with four. The other nominees were: William Wyler's social drama set in a New York City slum, *Dead End;* Frank Capra's utopian comedy *Lost Horizon;* and Henry King's romantic adventure *In Old Chicago.*

The political crusading drama reappeared in the late 1940s, when Hollywood began to explore racial discrimination, first against Jews, then against blacks and Native Americans. The 1947 Oscar-winning film was Elia Kazan's *Gentleman's Agreement,* based on Laura Z. Hobson's novel, adapted to the screen by Moss Hart. Gregory Peck plays a crusading journalist who decides to pose as a Jew so that he can experience first-hand racial prejudice. Like most serious films, *Gentleman's Agreement* also has a romance, here with the daughter (Dorothy McGuire) of Peck's publisher, who turns out to be bigoted herself.

The film is preachy, particularly in the lengthy dialogues between Peck and a Jewish military captain (John Garfield), who has just returned from occupied Germany. Even so, it was praised by most critics, with Howard Barnes finding it to be "more savagely arresting and properly resolved as a picture than it was as a book," and describing its script as "electric with honest reportage." *Gentleman's Agreement* won two other Oscars, for director Kazan, and for its supporting actress, Celeste Holm, who has the film's most pungent lines.

The major competitor for Kazan's agit-prop was Edward Dmytryk's *Crossfire,* which lost in each of its five nominations. Its screenplay, by John Paxton, was based on Richard Brooks's novel *The Brick Foxhole,* though in a typically cowardly Hollywood manner, the book's homosexual protagonist was changed into a Jew. *Crossfire* is a better film than *Gentleman's Agreement* in every aspect: characterization, acting, and visual style. It was directed by Dmytryk as a tense noir thriller about an obsessive, psychopathic sergeant (Robert Ryan, who specialized in this kind of role) who beats a Jewish ex-sergeant to death. Detective Finlay (Robert Young), helped by sergeant Keely (Robert Mitchum), sets out to trap the killer. Like *Gentleman's Agreement,* *Crossfire* is a message film replete with speeches against prejudice, but it boasts great acting by Ryan and Gloria Grahame, as a floozy dance hall girl; both were nominated for supporting awards.

That *Gentleman's Agreement* was voted Best Picture for ideological rather than artistic considerations is clear not only from its win over *Crossfire,* but also in its win over David Lean's masterpiece, *Great Expectations.* However, the Academy couldn't ignore *Great Expectations's* exquisite innovations, honoring its black-and-white cinematography and art direction and set decoration. Yet the Academy proved once again that, ultimately, a film's theme and content weigh far more than its cinematic style.

None of the late 1940s films dealing with racial prejudice against African Americans or Native Americans was nominated for Best Picture. Stanley Kramer's 1949 *Home of the Brave* began this cycle, which was followed by two other films released in the same year, *Intruder in the Dust* and *Pinky*. One of the first films about racial identity among blacks, *Pinky* was singled out for its acting. All three of its female performers were nominated: Jeanne Crain, as a light-skinned black trying to pass as white; Ethel Waters, as her benign grandmother; and Ethel Barrymore, as an old Southern matriarch.

Considered at the time "courageous," because of its subject matter, *Pinky* was not the first nominated film about interracial relations. That position is occupied by the first version of *Imitation of Life* (1934), starring Claudette Colbert and Louise Beaver, though that film was a lone voice at the time. In 1959, *Imitation of Life* was remade by Douglas Sirk as a glossy melodrama, starring Lana Turner and Juanita Moore. Moore and Susan Kohner, who played the black mother and daughter, earned supporting nominations.

Sidney Lumet's first feature, *Twelve Angry Men*, was nominated for the 1957 Best Picture, but did not win any award. A courtroom drama, it is confined to a jury room where twelve jurors debate the fate of a black boy accused of murdering his father. In the course of the tumultuous trial, Henry Fonda, as the liberal Juror No. 8, succeeds in reversing the majority's opinion.

In the following year, Stanley Kramer's Oscar-nominated *The Defiant Ones* was more successful, both critically and commercially, as an intriguing tale of two escaped convicts, one black (Sidney Poitier), the other white (Tony Curtis), forced to spend their short-lived freedom together because they are chained by the wrist. *The Defiant Ones* was cited as Best Picture by the New York Film Critics Circle and won two Oscars, for story and screenplay (Nathan E. Douglas and Harold Jacob Smith) and for Sam Leavitt's black-and-white cinematography.

Otto Preminger's *Anatomy of a Murder* and Robert Mulligan's *To Kill a Mockingbird* were Best Picture nominees in 1959 and 1962 respectively. Among other things, *Anatomy* contains one of the longest—over an hour—trial scenes in film history, in which James Stewart's small-town lawyer defends a white Army lieutenant (Ben Gazzara) accused of killing a black tavern owner for allegedly raping his wife (Lee Remick). Universal's *To Kill a Mockingbird* featured more prominently in the Oscar race than *Anatomy*, which did not win any award. Based on Harper Lee's Pulitzer Prize-winning novel, it cast Gregory Peck in his Oscar-winning role as a widowed liberal lawyer defending a black man against a rape accusation in a Southern town rampant with prejudice. Peck, in a perfectly suitable role, concentrated all his acting energies on the courtroom scene, the film's most powerful, a nine-minute close-up speech, delivered to the jury (i.e., the audience). *To Kill a Mockingbird* also won screenplay for Horton Foote, as well as black-and-white art direction and set decoration.

For unaccountable reasons other than a "noble" subject matter, Ralph Nelson's *Lilies of the Field,* was nominated for five awards in 1963. It won, however, only Best Actor to Sidney Poitier, who played Homer Smith, an ex-G.I. and light-hearted handyman who helps a group of nuns from behind the Iron Curtain build a chapel in the Arizona desert. Poitier thus became the first black actor to win an Oscar for a lead role and the second black, following Hattie McDaniel as supporting actress in *Gone With the Wind,* to ever win an Oscar. It would take another twenty years for the next black performer, Louis Gossett Jr. in *An Officer and a Gentleman* (1982), to win an Oscar, albeit a supporting one.

Black players and black-themed films about racial prejudice left their most impressive mark in 1967, with the release of three films, all starring Sidney Poitier: *To Sir, With Love; Guess Who's Coming to Dinner;* and *In the Heat of the Night.*

All of a sudden, black was not only beautiful but also good business at the box office. The Academy showered both *Guess Who's Coming to Dinner* and *In the Heat of the Night* with multiple nominations and awards. A verbose, rather explicit comedy, *Guess Who's Coming* centers on a liberal couple (Spencer Tracy and Katharine Hepburn), he a publisher, she an art gallery owner, whose value system is challenged when their only daughter (Katharine Houghton) announces out of the blue her intention to marry a famous black surgeon (Poitier). Nominated for ten Oscars, it won two: Best Actress to Hepburn, and screenplay and story to William Rose.

Norman Jewison's *In the Heat of the Night* is the only problem film about racial discrimination against blacks to have won Best Picture, though later pictures with similar issues, like Martin Ritt's *Sounder* in 1972, and *A Soldier's Story* in 1984, also directed by Norman Jewison, were nominated. But in 1967, the timing seemed "right" to honor a topical film, and *In the Heat of the Night,* about the evolving camaraderie between an initially bigoted police chief (Rod Steiger) and a black homicide detective (Poitier), won five Oscars, including Best Actor to Steiger.

Of the nominated films in 1967, the most exciting one was Arthur Penn's *Bonnie and Clyde,* an innovative film in every sense of the word. However, its romantic attitude toward its gangster characters and the fact that Hollywood-newcomer Warren Beatty served as producer and star all worked against it. To think that the Academy honored *In the Heat of the Night* for best editing and sound over the amazing achievements in these areas in *Bonnie and Clyde* is still shocking.

Aside from interracial issues, the serious winning films have dealt with such themes as adjustment to a changing postwar society, abuse of power, political corruption, urban alienation, and crime. Each of the Oscar-winning films was a representative, not always the best, of a larger cycle in which it was contained.

The Best Years of Our Lives, 1946's most honored film, received the largest number of awards to date, seven legitimate and two Special Oscars. This social drama captured the mood of postwar America so effectively that even the harsher critics failed to see its flaws at the time. Independent producer Samuel Goldwyn, who released the film through RKO, was inspired by an article in *Time* magazine of August 7, 1944, which recounted the homecoming story of war veterans. Goldwyn commissioned MacKinlay Kantor to write a screenplay, which was first published as a book, *Glory for Me,* then adapted to the screen by Robert Sherwood. Released on November 21, 1946, the movie was relevant and timely, with many Americans still struggling with painful readjustment to civilian life after the war.

In his rave review, James Agee thought that *The Best Years* was "profoundly pleasing, moving and encouraging," singling out the film's script, which was "well differentiated, efficient, free of tricks of snap and punch and over-design," and its visual style, which was of "great force, simplicity and beauty." Wyler's direction of *The Best Years* was described by Agee as being "of great purity, directness and warmth, about as cleanly devoid of mannerisms, haste, superfluous motion, aesthetic or emotional overreaching." The movie was photographed by Gregg Toland in black and white, stressing long shots, deep-focus, and crisp imagery. The acting was also superb, particularly by Fredric March, who won a second Best Actor for playing a mentally anguished banking executive and ex-sergeant, who realizes that in his absence his family—as well as society—have tremendously and irrevocably changed.

All the King's Men, a political drama about the corrupting nature of excessive power and the danger of populist dictatorship in America, won the 1949 Oscar. Broderick Crawford won Best Actor as Willie Stark, a self-styled demagogue, who starts as a self-made rural Louisiana lawyer and ends up building a fraudulent political empire, which results in his assassination. Mercedes McCambridge won supporting actress as his tough and unscrupulous secretary-mistress. The film drew on Robert Penn Warren's 1946 Pulitzer-winning book about the life of Southern Senator Huey Long. *All the Kings' Men* competed against four other films, each critical of some aspect of American life: two realistic analyses of men at war, *Battleground* and *Twelve O'Clock High,* a tale of a greedy courtship, *The Heiress,* and a satiric examination of bourgeois suburban life, *A Letter to Three Wives.*

James Jones's *From Here to Eternity,* about life in an Army base, was a best-seller before Fred Zinnemann decided to make it a big screen entertainment. Set in Hawaii prior to the Pearl Harbor attack, it captures the essence of military life in all its complexity and detail, centering on the conflict between individualism, embodied by Montgomery Clift's Private Prewitt, and rigid institutional authority, represented by the Army. Having once blinded a man in the ring, Prewitt refuses to fight for the unit's team, despite promises for rewards and then pressures from his officer. A stubborn yet decent soldier, he admires the Army, but is unwilling to compromise his notion that "if a man don't go his own way, he's nothin'," which sums up the film's message as well as director's Zinnemann's recurrent theme in all of his films.

Daniel Taradash's fine screenplay contains half a dozen sharply etched characterizations, including Burt Lancaster's Sergeant Warden, as an efficient but human officer; Clift's Prewitt, as an inner-directed man guided by his code of ethics; Frank Sinatra's Maggio, the cocky but honest Italian-American soldier; Deborah Kerr's Karen Holmes, the frustrated, adulterous wife married to a weakling (Philip Ober); and Donna Reed's Alma, a dance-hall hostess. Zinnemann's direction was tight and restrained, bringing to the surface the film's issues which, as Pauline Kael observed, represented new, more mature attitudes on the American screen and touched a deep social nerve. *From Here to Eternity* is candid in its treatment of life, military, personal frustrations, and most important of all, sexuality—the erotic beach scene with Lancaster and Kerr was daring and innovative at the time.

From Here to Eternity was nominated in 1953 along with two historical features, *Julius Caesar* and *The Robe,* George Stevens's classic Western *Shane,* and William Wyler's elegant comedy, *Roman Holiday.* Nominated in thirteen categories, *From Here* won eight, the largest number of awards for a film since *Gone With the Wind.* "The industry which voted the honors now merits an appreciative nod," wrote the *New York Times*'s Bosley Crowther, having convinced his peers earlier to honor the film, director Zinnemann and actor Lancaster with the New York Film Critic Awards. The casting and acting by each member was perfect, partly due to the fact that Zinnemann rehearsed the entire film with props, an uncommon practice in Hollywood, which gave the actors a sense of continuity. All five players were nominated, with Burt Lancaster and Montgomery Clift canceling each other out as Best Actors (the winner was William Holden in *Stalag 17),* but the film's supporting players, Frank Sinatra and Donna Reed, were honored with Oscars.

Political corruption, this time in the context of labor unions, was the topic of Kazan's *On the Waterfront,* the 1954 Oscar winner. The film works both as an expose of union racketeering and as a thriller, involving the murder of an innocent longshoreman. Filmed on location, *On the Waterfront* was photographed in a black-and-white, almost documentary style (Boris Kaufman won an Oscar), which suited its realistic subject matter and commonplace characters. Marlon Brando won Best Actor for one of his most touching and memorable performances as Terry Malloy, an ex-prizefighter, who transforms, with the assistance of his girl (Eva Marie Saint) and the neighborhood's priest (Karl Malden), from a passive dock worker into an active fighter against corruption in trade unions.

On the Waterfront won eight Oscars, for director Kazan, supporting actress Saint, story and screenplay to Budd Schulberg, art direction, and editing. The only category in which the movie lost was the supporting actor, probably because no fewer than three male roles were nominated. Rod Steiger was nominated for playing Brando's brother, an opportunistic lawyer working for the arrogant racketeer-boss, played by Lee J. Cobb, who was also nominated. Karl Malden was nominated for playing the militant, highly sympathetic Father Barry.

Much has been written about Kazan as a friendly witness testifying before the HUAC, in which he repudiated his leftist past and named names. The movie itself has been interpreted as a "McCarthy film" in favor of informing, though the analogy between informing on Communists and informing on corrupt crooks is problematic. But *On the Waterfront* is powerful and enjoyable even without this ideological reading, and it would have won Oscars regardless of its politics, considering the weak competition that year: a court drama based on Herman Wouk's *The Caine Mutiny*, starring Humphrey Bogart; Clifford Odets's stiff backstage melodrama *The Country Girl*, with Bing Crosby, Grace Kelly, and William Holden; MGM's musical *Seven Brides for Seven Brothers*, starring Jane Powell and Howard Keel; and the romantic comedy *Three Coins in the Fountain*, which did more for American tourism to Rome than for film art.

The urban crime drama, which had been very popular during the Depression, reemerged in the late 1960s. *Midnight Cowboy*, John Schlesinger's 1969 Oscar-winner, is a touching yet disturbing tale of the strange friendship that evolves between handsome Joe Buck (Jon Voight)—an uneducated and naive Texan, who, under the influence of radio and TV commercials fancies himself a stud, and Ratso Rizzo (Dustin Hoffman), a sickly and crippled poor drifter. The film captured the ambiance of night life in Times Square and its alienated, lonely creatures, but it also perpetuated the myth of New York as a sleazy, dehumanized, impersonal city. The acting of Voight and Hoffman, both of whom were nominated, was superb, and the screenplay (Waldo Salt won an Oscar), based on James Leo

Herlihy's novel, was witty and sharp. *Midnight Cowboy* surprised audiences with its blunt view of sex and daring dialogue—it is the only X-rated film to ever win an Oscar—though by today's standards, the film is rather mild.

The phenomenal success of *Bonnie and Clyde* revived interest in the crime-gangster-film. More crime films were nominated in the 1970s than in any other decade, and three won Best Picture: the action-thriller *The French Connection,* and the two Francis Ford Coppola crime sagas, *The Godfather* in 1972, and *The Godfather, Part II,* in 1974. Of the two, *The Godfather* was more critically acclaimed and more popular, grossing over eighty million dollars.

Less honored by the Academy than its sequel, *The Godfather* won a second Best Actor for Marlon Brando, as Mafia boss Don Vito Corleone, and screenplay, written by Coppola and Mario Puzo, upon whose best-seller it was based. Its major competitor in 1972 was Bob Fosse's musical *Cabaret,* which captured the largest number of awards, eight, including Best Director. Breaking new grounds in both thematic and artistic ways, the two *Godfather* sagas are still the only crime-gangster movies to have won Best Picture. *The Godfather, Part II,* which won the largest, six, number of awards in 1974, is the only sequel to have received an Oscar.

Despite anxious anticipation and pressures from the public, It took sixteen years for Coppola to make *The Godfather, Part III* (1990), which garnered Best Picture and other nominations. Again teamed with Puzo, Coppola extended his history-making Mafioso saga into an absorbing tale of Michael's (Al Pacino) attempt to remove himself from the world of crime, and how fate and circumstances draw him back in, with his trigger-happy nephew (Andy Garcia) and the rest of the family in tow. Longish (191 minutes), but masterfully told, the film had one nearly fatal flaw: the casting of Coppola's daughter, Sofia, in the pivotal role of Michael's daughter.

In the same year, Martin Scorsese made one of his best films, *GoodFellas,* which swept all the critics awards, but lost the Oscar to *Dances With Wolves.* Joe Pesci won a supporting Oscar for playing that year's worst human being in the movies, Tommy DeVito, a Mafia killer who gleefully enjoys his pasta while a dying victim is locked in his car trunk. As written by Scorsese and Nicholas Pileggi, based on the latter's book, *Wiseguy, GoodFellas* provides a fascinating look at the allure—and dark reality—of "routine" life in a Brooklyn Mafia family, based on experiences of Henry Hill (Ray Liotta), who wound up in the Federal witness protection program. The violence was necessarily harsh, but *GoodFellas* was brilliantly realized by Scorsese and cinematographer Michael Ballhaus. Pesci and Oscar-nominated Lorraine Bracco stood out in an exceptional cast that also included Robert De Niro.

Message Movies: Individual and the Family

Issue-oriented films have also dealt with individual problems such as alcoholism, physical deformity (deafness, blindness), mental anguish, and insanity.

Billy Wilder's *The Lost Weekend,* which won the 1945 Oscar, was the first major Hollywood film about alcoholism. Prior to that, alcoholics in film were either comic or secondary characters—but never the heroes. *The Lost Weekend* depicts the degradation and torment of Don Birnbaum (Ray Milland) who, unable to realize his writing ambitions, turns to the bottle. Despite a stark portrayal of alcoholism in all its misery and horror, the changes made in the adaptation of Charles Jackson's novel to the screen are instructive, because they shed light on Hollywood's morality standards at the time and on the conventions of portraying screen heroes. In the book, Birnbaum's frustration derives from an indecisive sexuality (he's a troubled bisexual), whereas in the film, he suffers from a writer's creative block. The movie also changed the book's ending, providing a hopeful resolution to his drinking problem, using the ploy of a patiently loving girl (Jane Wyman) who helps to rehabilitate him.

The Lost Weekend had earlier won the New York Film Critics Award, then under the leadership of Bosley Crowther, who found its "most commendable distinction," in being "a straight objective report, unvarnished with editorial comment or temperance morality." *The Lost Weekend* won over Hitchcock's *Spellbound* and Leo McCarey's *The Bells of St. Mary's,* both starring Ingrid Bergman. Surprisingly, it also appealed to large audiences, ranking as the year's ninth most popular film.

Suffering and victimization have been almost exclusively women's domain in the American cinema, as evident in the Oscar-winning performances of Jane Wyman's deaf-mute girl in *Johnny Belinda,* Joanne Woodward's schizophrenic Eve in *The Three Faces of Eve,* and Patty Duke's blind-deaf Helen Keller in *The Miracle Worker.* But it was due to the success of *The Lost Weekend* that pictures about mental illness could be made. Anatole Litvak's *The Snake Pit,* nominated for the 1948 Oscar, was based on Mary Jane Ward's partly autobiographic novel with screenplay by Millen Brand, about the harrowing experiences of a mentally ill woman (Olivia de Havilland) in an asylum. Considered at the time a breakthrough film, due to its more realistic treatment of insanity, it was honored with six nominations.

Hollywood has usually been careful in treating mental problems onscreen for fear of alienating its movie patrons. However, one such movie, *One Flew Over the Cuckoo's Nest,* the Oscar winner of 1975, was so popular that it even shocked its makers, producers Saul Zaentz and Michael

Douglas and director Milos Forman. Ken Kesey's 1962 novel, which was first adapted to the stage, was well-received, but it was Jack Nicholson's flamboyant performance as Randle Patrick McMurphy, a free-spirited, anti-establishment hero, which made the difference. The film's conflict between individualistic, nonconformist behavior (Nicholson's) and the repressive established society, represented by Nurse Ratched (Louise Fletcher), head of the mental ward, was embraced by younger audiences as timely, relevant and entertaining.

The *New York Times* critic Vincent Canby singled out the film's comic scenes, which he thought were the best, and the fact that Forman didn't patronize the patients as freaks, but presented them as variations of "ourselves," as ordinary human beings. *One Flew Over the Cuckoo's Nest* won all five major Oscars and became the most widely seen problem film, grossing over fifty million dollars at the box office, ranking second only to Spielberg's *Jaws* among the year's blockbusters.

The family is one of the most sacred and revered institutions in American culture, but family dramas, like other serious pictures, have appeared in cycles. *Cavalcade,* the Oscar winner of 1932–33, was Fox's most prestigious production to date. Based on Noel Coward's play, adapted to the screen by Reginald Berkeley, it is a tale of an upper-class British family, spanning thirty years, beginning on New Year's Eve of 1899, and continuing through the Boer War, the sinking of the Titanic, World War I, and the Depression. Diana Wynyard gave a wonderful (nominated) performance as the strong mother who loses both of her sons in tragic circumstances. *Cavalcade* won over nine other pictures, including *42nd Street, I Am a Fugitive from a Chain Gang, Little Women,* and *The Private Life of King Henry VIII.*

John Ford's 1941 Oscar-winning family drama, *How Green Was My Valley,* like *Cavalcade,* had been a smash hit at the box office even before earning a nomination. But unlike *Cavalcade,* it celebrates what Bosley Crowther described as "the majesty of plain people," and "the beauty which shines in the souls of simple, honest folk." The film reaffirmed Ford's populist ideology, propagated the year before in another Oscar-nominated family saga, *The Grapes of Wrath.* However, *How Green* was not associated with the leftist, angry politics of John Steinbeck's book. The story of a Welsh mining family narrated by its youngest son, it is one of Ford's most touching, if also sentimental, pictures. The critic Andrew Sarris has described *How Green* as an elegiac poem, with a portrait of a mining community's disintegration that is of epically heroic dimensions.

How Green won five Oscars, honoring Ford's direction, Arthur Miller's cinematography, and art direction. Sara Allgood was nominated for playing a gentle mother, and Donald Crisp won a supporting Oscar for his role as a stern father killed in the mine. Not to be underestimated is the fact that *How Green* was selected while the United States was already involved in the war. Its warm, sympathetic depiction of family unity must have hit deep chords in the country's collective consciousness, which may explain why its two major competitors, Orson Welles's masterpiece *Citizen Kane* and William Wyler's *The Little Foxes,* each with nine nominations, lost. Both *Citizen Kane* and particularly *Foxes,* were dark, somber visions of the American family. Once again, ideological considerations ruled; though in Ford's defense, *How Green* is as visually distinguished as thematically acceptable.

If Ford's *How Green* is one of the most stunning celebrations of ordinary life, the next winning film about ordinary, "little people," *Marty,* is possibly the most pedestrian, intellectually as well as emotionally. The competition in 1955 was one of the weakest in Oscar's history. Three of the nominees were screen adaptations of Broadway's stage hits, *Mister Roberts, Picnic,* and *The Rose Tattoo; Marty* was based on Paddy Chayefsky's television play. The fifth nominee was the romantic melodrama, *Love Is a Many Splendored Thing.* In this case, movie politics might give a clue as to why *Marty* was favored. *Marty* was the first American picture to win the Palm d'Or at the Cannes festival, a fact that couldn't be ignored by the Academy or the critics, as the film also won the New York Film Critics Award.

Marty tells the love story of its eponymous hero, a lonely bachelor-butcher from the Bronx (Ernest Borgnine), and Clara, a shy teacher (Betsy Blair), after they meet in a dance hall. Shot in the Bronx, its American-Italian locale was captured with attention, but the script patronizes its little, lonely protagonists, an attitude demonstrated in a scene in which Marty tells Clara, "You're not really as much of a dog as you think you are." Nominated for eight awards, *Marty* won four: film, director Delbert Mann, writer Chayefsky, and actor Borgnine. But the Oscar was not much help at the box office; *Marty* is still one of the least commercially successful Oscar-winners.

Two decades later, in 1976, an unemployed actor named Sylvester Stallone took some of *Marty's* ideas ,mixed them with conventions of the sports-prizefighting genre *(The Champ, Golden Boy, Champion,* and *Somebody Up There Likes Me),* and came up with the winningly formulaic *Rocky.* This movie proved the impossible by becoming the first, but not last, sports film to win the Best Picture; *Chariots of Fire* was the second. Along with *Bound for Glory,* the biopicture about singer-labor organizer Woody Guthrie, *Rocky* was an artistically weak, if popular, nominee.

Each of the other 1976 contenders was more interesting than *Rocky*. Alan Pakula's *All the President's Men,* produced by Robert Redford, was an effective political thriller about the Watergate scandal, based on the best seller by the two Washington Post reporters, Carl Bernstein (Dustin Hoffman) and Bob Woodward (Robert Redford). Sidney Lumet made an outrageous farce, *Network,* about the power of television that for some reason some critics perceived as a drama. Martin Scorsese followed up his breakthrough film, *Mean Streets,* with *Taxi Driver,* a disturbing anatomy of alienation, embodied by Robert De Niro in a forceful performance. Of the five, *Rocky*'s message, the rise to stardom of an obscure "nobody," which paralleled both the actor's life offscreen and President Jimmy Carter's 1976 election, was the most upbeat and also the most befitting of the nation's mood in the midst of its Bicentennial celebration.

The impact of *Rocky*'s success was felt for some time. The film made Stallone a popular star—the most dominant male image of the 1980s—surpassing the powerful persona of Clint Eastwood in his *Dirty Harry* films, and led to four sequels of the Rocky Balboa saga.

Rocky was not a family drama, but the romance between Rocky and Adrian, a shy, plain salesclerk (Talia Shire), whom he later marries, was conducted along the same movie lines of Marty and Clara in *Marty*. *Rocky* also paved the way to the production of other conventional, old-fashioned, movies about ordinary folks. Having been saturated for a decade with action-adventure "disaster" movies, the American public seemed to crave simpler, more humanistic fare.

Moviegoers must have noticed that the family has almost disappeared from American films for most of the 1970s. The last major pictures to have dealt with marriage and family were mostly negative portraits, such as Mike Nichols's nominated features, *Who's Afraid of Virginia Woolf?* and *The Graduate.* The reentrance of family dramas into mainstream Hollywood was gradual, with such romantic melodramas as *The Turning Point* and Paul Mazursky's social comedy, *An Unmarried Woman.* But it was Robert Benton's *Kramer vs. Kramer,* the 1979 Oscar-winner, which gave legitimacy and definition to the new cycle of family pictures. This cycle lasted about four years, during which two other family films won Best Picture, *Ordinary People* and *Terms of Endearment,* and five others were nominated, *Breaking Away, Coal Miner's Daughter, On Golden Pond, Tender Mercies,* and *Places in the Heart.*

Like other pivotal pictures that launched cycles, no one associated with *Kramer vs. Kramer* initially expected such extraordinary success. The film's carefully designed ad campaign, using different posters for different target audiences, proved this point. Nonetheless, based on Avery Corman's novel, it was a timely movie that described the confusion of women who wanted to establish a firm identity independent of their roles as wives-mothers. Evocatively shot on location in Manhattan, it featured a great cast, headed by Dustin Hoffman and Meryl Streep as the splitting couple, Justin Henry as their son, and Jane Alexander as their sympathetic neighbor. All four were nominated for their work, with Hoffman and Streep winning. The 1979 writing awards were divided between *Kramer,* which won best adapted screenplay, and *Breaking Away,* Peter Yates's family comedy set in working-class Bloomington, which won original screenplay for Steve Tesitch.

In 1980, a year after *Kramer*'s release, Robert Redford made a stunning directorial debut in *Ordinary People,* adapted to the screen by Alvin Sargent from Judith Guest's highly regarded novel. Emotional but decidedly unsentimental, *Ordinary People* concerned the disintegration of an upper-middle class suburban family which, following an accidental death of one son and a suicide attempt of another, is unable to communicate its feelings and deal with its strains. Redford's direction was restrained and the film was supported by an excellent cast, with Donald Sutherland as the sympathetic father, Mary Tyler Moore as the undemonstrative mother, Timothy Hutton as the surviving troubled youngster (who won an Oscar), and Judd Hirsch as the understanding Jewish psychiatrist. Amazingly, *Ordinary People* wasn't a big-budget film—it cost only six million dollars —but its domestic grosses, greatly assisted by the Oscar, surpassed twenty million dollars. By contrast, *Kramer vs. Kramer* would have become a box-office bonanza even without winning Oscars.

At first sight, Dustin Hoffman's first Oscar for *Kramer vs. Kramer* and his second, for *Rain Man,* have nothing in common but high-caliber acting. However, thematically, both films celebrate the sanctity of the America family. Indeed, the success of the 1988 Oscar-winning *Rain Man* could be attributed, among other things, to its ideological message, in this case, the rediscovery of sibling love between an autistic savant (Hoffman) and his hustler brother (Tom Cruise). At first, the younger brother, a fast-talking car salesman, wants to rob his elder of the inheritance his father has left, for which purpose he kidnaps him from an asylum. But gradually, he gets to know a brother of whose existence he has been completely ignorant, and both realize that they not only love but also need each other. Blending motifs of the comedy-drama and road picture genres, *Rain Man* propagated mainstream family values: the predominance of biological instincts and blood ties against all odds and the importance of protecting the nuclear family. The public embraced the film even before it was nominated for eight awards and won four: Best Picture, Actor (Hoffman), Director (Barry Levinson), and Original Screenplay (Ronald Bass and Barry Morrow).

With nine nominations, *Driving Miss Daisy* was the most nominated film in 1989, and went on to win Best Picture and three other Oscars: Best Actress to Jessica Tandy, Adapted Screenplay to Alfred Uhry, and Makeup. It competed against Oliver Stone's *Born on the Fourth of July,* Peter Weir's *Dead Poets Society,* Phil Alden Robinson's *Field of Dreams,* and Jim Sheridan's *My Left Foot.*

A virtuous, PG-13 movie, boasting values of decency and humanity, *Driving Miss Daisy* stood out by not featuring any sex or violence. As producer Richard Zanuck later said: "Anything that tugs at your heart and emotions has a good chance for Best Picture." *Driving Miss Daisy* had the cachet of being based on a Pulitzer Prize-winning play by Alfred Uhry. Its low budget (only $7.5 million) and the fact that it was made without stars also commanded the Academy's attention. Genteel, theatrical, and sporadically entertaining, it told the story of a simple black man (Oscar-nominated Morgan Freeman) who's hired as chauffeur for a cantankerous old Southern belle (Jessica Tandy) and winds up being her loyal companion. Directed by Bruce Beresford in a smooth and understated style, the film was elevated by fine performances from its leads, as well as a likable, Oscar-nominated turn from Dan Aykroyd in an unusual "straight" role as Miss Daisy's son.

The family featured prominently in a number of 1990s films. Barbra Streisand's *The Prince of Tides* (1991), *Forrest Gump* (1994), *Secret & Lies* and *Shine* (both in 1996), *As Good As It Gets* (1997), and *Life Is Beautiful* (1998), all had strong family plots or subplots in them, though, with a few exceptions, they were at once more and less than genre family movies.

The 1999 Oscar-winner *American Beauty* could be described as a dark seriocomedy about the American family and the American way of life. Offering a startlingly incisive view of suburban angst, it was superbly directed by Sam Mendes, with dynamic performances from its entire ensemble, particularly Kevin Spacey in a brilliant Oscar-winning turn. The low-budget (fifteen million dollars) movie was a triumph for DreamWorks, which was disappointed the year before, when Spielberg's *Saving Private Ryan* was reduced to also-ran status, losing to Miramax's more aggressively marketed *Shakespeare in Love.* In *Entertainment Weekly,* Mark Harris depicted *American Beauty* as "a film that has more laughs than any other in the Best Picture category and is indisputably the grimmest as well." Among other qualities, the film defines its title subject by a plastic garbage bag tossed in the wind, mesmerizingly capturing the loveliness of a fleeting moment.

It was the fourth time in the past five years that the Best Picture was based on an original script—good news for the speculation script market.

First-time scripter Alan Ball, who earlier won a Golden Globe and the Writers Guild prize, mines familiar suburban turf for profound pathos, vibrant characters, and one-liners. Released a year after *Happiness*, Todd Solondz's audacious exposé of a dysfunctional family, and two years after Ang Lee's *The Ice Storm, American Beauty*'s satire seemed facile. Even so, Ball took the concerns of a specific social class and turned them into a redemptive sermon on humanity, exploring the obvious comforts of living in an economic boom and the continuing struggle to discover the meaning of life.

Julie Hinds, the *San Jose Mercury News*'s critic, has compared *American Beauty* to *The Graduate,* made thirty years earlier. It's as if Kevin Spacey is playing Benjamin Braddock, now stuck in an unhappy marriage, ready to quit his job at a plastics manufacturer. For her, the movie was a time capsule and a work of art—it depicted what it is like to be alive at a specific time in America and the tendency to ignore the beauty of what's around you and dream instead of things you can't have.

Though British, Mendes showed instinctive understanding for American character, tone, and dialogue. The entire cast is impressive, from Thora Birch as Spacey's sullen daughter, to Wes Bentley as the mysterious neighbor with hidden depths of wisdom, to Mena Suvari's as Spacey's love interest, a girl who is not as precocious as she acts. *American Beauty* also had the distinction of being contemporary—dealing with the here and now. In the last twenty years, only four contemporary movies have won Best Picture: *Ordinary People* in 1980, *Terms of Endearment* in 1983, *Rain Man* in 1988, and *The Silence of the Lambs* in 1990.

In a year with a multitude of lengthy films, such as *Magnolia* and *The Green Mile, American Beauty* was just two-hours long (122 minutes to be exact).

CHAPTER 8

Oscar-Winning Films—Historical Epics

Historical epics have featured prominently in the Oscar competition, with no fewer than sixteen (22 percent) of the seventy-two Oscar winners: *Mutiny on the Bounty* (1935), *Gone With the Wind* (1939), *Hamlet* (1948), *Ben-Hur* (1959), *Lawrence of Arabia* (1962), *Man for All Seasons* (1966), *Gandhi* (1982), *Out of Africa* (1985), *The Last Emperor* (1987), *Dances With Wolves* (1990), *Schindler's List* (1993), *Forrest Gump* (1994), *Braveheart* (1995), *The English Patient* (1996), *Titanic* (1997), and *Shakespeare in Love* (1998). While not many epics are produced, those that do get made receive disproportionate attention from the Academy and stand a good chance to be nominated.

As a type of film, the epic deals with historical stories and characters, and has to do as much with locale as with scope and intent. Widely diverse in genre, epics tend to be big-budgeted, large-scaled, sumptuously mounted productions. Hence, an epic framework has been applied to Westerns *(Cimarron, Dances With Wolves),* war movies *(Saving Private Ryan, The Thin Red Line),* period romances *(Gone With the Wind, Out of Africa),* political dramas *(Gandhi),* disaster movies *(Titanic),* and even comedies *(Tom Jones, Shakespeare in Love).*

MGM's *Mutiny on the Bounty,* directed by Frank Lloyd, was based on the story of the famous 1787 mutiny aboard the British ship HMS *Bounty.* It features three great performances: Charles Laughton, as the ruthless and sadistic Captain Bligh, Clark Gable, as the dashingly romantic Christian Fletcher, and Franchot Tone, as the decent officer Byam. It's still the only film to have been honored by the Academy with nominations for all three of its actors, though none won. *Mutiny on the Bounty* was Gable's favorite film, because, as he once said, "it was something you could get your teeth into, for it was history, the struggle of real he-man, with a refreshing absence of the usual load of love-interest." Acclaimed by critics, the movie enjoyed popularity with audiences, but it won only one Oscar: Best Picture.

The Best Director and Best Actor went that year to John Ford and Victor McLaglen for *The Informer.*

Mutiny on the Bounty has withstood well the test of time, and it is vastly superior to its two remakes, the first by MGM in 1962, also nominated for Best Picture, starring Trevor Howard in the Laughton role and Marlon Brando in the Gable role. The second remake, produced by Dino De Laurentiis in 1984 as *The Bounty* and starring Anthony Hopkins as Captain Bligh and Mel Gibson as Christian Fletcher, may be more accurate than its predecessors to its source material, but it lacks the excitement and epic scale of the 1935 version.

Many expensive and expansive historical films have been nominated. Cecil B. DeMille, Hollywood's greatest showman, was represented in the Oscar contest with two epics: *Cleopatra* (1934), starring Claudette Colbert, and *The Ten Commandments* (1956), with an all star cast headed by Charlton Heston. *Cleopatra*, which won best cinematography, is far more entertaining than the later remake directed by Joseph L. Mankiewicz and starring Elizabeth Taylor, which was nominated in 1963. Nominated for multiple awards, *The Ten Commandments* won only for special effects, best applied to the scene depicting the parting of the Red Sea. DeMille's last picture turned out to be one of the top-grossing pictures of all time.

Historical epics were also the specialty of David Lean. Two of his epics won Best Picture: The war film *Bridge on the River Kwai* (1957) and *Lawrence of Arabia* (1962). A master filmmaker, Lean knew how to make grand-scale epic adventures populated by intriguing characters. *Lawrence of Arabia* represents grand filmmaking both visually and narratively. The complex persona of T. E. Lawrence, the British officer who organized Arab tribes in an effort to drive the Turks out of their lands, remains an enigma in the film, but the portrayal by Peter O'Toole, then a newcomer, is stunning. Produced by Sam Spiegel, *Lawrence of Arabia* won seven Oscars: Director, cinematography, art direction, editing, sound recording, and music score.

Lean was represented in the Oscar contest with two other historical epics: *Doctor Zhivago* (1964), based on Boris Pasternak's novel, which won five Oscars, and *A Passage to India* (1984), adapted to the screen from E. M. Forster's book, which won three, and became Lean's last picture.

MGM's *Ben-Hur,* the 1959 winner, boasted a number of records, including being the most expensive film of its time, with a budget of fifteen million dollars, one-fifth of which was allocated for a massive ad campaign. Producer Sam Zimbalist constructed three thousand sets in Rome, for which he employed more than fifty thousand people. *Ben-Hur* is still the first remake to ever win Best Picture, and it won the largest number of awards to date: eleven out of twelve nominations. The only category in which it lost was screenplay, credited to Karl Tunberg, though at least four writers worked on it: Maxwell Anderson, S. N. Behrman, Christopher Frye, and Gore Vidal, which might have been the reason for its loss; the winner was Neil Paterson for *Room at the Top*. The only historical spectacle in the 1959 contest, *Ben-Hur* was up against smaller, more intimate movies, such as Otto Preminger's *Anatomy of a Murder,* George Stevens's *The Diary of Anne Frank,* Fred Zinnemann's *The Nun's Story,* and Jack Clayton's *Room at the Top.*

Based on Lew Wallace's popular novel about the rise of Christianity, *Ben-Hur* features spectacular visual effects, and a stunning chariot race choreographed by Yakima Canutt. Its acting, by contrast, is not spectacular, and Charlton Heston, who was cast after Universal refused to loan out Rock Hudson, is just decent in the title role of a converted Christian in conflict with Massalla (Stephen Boyd), the Roman commander and former childhood friend. The shortcomings didn't matter, for the film was endowed with a visual sweep and enough pageantry to entertain audiences for an epic running time of 217 minutes. Overcoming MGM's fears, *Ben-Hur* was such an instant hit that its grosses were reported weekly to make it seem "a must-see" movie, which it became. With the assistance of good reviews and a positive word of mouth, it grossed over eighty million dollars in worldwide receipts.

Like other genres, historical epics have been more prominent in some decades than others. Their greatest representation was in the 1930s and then in the 1950s and 1960s. The 1930s were dominated by MGM's prestige literary adaptations, such as *Viva Villa!* (1934), starring Wallace Beery as the Mexican rebel; George Cukor's *David Copperfield* (1935), based on Charles Dickens's novel; Irving Thalberg's production of Shakespeare's *Romeo and Juliet* (1936), with Norma Shearer and Leslie Howard in the leads; *A Tale of Two Cities* (also 1936), based on Dickens's book with Ronald Colman; and the film version of Pearl Buck's *The Good Earth* (1937), starring Paul Muni and Luise Rainer as the Chinese farmers.

Based on classic novels, these movies were marked by literary values, though like most films at the time, they were made on the studio lot. Their budgets were immense by the time's standards. The cost of *The Good Earth* was three million dollars (the equivalent to sixty million at present), and the film was in production for three years, due to producer Thalberg's death and changes in directors: George Hill began and Sidney Franklin finished. *The Good Earth* won an acting award for Luise Rainer and best cinematography for the locust attack sequence, an impressive special effect by standards of the time.

Not many historical epics were made in the 1940s, which is why David Lean's masterpiece *Great Expectations* and Laurence Olivier's Shakespearean adaptations, *Henry V* in 1946 and *Hamlet* in 1948, stood out in the American scene and were honored by the Academy. *Henry V,* the more experimental and stylized of the two, was shot in Technicolor. The movie begins at the Globe Theater, where the actors prepare for the performance, then switches to a more realistic setting, including one spectacularly photographed battle scene. Nominated for four awards, *Henry V* won none, though Olivier received a Special Oscar for his effort.

Hamlet, the 1948 winner, was filmed in a different style, emphasizing the camera as an active participant in the narrative. The film was shot in black and white, based on Olivier's vision that "it was like an engraving rather than a painting." The Castle, with its massive and gloomy corridors, framed the human characters in a detached way—the Oscars for art direction and costume design were well deserved. Despite criticism of the adaptation, which omitted a number of characters and whole scenes, *Hamlet* is an exciting film with fine acting by Olivier and the very young Jean Simmons (Oscar-nominated for Ophelia).

In the 1950s, due to the fierce competition with the new medium of television, Hollywood believed that its survival depended on large-scale epic films, with production values that couldn't be seen on the small screen. Thus, almost every year saw the nomination of epic movies, though the field was dominated by MGM. This time, however, the epics were historical tales on the order of *Quo Vadis?* (1951), the most expensive film of its time, starring Robert Taylor and Deborah Kerr, or *Ivanhoe* (1952), a medieval romance, based on Sir Walter Scott's novel, also with Robert Taylor, but this time with two ladies, Elizabeth Taylor and Joan Fontaine. Each of these pictures was nominated in multiple categories but won few if any awards. *Quo Vadis?,* for example, received eight nominations, but no awards.

The trends of the 1950s continued into the 1960s. Along with David Lean's epics, the decade began with John Wayne's historical Western, *The Alamo* (1960), about Texas's 1836 battle for independence. In 1962, Lewis Milestone's version of *Mutiny on the Bounty,* was nominated for seven, but didn't win any awards. In 1963, *Cleopatra,* the picture that ultimately destroyed 20th Century Fox, was nominated for nine and won four technical awards. In the following year, the British film *Becket*—based on Jean Anouilh's stage play about the conflict between church, represented by the Archbishop of Canterbury (Richard Burton), and state, King Henry VII (Peter O'Toole)—was nominated in twelve categories, but won just one: Edward Anhalt's screenplay.

The most talked-about film in 1966 was Fred Zinnemann's *A Man for All Seasons,* based on Robert Bolt's stage hit, concerning the battle of will between Sir Thomas More (Paul Scofield), the Roman Catholic Chancellor, and Henry VIII (Robert Shaw), who broke with the Vatican and established the Church of England with himself as its head. Simplifying his own play, Bolt's script accentuated the differences between the characters, making More an utterly noble saint, thus lacking the play's dramatic wit. Zinnemann's direction was barely serviceable, but it was elevated by Scofield's dignified acting and Shaw's eccentric turn. Indeed, despite flaws, *A Man for All Seasons* was favored by the Academy for its human message over its major competitor, Mike Nichols's *Who's Afraid of Virginia Woolf?* The film won six awards: Best Picture, Director, Actor, screenwriter, cinematographer, and costume designer.

The critical and commercial success of these historical films encouraged producers to make other epics. Franco Zeffirelli's handsome production of *Romeo and Juliet* (1968), cast two unknowns in the lead roles and stressed visual excitement at the expense of Shakespeare's text. In the same year, James Goldman's play, *The Lion in Winter,* was transferred to the screen without its original players, Robert Preston and Rosemary Harris. A gossipy, modern version of Henry II's court intrigues, it was marked by such anachronistic dialogue as the Queen saying, "Hush, dear, mother's fighting," or "Well, what family doesn't have its ups and downs?" which recalled *The Little Foxes* and *Who's Afraid of Virginia Woolf?* But Douglas Slocombe's cinematography, plus O'Toole and Hepburn's acting, made viewing tolerable.

British royalty—this time the courtship between Henry VIII (Richard Burton) and Anne Boleyn (Genevieve Bujold)—featured again in the 1969 nominated film, *Anne of the Thousand Days,* which received only the costumes award out of ten nominations.

Of the two historical epics nominated in the 1970s, one, *Nicholas and Alexandra* (1971) was weak. James Goldman's script was based on Robert K. Massie's novel, which reconstructed the last years of Russian tsarist history, but despite a tragic fate, the characters weren't interesting or moving. Even the art direction and costumes (which won Oscars) weren't imaginative, and despite publicity campaigns and nominations, the movie died at the box office.

By contrast, Stanley Kubrick's *Barry Lyndon* (1975), based on William Makepeace Thackeray's eighteenth-century novel, represented a bold experiment in literary adaptations. Boasting a breathtaking visual vision, albeit lacking in dramatic momentum, the film won four awards, one for John Alcott's distinguished photography.

Roman Polanski's *Tess* (1980), inspired by Thomas Hardy's novel, and imbued with a contemporary viewpoint, excelled more in its production values—for which it won three Oscars—than in dramatic effect. *Reds* (1981), Warren Beatty's effort as producer, co-writer (with Trevor Griffith), director, and star, was an ambitious attempt to make an historical epic, romantic adventure, and political drama all in one film. The film was intelligent and original in the way it used informants, all contemporaries of John Reed, the adventurous journalist who was in Russia during the 1917 Revolution and wrote the influential book, *Ten Days That Shook the World*. *Reds* also provided good parts for Diane Keaton as Louise Bryant, Reed's lover and then wife, Jack Nicholson as Eugene O'Neill, and Maureen Stapleton as the revolutionary Emma Goldman, which won her a supporting Oscar.

Spanning two decades (1913 to 1931), *Out of Africa*, starring Meryl Streep as Danish writer Isak Dinesen, was a tedious rendition of what must have been a passionate romance. Unclear about its heroine's psychology, the film fails to provide clues about the meaning of Africa for Dinesen and how it made her the kind of writer she later became. Nor does *Out of Africa* work as a love story because there was no chemistry between Streep and Robert Redford, as the white hunter. Episodic rather than dramatic, and with cinematography which is beautiful in the manner of National Geographic, *Out of Africa* does have some redeeming qualities. A mature movie about adult characters for adult audiences, it stood out from the dominating teenage films at the time. Along with *The Color Purple*, the film was nominated for the largest (eleven) number of awards, winning seven, including Picture, Sydney Pollack's direction, Kurt Luedtke's adapted script, and David Watkin's cinematography.

Bernardo Bertolucci's epic *The Last Emperor* swept most (nine) of the 1987 awards. Boasting stunning cinematography (the film was shot in the Forbidden City), it suffers from an episodic narrative with no coherent story and no epic hero. Its protagonist, Pu Yi (who became emperor of China at the age of three), was a passive man who lacked any power over his life. This may have accounted for the fact that none of the performers was nominated, and the wins were mostly in the technical categories. But in terms of visual images, art direction, costumes, and editing, *The Last Emperor* was a treat to the eye. Bertolucci's win at his second nomination (the first was for *Last Tango in Paris)*, made him the first and only Italian filmmaker to receive a competitive Oscar.

Schindler's List, Spielberg's three-hour Holocaust epic, was his most mature film to date. Made on a small budget (twenty-three million dollars), and shot in black and white, it tackles an unusually tough subject matter. By holding himself back, Spielberg took a great leap forward, making a powerful yet restrained movie. The Academy finally "forgave" Spielberg for being the world's most commercially successful filmmaker and honored him with the Best Director accolade.

Spielberg and screenwriter Stephen Zaillian captured Thomas Keneally's 1982 book's matter-of-fact approach, making a film that's a huge canvas of locales, episodes, and characters. Schindler (Liam Neeson), a failed industrialist, takes over a major company that previously belonged to the Jews, and proposes to staff it with Jews—unpaid, of course. Schindler hires a Jewish accountant, Itzhak Stern (Ben Kingsley), and together they supervise a plant that becomes a major supplier of pots and pans for the German military. In the background is Krakow's disintegrating Jewish community, whose members are forced to identify themselves as Jews. The action switches from the liquidation of the ghetto—and annihilation of a whole culture—to the confined life within the Plaszow Forced Labor Camp.

Schindler is depicted as a persuasive man who knew how to manipulate the Nazi elite, but also willing to pay hard cash for every Jewish life saved. The portrait that Zaillian paints is far from heroic; there's no attempt to whitewash Schindler's motivation to be wealthy and live a good life. Ultimately, though, Schindler emerges as a complex character, torn by contradictory impulses. The most intriguing relationship in the film is between Schindler and Amon Goeth (Ralph Fiennes), the camp's vicious commander. Every frame of *Schindler's List* shows Spielberg's anger, his urge to chronicle a catastrophe that defies rational understanding. The existential issue of life and death—who survived and who was exterminated—often becomes a function of fate or sheer luck.

Spielberg's bravura technique is evident here in Janusz Kaminski's kinetic camera which records the traumatic events with the fury of a documentary. The film features top-notch, Oscar-nominated performances, with Neeson as Schindler; Ben Kingsley in an understated performance as the accountant who reluctantly becomes Schindler's employee and later confidant; and most impressive of all, Fiennes, as the Nazi commander whose portrait goes way beyond the nasty German officers seen in American movies. The ending, which was shot in Israel with the survivors from *Schindler's List,* is touching but a tad too soft. *Schindler's List* chronicles a genocide of unparalleled proportions, what Hannah Arendt called the banality of evil. But the movie contains a hopeful note and proof of humanity—after all, eleven hundred Jews were saved by a Catholic German.

The next year, Spielberg presented the Best Director Oscar to his protégé, Robert Zemeckis, for *Forrest Gump.* Zemeckis showed shrewdness and technical skill in turning morally dubious material into a uniquely poetic American comedy, whose phenomenal commercial success suggests that it touched a deep chord in the American public. The hero is a retarded man, but one blessed with innate decency and courage. Forrest is simple, but his heart is always in the right place. The film implies, as critic David Denby noted, that we the audience could be as good as Forrest if only we had the courage to be simple.

As a character, Forrest belongs to the same type of idiot- savant that defined the 1966 French film, *King of Hearts, Being There* (1979), with an Oscar-nominated role by Peter Sellers, and *Rain Man* (1988), which brought a second Oscar to Dustin Hoffman. Luckily, Forrest is embodied by Tom Hanks, the only star who could play the role without condescension. By 1994, a year after winning Best Actor for *Philadelphia*, Hanks had become America's favorite son. Hanks plays a character who is limited in consciousness but not in feeling, hence encouraging the audience to identify with him. (He is actually the glue that holds the episodic film together, never allowing Forrest's eccentricities to become a comic caricature.) The film's approach was so smart and funny that viewers ignored its sanctimonious tone, packaging innocence as a higher state of being.

Forrest's charmed life leads him everywhere, from the White House, where Presidents Kennedy, Johnson, and Nixon greet him amiably, to an Alabama boarding house, where he's seen shaking hands with the yet unknown Elvis Presley. A loose string of vignettes, presented at a brilliant pace by Zemeckis, the film establishes Forrest as an accidental emblem of his times: a timid Alabama boy whose slowness is balanced by a talent for running and a genuinely sweet nature. We follow Forrest from his childhood in the 1950s through the 1980s; along the way, he becomes a celebrity several times over, though no one remembers him from one instance to the next.

Framed as an autobiography, the film centers on Forrest's love for his childhood sweetheart, Jenny (Robin Wright)—she is the only constant thing in his life. His solid qualities never change, whereas Jenny is presented as a victim of shifting ideologies. Forrest's progress is contrasted with Jenny, who is involved in the era's trendy politics and fashions (a hippie who demonstrates against Vietnam, a disco-coke junkie); Forrest, through his dim naiveté, is immune to them. The movie implies that Jenny reacts to the Zeitgeist and gets nothing; Forrest stays out of it and gets everything. *Forrest Gump* was basically a lyric poem to America, a country that ambles along happily while everything around it falls apart. Former President Reagan must have admired the movie: Forrest ends up as a rich businessman, proving that Reaganomics works.

In 1995, Paramount topped the list of Oscar nominations with ten bids for *Braveheart*. The studio's heart was indeed brave, entrusting movie star

Mel Gibson with thirty-five million dollars for his second feature as a director. Gibson went from making an intimate little film, *Man Without a Face,* to an epic—the choreography of the battle scenes with masses of people and horses was impressive. There was plenty of action and romance in this high-schoolish pageantry—a thirteenth-century tale of the Scottish hero Walter Wallace (Gibson), who returns to his homeland after England's cruel king assumes power.

Braveheart became the fifth Best Picture in the last twenty years not to receive a screenplay Oscar—and deservedly so. Gibson became the fifth actor to win a directing Oscar, all in the past fifteen years, following Robert Redford in 1980, Warren Beatty in 1981, Kevin Costner in 1990, and Clint Eastwood in 1992. Gibson also had the distinction of being the fourth Oscar-winning helmer not to have won the Directors Guild Award. The DGA gave its prize to Ron Howard (who was not Oscar-nominated) for *Apollo 13,* his exhilarating chronicle of the ill-fated mission to the moon.

The 1996 Oscar-winning epic, *The English Patient,* was an intelligent adaptation by Anthony Minghella of Michael Ondaatje's novel about a mysterious man (Ralph Fiennes) who is badly wounded in a World War II plane crash in the African desert. A Canadian nurse (Oscar-winning Juliette Binoche) tends him in an abandoned monastery in Italy and slowly his story emerges. Fiennes and Kristin Scott Thomas are perfectly matched in this passionate romance about two people thrown together by chance during a tumultuous period. The story unfolds layer by layer. John Seale's striking photography draws in the viewer with its sensual images of the adulterous affair and jarring images of wartime brutality.

Upon winning Best Director, writer-director Minghella recalled: "Many people told me it was a novel that couldn't be adapted. Every day I felt I was hanging by my fingernails. I was helped by a great team, a great crew, and many of those people have been acknowledged by the Academy. The Oscar was "a vindication, due to the troubles of getting the film made," to producer Saul Zaentz, who acknowledged Sydney Pollack's help. After reading the script, Pollack "went out on a limb for us, and, finally, Harvey Weinstein listened to him." Sweeping most (nine) of the Oscars that year, *The English Patient* also won for sound, score, costume, and editing.

War Films

War films have featured poorly in the Oscar contest, amounting to only 5 percent of the 422 nominated movies. However, the ratio of the winning war films to those nominated is three to one, which shows the Academy's bias in favor of epic war films. All six Oscar-winning war films have boasted a grand epic scale: *Wings* (1927/28), *All Quiet on the Western Front* (1929/30), *The Bridge on the River Kwai* (1957), *Patton* (1970), *The Deer Hunter* (1978), and *Platoon* (1988).

With the exception of William Wellman, who was not nominated for *Wings*, all the other directors were honored: Lewis Milestone for *All Quiet*, David Lean for *The Bridge*, Franklin J. Schaffner for *Patton*, Michael Cimino for *The Deer Hunter*, and Oliver Stone for *Platoon*. Spielberg won a second directorial Oscar for *Saving Private Ryan*, but the movie lost the Best Picture to *Shakespeare in Love*.

Wings is the only silent picture to have won the Oscar. In production for over a year, due to its demanding aerial sequences, which are still exciting to watch, the film was the most expensive (two million dollars) at the time. The first collaborative effort between Hollywood and the Air Force, it enjoyed the latter's assistance on the condition that the movie projects\ a positive image of the military. This was just the beginning of a more intimate connection between the film industry and the Armed Forces that would develop during World War II.

If *Wings* celebrates heroism, action, and male camaraderie, the next winning film, *All Quiet on the Western Front,* has an antiwar message. Based on Eric Maria Remarque's novel, adapted to the screen by a team of writers headed by playwright Maxwell Anderson, it describes the initial excitement, then disillusionment of a group of German soldiers in World War I, none of whom survives. The text uncompromisingly depicts a bleak picture of fighting in trenches, stressing the inanity of war for both sides, the Allies and the German. *All Quiet on the Western Front* proved popular at the box office—it was Universal's biggest success to date. But the film was poorly received in Germany prior to Nazism and officially banned following Hitler's rise to power. Reissued in the United States in 1939 in a truncated version, the film enjoyed a second successful run.

As one might expect, the largest number (six) of war films were nominated in the 1940s, during World War II, but, interestingly enough, none won Best Picture. Furthermore, few of the nominees were action pictures about men in combat. Rather, most movies were concerned with the Home Front, such as *Mrs. Miniver,* the 1942 Oscar winner, about a "typical" British family during the Blitz. Or *The Human Comedy* (1943), based on William Saroyan's book about the lives of ordinary folks in a small California town, with Mickey Rooney as a Western Union messenger who delivers death telegrams.

In 1944, David Selznick produced an American version of *Mrs. Miniver,* which he entitled *Since You Went Away,* about a "typical"

American family during the war, with Claudette Colbert playing the kind of indomitable mother that Greer Garson had embodied in *Mrs. Miniver*. Most of Hollywood's examinations of the war and its effects were made after the war was over, like MGM's *Battleground* and Fox's *Twelve O'Clock High,* both nominated in 1949.

One exceptionally good film was Paramount's *Wake Island* (1942), a moving, though fictionalized, report of the defense of the Pacific Island base and the heroic gallantry of three Marines, played by Robert Preston, Brian Donlevy, and William Bendix, who won a supporting nomination. Despite the fact that they were shot in California, the battle scenes seemed convincingly realistic. The film received rave notices, though the reviews themselves were tainted by politics. *Newsweek*'s critic wrote that "Although the U.S. has been at war for nine months, *Wake Island* is Hollywood's first intelligent, honest, and completely successful attempt to dramatize the deeds of an American force on a fighting front." Bosley Crowther, who saw *Wake Island* in a Marine base, noted that the film-makers "deserve a sincere salute," predicting that the picture "should surely bring a surge of pride to every patriot's breast."

The British were represented with two war pictures in the 1940s. The first, *The Invaders,* made in 1941 and released in America a year later, deals with six survivors from a Nazi submarine attempting to cross the Canadian border to the United States. Its cast was wonderful: Laurence Olivier, Leslie Howard, Raymond Massey, and best of all Eric Portman as a heartless, relentless Nazi. The other, *In Which We Serve,* was the creative effort of Noel Coward who, inspired by the sinking of HMS *Kelly* off Crete, re-created the biography of a ship, from its building to its last battle, interspersed with flashbacks of its crew's lives at home.

The first Oscar-winning war films usually received a few awards. *Wings* won two Oscars, Best Picture and engineering effects, a category which was discontinued the following year. *All Quiet on the Western Front* also won two awards: Picture and Director. The tendency of one film to sweep many awards began with *Gone With the Wind* in 1939, and became a trend in the 1950s. David Lean's epic, *The Bridge on the River Kwai,* was showered with seven Oscars.

Like other Lean movies, *The Bridge on the River Kwai* is rich in characterization and ambiguous in point of view—evident here in the depiction of the conflict between Colonel Nicholson (Alec Guinness), a rigid British officer committed to the military code of integrity at all costs, the Japanese commander of the prisoners' camp (Sessue Hayakawa), and the American man of action (William Holden). The bridge's construction has different meanings for these men and, at the end, when the Colonel dies by falling on the detonator that destroys the bridge, the story's irony becomes explicit. Impressive as a psychological study of character, *The Bridge on the River Kwai* is also strong in suspenseful action and visuals. As the critic Ivan Butler suggested, it is one of those rare movies that satisfy audiences emotionally, cerebrally, and aesthetically.

In the 1960s, three big war movies were nominated, beginning with *The Guns of Navarone* in 1961, an action picture about a tough sabotage team sent to destroy giant guns on a Turkish Island in 1943. *The Longest Day*, in 1962, about the preparations and landings of the Allies in Normandy on D-Day, June 6, 1944, was more ambitious—were it not for the competition with *Lawrence of Arabia*, it would have probably won Best Picture. Of its five nominations, *The Longest Day* won two awards: black-and-white cinematography and special effects.

However, Fox's 1966 attempt to make another blockbuster war movie, *The Sand Pebbles*, failed. An unabashed publicity campaign got the film eight nominations, though it lost in every category. Writer Richard Anderson and director Robert Wise were not exactly sure what kind of message they wanted to send in their 1926 story about the involvement of an American gunboat patrol (led by Steve McQueen) with Chinese warlords trying to rescue American citizens and missionaries.

Patton, the 1970 Oscar film, was also ambiguous in message, attempting to please both right-wing and left-wing audiences by letting each group read the film the way it wanted to. But unlike *The Sand Pebbles*, the film works. Made on a twelve-million-dollar budget, with an original script by Francis Ford Coppola and E. H. North, it presents a multi-faceted view of General Patton as a noble hero, demented psychopath, genius strategist, megalomaniac devoid of any human feelings, and even a poet. In a brilliant performance, George C. Scott dominated every frame, to the exclusion of the other actors, whose roles were underwritten. The response of the country, then in the midst of the Vietnam War controversy, to this one-character, one-star movie was overwhelming: The picture grossed over twenty-eight million dollars. *Patton* won seven major awards out of its ten nominations, for director Franklin J. Schaffner, actor Scott, screenplay, art direction, editing, and sound.

In 1978, two major films about the Vietnam War competed for Best Picture: *The Deer Hunter* and *Coming Home*. Both films were set in 1968, though they differed in their narrative, orientation, and style. Michael Cimino's *The Deer Hunter* is more ambitious and multi-layered, dealing with five Russian-American friends and their harrowing experiences in Vietnam. The film starts with the depiction of ordinary life in a small Pennsylvania steel town, then sharply switches to Vietnam. It says something about male camaraderie, physical and moral survival, violence in political and personal contexts, and even family life. There was no doubt that the picture was stronger in its lyrical-expressive imagery than in story or ideas. Sweeping all major critics awards, *The Deer Hunter* also won five Oscars.

Francis Ford Coppola's *Apocalypse Now* (1979) was inspired by Joseph Conrad's *Heart of Darkness*. Though intellectually vapid and dramatically incoherent as a statement on the U.S. involvement in Vietnam, it was honored it with two Oscars for its major achievements, Vittorio Storaro's stunning cinematography (shot in the Philippines), and sound. The decade's other war nominated epic was a British film, Roland Jaffe's *The Killing Fields* (1984), about the civil war in Cambodia.

In the 1980s, the war genre was alive and well, judging by the crop of belated films about Vietnam, some of which were produced under the guise of action-adventures but were imbued with a strong political subtext, reminiscent of the anti-Communist Cold War movies of the 1950s. Prominent in this cycle were the Sylvester Stallone *Rambo* films, which, in their comic strip revisionism of the Vietnam War, proved to be bonanza at the box office, but were expectedly ignored by the Academy.

The 1986 Oscar-winning *Platoon,* honored with four Oscars out of its eight nominations, was different in texture and ideology. Based on director's Stone's tour of duty in Vietnam, it is an exploration of "the everyday realities of what it was like to be a 19-year-old boy in the bush for the first time." Narrowly focused on the routine activities of a single infantry unit, *Platoon* gets its dramatic shape from the battle between the "Evil" sergeant Barnes (Tom Berenger) and the "Good" sergeant Elias (Willem Dafoe) over the soul of an "innocent" grunt Chris (Charlie Sheen). It took Stone ten years to get his script produced due to the fact that the country seemed unwilling to deal with the issues of Vietnam. Released in December 1986, just as President Reagan's popularity began to decline, *Platoon* challenged the country's collective consciousness and its ambivalent feelings toward Vietnam and its veterans.

Repeating the 1978 pattern two decades later, two of the 1998 Best Picture contenders were combat movies: *Saving Private Ryan* and *The Thin Red Line,* both about World War II. Revisiting a genre that was all but dead, Spielberg made a great epic that neither looked nor sounded like any other war film. The shocking realization about *Private Ryan* is how experimental it is: Spielberg challenged the basic foundations of film grammar—image construction, montage, manipulation of sound and silence. As shot by Janusz Kaminski's piercing camera, the film's first twenty-three minutes represent the most revelatory battle ever recorded on-screen, a breathtakingly graphic portrayal of the violence and chaos at Omaha Beach on

D-Day. The intense violence set a new standard for Hollywood, which previously tended to sanitize and mythologize the war.

Just as *Schindler's List* shed insight on the Holocaust, *Private Ryan* confronts the sacrifices that Americans (and non-Americans) had to make during World War II. It was the fourth time that Spielberg explored this era—*1941, Empire of the Sun,* and *Schindler's List*—but each time, he depicts war on a grander physical scale while exploring its impact on individual lives. *Private Ryan* takes the genre's familiar conventions and looks at them afresh. Unlike most war movies, it does not suggest that American soldiers were fighting for patriotic causes, but shows that in combat there's only one ideology: survival. Refusing to glorify war, *Private Ryan* doesn't shy away from depicting the fear of getting killed, the hesitancy of taking a human life, even when it belongs to the enemy. Going beyond the realm of war, *Private Ryan* explores the burden of memory, the inevitable weight of the past on the present.

Tom Hanks, who once again played a sympathetic hero audiences and Academy voters could identify with, was nominated for Best Actor for the fourth time. Spielberg, already winning an Oscar for *Schindler's,* picked up his sixth nomination and second Oscar. Kaminski got a second Oscar (and a third nomination; the second was for *Amistad).* John Williams was nominated for his score—the composer has received thirty-six nominations and five Oscars, three of them in Spielberg movies. Editor Michael Kahn *(Raiders of the Lost Ark* and *Schindler's List)* also won an Oscar.

The Thin Red Line brought Terrence Malick (of *Days of Heaven's* fame) back to filmmaking after a twenty-year-hiatus. Naturally, there were high expectations ever since word leaked out that Malick was shooting the James Jones's novel. Unfortunately, Malick's concerns that his battle scenes would not match the intensity of *Private Ryan,* and that American viewers would not support two war movies proved valid. Additionally, the film's story line was too amorphous and its pacing too elliptical for Oscar's conservative voters.

The Academy proved again that it doesn't know how to handle an ensemble film—none of the cast members, Sean Penn, Nick Nolte, Elias Koteas, Ben Chaplin, or Jim Caviezel received a nomination. *The Thin Red Line* received seven nominations, including Best Picture, Director, and screenplay adaptation. Oscar-winning cinematographer John Toll *(Braveheart)* was up for his third nomination, but lost out to Kaminski *(Private Ryan). Thin Red Line* occupied the unfortunate position of being released after *Private Ryan,* which was a box-office bonanza, ever since its July opening.

Action-Adventures

Action-adventures have been popular with the public but unrespected by the Academy. With their ceaseless entwining of special-effects violence and simplistic one-liners, action movies are certainly not Oscar stuff. Indeed, only four adventures have won Best Picture.

The first Oscar-winning adventure was Cecil B. DeMille's *The Greatest Show on Earth* (1952), which also earned, for no apparent reason, the writing award. Produced by Paramount, it was the only DeMille film to win Best Picture. Its inspiration derived from the Ringling Bros., Barnum and Bailey Circus, and depicted a romantic triangle between a tough manager (Charlton Heston), his beautiful aerialist (Betty Hutton), and a trapeze artist (Cornell Wilde). The movie's most spectacular sequence is a train crash with hundreds of animals running around. A mass entertainment, *The Greatest Show on Earth* still ranks as one of the least accountable and least distinguished Oscar-winners. It is this film that began the tradition of honoring big-budget, special-effects blockbusters with a large number of nominations.

Cecil B. DeMille won his first and only directorial nomination for this picture, but the winner was John Ford for *The Quiet Man*. The Academy must have anticipated DeMille's failure to win a competitive award, for it honored him with a Special Oscar in recognition of *The Greatest Show on Earth* and other blockbusters. This tribute was well-timed: DeMille made just one more film, *The Ten Commandments,* before dying in 1959, at the age of seventy-eight.

Mike Todd's *Around the World in 80 Days* (1956), the second winning adventure, was directed by Michael Anderson and based on Jules Verne's best-seller about a Victorian gentleman (David Niven) and his valet (Cantinflas) who go around the world in eighty days on a wager. It was not the first film that used Todd-AO, which produced sharper images than Cinerama, but it was effective as an exciting travelogue that took audiences to exotic locales. With a budget of seven million dollars, well above the average at the time, the film boasts over fifty cameo appearances from famous stars such as Charles Boyer, Marlene Dietrich, Ronald Colman, Buster Keaton, Cesar Romero, and Frank Sinatra. Spotting the stars proved to be great fun for the audience, which set another trend: casting large ensembles of stars in small roles in episodic films, such as *The Longest Day, How the West Was Won,* and the disaster movies of the 1970s.

Around the World's five Oscars honored the adapted screenplay, color cinematography, editing, and musical score. Victor Young, the noted Hollywood composer, won his first Oscar posthumously, after nineteen nominations. The picture ranked second among the top-grossing films of the year, following *The Ten Commandments,* and was the most commercially popular Oscar film until *Ben-Hur* in 1959.

While it was in production, no one expected William Friedkin's *The French Connection* to either become such a major critical and commercial hit or to win the 1971 Oscar. But it did, capturing awards for its director, actor (Gene Hackman), screenplay (Ernest Tidyman), and editing (Jerry Greenberg). The Oscar legitimized *The French Connection*'s status as the decade's best "cop and caper" film. The movie contributed, as James Monaco has observed, to the resurgence of film noir in the 1970s and to the rise of a viscerally exciting visual style. Preceding the release of Clint Eastwood's *Dirty Harry* by a few months only, *The French Connection* made the cop film the most popular genre of the decade.

Every element in *The French Connection* is effective in its own right, but even better as a part of the movie as a whole. It has a serviceable screenplay, based on two real-life policemen, Eddie Egan and Sonny Grosso (who served as the film's technical advisers and also appeared in minor roles), who were obsessed with tracking down a large shipment of heroin hidden in a car transported from Marseilles to New York City.

In addition to being an exhilarating thriller, containing one of the best and most imitated chase scenes in American film, the narrative revolves around an interesting character. Popeye Doyle (Hackman) is a tough, vulgar, bigoted cop, obsessed with breaking up the international narcotic ring. To think that the filmmakers considered other actors for the role (Jackie Gleason and Steve McQueen, among others) is hard to believe, for it provided Hackman with the best role of his career. *The French Connection* also boasts breathtaking cinematography, the sounds of the streets of New York, and well-paced editing, all of which contributed to a well-made and entertaining movie. Praised by most critics, *The French Connection* went on to rank third among the year's top grossers.

The nominated adventures have appeared in two major cycles: in the 1930s and in the 1970s. No adventure films were nominated in the 1940s and 1960s, and few in the 1950s. Adventure films are always strong in production values and special effects, but there are differences between the 1930s and 1970s nominated adventures.

In the earlier decade, adventures had melodramatic stories and well-constructed, if contrived, plots. MGM's *Trader Horn* (1931) was a jungle melodrama distinguished by its on-location shooting in Africa, which was a novelty at the time, and cast, with Harry Carey as a white hunter pitted against hostile tribes. Another MGM production, the popular *San Francisco* (1936), featured the most spectacular earthquake ever recorded, lasting close to ten minutes of screen time. A well-made film, *San Francisco* tells an emotionally engaging love story about a tough saloon owner (Clark Gable) and a singer (Jeanette MacDonald), although a third character, a no-nonsense priest (Spencer Tracy), stole the show.

Warner's swashbuckling adventures of the decade, both starring Errol Flynn, were also nominated. *Captain Blood* (1935) didn't win any awards, but *The Adventures of Robin Hood* (1938), the first Technicolor version of the legend, won three: art direction, editing, and original score.

Paramount's adventure, *The Lives of a Bengal Lancer* (1935), for which Henry Hathaway received his only directing nomination, starred Gary Cooper, Franchot Tone, and Richard Cromwell as courageous British officers in India involved in treacherous border intrigues. One of the year's most nominated (six) pictures, it was honored with one Oscar, for best assistant direction.

The World War II years weren't particularly conducive to the production of adventures, which continued to be missing in the 1950s, with that decade's emphasis on historical epics. MGM's *King Solomon's Mines* (1950) stands out as the decade's most entertaining adventure, similar to the earlier *Trader Horn,* and marked by exquisite color cinematography of Africa's jungles by Robert Surtees, who won an Oscar, and impressive editing by Ralph E. Winters and Conrad A. Nervig, who also won.

After a decade of no adventures competing for Best Picture, the 1970s brought a new cycle of "action" films. Labeled "disaster movies," they depicted natural and man-made catastrophes set on earth *(Earthquake,* 1974), in the air *(Airport,* 1970 and its sequels), on the sea *(Jaws,* 1975 and its sequels) and under the sea *(The Poseidon Adventure,* 1972). This genre exploited its narrative possibilities in a few years, saturating the market so fast that it resulted in a hilarious send-up, *Airplane* (1980), of the "airport" movies.

The "disaster" adventures were commercially packaged products that flaunted all-star casts. Most proved to be popular with the public, at once cashing in on and promoting collective fears of such ordinary activities as flying *(Airport)*, swimming on Long Island's beaches *(Jaws),* and working in high-rise building *(The Towering Inferno)*. The pattern of these blockbusters was to receive a large number of nominations, in recognition of their technical aspects and commercial appeal, but only a few awards.

The disaster adventures provided employment to many actors, some who had been in forced retirement, but they were not generous to them—each actor had at best one or two good scenes. This explains the large number of technical nominations and the paucity of acting ones. The Academy usually singled out elderly performers in these films for sentimental reasons. Helen Hayes won a second (supporting) Oscar for portraying a compulsive stowaway in *Airport* who, upon being caught, says: "I don't think it would be very good public relations to prosecute a little lady for visiting her daughter." Reviewing the film in the *New York Times,* Vincent Canby wrote that Helen Hayes plays "with such outrageous abandon you believe she must have honestly thought it would be her last performance," which it was not, but maybe the Academy thought so. The Academy also nominated Maureen Stapleton, who played the slow-witted, distraught wife of a mad bomber, played by Van Heflin, who was also nominated.

The Poseidon Adventure honored Shelley Winters with her fourth nomination for playing a Jewish grandmother-passenger in a sinking ship. Sentimentality, on screen and off, also explains the first and only acting nomination of Fred Astaire, in *Towering Inferno,* as a widower who loses his friend (Jennifer Jones) in the disaster. The multiply nominated *Star Wars* received only one acting nomination for Alec Guinness as a whiskery wizard.

Star Wars began a new cycle of sci-fi films which, unlike its 1950s counterparts, was sophisticated in its technology and production values. The impact of *Star Wars,* its sequels, and imitators on pop culture has been immense, influencing fashion, interior design, TV programming, the toy industry, and even the way children are brought up. The Academy acknowledged its status with six competitive and one Special Award, but with respect to the other action-adventure blockbusters, *Star Wars* was the exception.

The Academy has shown its respect for these blockbusters in the nomination process, but when it came to the "real thing," the Oscar itself, a more cautionary vote was exercised:

> In 1970, *Patton* was selected over *Airport*
> In 1974, *The Godfather, Part II* over *Towering Inferno*
> In 1975, *One Flew Over the Cuckoo's Nest* over *Jaws*
> In 1977, *Annie Hall* over *Star Wars*
> In 1981, *Chariots of Fire* over *Raiders of the Lost Ark*
> In 1983, *Terms of Endearment* over *The Right Stuff*
> In 1993, *Schindler's List* over *The Fugitive*

The status of the disaster movie changed in 1997 with the release of James Cameron's two hundred million dollar *Titanic,* which blended successfully the conventions of the thriller, action-adventure, disaster movie and, above all, historical romance. With its huge number of nominations (fourteen), it tied *All About Eve* for the most nominations. Basically, *Titanic* faced only one serious competitor, Curtis Hanson's noir thriller,

L.A. Confidential. The other three nominees were small-scale, well-acted vehicles: *As Good As It Gets, The Full Monty,* and *Good Will Hunting.* After winning, Cameron reflected: "This movie touched a common chord. It has been connecting on a heart level in every country, and we can hardly take responsibility for it. We were just a conduit." The most popular Oscar winner ever, *Titanic,* has grossed globally over $1 billion.

Thrillers and Horror Flicks

Judging by the scarcity of nominations, suspense films, like action-adventures, are more appreciated by filmgoers than the Academy. Well-made thrillers are perceived in the industry as product of craftsmanship rather than art.

In the Academy's history, only two thrillers, Alfred Hitchcock's *Rebecca* (1940) and Jonathan Demme's *The Silence of the Lambs* (1991), have won Best Picture. Based on Daphne du Maurier's popular novel, *Rebecca* was Hitchcock's first American movie, in which he cast Laurence Olivier and Joan Fontaine in the starring roles. The film is distinguished by an exquisite cinematography (George Barnes won an Oscar), and great ensemble acting, headed by Judith Anderson as the malevolent housekeeper, in one of her most memorable portrayals.

In 1940, *Rebecca* competed against another Hitchcock film, *Foreign Correspondent,* which deals with espionage in Europe. The film was interpreted by some as an endorsement of the American involvement in the war, because its producer, Walter Wanger, was known for his antifascist views. Both *Rebecca* and *Foreign Correspondent* were popular; *Rebecca* grossed in rentals the then phenomenal $1.5 million.

Jonathan Demme began his career directing exploitation films for Roger Corman, but he gave *The Silence of the Lambs* the treatment of an art film. Based on Thomas Harris's best-seller, the suspenseful and gruesome thriller centers on the battle of nerves between an FBI trainee (Jodie Foster) and a diabolical psychiatrist-turned-cannibal in her efforts to hunt down a serial killer. The acting of the two stars was superb. Anthony Hopkins almost made a hero of out of Hannibal Lecter's sadistic, unruly demon, who becomes Clarice's sparring partner. As Clarice, Foster embodies the gentleness of an initially naive county girl who becomes susceptible to the advances of Hannibal Lecter. For some, the movie was too creepy and disconcerting in its hints of romantic attraction between Hannibal and Clarice.

Conservative viewers were outraged: First Lady Barbara Bush stormed out of the theater, protesting, "I didn't come to a movie to see people's skin being taken off." Then gay activists threatened to disrupt the Oscar show as a protest against Hollywood's representations of homosexuals in Demme's film, as well as in Oliver Stone's *JFK* (also nominated that year) and the Sharon Stone vehicle, *Basic Instinct,* which was released during the nomination period.

The first of the five nominees to be distributed theatrically, *Silence of the Lambs* opened at an unusual time, in February. By Oscar time, the picture has grossed $130.7 million, which made it the last successful release by the then-recently bankrupt Orion Pictures, the company responsible for the Oscar-winner of the previous year, *Dances With Wolves.* The bizarre situation was not lost on Demme, who remarked, "I know everyone feels the incredible irony of what's happened to Orion."

Silence of the Lambs swept all the major Oscars: Picture, Director, Actor, Actress, and Adapted Screenplay. Only two other films in the Academy's history have been recognized in all top categories: *It Happened One Night* in 1934, and *One Flew Over the Cuckoo's Nest* in 1975.

Except for Demme, no filmmaker has ever won a directorial Oscar for a thriller, including Hitchcock, the genre's acknowledged master. Hitchcock was nominated five times: for *Rebecca, Lifeboat* (1944), *Spellbound* (1945), *Rear Window* (1954), and *Psycho* (1960), his last undisputed success. Four Hitchcock films were nominated for Best Picture, the aforementioned *Rebecca* and *Foreign Correspondent, Suspicion* (1941), and *Spellbound.* Failing to give Hitchcock a legitimate Oscar, the Academy later compensated him with an Honorary Oscar.

Other filmmakers specializing in thrillers have met similar fates. Carol Reed established an international reputation with two extraordinary suspense films, both based on Graham Greene novels: *The Fallen Idol* (1949), starring Ralph Richardson, and *The Third Man* (1950), with Orson Welles. Both pictures boasted high production values; Robert Krasker won an Oscar for his black-and-white photography of Vienna in *The Third Man.* Reed received nominations for these films, but won the Oscar at his third nomination for a less characteristic movie, the musical *Oliver!*

Thrillers have also featured marginally among the nominees, amounting to 3 percent of all pictures, mostly in the 1940s. In addition to Hitchcock's films, they included John Huston's first and one of his best features, *The Maltese Falcon* (1941), George Cukor's gothic tale *Gaslight,* and Billy Wilder's *Double Indemnity,* both in 1944. No suspense films were nominated in the 1950s and 1960s, and only two in the 1970s: Roman Polanski's *Chinatown* and Francis Ford Coppola's *The Conversation,* both in 1974. Most of the nominated thrillers employed the thematic and stylistic vocabulary of film noir. Some, like *The Maltese Falcon* and *Double Indemnity,* have become classics of their genre.

"Craftsmanship, cultural impact, and box-office success. Now that's a trifecta Oscar may find hard to resist," is how *Entertainment Weekly* described the 1999 sleeper *The Sixth Sense*, a spiritual horror-thriller with strong performances from Bruce Willis (who was not nominated) and Haley-Joel Osment, who had the most memorable line in any movie that year: "I see dead people." The most successful horror film in the genre's history, and yet one of the gentlest, was directed by Indian-born M. Night Shyamalan, who, at twenty-nine, became one of the youngest Best Director nominees. *The Sixth Sense* made $284 million after its summer release, a level of success that must have deemed it too commercial for serious Oscar considerations.

The Academy's lack of respect for thrillers is also reflected in the under-representation of acting awards (less than 2 percent) in this genre. Not surprisingly, most of these roles were played by women, who typically played victims threatened with murder by their husbands-lovers, such as Joan Fontaine in *Suspicion* or Ingrid Bergman in *Gaslight* (see chapter 10).

Westerns

For decades, the Western, arguably the most uniquely American film genre, was regarded as the "bread and butter" of the industry. Year after year, numerous "B" Westerns, which functioned as the bottom of the double-feature bill, were made. In the 1950s, the best decade for "A" Westerns in the genre's history, the production of Westerns amounted to one-third of Hollywood's entire output. Yet, only three of the seventy-two Oscar-winning films have been Westerns: *Cimarron* (1932/33), *Dances With Wolves* (1990), and *Unforgiven* (1992).

Based on Edna Ferber's best-selling novel about the opening of the Oklahoma frontier, *Cimarron* covered three decades in the Cravat family, beginning with the gold rush in the 1890s. Directed by Wesley Ruggles, the sprawling saga provided good roles for Richard Dix, as a dashing, adventurously romantic hero, and Irene Dunne, as his indomitable wife Sabra, who starts out as fragile and dependent but later becomes the editor of a newspaper and then a congresswoman. *Cimarron,* which also won writing adaptation and art direction, was a blockbuster with the public.

Actor-director Kevin Costner proved his critics wrong, when *Dances With Wolves,* his epic ode to a West long gone, won seven Oscars, including Best Picture and Best Director. *Dances With Wolves* became the first Western since 1931's *Cimarron* to win the top prize. Costner directed himself as an idealistic officer whose solitary life at a frontier outpost is interrupted and then forever changed when he encounters members of the Lakota Sioux tribe.

When Costner was looking for finance, there was not much interest in a marathon-length Western featuring unknown actors speaking in a subtitled Lakota Sioux dialect. Hollywood skeptics, convinced that Costner had a flop the size of *Heaven's Gate* on his hands, had tagged his three-hour directorial debut, "Kevin's Gate." But by Oscar night, *Dances With Wolves* had accumulated more than $130 million in ticket sales. Michael Blake, who just a few years ago was washing dishes and sleeping on friends' sofas, won an Oscar for his script, based on his novel, which Costner had encouraged him to write.

The success of *Dances With Wolves,* which was Costner's first directing project, washed forgiveness over the much-scrutinized film. Despite his status as first-time helmer, the past shows that actors who direct stand a chance at grabbing the Oscar. Costner, in fact, became Hollywood's new Golden Boy. One studio head rationalized the effects that *Dances With Wolves* had in breaking every conceivable Hollywood rule: "When pictures like that explode—and they're rare—they do something to us: all of our notions have to be reconceived. Forget the success of the flick or the problems Costner had or his achievement. We're all thinking differently now. About Westerns. About subtitles. About the length a picture can be. About movies with quills."

Costner's main competition was Martin Scorsese and his crime gangster film, *GoodFellas,* which swept all the critics awards: Los Angeles, New York, and the National Society. The same year also saw the release of the third, eagerly awaited film of Coppola's 1970s crime saga, *The Godfather, Part III.* The other nominees were *Awakenings,* a psychological drama with Robin Williams and Robert De Niro, which received multiple nominations but was denied a nomination for its woman director, Penny Marshall, and the romantic blockbuster, *Ghost.*

Indeed, the great divide in 1990 was based as much on geography as on film sensibility. A New Yorker at heart, Scorsese was a graduate of NYU, and most of his films are set in New York. *GoodFellas,* like most of Scorsese's films, feels New York: sharp, urban, tough, and bloody. Costner hailed from California, and *Dances With Wolves* was a romantic epic about the West. Consensus held that *GoodFellas* was brilliantly crafted, but that the New York City gore and blood turned off the Academy voters, who are old and live in Los Angeles. An Academy voter reflected the opinion of many when he said: "If the whole Oscar show was done at Radio City, I think *GoodFellas* would win."

Unforgiven, Clint Eastwood's *chef d'oeuvre,* swept the major awards from the Los Angeles Film Critics before winning the Best Picture. A classic Western that is at once realistic and mythical, it boasted Eastwood's best work as an actor and director in a genre often regarded disreputable in Hollywood. Watching the film was particularly rewarding for those familiar with Eastwood's screen persona—*Unforgiven* deconstructs the myths of manhood and violence in the Old West. Eastwood set out consciously to humanize his superhero image in films that are not explicitly Westerns but have used elements of the genre, such as the *Dirty Harry* films, which are basically urban Westerns.

As the nameless gunslinger in Sergio Leone's spaghetti Westerns of the 1960s, Eastwood established himself as a tight-lipped, steely eyed icon. Now in the director's saddle, he turned that image on its ear with *Unforgiven*, in which he portrays William Munny, an aging pig farmer haunted by his blood-soaked desperado past, who emerges from retirement for one final bounty hunt—to avenge the two villains who cut a prostitute's face with a Bowie knife. A widower raising two children, Munny is doing it for the money he desperately needs for his farm. Based on David Webb Peoples's Oscar-nominated screenplay, *Unforgiven* is a debunking meditation on the irredeemable savagery of the West. A critical and box-office smash (one of the few Westerns to have grossed over a hundred million dollars domestically), the film earned four Oscars, including Best Picture and Best Director.

Of all genres, the Western has been the most peripheral in the Oscar contest. In addition to the three winning films, only seven Westerns have been nominated: *In Old Arizona* (1928/29), *Stagecoach* (1939), *The Ox-Bow Incident* (1943), *High Noon* (1952), *Shane* (1953), *How the West Was Won* (1963), and *Butch Cassidy and the Sundance Kid* (1969). With the exception of John Ford *(Stagecoach),* the other nominated Westerns were directed by filmmakers who didn't specialize in the genre, which may have had something to do with their gaining nominations. "Prestige" filmmakers, such as Fred Zinnemann *(High Noon)* and George Stevens *(Shane),* were rewarded for making one impressive Western in their careers. (Stevens would later direct *Giant.)*

A lack of respect for the genre is also reflected by the paucity of directorial Oscars for Westerns. John Ford, undoubtedly the master of Westerns, was nominated five times, but only once for a Western *(Stagecoach).* Ford failed to win a nomination for what's considered to be his masterpiece, *The Searchers* (1956). Significantly, Ford's four Oscars were for other genres: *The Informer, The Grapes of Wrath, How Green Was My Valley,* and *The Quiet Man.* Astonished by the Academy's biases, Ford bitterly noted: "I don't think a lot about honors, but I think it's demeaning to the Westerns that I have received honors for other films and none for my Westerns."

Other directors excelling in Westerns have similarly skirted the Academy recognition. Howard Hawks failed to get nominations for his two excellent Westerns, *Red River* (1948) and *Rio Bravo* (1959), but was nominated for the patriotic flag-waver, *Sergeant York*, though he did not win.

A typically masculine genre, the Western has offered better roles for men, which was acknowledged by the Academy: seven men, but no women, have won acting Oscars in a Western. The first was Warner Baxter, who played the legendary Mexican bandit the Cisco Kid in *In Old Arizona*. Gary Cooper gave one of his finest performances as Marshal Will Kane in *High Noon*. Lee Marvin played a dual part in *Cat Ballou* (1965): Kid Shellen, a whiskey-soaked gunfighter, and Shellen's antagonist, Tim Straun, a villain with a silver nose. *True Grit* (1969) provided John Wayne with one of the richest roles of his career, as the fat, aging, eye-patched marshal Rooster Cogburn, who helps a teenager avenge her father's death.

Four supporting awards honored Western roles, beginning with Thomas Mitchell as the drunken Doc Boone in *Stagecoach*. Walter Brennan won his third supporting Oscar for playing Judge Roy Bean in William Wyler's *The Westerner*. Burl Ives won for his patriarch landowner in *The Big Country*, another Wyler Western, and Gene Hackman won a second Oscar as the sadistic sheriff in *Unforgiven*.

Few players have been nominated for a Western, not for lack of distinguished performances, but due to genre's low prestige. Actors identified with some of the best Westerns failed to get recognition, including Henry Fonda, James Stewart, William Holden, Kirk Douglas, and Burt Lancaster. Moreover, those few who received recognition were nominated because of their status as players, not necessarily for a specific Western. Geraldine Page was nominated for a supporting role in a John Wayne Western, *Hondo* (1953), because it was her first movie upon arriving in Hollywood as Broadway's brightest star after *Summer and Smoke*. Jennifer Jones and Lillian Gish were nominated for King Vidor's *Duel in the Sun* (an erotic but silly Western) because it was a blockbuster. Julie Christie won her second nomination for playing the frizzy-haired, opium-smoking whore in Robert Altman's *McCabe and Mrs. Miller* (1971) because she was then in vogue.

Ironically, only when the Western became self-conscious, it began to win some respect. Lee Marvin won Best Actor for a Western spoof, *Cat Ballou*, which caricatured the traditional Western hero and was sold to the public as a "put-on" Western. John Wayne won acclaim only when he poked fun at his own screen image. Madeline Kahn received a supporting nomination for Mel Brooks's spoof, *Blazing Saddles* (1974), which poked fun at every convention of the genre. As Lily von Shtupp, Kahn payed tribute to the numerous cabaret singer roles played by Marlene Dietrich in *Destry Rides Again* and others.

CHAPTER 9

Oscar-Winning Films—
Comedies and Musicals

The Oscar Comedies

Compared with the number of films produced, comedy as a genre has been underrepresented in the Oscar contest. Year after year, the Academy has displayed biases against comedy films and comedic performances. Overall, comedies amount to about one-fifth of all 422 nominated pictures. But only ten out of the seventy-two Oscar-winning films have been comedies, and that figure includes such borderline cases as *The Apartment, Driving Miss Daisy,* and *American Beauty.*

It took seven years for a comedy to win the first Best Picture: Frank Capra's *It Happened One Night* (1934). And it won by surprise, as it was directed by a relatively unknown director and produced by a lesser studio, Columbia Pictures. For forty-one years, *It Happened One Night* held a record as the only film to have captured all five major awards: Picture, Director, Actor (Clark Gable), Actress (Claudette Colbert) and screenplay (Robert Riskin). In 1975, *One Flew Over the Cuckoo's Nest* became the second film to achieve that.

Structured as a "road" comedy, *It Happened One Night* concerns the evolving romance between a runaway heiress (Colbert) and a tough reporter (Gable) who, having been fired by his editor, plans a comeback by getting the exclusive story of the heiress's rebellious flight to marry a man her family doesn't approve of. The picture was rooted in the context of the Depression, embodying the values of upward mobility, individual success, and romantic love. But *It Happened One Night* was influential in other ways. It is credited with exerting impact on the fashion industry: when Gable took off his shirt and exposed his sexy bare chest, the sale of undershirts declined substantially. The comedy also boosted domestic tourism, with a tremendous increase in the number of women traveling by bus hoping to meet their white knights on the road.

The second Oscar-winning comedy was also directed by Capra for Columbia, *You Can't Take It With You* (1938), based on George S. Kaufman and Moss Hart's Pulitzer Prize-winning stage hit, adapted to the screen by Robert Riskin. This zany comedy centers on a madcap family that believes in free enterprise, with each member dedicated to his/her own crazy habits. Nominated for seven Oscars, the film won two: Picture and Director. The comedy boasts a large and excellent cast, of which only Spring Byington was nominated for a supporting role for playing Penny, the eccentric mother who begins writing endless plays when a typewriter is left at her house by mistake. None of the rest of the cast—including Jimmy Stewart and Jean Arthur as the romantic couple, Lionel Barrymore as the charming grandfather, and Edward Arnold as the stuffy millionaire—was singled out for their acting.

The 1940s saw only one Oscar-winning comedy, *Going My Way* (1944), directed by Leo McCarey and starring Bing Crosby—as a progressive priest who turns a group of delinquents into a choir—and Barry Fitzgerald—who plays the old and irascible priest still attached to his ninety-year-old mother. Both Crosby and Fitzgerald won acting awards, the former in the lead and the latter in the supporting category. *Going My Way* was the only nominated comedy in 1944; the other nominees were two film noir, *Double Indemnity* and *Gaslight,* and two patriotic films, *Since You Went Away* and *Wilson.* Sweeping seven Oscars, *Going My Way* proved to be a sentimental favorite of the public too, ranking as that year's top-grossing movie.

Not a single comedy won Best Picture in the 1950s, and only two were cited in the 1960s: Billy Wilder's comedy-drama, *The Apartment,* and Tony Richardson's historical adventure-comedy *Tom Jones.* Among other distinctions, *The Apartment* (1960) is the last black-and- white film to win Best Picture. Though not one of Wilder's best films, it still offers biting commentary on big business, the ethos of success, and adultery, a consistent theme in the director's screen oeuvre. Lacking a clear point of view, the movie vacillates between sympathy and pity for its protagonists. Nonetheless, the acting of Jack Lemmon as the young ambitious, upwardly mobile executive, and of Shirley MacLaine as the elevator operator in the office building, was superb; both were nominated, though neither won.

The Apartment opened to mixed reviews, ranging from outright rejection, with critic Dwight MacDonald charging that it lacked "style or taste," to moderate praise. Hollis Alpert regarded the film as a "dirty fairy tale, with a schnook for a hero and a sad little elevator operator for a fairy princess." But 1960 was not a particularly strong year, which may have accounted for its win. *The Apartment* is still one of the few winners whose Oscar wasn't much help at the box office; with grosses of $6.6 million, it was the least commercially successful Oscar-winner of the 1960s.

By contrast, *Tom Jones* was a commercial success prior to winning the 1963 Oscar and a smash-hit afterward—it is one of the most popular films of the entire decade. The first all-British film to win the Oscar since *Hamlet* in 1948, *Tom Jones* made its star, Albert Finney, a household name in America. Based on Henry Fielding's famous novel, which was adapted to the screen by playwright John Osborne (who won an Oscar), it features Finney as the adventurous, amorous illegitimate son of a servant in eighteenth-century England. All three supporting women were nominated: Dame Edith Evans as the intrepid aunt, Diane Cilento as the wild gatekeeper's daughter, and best of all, Joyce Redman as a lady of easy virtue who seduces the hero over a large meal in a seduction scene that became the film's best remembered sequence.

Production values were high, particularly cinematography by Walter Lassally (which won), editing, and music score. Influenced by the French New Wave, Richardson used his camera in a jazzy and dynamic manner. *Tom Jones* was far superior to all the other nominees in 1963: *America, America, Cleopatra, How the West Was Won,* and *Lilies of the Field.*

It took a whole decade for another comedy to win. Singling out George Roy Hill's *The Sting* (1973), the Academy found itself under severe attack by its more serious critics. Cashing in on the previous success of his comedy Western *Butch Cassidy and the Sundance Kid,* Hill reteamed its stars, Paul Newman and Robert Redford, in a Depression-era comedy set in Chicago, about the conceits of two con men (Newman and Redford) against a big-time racketeer (Robert Shaw). Released to mostly good reviews, *The Sting* ranks high on *Variety*'s All-Time Champions list. Abundant with charm, the movie boasts Scott Joplin's great piano rags, which were adapted by Marvin Hamlisch and became popular throughout the country. Still, many felt that blockbusters like *The Sting* had no business being nominated for Oscars in the first place, let alone winning.

Woody Allen's semi-autobiographic comedy, *Annie Hall* (1977), is a bitter-sweet, introspective look at the unstable affair between Alvie Singer (Allen), an anxiety-ridden Jewish comic, and Annie Hall (Diane Keaton), an insecure WASPish singer. The contrast between Jewish and Gentile lifestyles was both touching and poignant. At once funny and sad, free-wheeling and self-reflexive, *Annie Hall* was punctuated by Allen addressing the audience directly in witty monologues. Establishing Allen as a major director, *Annie Hall* ranks as one of his most popular movies; the other is the 1986 Oscar-nominated *Hannah and Her Sisters.*

Blending comedy and melodrama, *Terms of Endearment* (1983) was basically a TV sitcom expanded to a bigscreen format. James Brooks's triple win, as producer, writer, and director, represented an astonishing achievement, considering that the screenplay had been turned down by several studios before Paramount decided to finance it. In its sentimental tone and traditional view of women, *Terms of Endearment* resembled many old-fashioned, well-made movies. However, most audiences enjoyed the honest, loving relationship between a possessive mother (Shirley MacLaine) and her daughter (Debra Winger), and especially the amusing sexual encounters between MacLaine's middle-aged widow and her boozy ex-astronaut neighbor (Jack Nicholson).

The film's candid view of middle-age sexuality, expressed in the way that Nicholson courted MacLaine, was refreshing. *Terms of Endearment*'s release at a time when most Hollywood movies were either action-adventure or teenage fare may explain its acclaim by the Academy and its huge commercial appeal.

The latest comedy to win Best Picture was the crowd-pleaser *Shakespeare in Love* (1998), shrewdly directed by Brit John Madden in a manner that combines poetry, art, and entertainment. Screenwriter William Goldman has pointed out that no movie in the 1990s was such a valentine to the theater, depicting actors as romantic fools who can only be happy and alive on stage. Marc Norman's idea provides the basis for a clever script, co-written with Tom Stoppard: the Bard has a writing block. The movie presents a portrait of the artist (played by Joseph Fiennes) as a young hack struggling with creativity and affairs of the heart.

All the ingredients were right for the Academy voters' taste. The film's title had a cachet too. Who can resist Shakespeare? Shakespeare signals the beginning of modern drama and pop culture as well. The 435-year-old writer is "hot" in Hollywood, as evident in numerous Shakespearean productions, from an MTV-influenced version of *Romeo and Juliet* to modern-costume renditions of *Richard III* and *Love's Labour's Lost*. For director John Madden, "there was nothing remotely academic about the film, it's all about first love."

David Denby complained in the *New Yorker* that *Shakespeare in Love* has bad jokes, silly sword fights, and a weak ending, yet, overall, the picture is charming. The year's richest romantic comedy, *Shakespeare in Love* was made with exuberant theatricality and wit, a celebration of populist entertainment. A literary-erotic fantasy about the composition of the world's most famous love story, the film is a romantic romp about the Bard and his radiant muse. Gwyneth Paltrow, who won Best Actress for her irresistible Viola, gave a career-making performance in a role that was turned down by Julia Roberts. It's a great part, allowing Paltrow to be a boy and a girl, with moods swinging from passionate and sexy all the way to heartbroken.

Geoffrey Rush won a supporting nomination as a theater owner shaken down by Elizabethan money men, and Dame Judi Dench won a supporting Oscar for playing with authority Queen Elizabeth, a small but significant part. The result was massive box-office appeal and an Oscar bonanza, leading with thirteen nominations, and winning Best Picture. The intelligent characters and colorful sets and costumes certainly helped, but the real star of the picture was the feverish wordplay and whimsical plot by Tom Stoppard and Marc Norman, who won an Oscar. Norman is credited with the story, but it is Stoppard who mixes aspects of philosophy, literature, fact and fancy, with wit and derring-do.

The largest number (sixteen) of comedies were nominated in the 1930s, arguably the genre's golden age in the sound era. Every brand of comedy was made and nominated in this decade, including Mae West's 1933 sex farce *She Done Him Wrong,* which would not have been nominated a year later because of the Hays Office Production Code. In 1934, the most popular of the nominated comedies was MGM's comedy-mystery, *The Thin Man,* which made William Powell and Myrna Loy movie stars and role models for married couples across the nation. Charles Laughton gave a wonderful performance in Leo McCarey's 1935 political comedy *Ruggles of Red Gap,* which contrasted values of British aristocracy and American democracy. McCarey was also represented in the contest with the sophisticated marital comedy, *The Awful Truth* (1937), starring Cary Grant and Irene Dunne. Some of MGM's female stars also distinguished themselves in Oscar-nominated comedies: Jean Harlow in *Libeled Lady* (1936), Garbo in the Ernst Lubitsch romantic comedy, *Ninotchka* (1939).

Of the nominated comedies in the 1940s, George Cukor's *The Philadelphia Story* (1940), starring Katharine Hepburn in one of her greatest performances, assisted by Jimmy Stewart and Cary Grant, stood out in its subtle staging and flawless acting. In the same year, Charlie Chaplin's *The Great Dictator,* in which he plays a dual role, Adenoid Hynkel, the dictator of Tomania (standing in for Hitler), and a Jewish ghetto barber, won recognition as both slapstick comedy and political satire.

Columbia's *Here Comes Mr. Jordan* won the two writing awards of 1941, original story and screenplay, recounting a fantasy in which a prizefighter (Robert Montgomery) is sent by mistake to heaven and then back to earth in search of a new body. This popular film later served as the inspiration for Warren Beatty's 1978 *Heaven Can Wait,* which also received Best Picture nomination. The original *Heaven Can Wait* (1943) was Lubitsch's account of family life in nineteenth-century Hungary, with gorgeous sets and costumes.

In the same year, George Stevens's *The More the Merrier*, a war comedy about housing conditions in Washington, D.C., starred Jean Arthur as a civil servant renting her small apartment to an old gentleman (Charles Coburn) who in turn rents it to an attractive man (Joel McCrea). Coburn won a supporting Oscar for playing a daffy millionaire.

Not many comedies were nominated in the 1950s. The most commercial nominee was the service comedy *Mister Roberts* (1955), starring Henry Fonda in his best-known role, as the first officer on the *Reluctant*, a cargo ship miles away from the battle zone, whose route is described by him as "from Tedium to Apathy, and back again, with an occasional side trip to Monotony." The war is close to an end, and Roberts is anxious to get into combat before it is too late. Fonda's performance was unaccountably ignored by the Academy in a shameful oversight. By contrast, Jack Lemmon's Ensign Pulver, a flighty fellow assigned to laundry detail, won him his first (supporting) Oscar. Like Fonda, Rosalind Russell re-created her successful stage role in the 1958 film version *Auntie Mame*, which, with over nine million dollars, outgrossed the box-office receipts of the Oscar winner that year, *Gigi*.

The most original of the 1950s nominated comedies was George Cukor's *Born Yesterday* (1950), based on Garson Kanin's stage play, in which Judy Holliday's dumb-shrewd blonde Billie Dawn is victimized by a rough and rude junk dealer (Broderick Crawford) and educated by a sensitive Washington correspondent (William Holden). The first part of the picture is funny, and many wished Holliday's character didn't have to be socialized, because the romantically "educational" sessions with Holden drag the picture down.

The appeal of *Born Yesterday* was also due to its political message, the attempt of a scrap metal dealer to bribe a bill through Congress and the successful fight of a none-too-bright woman against political corruption, timely subject-matter after World War II, in that it condemned the dealers who profited from the war economy. Arthur Miller dealt with a similar issue in *All My Sons*, first as a Broadway play, then as a Hollywood movie.

The 1950s also saw their share of romantic comedies. William Wyler's stylish *Roman Holiday* (1953), starring Audrey Hepburn as a European princess, and Gregory Peck as an American reporter, was elegant and featured location shooting, albeit in black and white. In the following year, the Academy nominated Fox's romantic comedy, *Three Coins in the Fountain*, also set in Rome, which received a cinematography Oscar for its sumptuous color lensing. It also won Best Song, by Sammy Cahn and Jule Styne, which contributed to the film's popularity, showing, like *High Noon*'s ballad, how effectively a song can be used for the movie's marketing.

The comedies nominated in the 1960s were of great variability. In 1964, Stanley Kubrick's black comedy, *Dr. Strangelove; or, How I Learned to Stop Worrying and Love the Bomb,* was ahead of its time in its antinuclear message, depicting military generals as irresponsible puppets enamored of their limitless power. Peter Sellers excelled in playing three widely contrasting roles: the American President, a British RAF Captain, and best of all, a mad German scientist, whose heavy accent was inspired by the physicist Edward Teller.

The film was popular with audiences, though not as much as *Mary Poppins,* which was also nominated for Best Picture in 1964. It must have been a good year for comedies, for a third nominee was Michael Cacoyannis's *Zorba the Greek,* based on Nikos Kazantzakis's best-selling novel. Anthony Quinn was cast in what became his signature role, the no-nonsense, garrulous force of virility, contrasted in the picture with Alan Bates's British reservedness.

Toward the end of the decade, two comedies that reflected the new zeitgeist of youth culture and racial diversity were nominated. Mike Nichols's second feature, *The Graduate,* was nominated for seven awards, but won only Best Director. Nonetheless, it legitimized youth counterculture and the generation gap through the character of the nonconformist Benjamin Braddock, played to perfection by Dustin Hoffman. The other 1967 nominated comedy was Stanley Kramer's *Guess Who's Coming to Dinner* one of Hollywood's first films about interracial marriage. Both pictures aimed at younger audiences, and both were stronger in ideas than in artistic execution, which is the reason why neither, particularly *Guess,* holds up well.

Few comedies were nominated in the early 1970s. George Lucas's nostalgic view of youth, *American Graffiti* (1973), set in California in 1962, was used as a metaphor of "what we once had and lost." Made on a shoestring budget, it soon became a sleeper, launching a whole cycle of rock 'n' roll high school movies. But as the decade came to an end, more comedies were made and more were nominated. Paul Mazursky's *An Unmarried Woman* (1978), starring Jill Clayburgh, was a timely comedy which reflected the changing position of women in American society.

Of the cycle of comedies about the changing definitions of gender, masculinity, and femininity, Sydney Pollack's *Tootsie* (1982) was the most accomplished and also the most honored, with ten nominations. A witty, topical comedy, written by Larry Gelbart and Murray Schisgal, it provides commentary on love, sex, and friendship. It stars Dustin Hoffman as Dorothy Michaels, an unemployed actor who becomes daytime television's most popular star after disguising himself as a woman. All members of the cast played their parts to the hilt, and four received nominations: Hoffman, Teri Garr as Hoffman's unemployed and rejected girlfriend, Jessica Lange as the submissive and sexy actress, and Charles Durning as Lange's widowed father who falls for Hoffman.

No Respect for Comedy

The Academy has shown a consistent lack of respect for comedic performances. For some reason, they are considered to be "easier," more effortless than dramatic performances. Leading actresses have seldom won an Oscar for a role in comedy. It took twenty years after Audrey Hepburn's Best Actress win for *Roman Holiday* for the next actress to win an Oscar for a comedy, Glenda Jackson in *A Touch of Class*. Men winning for performances in comedies have not been much more visible. No Best Actor won for a comedy between Jimmy Stewart in *The Philadelphia Story,* in 1940, and Lee Marvin in *Cat Ballou,* twenty-five years later.

Supporting Oscars for comedies have been more prevalent. Peter Ustinov won a second supporting Oscar for playing a con man, talked into a robbery by Melina Mercouri in Jules Dassin's *Topkapi* (1964). Ustinov's misadventures as a tour guide afraid of his own shadow provided the most hilarious scenes in the movie. George Burns excelled in Neil Simon's *The Sunshine Boys* (1975), as a veteren vaudevillian reunited with his old partner (Walter Matthau) after decades of hostility.

Of the supporting comediennes, Josephine Hull gave a riotous performance in *Harvey* (1950), as Jimmy Stewart's distraught, scatter-brained sister who ends up in a mental institution she had intended for him. And Eileen Heckart received a well-deserved supporting Oscar as the overbearing, overprotective mother of her blind son in *Butterflies Are Free* (1972).

That comedy has been overlooked by the Academy is also reflected in the underrepresentation of comedy writers-directors. Take Charlie Chaplin, whose contribution to the genre is indisputable. Of Chaplin's major works, only *The Great Dictator* was nominated for Best Picture, though it did not win a single award. *The Circus* (1928), *City Lights* (1931), and *Modern Times* (1936) failed to receive nominations. Chaplin was nominated twice as Best Actor, for *The Circus* and, as noted, for *The Great Dictator,* losing on both occasions.

Preston Sturges, another extraordinary filmmaker, won only one Oscar, Best Original Screenplay, for his first film as a director, *The Great McGinty* (1940). Despite originality, urbane sophistication, and biting humor, none of Sturges's comedies was nominated for Best Picture, though at least three deserved serious consideration: *Sullivan's Travels* (1941), *The Palm Beach Story* (1942), and *Hail the Conquering Hero* (1944). The writers' branch was more appreciative of Sturges's work, and in 1944, he became the first scribe to have two scripts, *Hail the Conquering Hero* and *The Miracle of Morgan's Creek,* nominated for Best Original Screenplay; the winner was Lamar Trotti for the biopicture *Wilson.*

None of the "classical" clowns has ever won a legitimate Oscar or even a nomination. True, most of them did their best work in the silent era, prior to Oscar's birth, but even those who contributed to the genre later were overlooked by the Academy. The other members of the "clowns triumvirate" (which consisted, along with Charlie Chaplin, of Harold Lloyd and Buster Keaton), were also overlooked by the Academy, which later used its Honorary Oscars as corrective measures. In 1952, Lloyd was awarded a Special Oscar as "a master comedian and good citizen." Unlike Lloyd, Buster Keaton made some excellent comedies in the sound era, when he was under contract at MGM—*Cameraman* (1928) and *Spite Marriage* (1929)—but he never won the Academy recognition. Once again, a 1959 Special Oscar cited Keaton, the King of Comedy, for his "unique talents which brought comedies to the screen."

The popular comedy team Stan Laurel and Oliver Hardy was also underestimated during its lifetime. Joining forces in 1926, Laurel and Hardy delighted audiences with their inventive acts for decades. In 1960, three years after Hardy's death from cancer, the Academy honored his surviving partner, who had refused to perform after his colleague's death, with an Oscar "for his creative pioneering in the field of cinema comedy."

The Academy's bias against comedy was also apparent in the case of excellent comedians who had to deviate from this genre to gain the Academy's respect. The best example of these actors is Cary Grant, who distinguished himself in romantic as well as screwball comedies. It was comedy, beginning with *The Awful Truth,* which made him a star. The public preferred to see Grant in comedies, the best of which were those opposite Katharine Hepburn *(Bringing up Baby, Holiday)* and Rosalind Russell *(His Girl Friday),* but none of them brought him a nomination.

Grant had to step outside of his specialty to earn his nominations. The first was for a sentimental melodrama, *Penny Serenade* (1941), as a married man who loses his adopted daughter, and the second for a "serious-dramatic" role in Clifford Odets's *None but the Lonely Heart* (1944), as a Cockney drifter. No other actor of Grant's generation contributed more to screen comedy, but the Academy took for granted his acting, which appeared facile and natural. In actuality, it was a product of hard work and meticulous preparation. It took years of practice to perfect the genius timing, spontaneity, and naturalness in which Grant, Carole Lombard, Claudette Colbert, and others excelled. The Academy "corrected" this injustice by honoring Grant with a 1972 compensatory Oscar "for being Cary Grant."

Jack Lemmon's Oscars also show the Academy's biases against comedy. Lemmon began his screen career in comedies, often cast opposite Judy Holliday *(It Should Happen to You, Phfft)*. He later became the quintessential Billy Wilder actor, appearing in seven of his films, including *Some Like It Hot* (his first lead nomination) and *The Apartment* (his second). The Neil Simon comedies, *The Fortune Cookie* and *The Odd Couple*, further established Lemmon as one of the foremost comedians. Ironically, Lemmon received his acting accolades for straight "dramatic" performances, first for playing an alcoholic in *Days of Wine and Roses* (1962), a career breakthrough for which he earned a nomination. Lemmon won his Best Actor (and second) Oscar for *Save the Tiger* (1973), a film about the moral disintegration of a garment manufacturer who, in financial desperation, resorts to arson. For some reason, the character's self-pity and disenchantment with the American value system made Lemmon's acting seem more "serious" and "substantial."

Tom Hanks also won two Best Actor Oscars for dramas, for *Philadelphia* (1993) and for *Forrest Gump* (1994). In *Philadelphia*, he played the AIDS-stricken lawyer Andrew Beckett who fights for his human rights when he is fired from his job. Historically, Hollywood's top stars have steered clear from portraying gay characters, fearing it would harm their careers. *Philadelphia* was a bold departure for Hanks, then best known for his comedy skills in *Big, Sleepless in Seattle,* and *A League of Their Own.*

Hanks was nominated again for *Saving Private Ryan* (1998), for a role in which he delivered, as *Variety* wrote, "the kind of mature, thinking man's blend of guts and heart that the Academy loves." Lauren Shuler-Donner, who produced the Hanks vehicle *You've Got Mail,* said she would cast her vote for this comedy, because "Tom deserves another Oscar," but she conceded that Hanks would be nominated for *Saving Private Ryan,* because "the Academy goes for drama over comedy most of the time."

Underestimating comedy performers is not exclusive to the Academy. Other film associations have also failed to honor comedy films and performers. Neither Cary Grant nor Jack Lemmon have ever won the New York Film Critics Circle, for example. Steve Martin, honored in 1984 by the New York Film Critics and the National Society of Film Critics for his physical comedy in *All of Me* is the exception rather than the rule. Most performers know when they are cast in comedies that their films may be popular with the public but will not get Academy recognition. When British actress Julie Walters was nominated for *Educating Rita* (1984), in which she played a hairdresser eager to get higher education, her reaction was: "I won't win. They don't give Oscars for comedy."

The Golden Globes and the Tony Awards distinguish between comedy and drama to ensure that comedy gets its fair representation and due respect. However, by doing so, they increase the number of awards and diminish their relative prestige.

Musicals

In contrast to comedies, musical films have been overrepresented in the Best Picture category. Eight of the seventy-two winning films have been musicals. As a genre, musicals featured most impressively during the Great Depression—about half of all nominated musicals were made in the 1930s. By contrast, the weakest representation of musicals in the Oscar contest was in the 1940s, with only two nominees, *Yankee Doodle Dandy* and *Anchors Aweigh*. Hollywood was not willing to take risks with new ideas, and subsequently most of the nominated musicals from the 1950s on were based on Broadway hits. The few exceptions of Oscar-nominated musicals that originated on the big screen are *Seven Brides for Seven Brothers* (1954) and *Mary Poppins* (1964).

There is no logical link between the number or quality of musicals made and their representation in the Oscar contest. More musicals won Oscars in the 1960s than in any other decade, despite the fact that not many were made. Ironically, it seems that just as the musical genre began to decline, it gained in prestige. The Academy showed its dutiful respect for the effort involved in making musicals by honoring more of them.

The first Oscar-winning musical, *The Broadway Melody* (1928/29), was MGM's first musical and also the first talking film to be honored. Advertised as "All Talking, All Singing, All Dancing," it also featured the innovation of color: one number, "The Wedding of the Painted Doll," was presented in two colors. A backstage musical, it is the tale of two sisters (Bessie Love and Anita Page), who seek fame in the New York theatre, and in the process fall in love with the same song-and-dance man. By today's standards, the story and characters are cliché-ridden, but in 1929, the novelty of sound, color, and form proved winning.

Bessie Love's nominated performance as the older, wiser sister who sacrifices herself for her sister's career was truly touching. A big-budgeted film, close to half a million dollars, *The Broadway Melody* opened to rave reviews, soon becoming the season's second top-grosser with three million dollars in ticket sales. It was a good year for musicals: Fox's musical, *Sunny Side Up*, with Janet Gaynor and Charles Farrell at the height of their popularity, was 1929's most commercial movie.

The Broadway Melody was such a hit that MGM made three more *Broadway Melody* films, of which *Broadway Melody of 1936*, released in 1935, is considered to be the best. It is also one of the few sequels to be nominated for Best Picture. The supporting cast—particularly Jack Benny as the columnist, and June Knight as a no-talent who wants to become an actress—was more impressive than the leads, played by Robert Taylor and Eleanor Powell. The movie won one Oscar: dance direction for David Gould's sequence, "I've Got a Feeling You're Foolin'."

In the 1930s, most studios produced musicals, each developing its own distinct style. MGM was represented in the Oscars with *The Great Ziegfeld* (1936), the second Oscar-winning musical, and later with *The Wizard of Oz* (1939). Paramount participated with some sophisticated operettas that flaunted "the Lubitsch touch," such as *The Love Parade* (1929), *The Smiling Lieutenant* (1931), and *One Hour With You* (1934), all starring Maurice Chevalier. RKO left its imprint on the decade's musical map with the fabulous dancing of Fred Astaire and Ginger Rogers. Two of their musicals were nominated for Best Picture: *The Gay Divorcée* (1934) and *Top Hat* (1935).

Of Warner's major Depression musicals, only one was nominated, *42nd Street* (1933), with Warner Baxter, Ruby Keeler, and Dick Powell, though it did not win any award. Harry Cohn, head of Columbia Pictures, was not in favor of making musicals, yet having Grace Moore, the Metropolitan Opera diva, under contract convinced him to make *One Night of Love* (1934), a variation on the Svengali theme. Moore, as the rising star, was also nominated, and the film won sound recording and music score. *Alexander's Ragtime Band* (1938), 20th Century-Fox's big-scale musical, with a wonderful score by Irving Berlin and a cast headed by Tyrone Power, Alice Faye, and Don Ameche, also received a Best Picture nomination and an Oscar for Alfred Newman's musical direction.

In the 1940s and 1950s, MGM dominated the musical genre in the Oscar Awards. Of the six nominated musicals, four were produced by MGM, and the two of them were directed by Vincente Minnelli. *An American in Paris*, George Gershwin's musical about the romance of a young American painter (Gene Kelly) and a poor French girl (Leslie Caron), was the big winner of 1951, with six Oscars for story and screenplay (Alan Jay Lerner), musical scoring (Johnny Green and Saul Chaplin), and other technical awards.

The second Oscar-winning Minnelli musical was *Gigi* (1958), based on Colette's story, again set in Paris and starring Leslie Caron, as a shy girl groomed to become an elegant lady. Applying a uniquely French charm to the American-musical tradition, *Gigi,* an original movie musical, won the largest number (nine) of awards to date, including Director (Minnelli), Screenplay (Alan Jay Lerner), and color cinematography (Joseph Ruttenberg).

Paradoxically, more musicals won Best Picture in the 1960s, when the genre was in decline, than in any other decade. Four of the ten Best Pictures in the 1960s were musicals: United Artists's *West Side Story* (1961), Warner's *My Fair Lady* (1964), 20th Century-Fox's *The Sound of Music* (1965), and Columbia's *Oliver!* (1968), a British-made movie. All four musicals were based on Broadway hits, but each one involved a major cast change, the most publicized of which was the casting of Audrey Hepburn as Eliza Doolittle, a role played with great success by Julie Andrews on stage.

Each of these winning musicals represents some kind of landmark in the genre's history. Transporting Shakespeare's *Romeo and Juliet* to the slums of New York and boasting exuberant music by Leonard Bernstein and witty lyrics by Stephen Sondheim, *West Side Story* is the only winner in the Academy's history to receive awards in all (ten) but one of its multiple nominations. Furthermore, it is the only Oscar winner to be co-directed —Robert Wise and Jerome Robbins shared the directing award. *West Side Story* still ranks second, next to *Ben-Hur,* as the most Oscar-honored film.

The stylishly elegant *My Fair Lady,* which was nominated for twelve awards and won eight, was selected in 1964, a year that saw the decline of the classic musical and the rise of a new kind of musical, beginning with Richard Lester's Beatles vehicle, *A Hard Day's Night.* George Cukor, who won an Oscar at his fifth nomination, directed an opulent production in a grand manner, with fabulous costumes designed by Cecil Beaton. With the conspicuous omission of Audrey Hepburn in the lead role, its three British players, Rex Harrison, Stanley Holloway (as Alfred P. Doolittle), and Gladys Cooper (as Mrs. Higgins) were nominated, and Harrison deservedly won. *My Fair Lady* won over another musical, *Mary Poppins,* the first of two Walt Disney productions—the other is *Beauty and the Beast* in 1991—ever to be nominated for the top award, although *My Fair Lady* was much less commercially successful than the latter.

By contrast, the immense commercial success of the 1965 winner, Robert Wise's *The Sound of Music* became a desirable goal for every studio in Hollywood to emulate. Winning five of its ten nominations, it is, along with *Titanic* and *Gone With the Wind,* one of the most commercial

Oscar winners, grossing close to eighty million dollars in rentals. Based on Howard Lindsay and Russel Crouse's long-running Broadway musical, with music by Richard Rodgers and Oscar Hammerstein II, it represented Hollywood filmmaking at its most calculating.

Set in Austria in 1938, *The Sound of Music*'s narrative consists of stilted devices, each aiming to appeal to a different segment of the public. Advertised as entertainment for the whole family and a genuine celebration of life, it is high corn—American Kitsch. The motherless Von Trapp family of seven children, headed by Christopher Plummer, becomes a troupe of singers under the benevolence of Maria, the nun-turned-governess (Julie Andrews), thus eluding the Nazis and successfully escaping first to Switzerland and then to America.

Rather shrewdly, *The Sound of Music* includes two generational romances: Plummer and his haughty baroness (embarrassingly played by Eleanor Parker), whom he later deserts for the simpler and maternal Andrews; and a youthful romance. Ideologically, the musical cherishes family strength and religious benevolence, and is placed in a political setting imbued with anti-Nazi feelings. More importantly, it was shot in the stunning landscapes of the Austrian Alps and Salzburg. Ingeniously packaged and sold to the public, *The Sound of Music* was released in March, while Julie Andrews was still the talk of the town for *Mary Poppins,* and it became clear she would get the Best Actress in the upcoming ceremonies (in April). Andrews's win made *The Sound of Music* even more popular at the box office.

The 1965 competition for Best Picture was rather weak. Stanley Kramer's flawed and pretentious *Ship of Fools* and the screen adaptation of the Broadway comedy *A Thousand Clowns* stood no chance of winning. The other two contenders were made by British directors, David Lean's *Doctor Zhivago,* a romantic spectacle, and John Schlesinger's *Darling,* clearly the most innovative of the nominees, which was singled out earlier by the New York Film Critics. For most Academy members, the choice was between *The Sound of Music* and *Doctor Zhivago;* each received ten nominations. The awards were also equally divided, with each movie getting five, though, except for screenplay (Robert Bolt), *Doctor Zhivago* received mostly technical awards.

Fox hoped to repeat the success story of *The Sound of Music,* dubbed in Hollywood as "the sound of money," with two subsequent musicals that were poorly conceived and executed: *Doctor Dolittle* (1967), starring Rex Harrison, and *Hello, Dolly!* (1969), starring Barbra Streisand. These movies received multiple nominations, *Dolittle* nine and *Dolly* seven, not because of their merits but because of their shamelessly expensive campaigns (see chapter 14).

From 1970 to the present, only three musicals have been nominated for Best Picture: *Fiddler on the Roof* (1971), *Cabaret* (1972), and *All That Jazz* (1979). Michael Apted's *Coal Miner's Daughter* (1980), was a biopicture of country singer Loretta Lynn rather than a conventional musical. Similarly, *Amadeus,* the 1984 Oscar winner, was at once more and less than a genre musical, though one of its achievements was the way Mozart's music was integrated into the narrative.

The only musical to be nominated for Best Picture over the last two decades is *Beauty and the Beast,* in 1991. Disney's feature, co-directed by Gary Trousdale and Kirk Wise, became the first animated feature to get the top Academy recognition. Producer Don Hahn saw the film's Best Picture status as a "validation of animation as a legitimate way to tell a story," as well as a tribute to the long-lasting legacy of Disney. Cannily presented in the style of a Broadway musical, with a finely tuned script by Linda Woolverton, *Beauty and the Beast* racked up six nominations and won two Oscars for its music—Alan Menken's score and the title tune co-written with Howard Ashman. That Menken died of AIDS just before the ceremonies suggests that the awards show the Academy's sympathy for AIDS victims.

Up to the 1950s, the filmmakers of the winning musicals were not honored by the Academy. Vincente Minnelli was nominated for *An American in Paris,* but did not win; the winner was George Stevens for *A Place in the Sun.* Minnelli won his first and only Oscar for *Gigi,* at his second nomination. By contrast, all the directors of the winning musicals in the 1960s received an Oscar, some long overdue. George Cukor is the only filmmaker to have won the Oscar *(My Fair Lady)* at his fifth nomination. And British director Carol Reed was singled out for his direction of *Oliver!* at his third nomination. The separation between Best Picture and Best Director has been rare, but in 1972, the Academy chose Bob Fosse as Best Director for *Cabaret* and *The Godfather* as Best Picture; Francis Ford Coppola was nominated but did not win.

Musicals have not been generous to their performers as far as acting Oscars are concerned. Only a few players, mostly women, have won an Oscar for a musical role. Luise Rainer was the first to win Best Actress for a musical, as Ziegfeld's first wife, Anna Held, in *The Great Ziegfeld.* The next musical winner was Julie Andrews, almost three decades later, as the magical governess in *Mary Poppins.* Two winners have appeared in musical biographies: Barbra Streisand as Fanny Brice in *Funny Girl,* and Sissy Spacek as Loretta Lynn in *Coal Miner's Daughter.* One of the most brilliant performances in a musical was delivered by Liza Minnelli in *Cabaret,* as Sally Bowles, the ambitious night club singer in pre-Nazi Germany. The two male Oscar-winners in the musical genre have been Yul Brynner in *The King and I,* and Rex Harrison in *My Fair Lady.*

Most acting nominations in musicals were selected after 1950; Bessie Love and Gene Kelly *(Anchors Aweigh)* were the exceptions. Fred Astaire and Ginger Rogers were never nominated for any of their musicals. Rogers won Academy recognition only when she proved she could handle a dramatic role, as the Irish girl from the wrong side of the tracks in *Kitty Foyle* (1940). She herself was anxious to demonstrate that she was much more than Fred Astaire's dancing partner, though it is in this capacity she is best remembered today. The biases against musical performers have been similar to those against comedy performers.

What to Make of It

Going beyond analysis of genre, one might ask what are the most crucial attributes of Oscar-winning films? One way to answer this question is to examine the filmmakers who have dominated the competition. William Wyler, Fred Zinnemann, and David Lean have occupied special positions in the Academy annals in two ways: many of their films were nominated for Best Picture, and many performers in their films have received Oscar nominations and awards.

Of the three, Wyler is the most diverse, at least in genre, having directed serious dramas, Westerns, romantic comedies, and even musicals. Three of Wyler's films won Best Picture: *Mrs. Miniver, The Best Years of Our Lives,* and *Ben-Hur.* Wyler often brought out the best from his performers, with thirteen Oscar-winning roles in his films: Walter Brennan *(Come and Get It,* co-directed with Howard Hawks, and *The Westerner),* Bette Davis and Faye Bainter *(Jezebel),* Greer Garson and Teresa Wright *(Mrs. Miniver),* Fredric March and Harold Russell *(The Best Years of Our Lives),* Olivia de Havilland *(The Heiress),* Audrey Hepburn *(Roman Holiday),* Burl Ives *(The Big Country),* Charlton Heston and Hugh Griffith *(Ben-Hur),* and Barbra Streisand *(Funny Girl).*

Wyler was the Academy's most respected and most honored director: over half of his thirty-five sound movies brought their players nominations. Wyler's films may have contained the largest number of Oscar-winning or nominated performances due to his use, with cinematographer Gregg Toland, of long takes and deep-focus (in which characters appear in the same frame for the duration of entire scenes), thus enabling their actors to achieve continuity and coherence. These strategies required discipline and concentration on the part of screen players, most of whom were used to acting in bits and pieces, the predominant norm of shooting in Hollywood. A meticulous craftsman, Wyler was nicknamed "90-take Wyler" for the numerous takes he demanded. Accused of being a tyrant, Wyler often clashed with his actors, yet most of them have done their best work in his movies.

However, the Wyler films that won Best Picture and Best Director did not necessarily represent his most distinguished or characteristic work, among which are *Dodsworth, The Letter,* and *Little Foxes. Mrs. Miniver* won for political rather than artistic reasons, and the historical epic *Ben-Hur* did not bear Wyler's signature as a filmmaker, who was at his best in adapting literary works to the screen. Wyler's reputation suffered in the 1960s and 1970s, along with that of Zinnemann, when auteurist critics could not discern consistent or idiosyncratic elements in his work compared with those of the more obvious auteurs such as Fritz Lang, John Ford, and Howard Hawks. Yet as Vincent Canby observed, Wyler was best at "submerging his own personality to obtain the most effective realization of the work of others," and it is this "extraordinary consistency of purpose and achievement" that is his distinctive trademark.

If consistent artistic quality was Wyler's signature, Zinnemann's trademark was a middlebrow humanistic conception, which defined mainstream Hollywood in the 1950s and 1960s. Zinnemann directed two Oscar-winners, *From Here to Eternity* and *A Man for All Seasons,* and four Oscar-nominated pictures, *High Noon, The Nun's Story, The Sundowners,* and *Julia.* Considering the duration of his career, over half a century, his film oeuvre was rather small: twenty-two features. Nonetheless, the number of Oscar-winning performances in Zinnemann's films was disproportionately large. Eighteen players were nominated in his movies, some more than once, like Montgomery Clift in *The Search,* as a sensitive American soldier befriending an orphan in Europe right after the war, and in *From Here to Eternity,* as yet another sensitive soldier. Six of Zinnemann's actors won Oscars: Gary Cooper *(High Noon),* Frank Sinatra and Donna Reed *(From Here to Eternity),* Paul Scofield *(A Man for All Seasons),* and Vanessa Redgrave and Jason Robards *(Julia).* Some performers have done their best work in his films—Marlon Brando in his debut, *The Men,* Audrey Hepburn in *The Nun's Story,* and Julie Harris and Ethel Waters in *The Member of the Wedding.*

Zinnemann was considered to be a "dream director," due to his respect for actors. His movies were "perfect Oscar material," with their sensitive subject matter, humanistic orientation, and conflicted characters. Zinnemann's films also displayed thematic consistency. Asked to describe the narratives that attract him, he said: "I just like to do films that are positive in the sense that they deal with the dignity of human beings and have something to say about oppression. Moral courage has interested me the most. I look for the universal theme that will allow the audience to identify with the characters." What fascinated him about *Julia,* his last nominated film, was "the friendship of the two women and the issue of conscience. I always find questions of conscience very photogenic. That kind of interior drama is to me very exciting."

Zinnemann's early films were produced by Stanley Kramer, who was highly committed to problem films propagating liberal causes, such as racial equality *(Home of the Brave, The Defiant Ones),* political justice *(Judgment at Nuremberg),* and interracial marriage *(Guess Who's Coming to Dinner).* Kramer was one of the first Hollywood filmmakers to make mainstream movies about pressing social issues. Several of his films were nominated for Best Picture, despite unimaginative approaches and flat, static direction.

Ship of Fools was nominated for eight Oscars in 1965, including Best Picture, because it was considered to be "important," dealing with a group of passengers *("Grand Hotel* on water") aboard a ship bound for Germany in 1933. The movie was pretentious and technically crude and shapeless, yet a number of powerful performances and a symbolic message must have overshadowed its weakness, and the Academy proved again the primacy of subject matter over style and form. Like Zinnemann, Kramer was a "sociological" director, though he lacked the veteran director's command of technical skills.

Zinnemann's humanist approach to filmmaking is almost nonexistent in Hollywood today. In 1986, when British producer David Puttnam *(Chariots of Fire, The Killing Fields)* was appointed chair of Columbia, he hoped to reinstate Zinnemann's kinds of films. As he said, "If I had to characterize the films I like in terms of another filmmaker, they're not unlike Fred Zinnemann's films. They're about people finding within themselves resources they didn't know were there, and coming from the best of them." Puttnam didn't stay in power long enough to implement his ambitions, and it is doubtful that he would have succeeded even if he had.

One of the few filmmakers to combine intriguing issues, complex characters, and grand epic style was David Lean, whose work is a *perfect* example of the kinds of films that tend to win Oscars. Six of Lean's movies have been nominated, from *In Which We Serve,* co-directed by Noel Coward, through *Great Expectations, Doctor Zhivago,* and *A Passage to India.* Unlike other directors, Lean was also effective at making more intimate films *(Brief Encounter),* literary adaptations *(Oliver Twist),* and documentary-style narratives *(Breaking the Sound Barrier),* but he achieved international recognition when he switched to epic-style movies, beginning with *The Bridge on the River Kwai.*

The second crucial feature of Oscar films is glossy production values, expressed in sweeping visual style and epic vision—along with epic budget and epic running time. *Ordinary People* and *Terms of Endearment* were among the few "modest" films to have won Best Picture Oscars in the 1980s. The other winners have all been large-scaled and super-produced: *Chariots of Fire* in 1981, *Gandhi* in 1982, *Amadeus* in 1984, *Out of Africa* in 1985, and *The Last Emperor* in 1987.

Most Oscar-winning films have been big-budgeted, from the very first one, *Wings,* through *Gone With the Wind* in the 1930s; *Ben-Hur* in the 1950s; *Lawrence of Arabia* and *Tom Jones* in the 1960s; and *The Godfather* movies in the 1970s. If the 1940s are conspicuously underrepresented, it is due to the impact of an austere war economy on film production and the dominance of war pictures.

Lengthy running time has impressed not only moviegoers but also Academy members. The running time of over half of the winners has been in excess of the average 100 to 120 minutes. *Wings*'s running time was 136 minutes, *The Great Ziegfeld* 179, *Gone With the Wind* 220, *The Best Years of Our Lives* 182, *Around the World in 80 Days* 178, *Out of Africa* 150, *The Last Emperor* 166. This is especially true in the case of winners in the 1990s: *Dances With Wolves* 181 minutes, *Schindler's List* 195, *Forrest Gump* 142, *Braveheart* 177, *The English Patient* 162, *Titanic* 194.

Delbert Mann's *Marty* (1955) and Woody Allen's *Annie Hall* (1977) are still the notable exceptions: the former claims a running time of 91 minutes, and the latter, 93. Together, they are the shortest features of all Oscar winners.

CHAPTER 10

Oscar-Winning Roles

W hich screen roles tend to get Oscar nominations and awards? Is it possible to generalize about the kinds of roles that receive the Academy's attention? Have there been "typical" Oscar roles for men and for women?

Oscar-winning roles are usually contained in popular movies widely seen by the public, thus functioning as potential agencies of socialization, particularly for adolescents, who are the most frequent and avid moviegoers. From this perspective, the Oscar roles can serve as indicators of what the American cinema has been telling its audience about the appropriate (and inappropriate) behaviors for men and for women. Mainstream Hollywood movies are designed to appeal to the largest potential audiences, which means that filmmakers try to make movies that would be acceptable to them. The particular attributes of male and female Oscar-winning roles can therefore shed light on the cultural guidelines, proscriptions and prescriptions, that the American cinema has provided for male and female viewers.

Oscar and Genre

Favoring biopictures over fictional films, the Academy has rewarded actors who play biographical roles: about one-fifth of all Oscar-winning roles have been inspired by real-life personalities. Recreating real-life figures brings a measure of prestige to their performers, particularly if their characters were important in their time. However, a clear gender-related bias is in operation: the number of biographical Oscar roles is twice as large among the men than the women, particularly in the lead categories.

Male biographical roles have been more diverse, both historically and occupationally. Men have portrayed military figures, such as Gary Cooper as Alvin York, the Tennessee farmer who became a World War I hero in

Sergeant York, and George C. Scott as General Patton, World War II's controversial but brilliant strategist, in *Patton.* Historical figures have included Charles Laughton as the English monarch in *The Private Life of Henry VIII,* and Paul Scofield as Sir Thomas More in *A Man for All Seasons.* Men have also played political personalities, like George Arliss, as the British prime minister in *Disraeli,* and Ben Kingsley as the venerable Indian leader in *Gandhi.*

Women, by contrast, have mostly portrayed showbiz figures, like Luise Rainer, showman Florenz Ziegfeld's first wife in *The Great Ziegfeld;* Barbra Streisand as musical star Fanny Brice in *Funny Girl;* Sissy Spacek as country singer Loretta Lynn in *Coal Miner's Daughter,* and, most recently, Gwyneth Paltrow as the Bard's muse in *Shakespeare in Love.*

The underrepresentation of women in biopictures celebrating real-life achievements suggests that perhaps there have not been enough prominent women in science, politics, and literature for the movies to draw upon. But one could also argue that movies were reluctant to use real-life heroines for screen biographies, thus functioning as agencies of social control, keeping women "in their place" by confining them to the domestic arena or to show business, two traditional female domains.

Oscar roles have generally been contained in specific genres. The most frequent genre, for both male and female roles, is the serious drama, with 60 percent of all Oscar roles. Few of the Oscar roles have been in romantic melodramas, musicals, thrillers, and Westerns. But there has been unequal distribution of male and female roles in these genres, attesting to the prevalence of "masculine" and "feminine" genres. The second most frequent genre among the men is the action-adventure (including war films and Westerns), amounting to one-fifth of all male roles, with only a few female roles in this genre, usually in the supporting category.

The most "feminine" genre, the female equivalent of the action-adventure, is the romantic melodrama, particularly in the Best Actress category; no man has ever won an Oscar for such a film. In suspense films, there has been only one male winner, but four females, with women typically cast as victims, like Joan Fontaine in *Suspicion* and Ingrid Bergman in *Gaslight.*

Oscar and Gender

Actors tend to win the Oscar at an older age than actresses, which means that their winning roles are depictions of older characters. According to Oscar, the American screen heroine is typically young: three-fifths of all female Oscar roles have been young, compared with only one-sixth of the males. And conversely, over half of the male characters, but only one-fifth of the female, have been middle-aged. Characters in supporting roles, both male and female, have been older than those in leading roles.

Within each lead category, there is one dominant age group: young for women, middle-aged for men. American culture, as expressed in film, has prescribed consistent distinctions: screen heroines are much younger than screen heroes. Attached to these biological attributes are also aesthetic norms: leading ladies are young and attractive, whereas leading men are middle-aged and preferably but not necessarily handsome.

These normative guidelines have confined the range of screen roles allotted to women: lead roles are almost exclusively cast with young and beautiful actresses. Up to the late 1970s, leading actresses over the age of forty were forced to retire from the screen or to switch to playing character roles, which are usually smaller and secondary. Early retirement was not a matter of choice—actresses were forced to quit while at the peak of their careers. Deborah Kerr, a leading lady and a six-time Oscar nominee, retired in 1969—at the age of forty-eight—after appearing in Kazan's *The Arrangement* because she did not want to play aunts and grandmothers.

Oscar roles also reveal important information about patterns of marriage among men and women. Two-fifths of the female Oscar roles have been married compared with one-fourth of the men. And close to one-fifth of the male Oscar roles have made no reference to their marital status—in sharp contrast to the paucity of female roles with no information about their marital position. Clearly, if knowledge of gender roles were entirely based on information provided by the movies, it would be impossible to understand women without knowing whether they are single, married, divorced, or widowed. By contrast, marital status is less crucial to men's welfare or functioning, and statuses other than the marital are more important in understanding their place in society.

The proportion of male supporting roles with no reference to their marital status is five times greater than that of the female roles. These differences are relevant due to the fact that films usually do not provide much information about supporting roles, the screen time of which is limited. However, in the case of a female supporting role, even if the character has only a few scenes, there will be some reference to her marital status.

Furthermore, in the course of the plot, a woman's marital status tends to change more frequently than that of the man. These transformations (from single to married, from married to widowed) constitute the heart of melodramatic narratives, and they follow a consistent pattern: regardless of the heroine's initial status (single, widowed, divorced), by the end of the film she is either married, going to be married, or attached to one man. Most stories make a point, at times using the most illogical devices, to "resolve" their heroine's marital position if it is undetermined. This explains why the percentage of married or attached women is higher by the conclusion of the film than at its start.

The occupational portrayal of screen men and women as reflected in Oscar roles distinguishes between them even more sharply than their depiction in terms of age and marriage. The vast majority of the male roles have identifiable occupations and are gainfully employed. By contrast, over one-third of the female characters have no gainful work. It's inconceivable for screen males *not* to engage in gainful employment unless they are criminals or convicts. And whereas there's always a "good" reason for screen males not to work, there's nothing wrong with women who don't work. Moreover, the range of occupations is much wider for the men: Males have been portrayed in three times as many occupations than women, from the top of the hierarchy (kings, judges, governors, generals) to the least prestigious of occupations (butchers, miners).

Prevalent Male Roles

The men have been concentrated in authority positions that are in charge of maintaining law and order. The most frequent occupations among the male Oscar roles are soldiers, sheriffs, policemen, and politicians.

Fourteen men have won the Oscar for portraying a military figure: Emil Jannings in *The Last Command,* Gary Cooper in *Sergeant York,* Fredric March and Harold Russell in *The Best Years of Our Lives,* Dean Jagger in *Twelve O'Clock High,* William Holden in *Stalag 17,* Frank Sinatra in *From Here to Eternity,* Jack Lemmon in *Mister Roberts,* Alec Guinness in *The Bridge on the River Kwai,* Red Buttons in *Sayonara,* George C. Scott in *Patton,* Jon Voight in *Coming Home,* Christopher Walken in *The Deer Hunter,* Louis Gossett Jr. in *An Officer and a Gentleman,* and Denzel Washington in *Glory.* The number of screen soldiers among the Oscar nominees is even more substantial.

Law enforcers (sheriffs, detectives) have also been dominant among the males: Gary Cooper in *High Noon,* Lee Marvin in *Cat Ballou,* Rod Steiger in *In the Heat of the Night,* John Wayne in *True Grit,* Gene Hackman in *The French Connection,* and Sean Connery as the veteran Irish cop who takes Elliot Ness under his wing in *The Untouchables.* In 1992, the two male winning roles were Al Pacino's acerbic, blind lieutenant colonel in *Scent of a Woman,* and Gene Hackman's sadistic sheriff in *Unforgiven.* In the following year, Tommy Lee Jones won a supporting Oscar for playing the relentless Federal Marshal Sam Gerard in *The Fugitive.*

If all male roles concerned with the control of order are combined, their proportion amounts to over 40 percent of all Oscar roles. Along with military figures and sheriffs, this group include kings (Yul Brynner in *The King and I*), politicians (Broderick Crawford in *All the King's Men*, Ed Begley in *Sweet Bird of Youth*), freedom fighters (Paul Lucas in *Watch on the Rhine*), and judges or lawyers (Lionel Barrymore in *A Free Soul*, Walter Brennan in *The Westerner*, Maximilian Schell in *Judgment at Nuremberg*, and Walter Matthau in *The Fortune Cookie*).

Priests, who also help to define and control the social order, should also be counted. In *Boys Town*, Spencer Tracy's Father Flanagan creates a school for tough and poor street children, and Bing Crosby, in *Going My Way*, rehabilitates a group of juvenile delinquents by turning them into a choir. The Academy has honored four men with Best Actor nominations for playing presidents: Raymond Massey in *Abe Lincoln in Illinois*, Alexander Knox in *Wilson*, James Whitmore as Truman in *Give 'Em Hell, Harry*, and Anthony Hopkins in *Nixon*.

Most male roles have depicted men as highly committed to their careers, at times at the expense of having any personal or domestic lives. Rod Steiger's Billie Gillespie in *In the Heat of the Night* is a thick-witted, bigoted sheriff, investigating a murder in his small Southern town. The film deals with Gillespie's relationship with Virgil Tibbs (Sidney Poitier), a black homicide detective from the North who's brought to help him resolve the mystery. In the course of the movie, their relationship transforms from initial suspicion and contempt to mutual respect and understanding. *In the Heat of the Night* illuminates its male protagonists in terms of occupation and race, which are exclusively explored in the contexts of their jobs; nothing of their private lives enters into the narrative. Now try to imagine a female version of *In the Heat of the Night*, made in 1967. Wouldn't there be men and romantic affairs in the women's lives?

Similarly, *Patton* focuses on the career of the arrogant and authoritarian General who is in love with war and is incapable of coping with peacetime. In fact, *Patton* deviates from the conventions of biopictures by *not* presenting any information about its hero's personal life.

In the case of conflict between job requirements and family duties, priority is given to the job. Gary Cooper won a second Oscar for *High Noon*, playing Will Kane, a marshal facing a dilemma on his wedding day: Leave town, as his Quaker wife (Grace Kelly) initially urges him to do, or face the four outlaws by himself—nobody in this cowardly town is willing to help. Despite burdens of fear and isolation, the danger of losing his wife, and the fact that he has retired from the job, Kane decides to meet the challenge alone head on. "A man's got to do what a man's got to do," has been a consistent motto of screen heroes in all Hollywood genres, not just Westerns or war movies.

It is therefore revelatory that two out of the four male Oscar roles that primarily deal with their private life are of elderly or retired men. In *Harry and Tonto,* Art Carney's Oscar-winning role, Harry is an aging widower who, having been dispossessed of his New York apartment, goes on a transcontinental tour with his cat Tonto. And Henry Fonda's Norman Thayer, the protagonist of *On Golden Pond,* is an eighty-year-old retired university professor spending what seems to be his last summer with his spunky wife of fifty years.

Screen men have also enjoyed greater freedom from the legitimate social order, with several men winning Oscars for playing criminals. Marlon Brando and Robert De Niro won Oscars for playing the same screen role: the former portraying Vito Corleone in *The Godfather* and the latter played the same character as a young man in *The Godfather, Part II.* De Niro studied Brando's performance meticulously, as he later explained: "I didn't want to do an imitation, but I wanted to make it believable that I could be him as a young man." For De Niro, the challenge was similar to "a mathematical problem—having the result first and then figuring out how to make the beginning fit."

By contrast, there have been fewer Oscar roles of female deviants. Tatum O'Neal's 1973 supporting award in *Paper Moon,* as a tough-talking nine-year old girl who becomes an accomplice to a con man, a Bible sales-man (played by her real-life father Ryan O'Neal), is one exception.

As expected, there have been more nominations than actual Oscars for portraying criminals. Several actors have had to deviate from their screen image, if it were based on the crime genre, before winning the award. To get the Oscar, actors who began their careers as heavies and villains had to switch to playing heroes. Wallace Beery played a wide array of villains in his silent Paramount pictures, but with the advent of sound, he shook off his image and began to be cast as the "lovable slob," the "good-bad" guy, as in his Oscar-winning role in *The Champ,* in which he played an errant father, a drunk and gambling ex-champion who makes a comeback for the sake of his idolizing son (Jackie Cooper).

Ernest Borgnine's looks—wide face, beady eyes, gap between his teeth—made him a natural screen villain. As noted, Borgnine's appearance was exploited in his early years, when he was cast as a sadistic sergeant *(From Here to Eternity)* and other menacing villains *(Bad Day at Black Rock).* Nonetheless, Borgnine won the Oscar for a role that represented a change of pace: the lonely, utterly sympathetic and kind butcher in *Marty.*

Great performances in crime-gangster movies are either ignored by the Academy or at best earn nominations, but they seldom win Oscars. None of Warner's actors who specialized in gangster movies ever won an Oscar for such a role. James Cagney's image is closely associated with the gangster film, but neither his performance in *The Public Enemy,* the film which made him a star, nor his role in the Freudian gangster movie *White Heat,* were nominated. Cagney received two nominations for such movies: *Angels With Dirty Faces,* which also won him the New York Film Critics Award, and *Love Me or Leave Me,* as the tough racketeer Martin Snyder married to singer Ruth Etting (Doris Day).

But to win the Oscar, Cagney had to step outside his realm and portray patriotic showman George M. Cohan in *Yankee Doodle Dandy.* However, Cagney's 1942 role did not change his screen persona, as Frank S. Nugent wrote in the *New York Times:* "Mr. Cagney has the faculty of being taken for granted. Although he is not in the least public enemy-ish off the screen, he has done so well in the role that producers entered a happy conspiracy to keep him there. His few breaks for freedom—*Boy Meets Girl* among them—have not been successful, whether through Cagney's fault or our inability to adjust ourselves to seeing him without an armpit holster."

Paul Muni, another noted Warner's player, began his career in gangster films, delivering indelible performances in Howard Hawks's *Scarface* and others. But like Cagney, Muni won the Academy's respect when he played "important" historical figures, such as the French scientist in *The Story of Louis Pasteur,* his Oscar role, or the French writer-activist in *The Life of Emile Zola,* for which he received a nomination.

Perhaps most revealing is the career of Humphrey Bogart, who for a whole decade played villains usually shot down in the last reel; no other actor has died on-screen so many times. But after *High Sierra* and *The Maltese Falcon,* Bogart's screen image underwent a radical transformation, and he was rewarded by the Academy for his new tough-but-romantic persona in *Casablanca,* his first nomination and best-remembered film, and in *The African Queen,* for which he won the Oscar. Bogart was cast as Charlie Allnut, a tough, unshaven, gin-soaked riverboat captain who becomes a hero, helping a missionary (Katharine Hepburn) to torpedo a German battleship in Africa. As Andrew Sarris observed, the conservative Academy members are not likely to vote for anarchic, virile roles. The taming of Bogart by Hepburn in *The African Queen*—in one scene, she pours all his gin into the river—proves Sarris's point.

Until recently, mainstream roles rooted in dominant culture had better chances to be recognized than rebellious or anti-establishment roles. Take Dustin Hoffman's career, with its seven nominations and two Oscars. Hoffman received his first nomination for *The Graduate,* as the college graduate who first violates sexual mores and has simultaneous affairs with both mother and daughter, and then rejects the predatory older woman and the bourgeois lifestyle of his parents. Hoffman's second nomination, in *Midnight Cowboy,* was for playing Ratso, a drifter-outcast living at the margins of society. For his portrait of Lenny Bruce, Hoffman received a third nomination, though embodying the foul-mouthed comedian almost guaranteed he would *not* get the Oscar. Hoffman continued to play other counter-cultural roles, such as *Papillon,* as a prisoner on Devil's Island, and *Straw Dogs,* for which he was not nominated. It was only when Hoffman was cast in a mainstream role, in *Kramer vs. Kramer,* as a self-absorbed executive who learns how to become an affectionate and responsible father, that he won a long overdue Oscar.

For years, Hoffman was critical of the Oscar, which made him, along with other reasons, one of Hollywood's enfants terribles. However, when polls predicted his likelihood to win for *Kramer,* he mellowed his public utterances and also decided to attend the show. Hoffman was incorporated into mainstream Hollywood along with other Hollywood "rebels," such as Jane Fonda and Barbra Streisand. Anti–Hollywood and antiestablishment players are now all good citizens, abiding by the Academy and the industry rules. Their dissenting voices seem weaker and fewer—realizing that being rebellious has damaging effects on their careers and popularity. And the 1980s generation of stars, Meryl Streep, Sissy Spacek, Sally Field, William Hurt, have been "obedient" from the start, avoiding at all costs attacking Hollywood or the Academy. They either believe in the system or understand that to exercise power in Hollywood and win Oscars, they have to play by the rules of the game!

Female Stereotypes

Compared with the men, gainfully employed screen women are confined to stereotypical professions considered to be "appropriate" for women. Two lines of work for women rewarded with Oscars are in service (teachers, nurses) and in entertainment (actresses, singers, dancers). Indeed, the two most prominent professions among the female roles are actresses and prostitutes. One out of three gainfully employed women in the Oscar films is an actress or a prostitute, and at times both an actress *and* a prostitute.

In the two professions, a woman is paid, as critic Molly Haskell has observed, "for doing what already she did: prostitution, in which she was remunerated for giving sexual pleasure, and acting, a variant on natural role-playing." What's common to both lines is "playing roles and adapting to others, aiming to please." Moreover, neither acting nor prostitution enjoys high prestige in the occupational hierarchy, probably because it is possible to practice both without any formal education or training.

Actresses playing actresses stand the best chances to win nominations and Oscars. The Acting Branch has the largest number of members and can be biased toward portraits of showbiz personalities. Besides, playing a performer provides meaty and juicy parts that lend themselves to the display of histrionics and a wide gamut of intense emotion.

In Hollywood, there have been two common representations of screen actresses, both stereotypical. One role is that of the fading star, slipping from the top to skid row as a result of aging, declining looks, drinking problems, frustrated love, or an unhappy marriage. The other type is the reverse, the young, ambitious ingenue who gets her big break at the very last moment, usually on opening night when the veteran actress is unable to perform.

Some movies, like *All About Eve,* juxtapose the two stereotypes. Bette Davis, in the greatest performance of her career, plays Margo Channing, the aging star who cannot come to terms with her progressing age (forty), which by today's standards is young, but in the 1950s was considered old. Anne Baxter plays the young, driven Eve Harrington, scheming to take over everything that Margo has—her roles, her friends, and even her man.

Bette Davis specialized in portraying suffering actresses: Four out of her ten nominations were for such roles. In her first Oscar role, *Dangerous,* Davis plays Joyce Heath, a booze-swilling once-famous stage actress bent on her own destruction until she meets an admiring young architect (Franchot Tone) who sponsors her comeback. When her husband (John Eldredge) refuses Joyce a divorce so that she can marry the architect, she attempts to kill both of them by driving her car into a tree. They survive, but Joyce's husband is crippled for life. Returning triumphantly to the stage, she now understands the value of sacrifice.

In *The Star,* for which she received her ninth nomination, Davis's Margaret Elliot is a has-been, a former Oscar-winner who is now a pathetic, bitter and violent woman. As in *Dangerous,* an admirer (Sterling Hayden) saves Margaret by convincing her, as in *All About Eve,* to give up her career and live a more normal, that is, domestic, life.

Davis's last nomination was for the cult horror flick, Robert Aldridge's *What Ever Happened to Baby Jane?* She is cast as Jane Hudson, the genius child-star whose talent faded when she grew up, turning her into a demented alcoholic, sadistic toward her crippled sister (Joan Crawford). Davis gave a flashy, grotesque performance, which opened a new phase in her career as a horror queen.

Gloria Swanson created an indelible shading in *Sunset Boulevard* as Norma Desmond, the aging silent movie queen terrified of the camera but still dreaming of a big comeback. Geraldine Page did her best work, on stage and on screen, as Alexandra DeLargo in Tennessee Williams's *Sweet Bird of Youth,* as another aging, drug-addicted star, entertained by an opportunistic stud (Paul Newman), who finds out that her last film was not as disastrous as she had thought.

Screen actresses are not always tragic; the stereotype has been equally exploited in comedies, too. Maggie Smith won her second, supporting Oscar for Neil Simon's *California Suite,* playing British actress Diana Barrie, a hard-drinking and hard-talking performer who arrives in Hollywood for the Oscar ceremonies. Disenchanted after losing, Diana charges at her companion (Michael Caine): "Acting doesn't win Oscars—what I need is a dying father." Italian actress Valentina Cortesa was nominated for Truffaut's behind-the-scenes comedy *Day for Night,* in which she plays a fading movie star who hides a bottle on the set and cannot remember her lines.

The reverse stereotype, that of the young stage-struck ingenue, was embodied by Katharine Hepburn in her first Oscar-winning role in *Morning Glory.* She plays Eve Lovelace (note the name Eve), a naive Vermont girl who creates a sensation when she steps in for the recalcitrant lady on opening night. Some lines from this picture have entered into movie lore. "How many keep their heads? You've come to the fore. Now you have the chance to be a morning glory, a flower that fades before the sun is very high." Or Hepburn's vow, "I'm not afraid of being like a morning glory. I'm not afraid. I'm not afraid." And, of course, Adolphe Menjou, as a tough producer, telling Eve: "You don't belong to any man now, you belong to Broadway!"

The prostitute, with or without a "golden heart," is also one of the most enduring screen images, and the second most prevalent Oscar role for women. Elizabeth Taylor won her first Oscar for *Butterfield 8* (based on John O'Hara's novel) as Gloria Wandrous, a New York call girl. Gloria describes herself as "the slut of all times," but basically she is a good-natured woman whose main ambition in life is to gain respectability, marry a decent man, and live a suburban life. However, trapped in bad circumstances and unable to forget her past, there is no hope for Gloria and, after a disastrous affair with a wealthy, married Yale graduate (Laurence Harvey), she finds her death in a fatal car crash.

Jane Fonda's first Oscar, for *Klute,* is acknowledged a great performance. For no apparent reason, the film was named after its detective (played by Donald Sutherland), but it should have been titled after its heroine, Bree Daniel, a New York call girl. She may be a victim of her circumstances but also enjoys the power she possesses over her clients. *Klute* makes an explicit association between the two traditional female professions, acting and prostitution. When Bree complains to her analyst that she has had no luck as an actress, the latter responds, "What's the difference? You're successful as a call girl, you're not successful as an actress." Other films have also made similar links: Claire Trevor won a supporting Oscar for *Key Largo,* in which she's cast as a gangster's alcoholic mistress who's a faded torch singer.

More supporting than lead Oscars were given to actresses playing prostitutes. In *East of Eden,* Jo Van Fleet played James Dean's presumably dead mother, a woman who broke free of her family and is now a notorious madam. Dorothy Malone gave an intensely hysterical performance in Douglas Sirk's *Written on the Wind,* as a rich, frustrated nymphomaniac who seduces gas-station attendants in cheap motel rooms. Woody Allen's films abound with prostitutes. Mira Sorvino became the eighth actress to win an Oscar for playing a hooker, albeit a bright and cheerful one in Allen's 1995 comedy, *Mighty Aphrodite.*

Interestingly, some of these Oscars have rewarded actresses for deviating from their previously cleancut and wholesome screen image. Anne Baxter began her career as "the girl-next-door," in patriotic war films *(The Pied Piper, Crash Dive, The Fighting Sullivans),* but she won a supporting Oscar for a major departure from that image, in *The Razor's Edge,* playing a woman who becomes a dipsomaniac prostitute after the death of her husband and child in a car crash.

Donna Reed built a name for herself as a sincere, wholesome girl, as in *It's a Wonderful Life,* in which she plays Jimmy Stewart's loyal wife, but she won the Oscar for a role that was the exception, Alma, the "hostess" in *From Here to Eternity*. The film was less explicit than the book as far as Alma's line of work was concerned; in the book, she's a prostitute.

In 1960, the two female awards were given to actresses who played prostitutes: Elizabeth Taylor in *Butterfield 8* and Shirley Jones in *Elmer Gantry*. Jones was recruited to Hollywood from the Broadway stage, having established herself as a singer. At first, she played shy, romantic girls in musicals *(Oklahoma!, Carousel, April Love)*. However, only when Jones changed her image in *Elmer Gantry,* playing Lulu Bains, the good-hearted prostitute, did she earn the Academy's recognition. "I am sick of portraying ingenues with sunny dispositions, high necklines, and puffy sleeves, who are girlishly aggressive about happiness being just around the corner," Jones is reported to have said.

Other women's roles have conformed to familiar stereotypes of women as wives, mothers, and daughters. Family roles combined with sex and victimization have created some of the most enduring screen stereotypes: the adulteress, the self-sacrificing mother, the long-suffering wife, the oppressed spinster. These formulaic roles have persisted in mainstream American cinema for half a century with few, minor alterations.

The Southern belle is a uniquely American literary and cinematic type. Bette Davis won a second Oscar for *Jezebel,* as the rich, spoiled, and willful Julie Marsden, whose entire behavior is motivated by her failure to win the love of Pres Dillard (Henry Fonda). Pres breaks their engagement when Julie disregards the norms and wears a red gown to New Orleans's Olympus Ball; all the other girls wear a traditional white dress. Punished, Julie secludes herself, waiting for Pres to return, only to find out that he has married another girl. However, when Pres falls victim to a yellow-fever epidemic, Julie convinces his wife that *she* should accompany him to a quarantined island, promising to send him back if he survives.

Vivien Leigh gave a memorable performance as Scarlett O'Hara in *Gone With the Wind,* as a tempestuous and self-centered belle. Leigh's second Oscar was for playing Blanche DuBois in *A Streetcar Named Desire,* the sordid tale of the mental deterioration of a repressed Southern belle. Blanche DuBois, a challenge for every actress, is a perfect example of the kinds of screen roles that win Oscars, because it includes all the "necessary" ingredients of a substantial role, allowing for the display of a wide range of emotions and skills.

Tennessee Williams has written some of the most memorable female roles for stage and for screen. The eccentricity of his characters, their richly nuanced inner selves, often dominated by repressed sexuality, has called for distinguished acting. Not surprisingly, films based on Williams's plays have earned nominations and awards, mostly for their women. In *Baby Doll,* Carroll Baker was nominated for playing "white trash," a retarded, thumb-sucking child-wife, seduced by her husband's revenge-seeking rival. In the same film, Mildred Dunnock was nominated for playing a pathetically demented aunt.

Cat on a Hot Tin Roof was one of 1958's most nominated films, in which Elizabeth Taylor excelled as Maggie, the sexy wife punished by her alcoholic husband (Paul Newman, also nominated) who won't sleep with her. *Suddenly Last Summer,* a study of incest, cannibalism, and insanity, contrasted Katharine Hepburn, as a demented aristocratic mother in love with her homosexual poet-son, with Elizabeth Taylor, as her niece, who almost goes mad after witnessing her cousin's rape and murder. Both Hepburn and Taylor received Best Actress nominations, but neither won.

Vivien Leigh was not nominated for playing the widowed American actress who drifts into lassitude and moral decline in *The Roman Spring of Mrs. Stone,* but Lotte Lenya, playing a vicious female pimp, was. In *Summer and Smoke,* a drama about earthly and spiritual love, Geraldine Page was nominated as Alma, a sexually repressed spinster and minister's daughter. In addition to Page, *Sweet Bird of Youth* provided a nomination for Shirley Knight, who played the victimized daughter-girlfriend who had contracted syphilis from an irresponsible stud (Paul Newman). In *Night of the Iguana,* Grayson Hall received a supporting nomination as the leader of a group of vacationing schoolteachers whose animosity toward the defrocked priest (Richard Burton) was based on repressed lesbianism and an interest in the nymphomaniac teenager (Sue Lyon).

The spinster, or the old maid, is another enduring female stereotype. Olivia de Havilland won her second Oscar for *The Heiress,* as the timid, ugly-duckling daughter of a domineering father (Ralph Richardson). She is deceived and bitterly disappointed when she finds out that her admirer (Montgomery Clift) is a scoundrel interested in her wealth. Other frustrated spinsters who received nominations include Agnes Moorehead's neurotic and spinsterish aunt in *The Magnificent Ambersons,* and Joanne Woodward in *Rachel, Rachel,* who plays a spinster teacher in a small town, who has her first sexual encounter at thirty-five, only to be deserted by her lover.

Most of these screen spinsters have domineering mothers against whom they rebel, usually through the love of an older man. In one of Bette Davis's most popular roles, *Now Voyager,* she is cast as a desperately humiliated, mother-driven spinster who finds fulfilling love at a later age. In *Separate Tables,* too, Deborah Kerr starts as a timid, sexually repressed virgin, dominated by a cruel mother (Gladys Cooper), against whom she finally rebels.

Katharine Hepburn has had several phases in her lengthy career. In the earlier part, up to the 1940s, she played strongly independent attractive women *(The Philadelphia Story, Woman of the Year).* When she began to age, Hepburn continued to play strong-willed women, but they were now unglamorous and spinsterish. If Tracy Lord in *The Philadelphia Story* summed up the first part of Hepburn's career, *The African Queen* (her fifth nomination), in which she was cast as a missionary, offered a summation to the middle phase. Hepburn was cast in similar roles in *Summertime* (her sixth nomination), as a spinsterish teacher vacationing in Venice and falling in love with Rossano Brazzi. In *The Rainmaker* (her seventh nomination), she is a tomboyish girl whose womanhood is brought to the surface by a con man (Burt Lancaster).

Suffering and Victimization

Suffering and victimization have been the chief attributes of the female Oscar roles. According to Oscar, women have suffered a disproportionately large number of disasters, natural and man-made. While men are in charge of their lives, women exercise little or no control over their romantic, marital, and even familial bonds, all of which are causes for torment and anguish.

Sexual assault and rape are the most obvious forms of victimization. In *Johnny Belinda,* Jane Wyman plays a deaf-mute girl, a victim of a brutal rape by a drunken fisherman, who later attempts to steal her baby, which forces her to kill him and stand trial. Blanche DuBois, the genteel belle in *A Streetcar Named Desire,* is tortured and raped by her brutish brother-in-law, which drives her into insanity.

A larger number of Oscar roles depict women who are betrayed by their husbands. Adultery is one of the most consistent male privileges on-screen—and a continuous source of suffering for women. Janet Gaynor won Best Actress for *Sunrise,* in which she plays a farmer's loyal wife betrayed by her husband with a glamorous city woman, who almost convinces him to kill her. Luise Rainer's second Oscar was for *The Good Earth*, playing a selfless Chinese farmer's wife who is first neglected by her husband, then further humiliated when he marries a younger wife. Serafina Della Rose, Anna Magnani's Oscar role in *The Rose Tattoo,* is a tempestuous widow who idolizes her dead husband; she's the last to realize his unfaithfulness. A religious woman, she is obsessed with sexual memories to the point of becoming a reclusive, domineering mother.

Women's status in American film can be instructively examined through the "concept of stigma." Up until the 1970s, any attempt by screen women to deviate from prescribed stereotypical roles was consistently punished. Strong-willed heroines are not only depicted as deviants but are oppressed if their conduct is considered threatening to the status quo of male dominance. Forms of punishment range from the most extreme sanctions, such as death, to humiliation, ostracization, and relegation to domestic life.

Wearing a red gown, Bette Davis's Julie in *Jezebel* is punished for violating dress conventions. The film suggests that Julie destroyed her chances at real happiness, through marriage, by defying social norms. Sexual promiscuity by women is also regarded as a severe violation of mores. Most screen prostitutes (Elizabeth Taylor's in *Butterfield 8)* pay with their lives for engaging in such a disreputable occupation.

Death by accident is another fate of screen adulteresses. Gloria Grahame specialized in playing floozies and loose girls *(Crossfire, The Big*

Heat). Grahame received a supporting Oscar for *The Bad and the Beautiful*, playing a social-climbing wife, urging her screenwriter-husband to move to Hollywood and live a glamorous lifestyle. The ruthless producer (Kirk Douglas) considers her to be an interruptive force in her husband's creative career and arranges for her to have an affair with a Latin lover. Needless to say, she ends up in a tragic airplane crash.

Simone Signoret's Alice Abigal in *Room at the Top* finds her death in a fatal car accident. An aging, unhappily married actress, she is desperate for affection, but she falls in love with an ambitious working-class man (Laurence Harvey) who mistreats her. At the end, Alice is sacrificed by him for a younger woman, the daughter of the town's tycoon, and dies on his wedding day.

Screen death resolves the problem of having to deal with women as equal partners, particularly women who are actively involved in politics and the economy. Vanessa Redgrave's title role in *Julia* is of a young intelligent woman who rebels against her aristocratic family by becoming a fighter in the antifascist movement. She too is killed off in the course of the narrative, thus becoming a symbol of political heroism rather than a real living woman.

Screen death functions as a safety valve, permitting audiences to admire courageous and independent women as martyrs, while relieving men of the burden of dealing with them as equals on a realistic level. If *Julia*'s protagonist had been a man, he would probably have survived. Male screen fighters usually succeed in accomplishing their missions, as Paul Lukas's Oscar role in another of Hellman's works, *Watch on the Rhine*, shows. Lukas, in fact, plays a similar role to Vanessa Redgrave's in *Julia*, as an antifascist fighter.

Ambitious career women are consistently punished for stepping out of their place, entering into men's domain and thus competing with them for desirable jobs and rewards. In Joan Crawford's Oscar role as the suffering mother in *Mildred Pierce*, she plays a determined woman who builds up a chain of restaurants to provide her ungrateful daughter with all the rewards she was deprived of. Throughout the movie Mildred is penalized. Her younger daughter dies of pneumonia while she is spending her first weekend off from work with her lover. Mildred then throws herself into a second, loveless marriage with a playboy whom she ends up supporting. Her eldest daughter Vida (Oscar-nominated Ann Blyth) despises her mother's low-class origins and job as a waitress and flirts with her stepfather, whom she later kills out of jealousy. At the film's end, having lost everything, including her business, Mildred goes back to her first husband—and to a second life as a housewife, placed back where she belongs.

Mildred Pierce is by no means an exception. The portrayal of career women was quite consistent up to the late 1970s. That career women on-screen are typically single suggests that it is impossible for women to combine successful careers with satisfying personal lives—something screen men manage to achieve with relative ease. Even women choosing the perennial female occupation, acting, are single. In *All About Eve,* Margo Channing is unmarried while she's professionally successful; Eve is also by herself when her career begins to rise.

Screen career women are often ridiculed and condemned as grotesque, "unfeeling monsters." This dehumanization is illustrated in Louise Fletcher's Oscar role in *One Flew Over the Cuckoo's Nest,* as Big Nurse Ratched, a tyrannical nurse in charge of a mental ward. A severe, humorless woman, Nurse Ratched represents an oppressive establishment whose major goal is to tame patients—all of whom are men—using various controls, including electroshock treatment and lobotomy. Endowed with a bureaucratic personality, Nurse Ratched is rigid, indoctrinary, and adheres strictly to the rules. She is sympathetic to her patients only when it promotes her interests and her authority; she drives one of her young patients (Oscar-nominated Brad Dourif), a mother-fixated kid, into suicide by consciously playing on his guilt complex. The Nurse's character is not written or played on the same realistic level as her patients. She is more of an abstract symbol of sexual inhibition and repressive authority.

Faye Dunaway's Oscar role as Diana Christensen, a ruthless, power-hungry television executive in *Network,* is also more of an abstract type than a fully fleshed human character. Some believe that Dunaway was rewarded for being a good sport and poking fun at her own screen image as an ambitious career woman. In this film, Diana's chief goal is to upgrade the network's ratings, as she unashamedly boasts, "All I want out of life is a 30 share and 20 rating," for which she is willing to use illegitimate and disreputable means, such as co-producing a program with terrorists. Obsessed with her work, which permeates every aspect of her life, Diana talks about it nonstop, even during a sexual encounter. Diana is further ridiculed when she sets the tone and speed of this encounter with an older, sensitive married executive (William Holden). She sits on top of him and reaches orgasm prematurely, thus imitating what is considered to be a typically masculine sexual pattern. Efficient and rational, Diana is incapable of any human feelings. Neither Diana nor Nurse Ratched have any meaningful personal lives outside of the contexts of their work.

The most prevalent female screen stereotypes have combined showbiz with suffering. The prototype is still *A Star Is Born,* the story of a young actress who ascends to stardom while her husband's career goes on the skids. Janet Gaynor and Judy Garland were both Oscar-nominated for the same role in the 1937 and 1954 versions, respectively. Showbiz biopictures are based on simplistic formulas, the notions that achieving fame costs a high price, and that stardom doesn't last long due to its inevitably damaging effects on both career and personal life.

Consider the following Oscar-nominated roles:

Eleanor Parker, as the crippled singer Marjorie Lawrence in *Interrupted Melody*;

Susan Hayward, as the alcoholic singer Lillian Roth in *I'll Cry Tomorrow*;

Diana Ross, as the heroin-addicted, racially oppressed singer Billie Holliday in *Lady Sings the Blues*;

Bette Midler, as the drug-addicted rock star (loosely based on Janis Joplin's life) in *The Rose*;

Jessica Lange, as the doomed, anti-establishment actress Frances Framer in *Frances* who, tormented by an overbearing mother, turns to the bottle and is put in an asylum;

Mary McDonnell, as the paralyzed soap opera star in John Sayles's *Passion Fish*;

Angela Bassett, as the abused singer Tina Turner in the biopicture, *What's Love Got to Do With It*;

Miranda Richardson, as Vivienne Haigh-Wood, the socialite wife of poet T. S. Eliot (Willem Dafoe) in *Tom & Viv*, whose affliction was improperly diagnosed

The lovely British actress Emily Watson has elevated emotional instability to a high art, for which she was rewarded with two Best Actress nominations. The first one was for her astonishing performance as Bess McNeill in Lars Von Trier's emotional-spiritual drama, *Breaking the Waves* (1996). Two years later, Watson was nominated in *Hilary and Jackie* for playing Jacqueline du Pre, the world renowned cellist who led an outwardly glamorous life but whose desperation placed a strain on her family, particularly on her sister (played by Oscar-nominated Rachel Griffiths). Adding to her emotional problems, du Pre developed multiple sclerosis, which first took its toll on her musical career, and eventually took her life. To prepare for her role, Watson withstood three months of practice in a rehearsal room, and took three cello lessons per week. She also met with an MS doctor (and his patients) and a movement teacher to approximate du Pre's gestures.

Oscar, Hollywood, and Male Dominance

Film does not operate in a social or political void. Rather, it is interrelated with society's politics and with its dominant ideology. Hollywood is an industry whose products—movies—have a strong technological foundation but they are also transmitting cultural values. These two facets of movies, as ideological constructs and commercial products, are intertwined in Hollywood's popular movies. As such, they have expressed the ideological dominance of one powerful group: white middle-class men. This group has defined and controlled the normative order and has imposed it on less powerful groups, such as women and ethnic minorities. The notion of cultural hegemony is therefore crucial to the understanding of the specific images embodied by movies, best reflected in popular Oscar-winning roles.

Screen heroes and heroines have differed in age, appearance, marital status, and occupation. Male roles have been contained in serious dramatic pictures dealing with important issues such as racism and injustice. Assigned to roles which control the social order, men have perpetuated the status quo symbolically, on-screen, and pragmatically, offscreen. Female roles, by contrast, have been based on fictional figures mostly contained in romances and melodramas known as "women's films." According to Oscar-winning roles, women's contributions to society are mostly in the marital and familial arena, as wives and mothers, or in service professions, as entertainers and prostitutes.

The male Oscar roles can be described as *types,* whereas the female as *stereotypes.* Types are shared, recognizable, easily grasped norms of how people are expected to behave, whereas stereotypes are based on more stringent and confining guidelines. Stereotypes involve strong value judgments, both approval and disapproval, of particular ways of behavior. They imply that those who don't conform to the specified ways of appearing, feeling, and behaving are inadequate as males or females. Needless to say, stereotypes are often harmful, confining people to a narrowly defined range of behaviors.

The function of female stereotypes, from the point of view of the dominant ideology, is to keep women in their place, to reward them for accepting traditional roles—for *not* challenging the status quo. Women's dominant screen roles provide rationalizations that are needed to reconcile women to marriage and family life. All-embracing, these images go beyond the socio-economic area, offering a state of mind and a way of life for women. The persistence of these roles for half a century indicates that most moviegoers have accepted (at least passively) the ideological message of Hollywood movies.

However, the stereotypical portrayal of women also shows that Hollywood has been out of touch with reality, ignoring the progress women have made. This means that media images are not necessarily up-to-date: a "culture lag" often prevails between society's material conditions and its cultural representations. There has been such a gap between women's economic and occupational roles, and their ideological treatment by the movies. The most negative screen portrayals, trivializing women's domestic roles and condemning career women, occurred in the late 1960s and early 1970s—just when women were beginning to make their mark offscreen. Hollywood's ideological backlash in those years was manifest in at least three important ways.

First, there was a paucity of screen roles, particularly leading ones, for women. For a while it seemed as if women had disappeared from the American screen. The worst year in the history of the Best Actress Oscar, marked by extremely weak competition, was 1975, when members of the Acting Branch had difficulties coming up with five lead actresses. No wonder Louise Fletcher won—there was not much competition. Under normal circumstances, Fletcher's role in *Cuckoo's Nest* would have qualified as a supporting Oscar. The other nominees were: Isabelle Adjani in *The Story of Adele H.*, Ann-Margret in the musical *Tommy*, Glenda Jackson in the film version of Ibsen's *Hedda*, and Carol Kane in *Hester Street*. Ellen Burstyn, the previous year's winner, asked her colleagues in the Acting Branch not to nominate actresses in the lead category as a protest against Hollywood's marginalization of women.

Men dominated Hollywood quantitatively and qualitatively. The era's typical big-budget movies were action-adventures, focusing on male heroism, male friendship, and male courage. Major movies of that era usually featured two male stars in the leading roles, with few or no women in their narratives. The list of these movies is too long to reproduce here, but it is sufficient to name some Best Picture nominees: *In the Heat of the Night,* starring Rod Steiger and Sidney Poitier; *Midnight Cowboy,* with Jon Voight and Dustin Hoffman; *Butch Cassidy and the Sundance Kid,* with Paul Newman and Robert Redford; *MASH,* which boasted a male cast headed by Donald Sutherland and Elliott Gould; *Patton,* with George C. Scott and Karl Malden; *The French Connection,* with Gene Hackman and Roy Scheider; *Deliverance,* with Jon Voight and Burt Reynolds, *The Godfather, Parts I and II,* with an all-male starring cast, Marlon Brando, Robert De Niro, Robert Duvall, and Al Pacino; *The Sting,* with Paul Newman and Robert Redford; *The Towering Inferno,* with Paul Newman and Steve McQueen; *Dog Day Afternoon,* with Al Pacino, John Cazale, and Chris Sarandon; *Jaws,* with Richard Dreyfuss, Roy Scheider, and Robert Shaw; *All the President's Men,* with Robert Redford and Dustin Hoffman.

Finally, most box-office stars in the late 1960s and 1970s were men, with the exception of Barbra Streisand, the only woman among the ten Box-Office Champions. The industry's biggest names were all male stars with a tough "macho" image, such as Steve McQueen in *The Thomas Crown Affair* and *Bullitt,* Clint Eastwood in his *Dirty Harry* movies, Lee Marvin in *The Professionals* and *The Dirty Dozen,* and Charles Bronson in *Death Wish* and its variants.

Changes in Oscar Roles

Some significant changes in women's Oscar roles took place over the last two decades

Alice Doesn't Live Here Anymore (1974) signaled a major change, because it was a film with a strong central role for a woman that attempted to challenge male cultural dominance, on and offscreen. Ellen Burtsyn, who won Best Actress, was instrumental in bringing the project to the screen. Burstyn discovered Robert Gotchell's screenplay, persuaded a major studio, Warner, to distribute it, chose a rising director, Martin Scorsese, and even had a say in choosing its cast and crew. Thematically, however, *Alice* was compromising and far from the feminist film it intended to be. Its eponymous heroine is a recent young widow struggling to launch a new career as a singer and a new life for her and her son. But at the end, Alice becomes dependent again, settling into what seems to be a second, complacent relationship, albeit with a more sensitive man (Kris Kristofferson) than her husband. Even so, *Alice* showed that there is interest in women's stories and that such films are also commercially viable.

The turning point in Oscar roles occurred in 1977, when for the first time four of the five Best Picture nominees were about women and contained strong female characters. The Oscar winner was Woody Allen's *Annie Hall,* starring Diane Keaton, competing against Neil Simon's romantic comedy *The Goodbye Girl,* with Marsha Mason, and Fred Zinnemann's *Julia,* a picture about friendship between two women. The other nominee, *The Turning Point,* was about the costs and rewards of life choices, contrasting a dancer turned wife-mother (Shirley MacLaine) and an aging and lonely ballerina (Anne Bancroft).

In movies of the late 1970s, a new screen woman began to emerge: professional and career-oriented but without the dehumanization and condemnation of Fletcher's nurse in *Cuckoo's Nest* or Dunaway's TV executive in *Network.* The range of occupational roles widened considerably, going beyond traditional "female" professions of actresses, secretaries, or prostitutes. Glenda Jackson won a second Oscar for playing a fashion designer in *A Touch of Class,* Liv Ullmann was nominated for playing a psychiatrist in Ingmar Bergman's *Face to Face,* Ingrid Bergman was nominated for a concert pianist in another Bergman movie, *Autumn Sonata.* Geraldine Page excelled as an interior decorator in *Interiors,* and Jane Fonda received a nomination as an investigative reporter in *The China Syndrome.*

The new screen woman was concerned not only with her career, but with asserting herself as a worthy human being whose status neither derives from nor depends on her marital and familial roles. Meryl Streep won a supporting Oscar as Joanna Kramer in *Kramer vs. Kramer,* playing a woman who walks out on her self-absorbed husband, leaving him the responsibility of raising their young son alone. Joanna is depicted as a confused woman, deeply dissatisfied with her mother-wife chores. *Kramer* was the first major Hollywood movie to deal with a married woman who deserts her family in order to "find herself" and regain self-worth. In sharp departure from previous conventions, Joanna gives up her son willingly. After winning a cruel custody battle, she tells her ex-husband: "I came here to take my son home, and I realized he already is home." The movie also changed the traditional image of the husband-father, played by Dustin Hoffman, who won Best Actor. Ted Kramer starts out as an egotistic advertising executive, so engrossed in his career that he neglects his family and forbids his wife to work. But he is capable of changing and, by the film's end, he has transformed into a loving, caring father who learns some lessons about parenthood.

Screen women also began to show strong interest in the public and political domains. In the past, screen heroines were confined to their domestic lives, exhibiting little interest in what was happening in the outside world. But in the late 1970s, several new movies dealt with the process by which women gain greater political consciousness. At the center of Martin Ritt's *Norma Rae,* which gave Sally Field her first Oscar, is the politicization of a Southern working-class woman in a small dormant town, after meeting a Jewish labor-organizer (Ron Liebman) from New York. The movie describes Norma's feisty struggle to unionize a mill, which involves the organization of a strike. What is innovative from a gender point of view is that her relationship with the Jewish intellectual is neither romantic nor sexual, but based on mutual respect. At the end, they part with a friendly handshake rather than the clichéd kiss. Such camaraderie between unlikely partners (a simple, uneducated woman and a smart urban Jew) would have been impossible in years past, but in the context of this film, they are mutually engrossed, with each party learning and benefiting from the friendship.

The new screen woman also gained ground in sexual mores and conduct. In the past, it was the exclusive privilege of men to engage in illicit affairs. But recently women have become more sexually liberated—without being penalized. *Coming Home,* Jane Fonda's second Oscar, describes the change of Sally Hyde, a bored middle class wife married to a chauvinistic Marine captain (Bruce Dern, who was also nominated), into a politically aware citizen, while volunteering in a war veteran hospital, where she falls in love with a sensitive war paraplegic (Jon Voight). For a change, and it is a big change, the film does not condemn her adultery, which is favorably described.

There have also been changes in the perennial screen role of the mother. The new, liberated mother was no longer suffering and self-sacrificing, as Mildred Pierce or Stella Dallas were for the future of their children. She was no longer weak or submissive, but determined, in control of her life and in charge of her emotions. Sally Field won a second Oscar for playing Edna Spaulding in *Places in the Heart,* a Texan housewife whose husband-sheriff is killed in an accident. After fifteen years of marriage, Edna suddenly finds herself with no talent and no skills for anything except cooking and taking care of her children. But with will power, steadfastness, and hard work she faces a series of hardships: a foreclosing bank, a greedy cotton dealer, and a tornado.

A very similar type of mother was portrayed by Jessica Lange in *Country,* inspired by the farmers' plight in Iowa, and Sissy Spacek in *The River,* both of whom were nominated. These movies, labeled as "Hollywood's farm trilogy," also challenged the traditional screen images of men, depicting them as less committed, weaker, and often more emotional than their female counterparts.

A clear indication of changing gender roles—in both society and film—was evident in 1988, a particularly strong year for Best Actresses. The winner, Jodie Foster in *The Accused,* plays Sarah Tobias, a fast-food waitress (traditional female profession), who is gang-raped in a roadside bar (also a stereotype). However, in the course of the film, she transforms from a good-time, hard-drinking girl to a woman fighting (with the assistance of a female attorney) for the decency and self-esteem she was never accorded.

Like Foster, in *A Cry in the Dark,* Meryl Streep was cast as defiant working-class woman held responsible for the death of her baby girl. Based on the 1980 story of Lindy Chamberlain, the complex role shows her to be proudly stubborn, a victim of the sensationalistic and merciless Australian media (she was acquitted in 1987). In *Dangerous Liaisons,* Glenn Close's Marquise de Merteuil is another proud woman who refuses to live by the sexual mores of the ancient regime. "I was born to dominate your sex and avenge my own," she tells the Vicomte de Valmont (John Malkovich) with whom she engages in games of sex and power.

In her assured portrayal of the late anthropologist Dian Fossey, Sigourney Weaver dominated every frame of *Gorillas in the Mist,* a film about Dian's heroic struggle to save Africa's gorillas from poachers. Even Melanie Griffith's Tess McGill, in Mike Nichols's modern fairy tale *Working Girl,* pointed to a new direction. Tess begins as a Staten Island secretary, victimized by a female executive (Sigourney Weaver, in another role reversal), who decides to take charge of her life, and in the process also gets her boss's lover (Harrison Ford).

Changes in women's Oscar roles became more evident in the 1990s. Kathy Bates won the 1990 Best Actress Oscar for playing an obsessed fan in Rob Reiner's horror film *Misery,* a genre that has not done much for women. In her acceptance speech, Bates thanked her co-star, James Caan (who played the fiction writer she torments), apologizing for the chilling scenes in which she uses a sledgehammer to break his ankles. Ever since *Misery,* Bates has been subjected to a ton of jokes about sledgehammers.

In 1990, Bates had an edge over the other nominees, both because of her stage credentials and her Plain Jane publicity that indicated a serious dedication to her craft. Bates came out of nowhere, embodying the story of the duckling turning into a swan. When asked whether victory might encourage directors to cast lesser-known actors in major roles, Bates noted, "I'm not sure. I just happened to be in the right place at the right time."

Bates felt no animosity toward producers who passed her over for film roles she had earlier popularized onstage, such as *Frankie and Johnny,* in which the female lead was later (mis)cast with Michelle Pfeiffer. But she was proud to say, "This one is for the actors." Referring to her father, who died in 1988 at ninety, she said, "When I first decided to go to New York, he gave me the money and the encouragement. I just wish he could be here tonight."

Bates later won Golden Globes and Screen Actors Guild awards for her work in film *(Fried Green Tomatoes,* 1991), and television *(The Late Shift,* 1996). In 1998, Bates received a second, supporting nomination in *Primary Colors,* for playing a tough, openly lesbian character, based upon President Clinton's aide Betsy Drake, who was in charge of controlling what she once famously termed "bimbo eruptions."

Another atypical Oscar performance—by an obscure, out of nowhere actress—was Hilary Swank's Brandon Teena in *Boys Don't Cry* (1999). It was a truly revelatory performance, an indelible turn that won virtually every pre-Oscar trophy: the New York, Los Angeles, and Golden Globe Awards. It took years for director Kimberly Peirce to cast the role. Numerous actresses auditioned, but the director was determined to go with an unknown. For her test, Swank dressed as a boy. When shooting began, she cut her hair, bound her breasts, and "lost herself" completely, which was crucial to the role.

Swank has nudged Janet McTeer *(Tumbleweeds)* aside in the promising-newcomer sweepstakes with her portrayal of Brandon Teena, a doomed young woman who dresses and lives her life as a man. Swank beat out four actresses, and in so doing, she not only raised the profile of a tiny independent movie, but also transformed her career, which began inauspiciously with *The Karate Kid IV* and a part in TV's *Beverly Hills 90210*.

"The Oscars have always been such an exciting thing all throughout my life," Swank said before the ceremony. "I'm someone who tunes in every single year and watches these people who've inspired me. And I get nervous for them! To think that I'm actually going to be walking down that red carpet, sitting in that seat! I'm so blessed." "I pray for the day when we celebrate our diversity," Swank said in her acceptance speech. "I do feel like a princess. It's been quite an amazing journey," she told reporters backstage at the Oscars. "To see this movie get this recognition is quite spectacular."

In the same year, it seemed fitting that Catherine Keener's star-making role—and first Oscar nomination—came for an indie film, *Being John Malkovich*. Keener is a truly independent spirit, having brought her wit to such high-quality, low-budget productions as *Living in Oblivion, Walking and Talking,* and *Your Friends & Neighbors*. Maxine, Keener's alluring Machiavellian character in *Being John Malkovich*, is, as *Entertainment Weekly* pointed out, one of the most aggressively sexual characters—male or female—ever seen on-screen.

Seldom has the American screen seen a woman so confident of her attractiveness that she doesn't feel the need to be polite and can crush a man with an offhand remark. "If you ever got me," she teases John Cusack's smitten Craig, "you wouldn't have a clue what to do with me." Though Cusack plays a puppeteer, it is Maxine who pulls the strings. As she entrances Craig, his wife (Cameron Diaz), and the eponymous actor, Keener simultaneously seduces the audience with her off-kilter good looks and cut-to-the-quick delivery. And, together with Diaz and Malkovich, she engages in one of the most mind-blowing three-way sex scenes ever conceived.

Add to Swank's Best Actress and Keener's Oscar-nominated turn Angelina Jolie's supporting Oscar for *Girl, Interrupted,* in which she played a rebellious youngster in an asylum—the female equivalent of Jack Nicholson's role in *One Flew Over the Cuckoo's Nest*—and you get a sense of how much female screen roles have changed over the last two decades.

CHAPTER 11

Oscar as a Popularity Contest

Strictly speaking, the selection of winners should be determined by two factors: the quality of achievement and the intensity of competition in a given year. Indeed, logic dictates a strong correlation between the intensity of competition and the quality of winning achievements. In actuality, however, in years of fierce contest, the winning performance is not necessarily the strongest; at times, it is the weakest.

In 1940, the competition in the two lead acting categories was particularly intense. The nominees for Best Actress were: Bette Davis in *The Letter,* Joan Fontaine in *Rebecca,* Katharine Hepburn in *The Philadelphia Story,* Ginger Rogers in *Kitty Foyle,* and Martha Scott in *Our Town.* Consensus held that Hepburn gave the year's best performance, arguably the best of her career, for which she was cited by the New York Film Critics. The Academy winner, however, was Ginger Rogers, earning an Oscar for her first and only nomination. In the same year, James Stewart's winning performance in *The Philadelphia Story* was not the most distinguished, compared with Charlie Chaplin in *The Great Dictator* and Henry Fonda in *The Grapes of Wrath;* the two other nominees were Laurence Olivier in *Rebecca* and Raymond Massey in *Abe Lincoln in Illinois.*

In 1947, the most impressive male performance was delivered by William Powell in *Life with Father,* for which he won the New York Film Critics Award. Yet the Oscar winner was Ronald Colman in *A Double Life,* winning over stiff competition from Gregory Peck in *Gentleman's Agreement* and John Garfield in *Body and Soul;* the fifth nominee was Michael Redgrave in *Mourning Becomes Electra.*

The female category that year was not particularly strong. Winner Loretta Young in *The Farmer's Daughter* was up against Joan Crawford in *Possessed,* Susan Hayward in *Smash-Up: The Story of a Woman,* Dorothy McGuire in *A Gentleman's Agreement,* and Rosalind Russell in *Mourning Becomes Electra.*

Bette Davis was denied an Oscar for the greatest performance of her career, as Margo Channing in *All About Eve,* but she competed against her co-star Anne Baxter in the same category, as noted, which surely split the votes. It was a year of extraordinary performances, including Gloria Swanson's in *Sunset Boulevard.* The surprise winner was Judy Holliday in *Born Yesterday,* the only comedic role in a year of heavy dramatic roles; the fifth nominee was Eleanor Parker as the victimized wife in the prison drama *Caged.*

Ben-Hur was the biggest winner in 1959, winning eleven of twelve nominations, including Best Actor for Charlton Heston. An actor of limited range, Heston won his Oscar as a result of the patterned habit of the block vote, namely citing one film in most categories, deservedly or undeservedly. The Best Actor competition that year was extraordinary: Laurence Harvey in *Room at the Top,* Jack Lemmon in *Some Like It Hot,* Paul Muni in *The Last Angry Man,* and James Stewart in *Anatomy of a Murder,* who won the New York Film Critics Award.

Errors of Omission

The nominations have repeatedly been criticized for slighting or bypassing worthy achievements. The Academy's apologetic response has been consistent: there can be only five nominees and only one winner in each category. This inevitably means that not every worthy achievement will be nominated. Yet, errors of omission are particularly visible in years in which the nominated achievements are mediocre, compared with the excellence of those overlooked.

The most glaring omission is when a movie is nominated for Best Picture, but its director fails to be recognized. Lack of correlation between Best Picture and Best Director nominees is a function of the voting patterns. In 1995, although their films were cited in several categories, directors Ron Howard *(Apollo 13)* and Ang Lee *(Sense and Sensibility)* came up empty-handed. Instead, the two slots in the directorial category were filled by Mike Figgis, whose *Leaving Las Vegas* was nominated in major categories but not Best Picture.

All the winners of major critics groups who failed to receive recognition from the Academy probably deserved nomination. The most conspicuous omissions among performers cited by the New York Film Critics include: Greta Garbo in *Anna Karenina,* Ida Lupino in *The Hard Way,* Tallulah Bankhead in *Lifeboat,* Ralph Richardson in *Breaking the Sound Barrier,* Liv Ullmann in *Cries and Whispers* and *Scenes from a Marriage,*

John Gielgud in *Providence,* Glenda Jackson in *Stevie,* Norma Aleandro in *The Official Story,* and most recently, James Broadbent, as the eccentric and repressed Gilbert (of the team Gilbert and Sullivan) in Mike Leigh's *Topsy Turvy.*

Some players have been consistently passed over by the Academy. Edward G. Robinson was never nominated, despite a number of estimable performances, such as *Little Caesar,* and despite considerable range, excelling in playing men on both sides of the law, like his detective in *Double Indemnity.*

At least three of Jean Arthur's performances should have been recognized: *Mr. Deeds Goes to Town,* opposite Gary Cooper; *Mr. Smith Goes to Washington,* as Jimmy Stewart's secretary; and in George Stevens's Western *Shane,* with Alan Ladd and Van Heflin. All three movies were nominated for Best Picture and most of her co-stars earned acting nominations: Cooper in *Deeds,* Stewart and others in *Smith,* and Brandon De Wilde and Jack Palance in *Shane.* Vastly underestimated, Jean Arthur was nominated only once, in George Stevens's *The More the Merrier.*

Some films have earned nominations for several of their players, but excluded the one or two who deserved to be nominated but for some reason were not. Eleanor Parker and Lee Grant were nominated for *Detective Story,* but not Kirk Douglas, in one of his best roles, as the obsessively righteous detective. Burt Lancaster and Shirley Jones earned awards for *Elmer Gantry,* but Jean Simmons, who played a devout evangelist, was conspicuously omitted. Spencer Tracy received a nomination for the courtroom drama, *Inherit the Wind,* but co-star Fredric March did not. And Greer Garson was nominated for playing Eleanor Roosevelt in *Sunrise at Campobello,* but Ralph Bellamy, who re-created his Tony award-winning role as President Roosevelt, was not. *The Sundowners* was nominated in 1960 in many categories, including two acting nominations for Deborah Kerr and Glynis Johns, but not Robert Mitchum. In his entire career, Mitchum earned only one supporting nomination, in the war film *The Story of G.I. Joe.*

Year after year, critics compile lists of achievements bypassed by the Academy. Vincent Canby noted that in 1980 "there have been more glaring omissions than in any year in the recent past." On his list were six male performances, each of which he thought was more worthy than Peter O'Toole's in *The Stunt Man,* or Jack Lemmon's in *Tribute.* Canby singled out Alan King's tycoon in *Just Tell Me What You Want;* James Caan's blue-collar worker in *Hide in Plain Sight,* Michael Caine's psychiatrist in *Dressed to Kill,* Brad Dourif's anti-prophet in *Wise Blood,* David Bennent in *The Tin Drum,* and Anthony Hopkins's doctor in *The Elephant Man.*

Three of these, *Just Tell, Hide in Plain Sight,* and *Wise Blood,* were box-office failures; *The Tin Drum,* was a foreign film, and *Dressed to Kill* was a suspense-thriller, which might have explained their exclusion. The Academy is known for its biases against foreign films and thrillers. Many of the aforementioned omissions were in films that were commercially unsuccessful. Indeed, popular films and popular performers have often been nominated *because* of their popularity. There's no doubt that performers stand better chances to get nominated for lukewarm work in a blockbuster than for a distinguished performance in a fiasco.

Popularity Contest

Popularity with audiences rather than quality of performance have often been yardsticks for nomination. Bing Crosby was a dominant box-office draw in the 1940s, following his recordings and his "Road" movies with Bob Hope and Dorothy Lamour. His 1944 Oscar, *Going My Way,* and second nomination, *The Bells of St. Mary's,* were as much a reward to his long-enduring popularity as a tribute to his natural, effortless style of acting; it also helped that both movies were commercial hits.

Doris Day was the most popular female star in America for close to a decade. Her first and only nomination, for the comedy *Pillow Talk,* coincided with her appearance on the "Ten Most Popular Stars" poll in 1959. As she herself recorded: "I was surprised at being nominated for an Academy Award for my performance in *Pillow Talk,* and even more surprised to find that by the end of that year, I had shot up to number one at the box-office." Day's performance in this film didn't match her work in Hitchcock's *The Man Who Knew Too Much,* or the biopicture of singer Ruth Eting, *Love Me or Leave Me,* arguably the most accomplished of her career.

Robert Redford was catapulted to the pantheon of movie stars in 1969, after the success of *Butch Cassidy and the Sundance Kid,* co-starring Paul Newman. Four years later, the two stars were reteamed in a bigger hit, *The Sting,* proving that there was no need for a love interest to be in a film to make it a smash hit. Redford received his one and only nomination for *The Sting* (Newman did not), possibly because of its box-office appeal and Redford's appearance in another blockbuster that year, *The Way We Were.* Redford would have preferred to be honored for his work in Michael Ritchie's political satire *The Candidate,* and in Sydney Pollack's *Jeremiah Johnson.* But, by the time of the 1974 nominations, the Academy couldn't ignore that Redford ranked as America's most popular star.

Richard Dreyfuss's 1977 Oscar for *The Goodbye Girl* was probably also related to the fact that he had appeared in three of the all-time biggest blockbusters, *American Graffiti, Jaws,* and *Close Encounters of the Third Kind.*

Some actors would not have been nominated had they not appeared in a commercial hit. Ali McGraw, a beautiful if mediocre actress, began her career after a successful turn as a model, establishing herself as star material in *Goodbye, Columbus,* as the Jewish princess. McGraw's third movie, *Love Story,* based on Eric Segal's best-seller, opened to mixed reviews but was such a smash hit that it was nominated in every category: Picture, Actress, Actor (Ryan O'Neal), Director (Arthur Hiller).

Similarly, John Avildsen's *Rocky* would not have been nominated for ten awards, and won three, including Best Picture, had it not been the year's top money-maker, with over fifty million dollars in domestic rentals. Popular films make those associated with them appear more gifted than they are. Indeed, had Talia Shire's performance as Rocky's shy girlfriend been contained in another film, she would not have received a supporting nomination.

The choice of winners has often been based on a popularity rather than a talent contest since the final voting is by the Academy's entire membership. Consequently, many artists stress the nomination, because it is based on peer evaluation which is allegedly less biased. Since the final selections are made by a large and varied body, many irrelevant factors—ad campaigns, studio politics, the nominees' personality, popularity within the industry—come into play. And while there may be consensus over the deservedness of the five nominees, it is much harder to choose the *one.* Hence, almost inevitably, emotional and political factors impinge on the final selections.

The charge that the choices are based on the validity of the nominees' personalities offscreen rather than their on-screen work is double-edged. On the one hand, brilliant actors have been denied the Oscar (and nomination) because of real or alleged politics. But mediocre artists have won the award for sentimental and other personal reasons, such as an impressive comeback, career longevity, old age. In all of these cases, the Oscar is used as a symbol of social acceptance, granted to previously wayward members of the film colony.

Joan Crawford had been in Hollywood for twenty years, an MGM star for a decade, one of the highest-paid women in the United States, and an extremely ambitious actress, but she lacked one important thing—peer recognition as epitomized by the Oscar. In the 1940s, Crawford's career was in a rut and she was proclaimed a wash-out. In fact, Louis B. Mayer "released" her from her long-term contract after eighteen years of loyal service. For two years, she didn't make a picture until Warner came to the rescue with *Mildred Pierce*. Crawford demonstrated in this movie as much will power as acting talent, which was limited, in a perfect role that captured the essence of her offscreen life. She was as good as she could ever be, and the Academy rewarded her with an Oscar. The 1945 Oscar rejuvenated Crawford's career and she survived as an actress for decades beyond her MGM rivals; Greta Garbo and Norma Shearer both retired in 1942.

Olivia de Havilland, like Bette Davis, fought Warner for better roles and better contracts, for which she was occasionally suspended. At the end of De Havilland's seven-year contract, Warner refused to release her, demanding that the contract be extended to include the duration of her suspensions. De Havilland sued, winning a landmark victory with a court's decision setting the outside limit of a player's contract at seven years, including suspensions. Absent from the screen for three years, she celebrated her comeback with an Oscar for *To Each His Own*. Similarly, Gary Cooper's second Oscar for *High Noon* was also a comeback victory, after a faltering career in the late 1940s.

The impact of offscreen factors on winning the Oscar was abundantly clear in Ingrid Bergman's case. Bergman's career was severely damaged after she left her husband and daughter, and went to Italy to work with director Roberto Rossellini. Bergman's adulterous affair, bearing a child out of the wedlock, shocked the film community. After all, Bergman had been advertised as a "normal," "wholesome" star living an idyllic family life. Her screen roles, particularly Sister Mary Benedict in *The Bells of St. Mary's,* perpetuated this image.

Bergman's affair with Rossellini, while officially married to another man, made her the subject of a most vicious campaign. Fan magazines, the church, and even school organizations condemned her, and there was serious talk of boycotting her films in the United States. Senator Edwin C. Johnson denounced Bergman on the Senate floor as "a free-love cultist," "a common mistress," "a powerful influence for evil," and "Hollywood's apostle of degradation," demanding that she be barred forever from the country on grounds of "moral turpitude."

For almost a decade, Bergman was "persona non grata" in the United States. Unfortunately, none of the pictures she made with Rossellini was commercially successful. Neither artist benefitted from the professional collaboration; Bergman's star charisma was somehow foreign to Rossellini's neorealistic style that, among other things, relied on the use of nonprofessional actors. Soon the marriage itself was in troubled waters.

However, in 1955, producer Darryl Zanuck came to the rescue, offering Bergman the lead in *Anastasia,* as the the amnesiac refugee passing as

Tzar Nicholas and Alexandra's surviving daughter. This was done against the advice of Fox's executives, who believed that the American public had not forgiven Bergman yet. But with Zanuck's insistence and a new publicity campaign, now advertising Bergman as a courageous woman who sacrificed her career and family for the sake of love, her image began to change. Her comeback story reads like a Hollywood fairy tale. Ed Sullivan, the noted TV host, flew to London, where *Anastasia* was filmed to interview her, though not before soliciting his viewers' opinion concerning her return to America. Many believed that it was Sullivan's popular show that turned the tide of public opinion to her favor. Bergman's reputation was restored with a second Oscar for *Anastasia,* though she did not accept it in person. Bergman returned to the United States in 1959, when the Academy asked her to be a presenter on the show.

But in the 1950s, the very mention of Ingrid Bergman's name evoked negative response. Shelley Winters recalls that during her affair with Italian actor Vittorio Gassman, her Universal agents told her: "We have invested a great deal of money in you. And now you are destroying our investment." "You may not have noticed," they warned, "but Ingrid Bergman's career is finished in the United States and perhaps throughout the world. Are you ready to have that happen to you?"

Winters was also asked to keep a low profile during the 1951 nominations, to assure her placement on the ballots. Thus, a dispute with co-star Frank Sinatra on the set of *Meet Danny Wilson* infuriated Universal's Leo Spitz. "From all the rumors we hear," Spitz told her, "you're going to be nominated for Best Actress for *A Place in the Sun.* If you keep your publicity as dignified as possible—given your explosive personality—there's a good chance the Academy will vote for your performance, and you will get the Oscar." Winters was surprised to hear that "most of the newspapers owe us favors and we can keep all this nonsense out of the press."

Elizabeth Taylor's nominations and first Oscar were more dependent on events in her life offscreen than on-screen. Taylor's chances to win the award for her second nomination, *Cat on a Hot Tin Roof,* were good, because MGM's publicity had started an early campaign for her, and it was an estimable performance. Furthermore, the 1958 death of husband Mike Todd in a plane crash earned Taylor the sympathy of the industry and the press. However, a few months prior to the 1959 ceremonies, she broke up Eddie Fisher's marriage to Debbie Reynolds, one of Hollywood's most celebrated unions, immediately changing her public stature over her rush to marry him. Even so, Taylor was nominated in the following year for *Suddenly Last Summer,* but lost out to Simone Signoret in *Room at the Top.*

Once again, personal factors that had denied Taylor the 1958 Oscar operated in her favor in 1960, when she was up for *Butterfield 8*. This time, it was Taylor's almost fatal illness that brought sympathy—and the Oscar. The Academy, the press, and the public had forgiven Taylor's "sins," and her bout with death restored her to favor. Taylor herself believed that "the reason I got the Oscar was that I had come within a breath of dying of pneumonia." And although "it meant being considered an actress and not a movie star," she still felt "it was for the wrong picture, since any of my three previous nominations was more deserving." In retrospect, Taylor's winning performance was not all that bad—contrary to popular notions, it is not the worst performance honored by the Academy! Still, Taylor was delighted when she won her second Oscar for *Who's Afraid of Virginia Woolf?* since, as one critic put it, "it was for what happened on the screen rather than off." In this picture she demonstrated, once and for all to those who still doubted, that she could really act.

Reward for Mediocrity

"The curious thing about awards," composer Jules Styne once observed, "is that one receives them for work one does not expect to receive them for, and does not receive them for work one does." Styne received the Tony Award for *Hallelujah, Baby!* but not for *Gypsy*. Similarly, many performers have been nominated for mediocre work, not their best. And while there is an agreement over the candidate's talent, there is disagreement over the particular film for which they receive nominations or awards.

Lew Ayres was not nominated for playing the pacifist soldier in *All Quiet on the Western Front*, but for his doctor in *Johnny Belinda*, because that picture was nominated in every category. Cary Grant failed to earn recognition for any of his great comedies, *The Awful Truth, Bringing up Baby,* and *His Girl Friday,* or for his wonderful performance in Hitchcock's *North By Northwest*, but was nominated for two pedestrian movies, *Penny Serenade* and *None but the Lonely Heart*. John Wayne was not nominated for his excellent Westerns, *Red River* and *The Searchers*, but for the patriotic war film, *Sands of Iwo Jima*.

Lee Marvin undoubtedly gave a better performance in a more demanding role in *Ship of Fools*, as a vulgar Texan tycoon, than in *Cat Ballou*. Steve McQueen's one and only nomination was for his inscrutable, alienated sailor in the big-budgeted *The Sand Pebbles*, but not for his more interesting work in the more intimate and sensitive, *Baby, the Rain Must Fall Down*, Horton Foote's story of a violent parolee in a small Southern town.

Several British actors were nominated not for their good work in British films but for mediocre American movies. Sir Michael Redgrave was nominated just once, as Orin in *Mourning Become Electra,* but not for his teacher in *The Browning Version,* or for Oscar Wilde's *The Importance of Being Earnest.* Sir Ralph Richardson received his first supporting nomination for *The Heiress,* but not for his servant in *The Fallen Idol,* or *Breaking the Sound Barrier.*

More than a few winners have received the Oscar for average work in popular films. Even Oscar's supporters claim that while the winners might not be those who gave the best performance of the year, they are, nonetheless, Oscar-caliber artists, worthy of the award. The doubt is not over the award's deservedness, but over the *particular* achievement for which the award is given. Once again, the Academy claims that in the final account, the Oscars "even out the odds," honoring (sooner or later) artists who have consistently made Oscar-caliber films. Some members are known to vote for the *overall* quality of the nominee rather than the present nomination.

Bette Davis once said that her two Oscars, for *Dangerous* and *Jezebel,* didn't mean much because they were for the "wrong" films; she would have been more gratified to win for *The Letter* or for *All About Eve.* James Stewart gave a finer performance in *Mr. Smith Goes to Washington* than in his Oscar role, *The Philadelphia Story.*

The twelve-time nominee and four-time-winner Katharine Hepburn was nominated for distinguished roles, but won for merely good ones. Three of her nominated performances represent not only Hepburn's best but some of the best acting in American cinema: *Alice Adams, The Philadelphia Story,* and Mary Tyronne in Sidney Lumet's brilliant version of Eugene O'Neill's *Long Day's Journey into Night.* But Hepburn won for *Morning Glory, Guess Who's Coming to Dinner, The Lion in Winter,* and *On Golden Pond.*

Academy voters are naturally influenced by the selection of critics groups, such as the New York Film Critics Circle. Several players received the critics' award for a role which brought them a nomination—but not the award. Almost invariably, they later went on to win the Oscar for a lesser performance. Jon Voight was singled out by the New York Film Critics for his Jo Buck in *Midnight Cowboy,* for which he was also nominated, but he received the Oscar for *Coming Home.* Jack Nicholson won the New York Film Critics Award and an Oscar nomination for his private eye in *Chinatown,* but the Academy Award was given to him a year later, for *One Flew Over the Cuckoo's Nest.*

Some players actually won the Oscar for the weakest of their nominated performances. Jack Lemmon did not win for *Some Like It Hot, The Apartment,* or *Days of Wine and Roses,* but for *Save the Tiger.* Faye

Dunaway lost twice, as Bonnie Parker in *Bonnie and Clyde* and as the mysterious femme fatale in *Chinatown*, but she won for *Network*. Dustin Hoffman's first Oscar, for *Kramer vs. Kramer,* was not on par with his other nominated roles.

Reward for Eccentricity

Eccentricity, often manifested in physical transformation and heavy accents, is a common attribute of many male and female winning performances. "The best way to win awards in Hollywood," critic Andrew Sarris once observed, "is to plaster a young face with old-age makeup—artificial aging is interpreted as an infallible sign of 'character' for those who confuse the art of acting with the art of disguise." Players have used tricks other than heavy makeup to impress Academy voters. Such antics do not win awards in themselves but they contribute to the overall impact of performances, often making reasonable or passable work look more striking than it really is.

Heavy accents have been used to great effect as far as the Academy is concerned. Spencer Tracy sported a thick accent for playing the Portuguese fisherman in *Captains Courageous,* and Mischa Auer used a droll accent for his eccentric role in the screwball comedy *My Man Godfrey*. Loretta Young attempted a Swedish accent in *The Farmer's Daughter,* and Ingrid Bergman used her native Swedish for the role of the neurotic missionary in *Murder on the Orient Express;* in the same film, Albert Finney was unrecognizable, donning a wig and speaking in a Belgian accent as Hercule Poirot. Alan Arkin employed a Russian accent in *The Russians Are Coming,* and Michael Caine spoke directly to the audience with a Cockney accent in *Alfie*.

At present, twelve-time nominee Meryl Streep is nicknamed "the queen of accents," for using a different accent in almost every film, from Polish in *Sophie's Choice* to British in *Plenty* to Danish in *Out of Africa* to Aussie in *Cry in the Dark*.

Last year, Australian Toni Collette put on a Philadelphian accent for playing the mother in *The Sixth Sense,* which probably increased her chances of receiving a supporting nomination. Receiving accolades in the same category was British Samantha Morton, nominated for playing Sean Penn's randy and mute laundress-girlfriend in Woody Allen's *Sweet and Lowdown*.

The art of disguise derives from a long theatrical tradition, encouraging stage players to exploit mimicry and makeup as a form of sensationalism. In film too, heavy makeup and on-screen aging have been embraced by actors to impress the Academy. Fredric March's makeup transformation in *Dr. Jekyll and Mr. Hyde* was, of course, necessary, but it also contributed to the overall effectiveness of the film itself. Irene Dunne and Richard Dix aged extensively during the thirty-year-span of *Cimarron*. Greer Garson progressed from boarding-house slave to wealthy matriarch in *Mrs. Parkington*, a story that covered half a century.

Similarly, attractive leading ladies have been rewarded for deglamorizing their looks and for their willingness to appear drab or frumpy. Bette Davis wore paddings on her legs, donned glasses, and pulled her hair back tight in *Now Voyager*. Olivia de Havilland played an ugly duckling in *The Heiress*, and Grace Kelly won an Oscar for *The Country Girl*, as an embittered, humiliated wife, wearing the most unglamorized and unflattering wardrobe in her career. Similarly, Elizabeth Taylor portrayed an old, fat, harsh, and deglamorized woman in *Who's Afraid of Virginia Woolf?*

For a decade, Lynn Redgrave couldn't shake her image in *Georgy Girl*, as a pathetic ugly duckling weighing 180 pounds! In 1998, Redgrave won a second, this time supporting, nomination for *Gods and Monsters,* as director James Whale's housekeeper, for which she affected a thick Hungarian accent.

Men have also used tricks: Yul Brynner shaved his head for *The King and I,* and continued to flaunt it as a trademark for the rest of his career. Lee Marvin played a dual role in *Cat Ballou,* a drunken gunslinger and a killer with a silver nose. John Wayne put on an eye patch for *True Grit,* and Marlon Brando puffed his cheeks in *The Godfather.* Robert De Niro gained sixty pounds to play the gluttonous Jake La Motta in *Raging Bull,* and Jack Nicholson also bloated for *Terms of Endearment* and *Prizzi's Honor.*

Then there are men in drag, from Jack Lemmon as Jerry/Daphne in *Some Like It Hot,* to Dustin Hoffman as Michael Dorsey/Dorothy Michaels in *Tootsie.* Playing homosexuals, transvestites, or transsexuals has helped to get recognition through the eccentric, campy behavior of their characters, as shown by Robert Preston, who played Julie Andrews's mentor in *Victor/Victoria,* who has a flamenco-drag number; John Lithgow in *The World According to Garp,* as Roberta, the former football player who has undergone a sex-change operation; and Jaye Davison in Neil Jordan's romantic drama, *The Crying Game,* whose gender comes as a total surprise to both Forrest Whitaker and the audience.

Playing the opposite gender is a great challenge for actors. The latest screen characters who struggled with hiding their real gender include two Oscar-winning actresses: 1999's Best Actress, Hilary Swank, as Teena Brandon/Brandon Teena in *Boys Don't Cry,* and 1998's Gwyneth Paltrow as Viola De Lesseps/Thomas Kent in *Shakespeare in Love.* Barbra Streisand deserved to be nominated, but was not, for playing Yentl/Anshel in the 1983 gender-bending drama *Yentl*.

The Academy has always rewarded excessive performances that contain "big scenes," often hysterical ones. In choosing scripts, actors, too, are aware that it is the easily identifiable quality (or qualities) of their roles that will make their performances stand out—hence the questionable supporting nomination of Brad Pitt for Terry Gilliam's *Twelve Monkeys,* in which he played a rebel son escaping from an asylum. Pitt was also rewarded for becoming a hot box-office star. Or Diane Ladd, nominated for an over-the-top role as a wicked mother, smearing her face with lipstick and acting "big," in David Lynch's fable *Wild at Heart.* After being so out of control in *Wild at Heart,* critics were amazed the following year that Ladd could be so restrained in playing a sensitive and liberal wife-mother opposite Robert Duvall in *Rambling Rose,* for which she received a third supporting nomination.

Once in a while there are pleasant surprises. In *Georgia,* it was Jennifer Jason Leigh who had the role with the range people associate with Oscar-caliber performance. Leigh, who won the New York Film Critics Best Actress, was cast as an ungifted singer, jealous of her successful older sister, played by Mare Winningham, who received a supporting nomination. Subtle performances such as Winningham's, which accentuated the character's tense but repressed emotions, are often overlooked by the Academy since they look so easy. For many, Winningham personified the phrase "less is more," a quality rare in Oscar-winning performances.

Pitt and Ladd notwithstanding, most of the aforementioned eccentric roles have been good, if not distinguished. But they also raise an interesting, if not easily answerable, question: Is the written role in the scenario more important than the delivered on-screen performance? Sally Field said of her second Oscar-winning role: "The script of *Places in the Heart* is so well done that it brings more attention to the role. Edna is such a complex character that she gives the actor a lot to do." Vanessa Redgrave echoed the same feeling about her nominated role in *The Bostonians:* "All I've done is play the lady Henry James wrote." Is this modesty noblesse oblige on the part of performers, or *is* the scripted role more critical for winning an Oscar than the specific interpretation by a particular performer?

The Oscar as Compensation

Artists who have unaccountably lost the award are not forgotten—the Academy tends to compensate the losers, usually in the near future, with belated Oscars. These consolatory awards serve as corrective mechanisms to the imperfections of the Oscar as a reward system.

Bette Davis's award for *Dangerous* is believed to be a compensation for missing out on the previous year's nominations. The attempt to introduce new selection procedures in 1934, the write-ins, failed to get Davis a much deserved nomination for *Of Human Bondage*. In 1935, upon being nominated for *Dangerous*, Davis herself cited Katharine Hepburn's performance in *Alice Adams* as the year's best. Davis's Oscar is considered to be the first consolation or "hold-over" award.

Robert Donat's first nomination was for *The Citadel*, as the struggling doctor, but he lost out to Spencer Tracy in *Captains Courageous*. In the following year, this was "corrected" and Donat received the award for a nobler, but no better, performance in *Goodbye, Mr. Chips*. But by correcting this error, the Academy created a new error and a new "victim," Jimmy Stewart, who gave the best performance of 1939 in *Mr. Smith Goes to Washington*. Once again this was corrected, in 1940, when Stewart got the award for *The Philadelphia Story*. The fact that Stewart was already enlisted in the military, thus becoming Hollywood's first major star to join the war effort, was probably not unrelated to his win—Stewart accepted the award in uniform.

In 1964, the film musical *My Fair Lady* was nominated in every major category except Best Actress, despite an elegant performance by Audrey Hepburn as Eliza Doolittle. Production of this film was marked by resentment over Jack Warners's refusal to cast Julie Andrews in a role she had played to great acclaim on stage. Under other circumstances, Hepburn would have been nominated, but the Acting Branch expressed its indignation by denying her a nomination and by conferring on Julie Andrews the award for *Mary Poppins,* released the same year. It felt as if Andrews got the award for the wrong film—had she played Eliza, she would have won an Oscar. *Mary Poppins* served as an excuse to compensate Andrews for the injustice done to her by Warner.

Another corrective mechanism is to compensate artists who have been nominated multiple times. In theory, the number of nominations should not be a factor; in practice, however, chances to win increase with the number of nominations.

About one-tenth of all winners have received the Oscar upon their third or later nomination. Ellen Burstyn *(Alice Doesn't Live Here Anymore)* and Faye Dunaway *(Network)* won the Best Actress Award at their third nominations; their previous nominations must have had some effect. Susan Hayward won the Oscar for a very good performance in *I Want to Live!* at her fifth nomination, but her previous losses must have counted too. Robert De Niro officially won the Best Actor Award for *Raging Bull*, but how could the Academy forget his memorable performances in *Taxi Driver* and *The Deer Hunter* a few years before? Gregory Peck was honored with Best Actor for *To Kill a Mockingbird*, but the vote also acknowledged his status as a perennial nominee with four citations to his record.

The Academy has devised other mechanisms to counter the inevitable imperfections of its evaluation. The Honorary Awards, set apart from the competitive merit awards, are given "for exceptionally distinguished service in the making of motion pictures or for outstanding service to the Academy." The regulations also stipulate that they "are not limited to the awards year," and "shall not be voted posthumously."

Chaplin never won a legitimate award, but he was honored with three Special Oscars, the first of which in 1927/28 for his "versatility and genius," in writing, producing, directing, and acting in *The Circus;* Chaplin was nominated for this film in competitive categories, but did not win. Whenever the Academy sensed that a major contribution has no chances of winning a legitimate award, they vote a Special Oscar. Laurence Olivier received the 1946 Special Award for his first Shakespearean film, *Henry V.* "One of the greatest foreign films," the citation stated, "no play of classic theatre was ever translated to celluloid with such faithful flawless art." Olivier received nominations for this film, but did not win.

Similarly, when rumors circulated that Fred Astaire was going to retire, the Academy hurried and honored him with a Special Oscar in 1949, for "his unique artistry and contributions to the techniques of musical pictures"; Astaire had never been nominated for his musical films.

Greta Garbo, one of the screen's great actresses, was nominated three times but never won. In 1954, she received a Special Oscar, which she never even bothered to collect. In 1958, the Board voted a Special Oscar for French actor Maurice Chevalier "for his contribution to the world of entertainment for more than half a century." The Board denied rumors that there was a connection between the award and the fact that Chevalier failed to be nominated for *Gigi*, which swept most of the year's awards. But it was probably a compensation for this oversight as well as for having lost the Best Actor in 1929/30, when he was up for two films. Lillian Gish, another screen legend, received an Honorary Oscar in 1970 for her cumulative work. Gish was nominated only once, for a supporting role in *Duel in the Sun.*

A look at the Honorary Oscars shows that there is always some meaningful link with the legitimate Oscars. Edward G. Robinson, who was never nominated, received an Honorary award in 1973 for a half-century career. Unfortunately, the ceremonies took place just months after his death of cancer. A four-time nominee, Rosalind Russell was honored with the Jean Hersholt Humanitarian award in 1972 for her charity work. Barbara Stanwyck, a four-time nominee, received an Honorary Oscar in 1982, presented to her by William Holden, who made his film debut with her in *Golden Boy*. These have all been sentimental, but touching, moments in the history of the award.

Aware of their compensatory functions, most recipients of Honorary Oscars are sensitive about it. When Mickey Rooney, a four-time nominee, was given the 1983 Honorary Oscar, in recognition of his sixty-year career, which began at the age of two, he recited all the awards he had recently received so that the Academy would not think it was doing him a favor. "I'd been the world's biggest box-office star at 19 and, at 40, unable to get work," Rooney said, reminding his colleagues of the inherent instabilities in this glamorous profession.

Paul Newman, the recipient of the 1985 Honorary Oscar, was absent from the ceremonies; he was filming in Chicago. One of the Academy's great losers, Newman had received six Best Actor nominations. The special award was bestowed "in recognition of his many memorable and compelling screen performances and for his personal integrity and dedication to his craft." In his taped acceptance remarks, Newman made sure to state that unlike previous recipients, he was neither ill nor close to retirement. "I'm especially grateful that this did not come wrapped as a gift certificate to Forest Lawn, my best work is down the pike in front of me."

In the following year, injustice was corrected with a legitimate Oscar for *The Color of Money* (a sequel to 1961 *The Hustler*, which contains Newman's best work). Though Newman gave a decent performance as an aging pool player, doubts prevailed—was it a sentimental, compensatory vote for his previous defeats? The Academy could not do enough for Newman, and after winning an honorary Oscar in 1985, and a competitive Oscar in 1986, he was given the Jean Hersholt humanitarian award for years of donating money to various charities.

Deborah Kerr, a six-time Best Actress nominee, received an Honorary Oscar in 1993. Stanley Donen received the 1998 Honorary Oscar, "in appreciation of a body of work marked by grace, elegance, wit and visual innovation." Donen had produced and directed twenty-seven films, including *On the Town, Singin' in the Rain,* and *Charade,* yet had never been nominated for an Oscar.

Aside from Honorary Oscars, the Academy established in 1937 the Irving G. Thalberg Memorial Award, to honor "the most consistent high level of production achievement by an individual producer." Producer-director Stanley Kramer received this award in 1961, coinciding with the release of *Judgment at Nuremberg*, for which he received a Best Director nomination. Kramer had also been nominated for *The Defiant Ones*, but did not win. Alfred Hitchcock, a five-time directorial nominee, received the Thalberg award in 1967, and Mervyn LeRoy, nominated once for *Random Harvest*, in 1976.

In 1975 Howard Hawks, nominated in 1941 for *Sergeant York*, and French director Jean Renoir, also nominated once for his American-made *The Southerner* in 1945, both won Special Oscars for their cumulative work. King Vidor, who had been nominated five times as a director—for *The Crowd* in 1927/28, *Hallelujah* in 1929/30, *The Champ* in 1931/32, *The Citadel* in 1938, and *War and Peace* in 1956—received a Special Academy Award in 1978 to make up for all of these losses. Fellini, a four-time Oscar nominee, received an Honorary Award for lifetime achievements in 1992, two years before he died.

The Career Oscars

When the Oscar honors veteran artists who have been nominated several times, it is impossible to tell whether the award is given for a specific accomplishment or for an entire career of achievements. This is yet another corrective device, known as the "career Oscar." In such cases, the official reason and particular performance for which artists win serves as an excuse to reward them for careers full of contributions. The career Oscar is not well-respected, as recipients can never be sure if their win was based on sentimental or meritorious considerations. As one critic observed, the gesture has been dismissed as "more of a back-scratching symptom of the film capital's love of saying thanks for past services than a genuine tribute for current achievements."

The first player to have received a career Oscar was Mary Pickford, who officially won for *Coquette*, her first talking movie (and the first acting award for a sound film). In actuality, the honor paid Pickford a tribute for having been the first international movie star. Critics believe that the Oscar was "doubtless as much for past performances and for her service to, and eminence in, the industry, as for *Coquette*," particularly since the latter was not a very good performance.

Marie Dressler's award for *Min and Bill* can also be considered a career Oscar: she had been a famous screen (and stage) actress for decades. Winning at sixty-two, Dressler was the oldest female winner until Jessica Tandy won Best Actress when she was eighty-one. Both Pickford and Dressler retired from the screen shortly after winning; Pickford made only three more films before quitting in 1933, and Dressler's career was cut short by death that same year.

Ronald Colman had been an exemplary British actor in Hollywood for three decades, with fifty pictures to his credit, before winning for *A Double Life* in 1947. Colman had been one of the few players who became even more popular with the advent of sound, due to his marvelous voice and impeccable diction, both of which added immensely to his appeal. Colman was possibly rewarded for his enduring popularity in a medium marked by ephemeral success. And he may have also been compensated for previous nominations, in *Bulldog Drummond, Condemned,* and *Random Harvest.* His belated Oscar, at the age of fifty-six, was for a career in the silent and sound eras and for box-office popularity. After the Oscar, however, Colman's screen record was poor, making only a few films before his death in 1958, at the age of sixty-seven.

The 1969 vote for John Wayne's performance in *True Grit* was based on sentimental as well as on career-long achievements, though his work in this film was acclaimed by most critics. Wayne had been making films for over forty years, and had been a top star for twenty. With this Oscar, Wayne's colleagues essentially admitted that they had underestimated his acting skills. Wayne had been nominated once before, for his heroic role in *Sands of Iwo Jima,* which he lost to Broderick Crawford. Winning the Oscar at the age of sixty-two had no pragmatic affect on Wayne's career. But it was of great symbolic and prestige value to him.

Of Wayne's generation, Henry Fonda was the only major star without an Oscar. Fonda's first and only nomination was for his portrayal of Tom Joad in *The Grapes of Wrath* in 1940. In the late 1970s, the Academy and the American Film Institute realized that Fonda's achievements had never received their due recognition—and that he was not very healthy. Consequently, Fonda was showered with life achievement awards, from the American Film Institute in 1978, the Golden Globe in 1980, and an Honorary Oscar "for his life-long contributions to the art of filmmaking," in 1981. "It's been a very rewarding forty-six years for me and this has got to be the climax," Fonda said. But it was not the climax, though neither Fonda nor the Academy could have anticipated that a year later he would be named Best Actor for *On Golden Pond.* The Academy restored justice with the more prestigious legitimate Oscar at almost the very last minute. Daughter Jane Fonda received the Oscar for him in a lengthy and emotional speech. The cameras later followed Jane as she drove to her father's house to present the statuette in person. Henry Fonda died few months later.

Geraldine Page had been nominated eight times, five for Best Actress and three for Supporting Actress. Her winning role in *The Trip to*

Bountiful was good, though not her best. Some of her nominations, particularly for *Sweet Bird of Youth* and for Woody Allen's *Interiors,* were far more impressive. Like Katharine Hepburn, Page did not win for her best work.

The sentimentality factor is often reflected in the Academy's favoring older actors over younger and inexperienced ones, at times ignoring the performance's quality. Accused of erring on the side of conservatism at the expense of daring, the Academy has sometimes used the award as a compensation for survival in a volatile industry rather than as a merit award.

This charge bears some validity in the male acting categories. Of the sixty-six Best Actor winners, about eight were the youngest nominees in their respective years, like Marlon Brando (thirty) in 1954, or William Hurt (thirty-six) in 1985. But even Brando and Hurt were experienced performers, with notable work in the theater. In most years, the award was bestowed on older, at times the oldest, nominees. In the 1970s, the Oscar was conferred on older players, such as John Wayne at sixty-two; Art Carney at fifty-four; Peter Finch at sixty; Henry Fonda at seventy-six. Of the Best Actors, only Ernest Borgnine and Maximilian Schell were both young and unestablished. The preeminence of age over youth is consistent with other findings: Best Actors are older than Best Actresses at their film debuts, first nomination, and first win.

A totally different picture prevails among the Best Actresses, half of whom have been the youngest nominees in their respective years: Janet Gaynor was twenty-two, Katharine Hepburn twenty-seven, Claudette Colbert twenty-nine, Bette Davis twenty-seven. Only few Best Actresses have been the oldest, like Marie Dressler, Katharine Hepburn at her second win, Shirley MacLaine, and Jessica Tandy, but they are the exception. A large number of Best Actresses—Grace Kelly, Audrey Hepburn, Joanne Woodward, Gwyneth Paltrow, and most recently, Hilary Swank—had only brief film experience before winning.

The supporting winners, unlike the leading, have been either young and inexperienced or old and established. In both the male and female groups, for each young winner, there's a counter-example of an old player. George Chakiris was twenty-nine in 1961, but Ed Begley was sixty-one in 1962 and Melvyn Douglas sixty-two in 1963. As with the Best Actors, in the 1970s the pattern was to select old and established actors:

In 1968, Jack Albertson (58) won over Gene Wilder
In 1969, Gig Young (56) over Elliott Gould
In 1970, John Mills (62) over Richard Castellano
In 1973, John Houseman (70) over Randy Quaid

In 1975, George Burns (80) over Brad Dourif
In 1976, Jason Robards (57) over Ned Beatty
In 1981, John Gielgud (77) over Howard S. Rollins
In 1985, Don Ameche (77) over Klaus Maria Brandauer
In 1987, Sean Connery (57) over Albert Brooks
In 1991, Jack Palance over (72) over Michael Lerner
In 1992, Gene Hackman (62) over Jaye Davidson
In 1994, Martin Landau (66) over Samuel Jackson
In 1998, James Coburn (71) over Billy Bob Thornton
In 1999, Michael Caine (66) over Tom Cruise

Timothy Hutton, the youngest supporting nominee (twenty), and Cuba Gooding Jr. (twenty-eight) have been the exceptions.

Almost the same pattern describes the Supporting Actresses, who have been either very old or very young. However, there have been more inexperienced and younger winners among the supporting women than in any other category: Teresa Wright and Anne Baxter were each twenty-three, Patty Duke sixteen. But for each young recipient, there was an old one: Jane Darwell won at sixty, Ethel Barrymore at sixty-five, Josephine Hull at sixty-six, Margaret Rutherford at seventy-two. This conservative trend of honoring age over youth continued into the 1980s:

In 1968, Ruth Gordon (72) won over Lynn Carlin
In 1970, Helen Hayes (70) over Karen Black and Sally Kellerman
In 1972, Eileen Heckart (53) over Jeannie Berlin and Susan Tyrrell
In 1975, Lee Grant (46) over Ronnee Blakely and Lily Tomlin
In 1976, Beatrice Straight (60) over Jodie Foster
In 1981, Maureen Stapleton (56) over Elizabeth McGovern
In 1984, Peggy Ashcroft (77) over Christine Lahti
In 1989, Brenda Fricker (55) over Lena Olin

Inexperienced winners like Goldie Hawn, who was twenty-four, and Mary Steenburgen who was twenty-seven, were a rarity in the past. In 1993, at the age of eleven, Anna Paquin became the second youngest winner ever (after Tatum O'Neal, who was ten in 1973) to receive an Oscar, as Flora, Holly Hunter's jealous daughter in *The Piano*. Indeed, in the 1990s, younger winners such as Marisa Tomei, Mira Sorvino, Juliette Binoche, and most recently, Angelina Jolie (who was twenty-four when she won for *Girl, Interrupted*) have prevailed, perhaps reflecting the Academy's new demographics.

Overall, the best chances to win the Oscar at an early age and with brief film experience are for Best Actresses. The Academy's tendency to favor age over youth means that for veteran performers the Oscar has mostly symbolic effects—there's no denying that the Oscar is more influential when it honors young artists at the beginning of their career.

CHAPTER 12

The Meanings of Oscar

"There are two types of people," producer Dore Schary once observed. "One type asserts that awards mean nothing to them. The second type breaks into tears upon receiving an award and thanks their mother, father, children, the producer, the director, and—if they can crowd it in—the American Baseball League." As Howard Koch, former AMPAS president noted, the Oscar has been "sought and spurned, revered and reviled, called an incentive for excellence and a commercial tool."

Is grabbing an Oscar perceived to be the ultimate goal of every film artist? If so, what's the meaning of winning? What are filmmakers' subjective feelings toward the award? Is there complete embracing of the Oscar? ambivalence? cynicism? or outright rejection?

Total Embracement: The Oscar as Peer Recognition

Peer recognition is the primary reward in the acting profession. Most actors regard the winning of an Oscar as a great accolade, a supreme praise from colleagues. William C. DeMille, the second Academy president, explained in 1929: "The most valuable award a worker can get is to have the acknowledged praise of his fellow workers. It means a great deal more to us than just the acclaim of the public." The Oscar was considered to be the first occasion in film history in which "individual creative work is recognized, and meritorious achievements are passed upon by experts."

The very nomination for an Oscar is perceived to be an important achievement in its own right. In 1930, the Academy Board announced: "Regardless of which ones of the nominees are finally chosen by the Academy to win the statuette trophies, there will be undeniable distinction in winning the preliminary nominations at the hands of their fellow workers." In the first year, all the nominees received an honorable mention, a practice that was later dropped. The Academy still emphasizes the prestige of being nominated, conferring on every nominee a Certificate of Nomination. The nominees' luncheon, which takes place two weeks before the Oscar ceremonies, is designed to encourage esprit de corps among the contenders.

The first nomination serves as a formal acknowledgment of talent by peers. Penelope Milford, one of the youngest nominees *(Coming Home)*, recalls: "The minute the nominations were announced, the telephone started ringing. A lot of people now are telling me they always knew I had talent and how wonderful it is that I've been nominated. They're the same guys who wouldn't take a phone call from me last week. I'd like to blast them . . . but let's face it, that's not the way to play the game. You've got to keep cool." After the nomination, Milford realized she had become "a known and valued commodity."

Pride often comes along with tremendous anxiety. Whoopi Goldberg remembers that after her first nomination, for *The Color Purple* in 1985, "I gave myself the hives. I got them so bad, I had to go to the dermatologist. I was totally freaked out."

Cicely Tyson took great pride in her first nomination *(Sounder)*: "I'm proud and I want every person in the world to see the film." It was a special honor for a black actress to be nominated, and in a year in which Diana Ross was also a nominee, it was a double honor. Paul Winfield, Tyson's co-star in *Sounder*, also delighted in his nomination, because he was up against "heady competition" (Marlon Brando, Michael Caine, Laurence Olivier, and Peter O'Toole). Even though Winfield lost, he felt he had won, because the nomination came so soon and took him by surprise.

The significance of the first nomination is vividly recalled by Ray Milland. Apparently it was the sound mixer of *The Lost Weekend* who was the first to bet that Milland would be nominated and win. Milland drove home that night "in a very bemused state, trying not to think about it, but it kept filtering back. 'Could this wonderful thing possibly happen to me? To be acclaimed by one's colleagues in all the cinema crafts, for having given the best performance of the entire year? No! No, stop it! Don't even think about it. Think of the disappointment if nothing happens.'"

Even before the nominations were announced, Milland sensed a change of attitude: "I had been getting smiles from people I didn't know, a little more deference from the people in the mailroom, and an unaccountable query from the studio operations wanting to know if I'd prefer a parking lot right outside my dressing room instead of the one I now had."

The day the nominations were announced was considered "judgment day," on which "five actors would be in purgatory until the 'Night' four weeks later." Early in the morning, Milland saw his wife, son, cook, butler, and nurse all sitting in the dining room with their eyes glued to the window. He asked them, "what was going on, why they were up so early. As one they replied: 'Same as you. Waiting for the paper.'" Later on, "with the long-suffering look of a man forced to live with mental defectives, I went in to my breakfast. I was just lifting the cup to my lips, when I heard the scramble of the front door, and I froze. There was a moment of silence and then one big yelp of exuberance as they all came barreling through the door yelling, 'You made it? You're nominated!'"

The nomination gives actors a measure of assurance, a standard of gauging the quality of their work. As Milland recalled, before the opening of *The Lost Weekend,* "I didn't know whether what I'd done was good or bad, a subject of this kind (alcoholism) hadn't been done before. I had no standards, and it had depressed me terribly." For Milland, the nomination's most important effect was that "although I had been termed a movie star in the usual magazine concept for five or six years, I was now being accepted as an actor with dramatic merit. It was a wonderful feeling."

That peer esteem is one of Oscar's most vital functions, even for veteran players, is easy to document. James Cagney believed that "praise from your peers generates a special kind of warmth." "I've always maintained," Cagney said in his *Yankee Doodle Dandy*'s acceptance speech, "that in this business, you are only as good as the fellow thinks you are."

Peer recognition was also the most valued reward for the young and inexperienced Mercedes McCambridge *(All the King's Men)*. The Oscar literally changed McCambridge's life: her salary skyrocketed overnight, she got more publicity, more invitations to parties, and an active social life. All of these changes were "highly enjoyable fringe benefits, but, best of all, was the knowing that you earned it from your peers, that actors voted for *your* acting."

Theater awards perform the same vital role. "There is something very special about having your work acknowledged by your peers," Joel Grey said after winning a Tony for *Cabaret.* "It is a milestone to work for, and the first time something like this happens to you, it is deeply satisfying."

Other film forums perform the same function without conferring prizes. For Martin Scorsese, whose third feature, *Mean Streets,* was selected for the 1973 New York Film Festival, "it was the most important time of my life. The festival was a launching pad for my work." This kind of acknowledgment is crucial for artists who are at the beginning of their careers: "The Festival can make the difference between recognition and disappearance."

The Oscar legitimizes the talent of popular movie stars who have not previously enjoyed respect from colleagues. "Before I made *Two*

Women," (her Oscar-winning film), Sophia Loren said succinctly, "I had been a performer. Afterward, I was an actress." Loren had been a box-office star in Italy and America, but her 1961 Oscar assumed a special meaning: "I know some actors have deprecated the value and purpose of the Academy Award, but I'm certainly not one of them. As far as I'm concerned, if you are a professional actor who has pride in his work, the judgment of your peers should be important to you." Loren treasures each and every award she has ever received, and her Oscar is "in a place of honor."

The Oscar also reinforces the determination of players to pursue careers in a profession that's inherently unstable. Asked how *Gandhi* changed his life, in addition to the resulting barrage of scripts and a constantly ringing telephone, Ben Kingsley said, "I profoundly believe I'm an actor now. I'm not saying I believe I'm a good actor. I just believe there is nothing else in the world I should be than an actor." The Oscar made Kingsley see the tip of the iceberg, as he said: "I know it's there and it's real."

Mercedes Ruehl, who won a supporting Oscar for playing a video store owner who nurtures a burned-out radio talk-show host in *The Fisher King*, recollected that success has not come easily. However, "in light of the Oscar, all of these sort of doleful memories transform themselves into amusing and charming anecdotes for my memoirs."

Contrary to popular notions that stress commercial success, given the choice, most artists would favor peer recognition. When Peter Finch's publicist first met her client, she asked him what his ambition was. Finch replied unequivocally that the only thing he really wanted was that when he died they would write on his tombstone: "He was a good actor." Finch's wish came true, though he didn't live to see it happen; his Oscar for *Network* was awarded posthumously.

Another star, Ingrid Bergman, indicated long before she died that she wanted her tombstone to read, "she acted on the last day of her life." Which she did: Bergman's last big-screen appearance was in *Autumn Sonata,* for which she received the New York Film Critics Award and her sixth Best Actress nomination. Her last acting job was in the TV mini-series *Golda,* shown after her death. Bergman's self-chosen epitaph was: "Here lies a great actress."

The Oscar is not an achievement that just happens. Rather, it is on actors' minds early on in their careers as the ultimate symbol of success. Loretta Young, who began her career as a child but won an Oscar after nineteen years of acting, sang out "At long last," when her name was announced. And Shelley Winters shouted, when she won her first supporting Oscar, "I've waited fifteen years for this."

Susan Hayward was determined to get an Oscar ever since she made her debut. When she was defeated *(Smash-Up: The Story of a Woman)*, she tried to take it with a sense of humor. But the defeat made her even more committed: "I'll be nominated for an Oscar again. Maybe the next year. Maybe I'll have to wait until the fifties. But I intend to win some day. That's my goal." After winning *(I Want to Live!)*, at her fifth nomination and following years of hard work, producer Walter Wanger commented: "Thank heaven, now we can all relax. Suzie got what she's been chasing for twenty years." Hayward herself was convinced that she now had everything she had ever wanted in life. "I used to make pictures for Academy Awards," she confessed, but, "I'm not concerned about winning Oscars anymore. I'm not retiring, but now I'll act for the joy of it and for the money."

While Hayward's story is by no means unique, it attests to a displacement of goals—the Oscar was originally designed as a local gesture by Hollywood's artists to honor film achievements. The Oscar was an afterthought on the Academy's agenda, barely mentioned in the 1927 statement of goals. No one could have anticipated that it would become such a "sacred" end in its own right. It's no secret that artists set out consciously to make an "Oscar-winning" film, or give an "Oscar-winning" performance. For better or for worse, winning an Oscar has become a major motive for choosing projects, based on the knowledge of which films are likely to get nominations and awards.

Shirley MacLaine turned down the title role in *Mistinguette,* a biopicture about the legendary French performer, in order to accept the part of the eccentric and possessive mother in *Terms of Endearment*. It was a conscious and rational decision. Two years before it was made, MacLaine had told her friends that the role might bring her an Oscar. "That's one reason I waited," MacLaine told the press, "and didn't work anywhere else for two years." MacLaine confessed she would like to win an Oscar and if she did, "I would think I deserved it." She could not have been more perceptive: *Terms of Endearment* provided the best part of her career—and the coveted Oscar.

It's no secret that actors wish to win the Oscar for a role they consider consequential, one for which they feel strong professional or emotional affinity. Bette Davis said that she won her two Oscars *(Dangerous* and *Jezebel)* for the "wrong" films; she would have preferred to win for *All About Eve*. By contrast, Gig Young, was "crazy" about his part as the marathon dance emcee in *They Shoot Horses, Don't They?* and considered himself "lucky enough to win for the right picture." Young summed up his career as "Thirty years and fifty-five pictures, of which there were not more than five that were any good, or any good for me."

The Oscar assumes a special meaning for players who worked indefatigably on their winning film, like Charlton Heston, who said he had never worked so hard on a picture as he did in *Ben-Hur*. The Oscar never loses its value, even for those who have won one. When Billy Wilder received his second directorial Oscar *(The Apartment)*, Charlton Heston remarked, "I guess, this is old hat to you." To which Wilder replied, "It never gets old hat!"

Receiving an Oscar not only puts pressure on the winners to show that they have been worthy of it, but also motivates them to win another one, to prove that the first win was no accident. When Sally Field won her second Oscar *(Places in the Heart)*, she shouted: "I've wanted more than anything to have your respect. And I can't deny the fact that you like me now. You really like me!" Field later told the *New York Times* that her response was emotional due to her "unorthodox career," having started on TV in *Gidget*. Noted Field: "The first 10 years of my career were in television and it wasn't the finest television. It's taking me a while to get over that feeling."

The Oscar serves as a metaphor for glamour as well. Shelley Winters recalls that upon being introduced to Mrs. Roosevelt and Mrs. Stevenson, who congratulated her and Vittorio Gassman for their films, Vittorio behaved "as if we both has just won Oscars." Winters believes that there are "very definite rules" for public appearances in Hollywood's parties and opening nights: "You must always look beautiful and gloriously happy, and you must be photographed with someone more important than yourself, like people who have won Oscars."

The statuette gets royal treatment from the winners. Joan Fontaine recalls "cradling it like a doll in my arms." Ray Milland drove after the ceremonies to Hillcrest, where "with the golden Oscar in my hand, I walked to the edge of Sunset and looked down at the lights. They seemed very bright that night. After a few moments, I quietly said, 'Mr. Navarro. Tonight they belong to me!'"

Asked if she had a mantel on which to put the Oscar, Mercedes McCambridge said, "Got one? I'll build one." And when a photographer asked McCambridge to pose while washing the Oscar in a basin, she refused, because she couldn't make fun of it. Regarding the statuette as "a remarkably beautiful piece of furnishing," McCambridge kept it in front of a mirror so that "it looked like two," a gimmick that was also used by Louise Fletcher and other winners. For years, McCambridge wore a miniature Oscar on a golden chain around her neck.

Shelley Winters promised to donate her first Oscar (for *The Diary of Anne Frank*) to the Anne Frank Museum in Amsterdam after Otto Frank, Anne's father and the family's only survivor, visited the set and predicted she would win an Oscar. But after winning, Winters kept it on a mantel for fifteen years, because she couldn't bear to part with it—"I thought the other one (for *A Patch of Blue)* would get lonely!" Years later, Winters brought the Oscar in person to Amsterdam. Initially, the statuette was put on public display, but it became such an attraction, with people touching and holding it, that after three days, it was put inside a glass case.

Peter Ustinov, a two-time Oscar and two-time Emmy winner, had on his desk "two emasculated gentlemen and two emasculated ladies," with the four of them making "a fine mixed-double match." Upon winning his third Emmy, Ustinov felt that he had built "an entire empire." Sophia Loren's Oscar was stolen by thieves who believed it was all solid gold. For a sixty-dollar check, she got a replacement from the Academy. Strange, thought Loren, how hard it was to win the Oscar, and how easy to replace it!

Ambivalence and Rejection

Most film artists embrace the Oscar completely, with no criticism, but some show a more cynical attitude toward its merits and fairness. Ambivalence toward the Oscar characterizes players who have been nominated multiple times, but never won. Others are critical—until they win, at which time their criticisms mellow. Total rejection of the Oscar describes the reaction of a small minority of filmmakers.

Humphrey Bogart's cynicism toward the Oscar mellowed the moment he won the award. Bogart was the kind of actor who detested Hollywood's phoniness, but was extremely conscientious about his work and one of the few men to be really proud of his profession. However, the idea of awards was "diametrically opposed to his concept of noncompetitive acting." Bogart held that "awards are meaningless for actors, unless they all play the same part." For him, the only true test of ability would be to have all the actors don black tights and recite Hamlet.

Bogart was first nominated for *Casablanca,* then for *The African Queen.* He lost the first time to Paul Lukas, and the 1951 pre-Oscar polls predicted that all four actors of *A Streetcar Named Desire* would win. Bogart's friends were certain he would beat Brando, and he was just as certain he would lose. When Bogart's friends asked him what he would say in his speech, if he won, he replied, "I'm not going to thank anyone; I'm just going to say I damn well deserve it." Bogart believed that he "owed nobody nothing," that his achievement was due to his own hard work. This attitude, as one critic suggested in the *New York Times,* was "in part making a shrewd bid for publicity, and in part he was giving irascible voice to his honest hatred of the crass and phony side of motion pictures." Before winning, Bogart described the Oscar as "silly" and "all bunk," and once even called it "a fake."

However, when Greer Garson announced his name, Bogart, stunned, rushed onto the stage, took the Oscar gently, as though it were a newborn baby, and said, "It's a long way from the Belgian Congo to the stage of the Pantages, but it's a lot nicer here." He then proceeded to thank his colleagues: "No one does it alone. As in tennis, you need a good opponent or partner to bring out the best in you. John (Huston) and Katie (Hepburn) helped me to be where I am now."

Wife-actress Lauren Bacall claims that in spite of Bogart's seeming cynicism, he was very emotional and very humble. Bogart had really wanted to win—"for all his bravado, when push came to shove, he did care and was stunned that it was such a popular victory. He had never felt people in town liked him much and hadn't expected such universal joy when his name was called." Bogart, too, used the Oscar as a metaphor of achievement. Indeed, Richard Burton recalls that once, when he "dared to challenge Bogart over acting, Bogart stormed out of the room and came back with his Oscar, which he thumped down on the table. 'You were saying?' he growled."

John Wayne was another cynic who deprecated the value of the Oscar before he won. Asked how he felt about the possibility of winning, he would say, "You can't eat awards. Nor, more to the point, drink them." "My pictures don't call for the great dramatic range that wins Oscars," the Duke used to say, which was based on the unfortunate reality that his specialty, Westerns, have always been overlooked by the Academy. In 1969, however, when prospects to win for *True Grit* seemed good, Wayne became more cautious in his public utterances. After winning, he praised the award as a great accolade: "The Oscar is a beautiful thing to have. It symbolizes appreciation of yourself by your peers. The Oscar means a lot to me, even if it took the industry 40 years to get around to it."

Before Jane Fonda won her first Oscar *(Klute)*, she used to say: "I don't care about the Oscars. I make movies to support the causes I believe in, not for any honors." But people close to her believed she was extremely disappointed to have lost the award for *They Shoot Horses, Don't They?* Indeed, despite her radical politics, she accepted the New York Film Critics Award for *They Shoot Horses* appreciatively: "It's the biggest accolade I've ever been given. One tries to be blasé about things, but now that it's happened, it's very nice."

George C. Scott and Marlon Brando received a lot of publicity for refusing the Oscar, but they were not the first to have done so. Dudley

Nichols, winner of best screenplay *(The Informer)* refused his Oscar in 1935. A militant member of the Screen Writers Guild, Nichols resigned from the Academy, along with other members, during the 1933 labor crisis. The relations between the Academy and the Screen Guilds reached a low point at the eighth annual banquet (March 5, 1936), when the Guilds asked their members to boycott the ceremonies. Bette Davis and Victor McLaglen, the winners of the acting awards, attended, but Nichols and director John Ford, also a winner, boycotted the show. Nichols felt that, "to accept the Oscar would be to turn my back on nearly a thousand members of the Writers Guild."

Nichols's negation was a minor incident compared with the controversy over George C. Scott's rejection. In 1971, upon notification of his nomination for *Patton,* Scott sent the Academy a telegram requesting that his name be withdrawn from the nominees. "I mean no offense to the Academy," wrote Scott, "I simply do not wish to be involved."

Scott had not denied his first nomination for *Anatomy of Murder;* many believed he gave the year's best performance, but the winner was Hugh Griffith for *Ben-Hur,* which swept most of the 1959 awards. Scott's friends said it was important for him to win, but after witnessing the fierce campaigns for votes by his peers, Scott determined never again to have anything to do with the Oscar "meat parade."

In 1962, Scott was nominated again for a supporting award *(The Hustler).* This time, however, he asked the Academy to withdraw his name from the nominees, but his request was denied by Academy President Wendell Corey. "You were nominated by a vote of your fellow-actors," Corey stated, "and the Academy can not remove your name from the list of the nominated performances. The Academy nominates and votes awards for achievements as they appear on the screen. Therefore, any one person responsible for achievement cannot decline the nomination after it is voted." But Scott was told he could refuse the award, if he won. He lost, again undeservedly; the winner was George Chakiris in *West Side Story,* which, like *Ben-Hur,* received most of the Oscars.

Scott regarded Oscar politics as "offensive, barbarous, and innately corrupt," encouraging the public to think that awards are more important than the work itself. Thus, when he received his third nomination for *Patton* he declined it again: "Life isn't a race, and because it is not a race, I don't consider myself in competition with my fellow actors for awards or recognition." "I don't give a damn about the Oscar," Scott later told the *New York Daily News,* "I'm making too much money anyway." Daniel Taradash, then Academy President, ignored Scott's protests and made it clear that it was not Scott but his *performance* that was nominated.

Taradash felt that to agree to Scott's demand would be demeaning to his fellow artists. Many actors believe that this was one of the Academy's finest hours, demonstrating that the vote was not personal but dispassionate—the kind of vote that could not have happened during the studio system.

Scott's attack on the film colony, thumbing his nose at the awards, had no damaging effects. He won for *Patton* and a year later was nominated for *The Hospital,* which has been interpreted as a positive sign of the Academy freeing itself from personal favoritism. Scott claimed he did not really mean to create a furor by his conduct. Indeed, when the scandal grew to unprecedented proportions, he decided that if he would ever be nominated in the future, he would accept it. It was too much trouble *not* to accept.

The second actor to refuse an Oscar was Marlon Brando, when he was cited for *The Godfather.* Brando's rejection, however, differed from Scott's: he protested against the mistreatment of Native Americans on screen and off. Brando did not refuse his first Oscar for *On the Waterfront,* even though his critical views of Hollywood were already established. And, as in Scott's case, Brando's refusal had no impact on his standing, as a year later he was nominated for *Last Tango in Paris.*

Katharine Hepburn has been ambivalent toward the Oscar, though she didn't reject any of her four Academy Awards. Her form of protest (some say eccentricity) was not to attend any ceremonies until 1968, when she broke her long-standing vow and appeared in a pre-recorded segment for the fortieth anniversary show. Hepburn made her first appearance at the 1974 ceremonies, when she presented a special Oscar to her friend, producer Lawrence Weingarten. "I'm a living proof," she said, "that someone can wait forty-one years to be unselfish."

Dustin Hoffman attended the ceremonies when he was nominated for *The Graduate,* but claimed to have been uncomfortable about it. "I hope to God I don't win an Oscar," he said. "It would depress me if I did. I really don't deserve it." In 1975, an interview taped earlier aired on CBS a few hours before the show, in which Hoffman voiced his contempt, calling the Oscar "ugly and grotesque." Frank Sinatra, one of the show's emcees, scolded him publicly for these remarks. For his part, Hoffman made a point not to show up at the awards presentations for his next two nominations.

Hoffman created another uproar when he questioned the validity of awards at the 1980 Golden Globe ceremonies. "I think that awards are very silly," he said, accepting an award for *Kramer vs. Kramer,* "They put very talented and good people against each other and they hurt the hell out of the ones that lose. And I think they relieve us that win." Addressing his fellow-nominees, Hoffman asserted that "awards make more sense when they are given for a life achievement to a man like Mr. Fonda" (recipient of the Cecil B. DeMille Career Achievement Award) "and particularly to a man like Mr. Lemmon, who recently gave one of the great performances of his life" in *The China Syndrome.*

Hoffman's criticism was similar to Scott's, deploring the demeaning effects of the Oscar race. Both protested, as Scott said, that actors felt obliged to enter into a competition with each other that has nothing to do with acting. They also resented the idea that actors have increasingly become award conscious. Unlike Scott, Hoffman didn't refuse his award, but he repeated his criticism in his Oscar speech, expressing resentment over the Academy's spotlit competition among fellow artists. "I refuse to believe that I am better than Jack Lemmon, Al Pacino, and Peter Sellers, and I refuse to believe that Robert Duvall lost. We are part of an artistic family and I am proud to share this award."

There is no doubt that Hoffman meant what he said, and there is no doubt that he expressed the opinions of many other artists. Yet it is doubtful that this kind of criticism will change the Oscar's operations and effects. The excitement over the Oscar depends and even thrives on individual competitiveness in all its nasty and cruel manifestations.

Reaction to Winning

Winning an Oscar is considered to be a career climax, sometimes the greatest achievement of a film artist's life. Immediate reactions to winning which follow a long period of anxiety, the six weeks between the nominations and the awards ceremonies, are revelatory since they are more spontaneous or less fabricated than is the norm in Hollywood. With all the preparations to win, there are always elements of unpredictability. Ever since the awards telecast, the reaction to winning (and losing) are shown live to a billion viewers all over the world, which is exciting for the winners but could be terribly embarrassing for the losers.

In the first years, neither the ceremonies nor the award were publicized. Charles Laughton could not attend the 1933 banquet, as the ceremony was called in the 1930s, because he was working in London. The Academy's telegram, congratulating him for winning for *The Private Life of Henry VIII,* was put on the board, and Laughton made no big fuss over it, partly because he didn't comprehend its meaning and partly because the award itself didn't have much effect.

Joseph Schildkraut *(The Life of Emile Zola)* didn't attend the banquet either. "My agents discouraged me from going to the affair," he recalled, "because they thought the recipient would be Ralph Bellamy or Thomas Mitchell." Schildkraut was already in bed, when the telephone rang and "the excited voice of a man who did not even bother to introduce himself bellowed: 'Where in the hell are you? Why aren't you here? The awards are about to be handed and you are not here.'"

Thinking it was some practical joke, Schildkraut blurted out, "If you don't tell me, I won't come." Then, the anonymous man replied, "Yes, you son of a gun, you won it. Get down here!" Schildkraut dressed in style, ordered out the car, and went to the Biltmore Hotel. He arrived just in time to be seated at the Warner's table and to accept the Oscar from Frank Capra for his portrayal of Dreyfus.

Similarly, fearing rejection, Joan Crawford decided not to attend the 1946 ceremonies. "I know I'm going to lose," she told her publicist, Henry Rogers. Even if she won, Crawford dreaded the idea of having "to get up in front of all those people and make a speech," worrying that she would be "tongue-tied and make an ass of myself." Neither her publicist nor producer Jerry Wald could persuade Crawford to go. However, Rogers, who had started an Oscar campaign earlier, arranged for photographers from all the fan magazines to be at her home.

When Charles Boyer announced on the radio that Crawford won, cheers erupted over the radio from the Graumann's Chinese Theater, and Crawford exclaimed, "This is the greatest moment of my life." Director Michael Curtiz, who had accepted the award for Crawford, came to her house to present it personally. The next morning, newspapers all over the world printed front-page stories of how Hollywood's Cinderella won the prize without even going to the ball. Highly moved, Crawford responded with a personal signed letter to each sender of flowers and telegrams.

Ingrid Bergman did not attend the 1957 show, when she was up for *Anastasia*. Performing in Paris, she asked Cary Grant to stand by, just in case she got lucky. After her performance, Bergman went to her hotel, only to be awakened at seven o'clock in the morning by a Fox publicity man shouting into the phone, "You've won! You've won!" Later, Bergman listened to a repeat of the ceremony over the French radio, and was taking a bath when Cary Grant began his speech, "Dear Ingrid, wherever you are in the world" (and she was saying, I'm in the bathtub!), "we, your friends, want to congratulate you, and I have your Oscar here for your marvelous performance, and may you be as happy as we are for you."

When Sophia Loren heard she had been nominated for *Two Women*, she ecstatically announced that she would attend the Hollywood ceremonies. "I felt that just being nominated was an honor in itself and a rare one at that for an Italian-speaking actress in an Italian film." But then, upon reflection, Loren changed her mind, as she recalled: "My competition was formidable (Audrey Hepburn, Piper Laurie, Geraldine Page, and Natalie Wood). Besides, the plain fact was that in its long history, an Oscar had never been given to an actor or actress in a foreign-language film." Loren determined: "I could not bear the ordeal of sitting in plain view of millions of viewers while my fate was being judged. If I lost, I might faint from disappointment; If I won, I would also very likely faint with joy. Instead of spreading my fainting all over the world, I decided it was better that I faint at home."

Loren had no real expectations of winning. But, as she recalled, "hope being the eternal rogue that it is, on the night of the Awards, I was too nervous to sleep." Photographer Pier Luigi came to Loren's Rome apartment to keep the vigil with her. At three o'clock in the morning, "I tried to go to bed, but my eyes would not close and my heart would not stop pounding, so I went back to the living room to talk to Pier." There was no coverage then of the Awards on Italian television or radio. By six o'clock, Loren knew the ceremony was over and was sure she had not won. However, at 6:45 she was awakened by Cary Grant's pleasant voice telling her the good news. "I didn't faint," Loren recalled, "but I went rather giddy. It was incontestably the greatest thrill of my life."

The anxiety during the Oscar ceremonies is immense—all the nominees report that the show seems endless—that is, until winners are announced in their categories. As Ray Milland recalled: "And we sat, and we sat, through the interminable minor awards, applauding dutifully each recipient and the endless speeches of acceptance." He remembered that after Ingrid Bergman tore the envelope open and a great big grin appeared on her face, he knew he hadn't won, because "she was smiling and I'd never even met her." But then "dimly, I heard the words, 'Are you nervous, Mr. Milland? It's all yours!'" In the applause that followed, Milland just sat there: "I never thought to move until I felt Mal's elbow in my ribs, a blow which I still feel to this day when it's raining. Get up there sweetheart!" his wife said. "Get up there! It's you! It's you!" Milland doesn't remember much of what happened after that, except for "a jumble of handshakes, microphones, people with notebooks and pencils, and flashing camera bulbs."

Gig Young, the 1969 supporting winner, also kept looking away from the program, because he didn't want to know exactly when his category would be called. He kept telling himself, "I mustn't jump up if they call somebody else's name. I mustn't jump up."

Joan Fontaine recorded her experience of Oscar Night, when she utterly froze: "I stared across the table, where Olivia was sitting directly opposite me. 'Get up there, get up there,' she whispered, commanding. Now what had I done! All the animus we'd felt toward each other as children, the hair-pullings, the savage wrestling matches, the time Olivia fractured my collar bone, all came rushing back in kaleidoscopic imagery. My paralysis was total." Fontaine also remembers that "cries of 'Speak, Speak!'" echoed through the room as she tried to find her voice. She doesn't have "the faintest idea" of what she said in her acceptance speech—"God knows I hadn't rehearsed anything."

It's not always easy to predict the winner. When Broderick Crawford *(All the King's Men)* was asked about his view of the polls which had predicted he would win, he snapped: "Polls! The polls predicted Dewey would win too!" referring to the failure of the presidential candidate. "I have no blood," Crawford said after the ceremonies, "I feel like I've been under an anesthetic all day." Crawford's wife was already in the car, with the motor running, "taking no chances on a recount."

Year after year, film critics, public opinion polls, and moviegoers try to predict the winners. In some years, all pre-presentation favorites come through as expected. In others, though, there are major surprises, even shocks. In 1956, Anthony Quinn's win *(Lust for Life)* upset the pre-Oscar favorite, Robert Stack *(Written on the Wind)*. In 1963, Sidney Poitier *(Lilies of the Field)* won to almost everyone's surprise; Paul Newman *(Hud)* and Albert Finney *(Tom Jones)* were considered more likely candidates.

In 1965, Rod Steiger *(The Pawnbroker)* was the critical favorite, and Richard Burton *(The Spy Who Came in from the Cold)* a runner-up, but the winner was Lee Marvin *(Cat Ballou)*. In 1968, Peter O'Toole *(The Lion in Winter)* was considered the sure winner, but the Oscar went to Cliff Robertson *(Charly)*. In 1974, most predictions chose Fred Astaire *(The Towering Inferno)*, a sentimental favorite, but the winner was Robert De Niro *(The Godfather, Part II)*. In the same year, most polls predicted Jack Nicholson *(Chinatown)* would win, but Art Carney *(Harry and Tonto)* was the surprise winner.

In 1976, Liv Ullmann *(Face to Face)* was expected to win; the winner, instead, was Faye Dunaway *(Network)*. "I didn't expect this to happen quite yet" said the overwhelmed Dunaway. In 1985, William Hurt *(Kiss of the Spider Woman)* was the surprise honoree; Jack Nicholson *(Prizzi's Honor)* was expected to win.

Actors themselves have been surprised by the nomination and Oscars. Simone Signoret had no notion, when she agreed to appear in *Room at the Top,* "that this train I was boarding would lead me to my saying thank you in April 1960 in front of millions of TV viewers, to three thousand people seated in red-velvet seats in a Hollywood cinema." The critical acclaim shocked Signoret: "We had made this movie hoping that a few friends would like it." The picture's success in America came as a total surprise to her.

The uncertainty prior to the ceremonies adds excitement. "When the presenter finally gets the envelope open and the winner is you," Mercedes McCambridge recalled, "the giddiness of delirium sets in, and the long walk to the stage is anesthesia. The dosage diminished slowly, its effects taking weeks to wear off."

Charlton Heston recorded in his diary, on April 4, 1960: "I made it. Looking across the orchestra, just before Susan (Hayward) read it off, something popped in my head, 'I'm going to get it.' And I did. I kissed Lydia and walked to the stage dripping wet, except for a pepper-dry mouth: classic stage fright. I'll never forget the moment, or the night, for that matter."

Rita Moreno *(West Side Story)* was sure Judy Garland *(Judgment at Nuremberg)* would win the 1961 supporting Oscar. Extremely emotional and practically in orbit when her name was announced, she shouted, "I can't believe it! Good Heavens." "I never thought I'd win," she said after the awards, "yet, at the same time I was wishing I would win. It's a strange emotional feeling to go around with for days. I'm glad it's over." Gregory Peck was trying "not to work up either undue excitement or nerves," when he earned his fifth nomination for *To Kill a Mockingbird*—he had lost before and fully expected to lose again.

Sidney Poitier didn't expect to be nominated for *The Defiant Ones* nor to win for *Lilies of the Field*. "My anxiety mounted until it was unbearable," he said of the 1964 Oscar Night. "I was sitting there being ripped up internally . . . absolutely beside myself with nervousness." Poitier understood "this is an important moment and I have to be here and in fact I want to be here for what it means to us as a people," but he also decided, "never again, under no circumstances, am I going to come here again and put myself through this." Although winning seemed a "long shot dark horse, I was switching from no chance at all to writing my acceptance speech."

When John Mills was watching the rushes of his scene with the lobsters in *Ryan's Daughter,* director David Lean asked him, "Johnny, have you ever won an Oscar?" to which the actor said, "No, I haven't. Why?" "Nothing," said Lean, "I just wondered." A year later, Mills received a cable from the Academy congratulating him for his supporting nomination.

After the nomination, Mills recalled, "I [did] my best, because I wanted the damn thing so desperately, to persuade myself that I really didn't care, and that I had very little chance." He knew that his part, the village's idiot, was small and "without a single line of dialogue." One day, Mills's daughter, Juliet, called from Hollywood to tell him that he had been awarded the Golden Globe. After that, Mills was even more anxious because he realized "that the recipient of the Golden Globe Award becomes a top tip for the Oscar."

On Oscar day, "the phone rang continually, reporters, gossip writers. Several of them told me that the rumors circulating around town made me favorite. The more of the stuff I listened to, the more convinced I was that I really didn't stand a chance." On Oscar Night, Mills tried "to look cool and totally relaxed," but he failed. He desperately wanted the Oscar, "knowing that at my age (sixty-three), it was in all probability my last chance of winning one." After "what seemed like an eternity, the moment arrived." Maggie Smith, the award's presenter, opened the envelope and smiled broadly, "I knew before she made the announcement, I'd made it."

To Mills's British colleague, Dame Judi Dench, the Oscar ceremonies were also "unbelievable." As she recalled: "The first time I took my daughter and it was so larky. I'm always terribly starstruck. We were black-and-blue from nudging each other the whole time, trying to draw attention to people. The next time we went, we were all rather blasé about it. Our car was late. We got there and the place was all locked up. Somebody said, 'Oh, God, they want a shot of her while Whoopi Goldberg arrives as Elizabeth II.' So we were smuggled in."

For Dench, it was not revenge to win after being passed over for *Mrs. Brown,* because she really didn't think she was going to win either year. Dench doesn't remember much, "except my husband Mikey saying to me, 'I think you've won, Jude.' I don't remember getting up there. I remember Robin Williams curtsying. I remember crying in a lift. And then I remember meeting the Italian man Benigni."

I Would Like to Thank

Nowadays, the Oscar thank-you speeches, often the most remembered part of the awards show, tend to sound like a speed-read version of the telephone book. Even Fellini had to shout his unintelligible last words off camera, without benefit of a microphone, when he overstayed the welcome norm of one minute per speech. This is one aspect of the show that has changed a lot over the years.

Acceptance speeches used to be modest prior to the public broadcasts of the show. Janet Gaynor, the first winner, simply said, "I am deeply honored," but she couldn't continue as her voice cracked and tears filled her eyes, thus setting a standard for future speeches by female winners. Embarrassed, she later sent a letter to the Academy: "This is an honor that I deeply appreciate. I regard the opinion of the Academy as so expert and unbiased that to be recipient of the award makes me very happy indeed."

Speeches have varied in length, content, and originality. Some were brief, as Vivien Leigh's 1940 remarks, in which she thanked "Mr. Selznick, all my co-workers and most of all Miss Margaret Mitchell."

Others, such as Greer Garson's, were extremely long, thanking everyone, including "the doctor who brought me into the world." "I walked into the wings," she later recalled, "and a man said, 'you spoke for five and a quarter minutes.'" Garson realized she had broken "a sacred rule," since "leading ladies aren't supposed to get further than, thank you, thank you, and burst into tears." Garson's speech soon became a joke in Hollywood, endlessly imitated at parties; in the next decade, she refused to speak in public at all. This kind of speech is impossible at present, in the age of television, when every minute of advertising costs a fortune. Still, in recent years, Beatrice Straight's speech was almost as long as her part in *Network*, practically two scenes.

The "Thank You" note has been customary in every speech, but different people have been thanked. Wearing a military uniform, Jimmy Stewart *(The Philadelphia Story)* thanked the entire film industry: "I assure you this is a very important moment in my life. As I look around this room, a warm feeling comes over me, a feeling of satisfaction, pride, and most of all, gratefulness for the encouragement, instruction, and advantage of your experience that have been offered to me since I came to Hollywood, and with all my heart I thank you."

Joanne Woodward tearfully expressed her thanks to Nunnally Johnson, who wrote, produced, and directed *The Three Faces of Eve,* "for having more faith in me than I ever knew anyone could have." Charlton Heston *(Ben-Hur)* thanked "the first secretary in a Broadway casting office who let me in to get my first job." In the same year, Shelley Winters thanked her agent for getting her the part in *The Diary of Anne Frank*. But Maureen Stapleton *(Reds)* outdid them all, thanking everyone she has met in her life.

Audrey Hepburn's choice as presenter of the 1965 Best Actor Award was ironic. She had not been nominated for *My Fair Lady,* but her co-star Rex Harrison was and his chances to win were excellent. "It was a strange evening," Harrison reported. "I knew that if I won the award I would be on the stage with two Fair Ladies. Julie Andrews had been nominated *(Mary Poppins)*; Audrey Hepburn had not, but she was in Hollywood to present the awards to the winners." It all happened—"I won it and Julie won it and things were fairly hectic backstage, trying to keep the factions in the right place for the photographs and interviews. The public relations people had a difficult time, but they are well equipped to for this." "I have to thank two fair ladies," Harrison said in his speech. Hugged by Audrey Hepburn, the TV camera caught a close-up of Julie Andrews extremely upset.

In the following year, when Harrison presented the Best Actress Award, another interesting incident happened. The two major contestants were both named Julie and both were English: Julie Christie *(Darling)* and Julie Andrews *(The Sound of Music)*. Harrison ripped open the envelope and said with lips pursed, "Julie," then paused for another second and said, "Christie." Christie, who had been trying to sit calmly, ran to the stage crying, clutching the Oscar and Harrison at the same time.

Burt Lancaster's speech evoked laughter and applause when he thanked those who worked with him in *Elmer Gantry,* those who voted for him, and those who didn't. Similarly, Sean Connery *(The Untouchables)* began his speech by saying, "Ladies and gentlemen, friends, and a few enemies." Connery then noted: "I realized just the other day that my first one and only attendance was 30 years ago—patience is truly a virtue."

Rod Steiger was gracious when he thanked his co-star in *In the Heat of the Night,* Sidney Poitier, "whose friendship gave me the knowledge to enhance my performance—and we shall overcome." Gene Hackman *(The French Connection)* thanked his director, William Friedkin, who "brought me through this when I wanted to quit." Jack Nicholson thanked "Mary Pickford who, incidentally, was the first actor to get a percentage of her pictures." "Speaking of percentages," he continued, "last but not least, I thank my agent, who about ten years ago said I had no business being an actor." Jason Robards took the award "in honor of my producer, Robert Redford, who showed such integrity and perseverance" in creating *All the President's Men.*

One of the more charming speeches was given by Mary Steenburgen, who thanked "my patron, Jack Nicholson, for casting me in my first film, *Goin' South.*" She concluded by thanking her then husband, actor Malcolm McDowell, "for making life so nice." "I feel like tap dancing," she said, quoting from her role in *Melvin and Howard.*

Fredric March, who split the 1931/32 award with Wallace Beery, said: "It just happened that this year Mrs. March and I adopted a child and Mr. and Mrs. Beery adopted a child. And here we are, both, getting awards for the best male performance of the year." Claudette Colbert was boarding the Santa Fe train to New York when she was announced winner. The Santa Fe officials held up the train and she was taken by taxi to the ceremonies at the Biltmore Hotel. "I'm happy enough to cry," she said, "but I can't take the time to do so. A taxi is waiting outside with the engine running."

Bing Crosby thought he had only slim chances to win and subsequently decided to stay at home. However, around six o'clock in the evening of the awards, when Paramount learned that he might win, the executives had to convince him to go. It was not an easy task. "All I can say," Crosby commented, "is that it sure is a wonderful work when a tired crooner like me can walk away with this hunk of crockery." Edmund Gwenn, who won for his Santa Claus in *Miracle on 34th Street,* said: "Now I know there is a Santa Claus." Jane Wyman, winning for playing a deaf-mute in *Johnny Belinda,* said: "I accept this very gratefully for keeping my mouth shut; I think I'll do it again."

Eva Marie Saint *(On the Waterfront)* was in an advanced pregnancy and feared "I may have the baby right here out of excitement." "I hope this is not a mistake," Yul Brynner *(The King and I)* said, "because I won't give it back for nothing." And the same concern was expressed by Alec Guinness, recipient of the 1980 Special Oscar for career achievement, "I'm grabbing this while the going is good."

An excited David Niven *(Separate Tables)* admitted, "I'm so loaded down with good-luck charms I could hardly make the steps." The following day, he published a big "Thank You" in the trade magazines:

> In the full glare and under the stress of "Oscar Night" (if one is lucky enough to be the winner), it is almost impossible not to be corny in the wording of one's thanks. May I now, in the cold light of the morning after, thank from the bottom of my heart, not only those who voted for me, but those who did not vote for me, those who could not vote for me, and those who would not have voted for me in a million years even if they could have voted for me. In other words, I want to thank all show business where, in the midst of the most wonderful and crazy people, I have spent the happiest years of my life.
>
> Love to All
> David Niven

Lee Marvin broke with the tradition of speeches when he simply said, "Half of this (Oscar) belongs to a horse someplace out in the valley," which helped him win in *Cat Ballou.* Gene Hackman suggested, in the same vein, "maybe the award should really go to my car," referring, of course, to the breathtaking chase scene in *The French Connection.*

Estelle Parsons caused a wave of laughter when she gasped, "Oh, boy, it's heavy!" as she took the statuette from Walter Matthau. Her Broadway show, *The Seven Descent of Myrtle,* closed down for the night so she could attend the event.

Barbra Streisand simply looked at the statuette and said, "Hello, gorgeous," her line from *Funny Girl.* In the following year, Streisand saw tears in John Wayne's eyes when she presented him the award for *True Grit*. Yes, the symbol of "macho" broke down crying. "I thought some day I might win an award for lasting so long! But I never thought I would get this particular award," Wayne said. "I feel very grateful, very humble." And he concluded: "If I'd known what I know now, I'd have put a patch on my eye thirty five years ago."

The winners for *One Flew Over the Cuckoo's Nest* referred in their speeches to the setting of their movie. "I spent more time in mental institutions than the others," said director Milos Forman. "I guess this proves there are as many nuts in the Academy as anywhere else," Jack Nicholson commented. And Louise Fletcher said, "It looks like you all hated me so much that you are giving me the award for it, and I'm loving every minute of it. All I can say is, I've loved being hated by you."

With all the delirium, acceptance speeches cannot conceal completely persistent doubts. Olivia de Havilland spoke of the confidence placed on her ability to maintain a high standard of acting when she first won *(To Each His Own)*. "Thank you for your very generous assurance that I haven't failed to do so," she said. José Ferrer *(Cyrano de Bergerac)* also spoke of the Oscar as a vote of confidence: "It is more to me than an honor accorded to an actor. It's a vote of confidence in me. Believe me, I'll not let you down." Deeply moved upon winning his second supporting award in *Lust for Life,* Anthony Quinn noted: "I want to say humbly to my colleagues that acting has never been a matter of competition, but a fight with myself. And I thank you for letting me win that fight."

A word of consolation to the yet-undiscovered also appears in the speeches. Mercedes McCambridge, who won for her first film encouraged other young actors: "Mostly I want to say to every waiting actor, hang on! Look what can happen!" She later explained, "I meant it with my heart, as a message to all those other actors in the cattle call that day back in New York. I got it that time. Maybe their turn is next. The hanging on is the hard part." Dustin Hoffman also spoke of actors as members of an intimate community: "How many other Oscar-caliber actors are out there, undiscovered?"

An exceptionally honest speech was given by Ingrid Bergman, shocked upon learning of her fifth nomination for *Murder on the Orient Express:* "To be nominated for something so small; I really had only one scene." Upon winning, Bergman rushed up to the stage and said: "This is unfair. I want this award to go to Valentina Cortesa," nominated for *Day for Night*. The spotlights and cameras swept across to Valentina, who stood up and blew kisses at Bergman. "It was really sad that she hadn't gotten it," Bergman thought, "because she deserved it." "Please forgive me

Valentina," she apologized, "I didn't mean to." Later, Bergman realized that it was not "quite the right thing to say as the movie industry is supposed to be impartial." And there were three other supporting actresses, beside Cortesa, who did not win.

Defeat in the Public Eye

Since it is not easy to face failure, some film artists cling to the importance and prestige of the nomination itself. "My own disappointment," Gene Tierney observed, "was lessened by the conviction, new to me, that I had developed a difficult character *(Leave Her to Heaven)*, not just a pretty face on the screen." "I had been challenged by the role," she explains, "and to have been nominated for an Oscar was excitement enough." Joan Fontaine lost at her first nomination *(Rebecca)*, but she was not disappointed, because, "to have won it with my first good role would have been precipitous. The voters might well have thought Hitchcock was my Svengali, that after so many undistinguished performances in the past, surely it was Hitchcock who had mesmerized me into the performance I was nominated for."

Four-time nominee, and thus one of the Academy's greatest losers, Rosalind Russell recalled of her first nomination for *My Sister Eileen*: "Glad as I was about it, the honor put me under heavy pressure. It means too much to the studios to have their people win; I still can't think of the tension surrounding these races without breaking into a sweat." Of her subsequent nominations, Russell observed, "Half a loaf can feed you *(Sister Kenny* and *Mourning Becomes Electra* had both been critical successes, bringing me two more Oscar nominations), but when you get the whole loaf, you know the difference." Apparently, Russell's 1947 loss threw her into a complete state of shock; some suggested cynically that RKO changed *Mourning Becomes Electra* to "Mourning Becomes Rosalind Russell." And if three misses were not enough, Russell lost a fourth race in 1958 for *Auntie Mame*.

That players are expected to care about the award is clear from Gloria Swanson's testimony of her *Sunset Boulevard* experience: "I surprised everyone, except Bette Davis, probably, and Judy Holliday, who sat next to me, by losing." Swanson could not attend the ceremonies because she was performing in New York, but she listened to the broadcast. "I honestly didn't care, but I could see in the faces of everyone at La Zambra, and everywhere else I went in the weeks after that, that people wanted me to care. In fact, they seemed to want more than that. They expected scenes from me, wild sarcastic tantrums. They wanted Norma Desmond, as if I had hooked up sympathetically, disastrously, with the role by playing it." It soon became a problem, "if I said I didn't care, people would pity me and say I had a bad case of sour grapes. If I told them I was an Aries, that it was not in my nature to be dejected, they would think I was mad, and the Gloria-Norma identification would be made forever in the eyes of the press. It was easier to say nothing."

It is especially hard to accept failure for those nominees expecting to win. Shelley Winters was sure she would win at her first nomination *(A Place in the Sun)*. On Oscar Night, as she described, "I was a wreck," and "the show seemed interminable." When Ronald Colman opened the envelope, Winters was sure he announced her name and was almost on the steps leading to the stage, when her beau Vittorio Gassman tackled her. She remembered that "as we lay on the floor of the aisle, I thought he'd gone insane." Gassman whispered, "Shelley, it's Vivien Leigh," and they managed to crawl back to their seats "as inconspicuously as possible." But Winters could not believe it, "the rest of the evening I felt as if Ronald Colman had betrayed me. He could at least have said my name and swallowed the card, if he were any kind of English gentleman." Later, they went to the Governor's Ball, but "I don't remember anything about it. I just knew that the gold statuette was not on *my* table." Winters believes to this day that Vivien Leigh had "taken my Oscar."

Frank Capra, whose *Lady for a Night* got four nominations, was extremely excited—"I became impossible to live with. I kept telling myself I would win four awards." In preparation for the event, Capra wrote and threw away dozen of speeches. "I ordered my first tuxedo, rented a plush home in Beverly Hills to be seen, sway votes in bistros." When presenter Will Rogers said, "Well, well, well, what do you know. I've watched this young man come up from the bottom, and I mean the bottom," Capra was sure Rogers was talking about him. "It couldn't happen to a nicer guy," Rogers continued. "Come up and get it Frank." Capra rose and headed toward the spotlight, only to realize the winner was Frank Lloyd for *Cavalcade:* "I stood petrified in the dark, in utter disbelief, as I began the longest, saddest, most shattering walk of my life. I wanted to crawl under the rug. All my friends at the table were crying."

After this awkward experience, Capra vowed that "if they ever did vote me one, I would never, never, NEVER show up to accept it." But, as could be expected, Capra did not live up to his vow, and two years later, his dream materialized when *It Happened One Night* set a record, getting all five major awards.

Judy Garland experienced several Oscar defeats. Of her first nomination *(A Star Is Born),* biographer Gerold Frank writes: "It was inevitable that Judy be nominated, with almost everyone agreeing she was sure to get it. Though she had received a juvenile award for *The Wizard of Oz,* this was the real thing, and if it were to come true, what a triumph after everything." Prior to her nomination, husband Sid Luft went to an analyst, to help him cope with Judy "as the time drew nearer not only to the birth of her third child but to the resolution of the mounting uncertainty as to whether she would win the Oscar."

Garland was determined to attend the ceremonies, but, unexpectedly, gave birth on March 29, 1955, the night before the Oscar show. Extensive preparations were made at the hospital, with television cameras in her room. The idea was that if Garland won, she would talk to Bob Hope from her bed. After she learned of her loss (to Grace Kelly in *The Country Girl)* Garland said: "I knew I wouldn't get it. They wouldn't give it to me, although I deserved it." Her consolation was her newborn son, whom she labeled "My Academy Award." Garland's disappointment was profound— she accepted what was much more of a disaster to her than everyone knew. Comedian Groucho Marx sent her a consolatory telegram: DEAR JUDY. THIS IS THE BIGGEST ROBBERY SINCE BRINK'S.

Even players who eventually won the Oscar had a hard time accepting earlier defeats. Susan Hayward took her first failure with humor. However, when she was nominated for the fourth time *(I'll Cry Tomorrow)* and lost, she confided: "I managed not to shed any tears until everything was over. Then I sat down and had a good cry and decided that losing was just part of the game."

Rod Steiger, who most people believed would win for *The Pawnbroker,* was bitterly offended to have lost to Lee Marvin in *Cat Ballou.* Sylvia Miles, nominated for *Midnight Cowboy,* reacted similarly: "People think I was mad when I didn't win, but they're wrong. It's not that I mind losing, but losing to Goldie Hawn *(Cactus Flower).* That was an insult."

Peter Sellers saw his role in *Being There,* as Chance Gardiner, the simple-witted fool who becomes politically powerful in Washington, as an "all-out bid" for an Oscar. Driven by an "obsessive quest" to make the film for seven years, he hoped this part would "purge him of the coarse and exploitative roles he had taken in other films. He would finally achieve the perfection that had eluded him." It was a simple, understated performance, devoid of tricks, accents, and multiple impersonations that had made Sellers rich and famous in the *Pink Panther* movies, as Inspector Clouseau. In public, Sellers treated his loss to Dustin Hoffman *(Kramer vs. Kramer),* with "little show of emotion, but deep down inside, he was tremendously disappointed."

Elizabeth Taylor, who won her second Oscar for *Who's Afraid of Virginia Woolf?* was upset that her then husband, Richard Burton, lost, believing that he gave the best performance of the year. Burton knew he had no chance of winning after Paul Scofield was cited by the New York Film Critics. To his credit, Burton didn't try to conceal that he was hurt, having lost out on six previous occasions. "I want the Oscar," he told close friends, "I've won all kinds of little Oscars but not the big one."

Burton talked his wife out of attending the ceremonies, despite promises made to Jack Warner. The excuse given by Hollywood's royal couple was their need to be on the settings of their new film, *The Comedians*, in France. Taylor rationalized their decision: "I've gone to those award dinners four times, won it once, for not dying. The only time I didn't go was when I was nominated for *Raintree Country* and the dinner was just two weeks after Mike (Todd) was killed. They didn't expect me to go. But most of the time you're supposed to, if you possibly can, whether you've got a chance of winning or not. It's for the industry." Anne Bancroft accepted the award for Taylor, which prompted emcee Bob Hope to quip: "It must be nice to have enough talent just to send for one."

Taylor's absence was criticized since all pre-award polls predicted she would win. "Everybody was talking about it backstage," Walter Matthau, the supporting winner that year *(The Fortune Cookie)* recalled. "When the winners aren't present, it denigrates the whole thing, it cheapens it, it lessens the value, the drama, the excitement." In the same year, the other supporting winner, Sandy Dennis *(Who's Afraid of Virginia Woolf?)* also didn't attend the show because she was performing in New York and, besides, she hated flying. "It's much easier to go than raise a storm of criticism," she later admitted.

Contestants in all categories are expected to attend the ceremonies regardless of their chances to win. Indeed, in the last decade most have been present. Even so, the Oscar show, more than other awards, is fun for the winners, but not for the losers, as every gesture is mercilessly recorded and instantly broadcast all over the world.

Mary Pickford, "America's Sweetheart," in her Best Actress role in *Coquette* (1928/29), the only departure from her screen image, cast as an impetuous belle. Her win was not unrelated to her husband Douglas Fairbanks Sr. being the Academy's president. (Courtesy of The Museum of Modern Art/Film Stills Archive)

Katharine Hepburn and Adolphe Menjou in *Morning Glory* (1932/33). Hepburn's first Oscar was for playing a rising actress, one of the most enduring female roles. (Courtesy of The Museum of Modern Art/Film Stills Archive)

Joan Crawford in her Oscar-winning role in *Mildred Pierce* (1945), her most famous film; Bette Davis and Barbara Stanwyck had turned down the role. (Courtesy of The Museum of Modern Art/Film Stills Archive)

Jane Wyman deviated from her previous glamorous roles and won the 1948 Best Actress in *Johnny Belinda*, as a deaf-mute girl and rape victim, a stereotypical female role in the 1940s. (Courtesy of The Museum of Modern Art/Film Stills Archive)

Broderick Crawford and Judy Holliday, the 1950 Best Actress, as the "dumb-intelligent blond," in George Cukor's political comedy *Born Yesterday*. (Courtesy of The Museum of Modern Art/Film Stills Archive)

Playing Southern belles became a specialty for British player Vivien Leigh, here with Marlon Brando in her second Oscar-winning performance in *A Streetcar Named Desire* (1951), based on Tennessee Williams's prize-winning play. (Courtesy of The Museum of Modern Art/Film Stills Archive)

Anna Magnani (left) in her 1955 Oscar performance in *The Rose Tattoo,* the first Italian actress to win an Oscar, though in an American movie. (Courtesy of The Museum of Modern Art/Film Stills Archive)

Susan Hayward was one of the few women to win Best Actress for playing a criminal, as Barbara Graham in *I Want to Live!* (1958). (Courtesy of The Museum of Modern Art/Film Stills Archive)

Jane Fonda's first Best Actress was for playing a New York call girl in *Klute* (1971), one of the most complex female characterizations and one of the best performances of the whole decade. (Courtesy of The Museum of Modern Art/Film Stills Archive)

Sophia Loren won Best Actress in *Two Women* (1961), a film that made a career difference, changing her image from a sex symbol to a serious dramatic actress. (Courtesy of The Museum of Modern Art/Film Stills Archive)

Katharine Hepburn received a ninth Best Actress nomination for portraying Mary Tyrone in Sidney Lumet's version of Eugene O'Neill's *Long Day's Journey Into Night* (1962). Her superlative acting in this movie surpasses each of her four acting Oscars. (Courtesy of The Museum of Modern Art/Film Stills Archive)

The two female awards in 1962 honored Anne Bancroft (as Anne Sullivan) and Patty Duke (as Helen Keller) in Arthur Penn's *The Miracle Worker.* Bancroft had earlier won a Tony award for playing the role on stage. (Courtesy of The Museum of Modern Art/Film Stills Archive)

Ellen Burstyn (right) received Best Actress and Diane Ladd a supporting nomination in Martin Scorsese's *Alice Doesn't Live Here Anymore* (1974), which resurrected the woman's film in the 1970s. (Courtesy of The Museum of Modern Art/Film Stills Archive)

Faye Dunaway parodied her own screen image, as a ruthlessly ambitious television executive, in Sidney Lumet's political farce *Network* (1976), winning Best Actress at her third nomination. (Courtesy of The Museum of Modern Art/Film Stills Archive)

Sally Field gave a stunning performance, as a working-class woman who gains political consciousness, in Martin Ritt's *Norma Rae* (1979), for which she was rewarded with her first Best Actress Award. (Courtesy of The Museum of Modern Art/Film Stills Archive)

Meryl Streep won her second Oscar as the doomed Polish Holocaust survivor, pictured here with Kevin Kline, her tormented lover, in Alan J. Pakula's *Sophie's Choice* (1982). (Courtesy of The Museum of Modern Art/Film Stills Archive)

Leonardo DiCaprio and Kate Winslet atop the sinking ship in *Titanic* (1997), a fictionalized account of the 1912 accident that became the most successfully commercial Oscar-winning film due to director James Cameron's shrewd manipulation of technology and focus on romance rather than disaster. (Courtesy of The Academy of Motion Picture Arts and Sciences)

Gwyneth Paltrow, who won the Best Actress Oscar, and Joseph Fiennes in John Madden's *Shakespeare in Love*, a crowd-pleasing romantic comedy and the surprise 1998 Oscar winner due to Miramax's savvy marketing campaign. (Courtesy of The Academy of Motion Picture Arts and Sciences)

In its critique of family and suburban life, the 1999 Oscar-winning *American Beauty* didn't break new thematic ground, but Sam Mendes's direction was smooth and the acting nearly flawless, particularly by Kevin Spacey here with Annette Bening. (Courtesy of The Academy of Motion Picture Arts and Sciences)

CHAPTER 13

Oscar's Impact

Accumulative advantage, summed up in the expression, "the rich get richer and the poor poorer," describes the distribution of rewards in the film industry. The Oscar perpetuates the inequality that prevails in Hollywood between the haves and have-nots in terms of money, prestige, and power. More specifically, how pervasive are the Oscar's effects on the winning and nominated films? Is the impact felt in the short run or in the long run? Some observers have stressed the "overnight success" syndrome, the winner who becomes an international star. Others talk about the Oscar's negative impact, or the Oscar as a jinx: winners who become "victims" after winning.

Impact on Films

The goal of every studio in Hollywood is to receive a nomination for and win the Best Picture Oscar, because the top prize carries with it cash and prestige. The first film to benefit directly from winning, though not from Best Picture, was John Ford's *The Informer,* which opened to good reviews but was not popular at the box office. However, after winning four Oscars, the largest number of awards for any film in 1935, including Director and Actor, it became a hit.

A more dramatic impact was felt in 1947, when *The Best Years of Our Lives* turned out to be the most commercial Oscar-winner of its time, grossing in domestic rentals over eleven million dollars. The Best Picture and other awards translated into at least two more million dollars at the box office.

Even when the Oscar doesn't turn the winning movies into blockbusters, it still has *some* effect. A success d'estime, *Hamlet* was initially intended for select audiences in the arthouse circuit. But its surprise Best Picture Oscar made it a bigger draw, particularly for audiences who would not have seen it otherwise.

Oscar's commercial value in the first two decades wasn't immense. In the 1930s, the average domestic rentals of an Oscar-winner was about $2 million. *Cimarron,* the 1930/31 winner, became the year's top money-maker with $2 million in rentals. *Grand Hotel,* the 1931/32 winner, was also that year's top grosser, with $2.25 million. *Cavalcade,* in 1932/33, ranked second among the season's blockbusters with $3.5 million, which made it the decade's second most popular Oscar-winner, after *Gone With the Wind* in 1939.

In the 1940s, the average box-office performance of the Oscar winners was $4.6 million, or twice as much as that of the 1930s. The three most commercial Oscar films of the 1950s were: *Around the World in 80 Days* with $23 million in domestic rentals; *The Bridge on the River Kwai* with $17 million; and *Ben-Hur* with $36 million. Each of these movies was a blockbuster prior to the nominations, but became a bonanza after winning the Oscar.

The Academy continued to honor "smaller" pictures whose Oscar had modest influence on their box-office standing. Contrary to public opinion, *All About Eve* was not a huge hit—it ranked eighth with $2.9 million. On the other hand, it is doubtful that *Marty* would have grossed $2 million in 1955 without the Oscar. MGM's 1958 musical *Gigi* was commercially successful before winning Best Picture, but the award added about $2 million to its grosses, thus making it the fifth top-grosser of the year, with $7 million.

Oscar's financial impact became more apparent in the 1960s. Billy Wilder's *The Apartment* was the only Oscar-winner in the entire decade to have grossed less than $10 million; the average was $21 million. True, more blockbusters were nominated for Best Picture than ever before, which means that most winners were hits even before the nominations. *The Sound of Music* didn't need the 1965 Oscar to become the decade's block-buster, but the 1966 Oscar for *A Man for All Seasons* doubled its domestic receipts to about $13 million , a phenomenal amount for a historical film that lacked high production values.

In the 1970s, the cash value of the Oscar ranged from five to thirty million dollars in the United States. The 1971 Oscar for *The French Connection* added at least $15 million to its grosses. *Annie Hall,* the 1977 winner, had finished its major run by nomination time with $12 million, but the film was rereleased after winning Best Picture, which added at least five more million dollars to its rentals. The two films that benefited the most from their Oscars in the 1970s were: *One Flew Over the Cuckoo's Nest* and *The Deer Hunter:* about half of the former's $59 million and about half of the latter's $30 million could be attributed to the award's impact.

Two blockbusters were nominated for the 1973 Best Picture: William Friedkin's horror movie, *The Exorcist,* and George Roy Hill's adventure comedy, *The Sting,* which won. Both films were released in the prime time movie-going season, at Christmas. In their first fourteen weeks, *The Exorcist* had a clear lead, grossing close to fifty-three million dollars, while *The Sting* followed with thirty million dollars. However, in the first eight weeks after the Oscar, *The Sting* doubled its pre-Oscar weekly pace and made thirty million dollars more, whereas *The Exorcist* made twelve million dollars more. The difference between these movies' box-office status is attributable to *The Sting*'s multiple Oscars, which made it one of the all-time box-office champions in American film.

The value of Best Picture goes beyond box-office appeal, bestowing prestige on its filmmakers and turning the winners into more visible and accessible movies. After winning, they become must-see movies to a larger public that would not have seen them otherwise. The Oscar provides a legitimacy of approval, as director Martin Scorsese once observed: "When people see the label Academy Award winner, they go to see that movie." This may have negative effects too, as Scorsese noted, "the Academy voters feel a sense of responsibility," which means that they tend to choose movies by their "proper" subject matter rather than artistic merit.

Of course, the extent of Oscar impact depends on the kind of film nominated. *Reds* was perceived as high-brow fare because of its political content. Warren Beatty, its director, hoped that the Oscar would elevate and broaden its visibility. But failing to win Best Picture, *Reds* didn't even recoup its budget.

However, in the case of *The Turning Point,* just receiving a 1977 Best Picture nomination made the difference. Herbert Ross's dance film made more money in its second round, after it was nominated in eleven categories, than in its initial run. The nominations were helpful in getting booking dates across the country as the film's specialized milieu, the classic ballet world, was initially an obstacle in attracting the mass audience.

Oscar nominations performed a similar function for *The Elephant Man,* which, initially, Paramount released mostly in "sophisticated neighborhoods," based on the belief that the appeal of David Lynch's period, black-and-white saga was confined to educated audiences. But after receiving Best Picture and other nominations, *The Elephant Man* went into wider distribution.

For smaller films, a Best Picture nomination is of major help at the box office. Louis Malle's *Atlantic City,* which was nominated in 1981 for five awards and was cited as best film by the National Society of Film Critics, also gained from its reissue after the Oscar nominations. Opening on April 3, *Atlantic City* completed its run before the end of the year with $3.3 million in domestic rentals. After the nomination, it was rereleased and made another $1.7 million, about one-third of its total grosses.

Timing of release is also a crucial variable. A December release, *Shakespeare in Love,* the 1998 Oscar-winner, enjoyed a significant box-office boost over the first post-Oscar weekend, with a three-day gross of $4.4 million, up 48 percent from the previous weekend. Miramax then widened the film's number of screens by 52 percent, from 1,266 to 1,931 play-dates, in an effort to capitalize on *Shakespeare*'s seven Oscars. By contrast, *Saving Private Ryan,* which opened in July 1998, went into the Oscar show with roughly $210 million in domestic ticket sales, so obviously its three Oscars, including Spielberg's Best Director, were of lesser impact.

The 1999 Oscar winner *American Beauty,* which had opened in September, saw the material benefits of its five Oscars the day after the ceremonies. The film grossed $727,544 on Monday, a day after taking Best Picture, Director, and Actor trophies. This represented a 132 percent surge from its total of $313,542 on the same day a week before. Monday is historically the weakest day of the box-office week. The post-Oscar start lent credence to DreamWorks' projections that *American Beauty* would add about $15 million to its domestic tally. As it turned out, reality proved much rosier for DreamWorks: by June 1, the picture's domestic grosses reached over $130 million.

Oscar effects are particularly noticeable for specialized arthouse films. The other 1999 Oscar favorites, Miramax's *Cider House Rules,* which won best screenplay and Supporting Actor for Michael Caine, and Fox Searchlight's *Boys Don't Cry,* for which Hilary Swank won Best Actress, also saw a box office boost. *Cider House Rules* collected $309,000 on Monday, up 35 percent from the Monday before, and *Boys Don't Cry*'s receipts roughly doubled, to an impressive $136,000.

Up to the 1980s, winning the top award almost always led to the reissuing of the honored films. *It Happened One Night,* the 1934 winner, was successful in its initial run in February, but a week after the 1935 ceremonies, it was rereleased by Columbia, on the strength of its multiple Oscars, and enjoyed a second successful run.

However, at present, it takes three to five months for new movies to come out on video, which minimizes the reissuing prospects of Oscar-winning films. *Prizzi's Honor,* a 1985 Best Picture nominee, was available on video shortly after the Oscar show, which means that even if it had won Best Picture, it would have been a moot point to rerelease it theatrically.

Winning an Oscar for the Foreign-Language Picture is also commercially beneficial, though with considerably less impact. The 1959's winning French film, *Black Orpheus,* benefited in several ways: at least a 50 percent increase in bookings, particularly in cities seldom showing foreign fare, and a double in its gross at the box office. Pedro Almodovar's comedy-drama,

All About My Mother, also added two to three million dollars to its box office after grabbing the 1999 Best Foreign-Language Picture Oscar.

Winning the Best Foreign-Language Picture, or even a nomination, makes the directors of these movies instantly and internationally marketable. Polish director Agnieszka Holland, whose *Angry Harvest* was nominated for the 1985 Oscar, found it much easier to get funding for her future work. Nominated director Mike Figgis refused to view the omission of *Leaving Las Vegas* from the 1995 Best Picture nominees as a snub, claiming: "Everything is a bonus. The awards will provide the film with an exposure to audiences it would not have otherwise had."

Aside from *Leaving Las Vegas* in 1995, the movies with the most to gain overseas were *Sense and Sensibility, Dead Man Walking,* and *Nixon.* The foreign distributors held off on their theatrical release until Oscar time: industry recognition, by way of Oscar nominations and awards, increased the commercial prospects of these pictures overseas.

The acting Oscars are less influential, though still instrumental for films that deal with unusually tough topics, or films lacking an immediate box-office appeal. Meryl Streep's 1982 Best Actress for *Sophie's Choice,* a film about a doomed Polish Holocaust survivor, is estimated to have increased box-office receipts by at least four million dollars, and Geraldine Page's 1985 Best Actress did a lot of good for *The Trip to Bountiful.*

No one expected *Kiss of the Spider Woman* to be nominated for the 1985 Best Picture, but it was, and William Hurt's Best Actor Award contributed about two million dollars to its overall box office. The very fact that clips from the movie were shown during the Oscar show brought *Kiss of the Spider Woman* to the awareness of millions of viewers, who made a point to see the movie or rent it on video. Similarly, there's no denying that Hilary Swank's Best Actress Award for *Boys Don't Cry* is responsible for doubling the picture's grosses.

Another bonus is that producers of Oscar-winning pictures get better deals for their films when they are sold to television. In 1984, CBS paid $4.5 million to show the 1981 winner, *Chariots of Fire,* and NBC paid more than $12 million for the Oscar-nominated *On Golden Pond.* Enormous amounts were paid despite the fact that both films had enjoyed healthy theatrical runs and both were previously shown on HBO or Cinemax.

Additionally, Oscar nominations and awards also increase the revenues of the video companies that release the winning movies. Retailers ordered more rental copies of *American Beauty, Cider House Rules,* and *Boys Don't Cry.* To video retailers, the Oscar nominations are prime marketing tools that can trigger rental surges. Retailers benefit the most when nominated movies come out on video just before the nominations are revealed, allowing them to profit from the media blitz that continues for the weeks leading up to the ceremonies.

Oscar's Career Impact

Next to Best Picture, the other awards with strong impact are the lead acting Oscars, Best Actor and Best Actress, which have both symbolic and pragmatic effects on the winners' careers.

Skyrocketing Pay

One of Oscar's immediate effects is financial: every winner gets better pay after winning. "Was my life changed by winning?" notes Mercedes McCambridge. "Oh, yes, yes indeed, if 'change' means money. Salary rocketed overnight, literally overnight."

The Oscar always had cash value, but in the first two decades it was not discussed or revealed publicly. Claudette Colbert's pay jumped from $35,000 to $150,000 per picture after winning the Oscar for *It Happened One Night*. In 1936, Colbert became the highest-paid individual in the United States, based on her $302,000 yearly income.

Not every winner reaped the benefits of winning during the studio system. Joan Fontaine was under contract to producer David O. Selznick, who made huge profits from loaning her out to other studios. Fontaine's loan-out fee jumped from $25,000 to $100,000 after her first nominated film, *Rebecca,* but she was still paid her usual fee, $1,200 per week. After Fontaine's Oscar for *Suspicion,* her fee went up, but she received only $100,000 out of the $385,000 that Selznick made. Fontaine's value, like that of other winners, went up, but she didn't enjoy it due to her exploitative contracts. Furthermore, Fontaine didn't work for long periods because Selznick was holding out for higher fees, cashing in on her Oscar status.

Marlon Brando was paid $40,000 for his first film, *The Men,* and $75,000 for his second, *A Streetcar Named Desire.* This Oscar-nominated role brought his salary up to $100,000 for his third picture, *Viva Zapata.* In 1960, six years after his first Oscar for *On the Waterfront,* Brando was earning $1 million per picture. And after his second Oscar for *The Godfather,* his pay rose again. For *The Missouri Breaks,* he was paid $1.5 million and a percentage of the profits.

It is hard to believe that Dustin Hoffman was paid only $17,000 for his first film, *The Graduate,* which made him an instant star and also brought him his first nomination. Two years later, Hoffman received $400,000 for

Midnight Cowboy, earning another nomination. In the 1970s, Hoffman commanded over $1 million per picture, and for *Tootsie,* his first movie after winning an Oscar for *Kramer vs. Kramer,* he was paid $5 million.

At times, Oscar's monetary gains could be dramatic. Within a decade after Julie Christie's debut, *Billy Liar,* for which she was paid only $3,000, her salary was over a hundred times as great. For her Oscar-winning role in *Darling,* Christie was paid the meager sum of $7,500, but for her next film, *Doctor Zhivago,* she received $120,000. In the late 1960s, Christie commanded $400,000 or a percentage of the film's grosses, whichever was higher.

The award's cash value is enjoyed by all winners, lead and supporting. "All they wanted to know," said Martin Balsam, the 1965 supporting winner, "was how much more money I wanted for my next project." The scripts Balsam received were the same, but everything was reduced to money, or, as he put it, "I was an exploitable item." Tatum O'Neal also saw a dramatic increase in her fee after winning the supporting Oscar for *Paper Moon,* commanding $300,000 and 9 percent of the net profits of *The Bad News Bears,* thus becoming the highest-paid child actress in Hollywood.

The nomination itself could have sudden impact on actors' box-office worth. Faye Dunaway's third film, *Bonnie and Clyde,* for which she received her first nomination, changed her status, with her pay rising from $30,000 to $300,000. The enormous success of—and nominations for—*Love Story,* for which Ryan O'Neal earned only $25,000, resulted in his fee-jumping to half a million against 10 percent of the gross profits. Mostly known as a TV actor *(Peyton Place),* O'Neal became a bankable star whose name alone was sufficient guarantee to obtain financing.

International Stardom

The Oscar catapults the winners into the media spotlight, with extensive coverage of their on- and offscreen lives. For some, this effect is more important than the pecuniary benefits. As director Frank Capra observed: "Those who grabbed off the little statuettes didn't give a hang how they got them. They just knew an Oscar tripled their salaries and zoomed them to world fame. Salary increase didn't whet my appetite, but world fame—wow!"

The Oscar's media effect is sudden and quite shocking to most achievers. Joan Fontaine didn't exaggerate when she describes Oscar winners as "minor members of royalty suddenly elevated to the throne." After her win, "the press clamored for some sittings, still photos, and a scrap or tidbit to fill the endless gossip columns, fan magazines, Sunday supplements."

Elevated recognition has "pragmatic" benefits too, such as "the best table in restaurants, preferential treatment whenever one traveled." For Fontaine, this "was a fishbowl experience until the next year's awards, when a new winner would occupy the throne."

Mercedes McCambridge also realized she was "really in the big leagues," after winning. Going to New York on a publicity tour, she was amazed to find out that, "for the first time in my life a baggage porter recognized me!" This meant, as she noted, that "I had moved into a new dimension: from now on my gratuities to such people would have to be stepped out to keep pace with my exalted station!" Indeed, in the disgracefully broken-down taxi, the driver knew who she was, and his flattery cost her another five bucks.

Veteran star John Wayne had never realized the world-wide importance of the Oscar—until *True Grit.* "What opened my eyes to how much it means to people," he said, "was the flood of wires, phone calls, and letters I've been getting from all over the world." Wayne regarded them as "a tribute to the industry and the Academy." It reinforced his belief: "Never underestimate the power of the movies." After claiming for years, "I really didn't need an Oscar, I'm a box-office champion with a record they're going to have to run to catch," the Duke conceded that he was shocked by the massive media attention accorded to him. For Charlton Heston, too, the day after his Oscar for *Ben-Hur* was "a fabulous round of phone calls and wires pouring in. It gets kind of frantic, but I wouldn't miss a minute of it."

The Oscar's impact is more intense for lesser-known players. Few movie-goers knew who Audrey Hepburn, Joanne Woodward, or last year's Hilary Swank were *before* the Oscars. Audrey Hepburn made her screen debut with a walk-on part in a British film, *Laughter in Paradise,* then appeared in a few more movies, but after her Oscar for *Roman Holiday,* she became an international star. Hepburn would have become a star without the Oscar, but the award made her status official and legitimatized her talent. Joanne Woodward was virtually unknown before making *The Three Faces of Eve,* a film that put her in the front rank of leading actresses.

Lee Marvin had also been relatively obscure until *Cat Ballou,* which made him an instant star. Marvin began his career as a supporting actor, specializing in Westerns and crime pictures usually as the villain, but the Oscar led to a new screen image as a leading man and to box-office popularity, with such films as *The Dirty Dozen* and *The Professionals.*

Several respectable actors became box-office attractions only *after* winning the Oscar. Fredric March enjoyed a reputation as a stage actor, but the Oscar for *Dr. Jekyll and Mr. Hyde* made him a full-fledged movie star. Marie Dressler was unlikely star material, but after the Oscar for *Min and*

Bill, she became the top female star in America for four years. Some of these players would have become stars without the Oscar, but the award expedited the process and made them *internationally* popular.

Sidney Poitier's first nomination for *The Defiant Ones* was a turning point in his career, winning him recognition as a dramatic actor. Poitier's popularity rose gradually after winning the 1963 Oscar for *Lilies of the Field,* until he was named the 1968 box office champion after the tremendous success of *To Sir, With Love* and *Guess Who's Coming to Dinner,* which were released back to back in 1967.

The Oscar can also revitalize dwindling and faltering careers. In the late 1940s, Frank Sinatra enjoyed success on stage, radio, and in musical films. In 1952, however, he was dropped by RCA when his vocal cords abruptly hemorrhaged. Sinatra's career seemed finished. But he fought back, literally begging Columbia to cast him as Angelo Maggio in *From Here to Eternity,* for which he was paid as little as eight thousand dollars. The supporting Oscar for this performance salvaged Sinatra's career, establishing him as a dramatic actor with a wider range.

Oscar's surprising effects were also experienced by veteran comedian George Burns. In his autobiography, appropriately titled *The Third Time Around,* Burns writes in a chapter called, "A 79-Year-Old Star Is Born": "I hope the title of this chapter doesn't make you think I'm egotistical, calling myself a star, but I can't help it. That's what it says on my stationery." Burns explained: "I was seventy-nine years old when they asked me to play the part of Al Lewis in *The Sunshine Boys.* And it did start a whole new career for me." Burns didn't stop working, playing a variety of roles, including God in the *Oh, God!* comedies.

Stronger bargaining power for better films also comes with winning the Oscar. This power, which translates into a forceful say over the choice of projects, directors, and co-stars, is just as important as better pay and increased international visibility. In Hollywood, power is the most crucial reward, even if it doesn't last long.

Meryl Streep's supporting Oscar for *Kramer vs. Kramer* and growing prestige as an actress helped to finance *The French Lieutenant's Woman,* based on John Fowles's novel and directed by Karel Reisz. Other noted directors, like Mike Nichols and Fred Zinnemann, had tried to bring the project to the screen, but no studio would finance it. Streep's star power was a crucial factor in convincing a major studio, United Artists, to invest ten million dollars in the production.

Streep also had a say over the choice of her leading man, opting for English actor Jeremy Irons. After winning a third nomination for this film and a second Oscar for *Sophie's Choice,* Streep became one of the few women in Hollywood with the ability to command any screen role. Streep's power has also allowed her to demand—and get—changes in screenplays submitted to her. Robert Benton, who directed Streep for the second time in *Still of the Night,* observed after the experience: "Giving her a script is like giving it to a second author."

James Brooks noted after winning the Best Director for *Terms of Endearment:* "The Oscar gives you the right to make whatever movie you want next." This freedom could be positive as well as negative. Richard Attenborough fell flat on his face with the musical version of *A Chorus Line* (1985), an unsuitable film for his talents and skills that he was only able to make on the strength of winning an Oscar for *Gandhi* three years earlier.

Oscar's Cumulative Advantage

The multiple effects of the Oscar Award point to a broader social phenomenon, known as the principle of cumulative advantage. This process, which both creates and maintains inequality within a profession, means that those who have done good work and earned peer esteem get more prestige and more recognition for their new work, and they get it faster than they would had they not been honored for their previous achievements. In other words, the rich and famous get richer and more famous, and the poor get poorer. The Oscar winners and, to a lesser extent, the nominees, get better roles, higher pay, and more publicity at a rate that makes them even more famous and successful, while making other players less and less successful.

The accumulation of advantage begins to operate once an actor "has made it," which can happen with a single movie, even the first one. Almost every player can point accurately to his or her "breakthrough role" or "turning point." However, an effective film debut is neither sufficient nor a guarantee for a successful career. Many prominent players didn't make strong impressions in the early phase of their careers and had to wait for years for their breakthrough.

Jane Wyman made two abortive attempts to break into Hollywood: the first at the age of eight, the second at twenty-two. After the first effort, Wyman turned to radio, using the name of June Durrell. But she didn't despair, and in 1934, she tried Hollywood again—her small part in *My Man Godfrey* led to a contract with Warner. After a long apprenticeship at Warner, playing chorus girls and other bit parts, Wyman was cast as Ray Milland's patient girlfriend in *The Lost Weekend.* This was a turning point, and three years later, Wyman was given the chance of a lifetime in *Johnny Belinda,* her Oscar-winning role that made her a top actress.

Anne Bancroft began her career in television in 1950, when she was nineteen, under the name of Anne Marno. Two years later, she made her film debut in *Don't Bother to Knock,* followed by a succession of B films for another six years. In 1958, disillusioned with Hollywood, Bancroft went back to New York and scored a huge success in *Two for the Seasaw* opposite Henry Fonda. She received a Tony Award for this part and a second Tony the next year for her performance as the devoted teacher, Annie Sullivan, in *The Miracle Worker,* which she repeated on screen, earning an Oscar for it.

Ellen Burstyn left her Detroit home when she was eighteen, determined to seek fame and fortune in New York. At first, she worked as a chorus dancer in nightclubs, but in 1957, she landed a part on Broadway in *Fair Game.* Burstyn's study at the Lee Strasberg Actors Studio improved her skills and made her more committed to acting. Her first important role was playing the bitter mother in *The Last Picture Show,* earning for it a supporting nomination and the New York Film Critics Award. By the time she had "made it," Burstyn was thirty-nine, claiming three different screen names to her credit.

The Oscar's effects are much more dramatic for the winners, whose increased popularity and prestige lead to additional nominations: about half of all winners have earned another Oscar and/or another nomination. This is particularly the case of the lead players: 59 percent of them, but only 30 percent of the supporting players, have won another Oscar and/or another nomination.

Among the supporting actors, only Walter Brennan received two more awards *(Kentucky, The Westerner)* and a nomination *(Sergeant York)* after his first Oscar. Five supporting actors have received a second Oscar: Anthony Quinn, Melvyn Douglas, Peter Ustinov, Jason Robards, and most recently, Michael Caine. Caine's first Oscar was for *Hannah and Her Sisters,* in which he played an adulterous husband, and the second was for *Cider House Rules,* for playing a humanist doctor performing illegal abortions.

Only two supporting actresses have received a second Oscar. Shelley Winters won a second supporting award for *A Patch of Blue,* in 1965, and another nomination for *The Poseidon Adventure* in 1972. The two supporting Oscars collected by Dianne Wiest are for appearances in Woody Allen movies: *Hannah and Her Sisters* in 1986, and *Bullets Over Broadway* in 1994.

Of the four acting categories, the Oscar has been the most influential for the Best Actresses. Twice as many Best Actresses (28 percent) as Best Actors (13 percent) have received a second Oscar. Four-fifths of the Best Actresses, but only two-fifths of the Best Actors, have been nominated again.

These variations arise from the fact that most Best Actresses have won the award at their first nomination, whereas Best Actors have been nominated two or three times before winning. Indeed, while there is no difference between men and women in the *number* of nominations, there are differences in the *timing* of these nominations. The Best Actors earn multiple nominations *before* their first win, whereas Best Actresses receive them *after* that.

Katharine Hepburn received three Oscars and eight nominations after her first win, and Bette Davis another Oscar and eight more nominations. Ingrid Bergman got two more Oscars and two nominations, and Jane Fonda a second Oscar and four nominations. The same players are repeatedly nominated and repeatedly win. Indeed, 1961 stood out because it was the first time in which all four winning actors (Maximilian Schell, Sophia Loren, George Chakiris, and Rita Moreno) won Oscars at their first nomination. At times, previous winners amount to half of the nominees in a given year. In 1964, for instance, five of the twenty acting nominees were former winners and six were previous nominees. In 1982 too, five of the nominees were former winners and four had been nominated before. The 1985 Best Actress nominees, Anne Bancroft, Whoopi Goldberg, Jessica Lange, Geraldine Page, and Meryl Streep, have collectively been nominated twenty-four times!

Cumulative advantage is also manifest in the distribution of honorific awards. Oscar winners are the recipients of awards from film critics, film festivals, and other associations. Most of these awards are announced in late December, about six weeks before the nominations in mid–February, thus inevitably affecting both the nominations and the final selections.

A reasonable consensus prevails between the Academy's and the New York Film Critics' choices: about one-third of all Oscar-winners have also won the Gotham Awards. The correlation between the two lead awards is even stronger: about half of all lead players have won both prizes. Some Oscar winners have been recipients of multiple critics' awards. Ingrid Bergman, Laurence Olivier, and Burt Lancaster hold the record with each winning three New York Film Critics Awards.

The Golden Globes are announced in late January, but their nominees are announced in mid-December, before the Academy nominations. About half of all Oscar winners have also received the Golden Globes, with a higher percentage among the lead categories. The stronger link between the Oscar and the Golden Globes, compared with that of the New York Film Critics, is due to the fact that the Globes are awarded by journalists rather than critics. The Academy's large size and diverse membership like those of the Hollywood Foreign Press Association, often lead to choices that are not entirely based on matter-of-fact considerations.

Multiple awards are often given for the same performances. Again, about one-third of the New York Film Critics winners have been cited for the same role which won them the Oscar. As Ray Milland observed in 1945: "I found myself the recipient of more awards than I ever knew existed." For his portrait of the alcoholic writer in *The Lost Weekend,* Milland received the Oscar, the New York Film Critics Award, the Golden Globe, the *Look* magazine award, and a citation from the Alcoholics Anonymous Unwed Mothers of America. Mercedes McCambridge was also surprised that "for the same short performance, I had already won two Golden Globes, one for Best Supporting Actress and one for Best Newcomer, the *Look* award, and there were lesser ones."

There are so many film awards that actors can collect six or seven prizes for the same role. For her portrayal of the petty criminal Barbara Graham in *I Want to Live!* Susan Hayward won the Oscar, the New York Film Critics, the Golden Globe, the Cannes festival, and the Donatello (the Italian Oscar) awards. George C. Scott was singled out for *Patton* by the Academy, the New York Film Critics, the Hollywood Foreign Press, the National Society of Film Critics, the National Board of Review, and the British Film Academy.

The Triple Crown: Oscar-Tony-Emmy

A large number (one-third) of Oscar winners and nominees are distinguished stage actors and recipients of the Tony Award, the top award in Broadway theater. But, once again, the largest number of Tony winners and nominees is among the Best Actresses: more women than men have won or have been nominated for Tonys. As in film, a smaller number of women dominate the theatrical world, with the interesting stage roles circulating among them.

About a dozen players have won the Oscar and Tony awards for the same role. The Tony precedes the Oscar since motion picture rights are purchased after a play is proven to be a commercial success on Broadway. This lucky group includes: José Ferrer *(Cyrano de Bergerac),* Shirley Booth *(Come Back, Little Sheba),* Yul Brynner *(The King and I),* Anne Bancroft *(The Miracle Worker),* Rex Harrison *(My Fair Lady),* Paul Scofield *(A Man for All Seasons),* Jack Albertson *(The Subject Was Roses),* and Joel Grey *(Cabaret).*

The "success syndrome" in both the theater and film worlds often occurs within a short period of time. Shirley Booth won her first Tony for a featured role in *Goodbye, My Fancy* in 1949, then a second Tony as Best Dramatic Actress in *Come Back, Little Sheba* in 1950, an Oscar for the same role in 1952, and a third Tony for *Time of the Cuckoo* in 1953.

Half a dozen players have won the Oscar and Tony awards in the same year. Fredric March was the first to claim both prizes in 1947, winning a second Oscar for *The Best Years of Our Lives* and a second Tony for *Years Ago.* Audrey Hepburn's 1954 Tony for *Ondine* followed the Oscar for *Roman Holiday* by only a few weeks. Ellen Burstyn's career peaked in 1975 when she won Best Actress for *Alice Doesn't Live Here Anymore* and the Tony for the comedy *Same Time Next Year,* which she later re-created on the screen. The record holder is Bob Fosse, who, in 1973, became the only person in showbiz to win the Tony for the musical *Pippin,* the Oscar for the film *Cabaret,* which he didn't direct on stage, and the Grammy for the album *Liza with a Z.*

Dame Judi Dench is still in awe of her meteoric rise to stardom. Although the movies are overrun nowadays by hot young up-and-comers, Hollywood has "discovered" Dench while in her sixties. In 1997, Dench became a star with her Oscar-nominated performance as Queen Victoria in *Mrs. Brown.* The next year she played another queen, Elizabeth, in *Shakespeare in Love,* and won a supporting Oscar. Dench followed with a Tony for *Amy's View,* her first Broadway play in forty years, though she has been a staple of the London stage. Dench was on screen for only eight minutes in *Shakespeare in Love,* and yet she was unforgettable. She fondly recalled: "I just played her like I imagined she would be. She was a fierce woman. People didn't like messing with her. I was in all those clothes and I couldn't do much but stay very still and pray I didn't have to go to the loo in the middle."

Successful players "commute" effectively between stage and screen, and between the big and small screen. This is yet another indication of "accumulative advantage" in the entertainment world. There is no short supply of talented actors, but those who are both talented and popular are in high demand. Theatergoers want to see the "hot" actors, and actors often become hot after winning an Oscar Award or a nomination, such as Glenn Close or Linda Hunt.

Popular screen players, like Vanessa Redgrave, Meryl Streep, and Jessica Lange, have also played interesting roles in television, often winning the Emmy, the most prestigious prize for television work. Two fifths of all Oscar winners have either won or have been nominated for an Emmy. And again, lead players have an advantage over supporting ones, and more women than men, particularly in the lead categories, win Emmys.

Awards in the performing arts are concentrated within a small clique of actors whose success in one medium often leads to success in other media. It's no longer true that most players begin their careers in the theater, then moved on to film and television. It's impossible, in fact, to discern one dominant route, beginning, say, with winning a Tony, then an Oscar, and then an Emmy.

The strong correlation among the various awards points to the existence of what could be called *media stars*—celebrities who are equally successful in all the media. This small minority is headed by winners of the "triple crown," the Oscar, the Tony, and the Emmy. Helen Hayes, Thomas Mitchell, Ingrid Bergman, Shirley Booth, Melvyn Douglas, Jack Albertson, Paul Scofield, Anne Bancroft, Liza Minnelli, and Dame Judi Dench have all been media stars.

Barbra Streisand became "the queen of the entertainment industries," because, as one observer noted, at the staggeringly unprecedented age of twenty-seven, "she accomplished an unheard of, indeed, undreamed of feat. She was the only person, male or female, to have won every major entertainment award." Early on, Streisand vowed to scoop all major awards, a feat that she achieved in only five years. She was nominated for a Tony for her role as Fanny Brice in *Funny Girl,* which provided her screen debut and earned her an Oscar in 1968. Streisand won a Special Tony in 1970, as "the Actress of the Decade," an extensive, multi-million dollar contract, and a string of recordings and successful TV specials which earned her Grammys and Emmys.

Henry Fonda, one of America's most beloved actors, was a media star in the full sense of the term, though he considered himself primarily a stage actor. One of the first screen stars to make a successful transition to stage and television, Fonda alternated regularly among them. In 1959, he appeared in the TV series *The Deputy,* two theatrical films, *Warlock* and *The Man Who Understood Women,* and a Broadway play. Fonda's string of prestigious awards included a 1948 Tony for *Mister Roberts,* a 1982 Oscar for *On Golden Pond,* Emmy nominations, and numerous career-achievement awards.

No showbiz personality validates the principle of accumulative advantage better than Meryl Streep, Hollywood's "hottest" actress of the 1980s. Streep has achieved stardom on stage, television, and film in an astonishingly brief time. Upon graduation from the Yale School of Drama, she appeared in repertory at the Public Theater. For her Broadway debut, in the Phoenix Theater's production of Tennessee Williams's *27 Wagons Full of Cotton* and Arthur Miller's *A Memory of Two Mondays,* she received Tony and Drama Desk nominations and the Outer Critics Circle and Theatre World awards. This auspicious beginning led to a bit part in the film *Julia* and to a major role in the TV series *Holocaust,* for which she received an Emmy. In 1978, Streep earned her first supporting nomination and the National Society of Film Critics Award for *The Deer Hunter.*

The turning point in Streep's career occurred in 1979, with the release of Woody Allen's *Manhattan* and Robert Benton's *Kramer vs.*

Kramer, which brought Streep her first Oscar and established her as a household name. In 1981, Streep made a successful transition from supporting to leading roles in *The French Lieutenant's Woman,* which earned her a first Best Actress nomination. In the following year, there was critical consensus that her doomed Polish heroine in *Sophie's Choice* was the best performance of the year, for which she won the Oscar and practically every possible film award. In 1983, Streep won her fifth nomination for playing the title role in *Silkwood,* and two years later she was singled out by the Los Angeles Film Critics for her work in *Out of Africa,* winning for it her sixth Oscar nomination and the Cannes Festival Award.

Over the last decade, Streep has been labeled the queen of Oscar because of her spate of nominations: *Ironweed* in 1987, *Cry in the Dark* in 1988, *Postcards from the Edge* in 1990, *The Bridges of Madison County* in 1995, *One True Thing* in 1998, and *Music the Heart* in 1999. Chances are that Streep will surpass the critical recognition of Katharine Hepburn, with whom she holds the all-time record with twelve acting nominations.

For Helen Hunt, too, the Oscar arrived on a day when her blossoming movie and TV careers came together. Early one day, Hunt announced she would return for another year of her hit NBC sitcom, *Mad About You,* and in the evening, she won Best Actress for *As Good As It Gets.* Hunt's movie and TV career complement each other, and she has three movies in development with Sony. In the past, TV actors were virtually "blacklisted" from Oscar consideration. "I think the industry is finally changing," Hunt said when asked about her crossover appeal. The experience of making *As Good As It Gets* was "thrilling and fun and brutal and hard, a one-of-a-kind experience." Asked to compare her Oscar with her Emmys, Hunt joked: "Thinner? Without wings. They are two projects close to my heart."

Oscar's Negative Effects

The Oscar can also bring negative effects on the winners' careers. Some winners become victims of their success when they are rushed by their agents into a succession of films designed to cash in on their new popularity. After her stunning performance in *I Want to Live!,* Susan Hayward made mostly B movies, which were meant to exploit her status as an Oscar-caliber winner. The studios held up the release of *Thunder in the Sun* and *A Woman Possessed* hoping that audiences would flock to see them regardless of their merits. They were wrong, both pictures did poorly, and Hayward never had another critical success before her retirement from the screen in the late 1960s.

Quick attempts at reuniting Oscar winners to cash in on their visibility have mostly failed. The two 1961 Oscar winners, Maximilian Schell and Sophia Loren, were cast in *The Condemned of Altona,* based on Jean-Paul Sartre's play, but the film failed both artistically and commercially.

A rare, fortunate film was *The Bells of St. Mary's,* which reteamed three of the 1944 Oscar winners: Bing Crosby, Ingrid Bergman, and director Leo McCarey. Since Crosby played a priest who was similar to his Oscar role in *Going My Way,* audiences believed that *The Bells of St. Mary's* was a sequel. It is one of the few sequels whose success surpassed that of the original movie on which it was modeled.

It is easy but unfair to charge the Oscar with actually causing winners' dwindling careers. For every case of an Oscar "casualty" or "victim," there has been a counterexample of an Oscar winner whose career has been rescued and revitalized by the Academy Award. Faltering careers are seldom the direct result of winning an Oscar. Hence, some Oscar winners were not distinguished performers in the first place. Jennifer Jones was never a formidable actress, but when cast in the right role and working with a strong director she could give a credible performance, like her Oscar-winning role in *The Song of Bernadette.*

Indeed, it is possible to distinguish between Oscar-caliber performers, who have given many good performances, and performers who have excelled in one role for which they received an Oscar. Louise Fletcher has excelled in only one film, *One Flew Over the Cuckoo's Nest,* for which she was singled out by the Academy. By contrast, Vanessa Redgrave, Jane Fonda, Sissy Spacek, Meryl Streep, Holly Hunter, and Julianne Moore are Oscar-caliber actresses who have consistently rendered high-quality work.

Many players reach the apogee of their careers with their Oscar-winning roles, and subsequently are unable to surpass or match that quality. Sophia Loren *(Two Women),* Julie Christie *(Darling),* and Elizabeth Taylor *(Who's Afraid of Virginia Woolf?)* have earned Oscars for their finest performances, which have been hard to match, let alone surpass. Sophia Loren seldom reached the heights of her Oscar-winning role and, with the exception of her films opposite Marcello Mastroianni, *Marriage Italian Style* and *A Special Day,* made mostly mediocre pictures.

Julie Christie is an Oscar-winner who has never reached the artistic heights expected of her after *Darling,* though she appeared in many commercial hits, such as *Doctor Zhivago* and *Shampoo.* Critics still wonder whether *Darling,* and to a lesser extent *McCabe and Mrs. Miller* and *Afterglow*—a comeback performance for which Christie won a 1997 Best Actress nomination—were the only vehicles that brought out her distinctive talent and intelligence as an actress.

Yet, given the ratio of acting talent to the number of films produced, it is not surprising that gifted actors end up making bad pictures. Broderick Crawford began and unfortunately ended his career making B movies; his Oscar-winning role in *All the King's Men* was the notable exception.

The most devastated Oscar victim in Hollywood mythology is still Luise Rainer, whose career prompted gossip columnist Louella Parsons to coin the often-used phrase, "the Oscar as a jinx." or the Oscar as a curse. Rainer was brought to Hollywood by Irving Thalberg to join MGM's great roster of female stars, headed by Greta Garbo, Norma Shearer, and Joan Crawford. Rainer's career took off immediately, and she became the first actress to win two successive Oscars, for *The Great Ziegfeld* and *The Good Earth*.

"Those two Academy Awards were bad for me," Rainer later observed. Expectations of her work were so unrealistically heightened that when her next film failed, "I was treated as if I had never done anything good in my life." Rainer made only a few films after her second Oscar and her career terminated abruptly with her last MGM film, *Dramatic School*, in 1938. "After Academy Awards, you cannot make mistakes," she complained. "In my day, making films was like working in a factory. You were a piece of machinery with no rights."

Some say Louis B. Mayer lost interest in Rainer after her MGM sponsor, Irving Thalberg, died. Others put the blame for her premature retirement on poor choice of roles and bad advice from her husband, playwright Clifford Odets. But judging by the quality of her Oscar performances, Rainer was not a major talent, and the fact that she won two years in a row had to do more with studio politics than genuine acting skills.

Decline in the quality of Oscar-winners' work may be the result of rushing actors into film projects and indiscriminating choices by the actors themselves. Even so, the chronic imbalance between the supply and demand of acting talent may also account for low quality. The abundant supply of gifted players—in relation to the volume of films made and percentage of good films—results in many actors being miscast, misdirected, or just giving decent performances in bad films.

The Curse of Typecasting

Typecasting actors in roles similar to their Oscar-winning roles is another negative effect of an Oscar win. Actors complain that they tend to receive scores of roles identical or similar to their winning one, and that it is impossible for them to break away from the mold, often created or reinforced by the Oscar itself.

Most actors are aware of their potential range and of what audiences expect of them. "When I appear on the screen," Cary Grant once said,

"I'm playing myself," though he believed that "it's harder to play your-self." Grant attributed his success to his conformity to audiences' expec-tations. Hence, his philosophy was: "Adopt the true image of yourself, acquire technique to project it, and the public will give you its alle-giance." Indeed, if it is possible to describe Grant's or Wayne's screen per-sona, it is because of their durable coherence and consistency. Actors understand the different responsibilities and rewards involved in being actors and in being movie stars. The Critic John Russell Taylor once described "the penalty" of being a star by saying that "an actor is paid to do, a star is paid to be."

Indeed, some actors have come to resent the screen image imposed on them by the public because it limits their range. Mary Pickford was best loved for playing the naive and innocent girl, for which she was dubbed "America's Sweetheart." Occasionally, Pickford would try to deviate from her standardized roles, but under public pressure she would be forced to play them again. As late as 1920, when she was twenty-seven, Pickford was still playing teenagers in the mold of *Pollyanna*.

Interestingly, Pickford was cast against type in her Oscar-winning role, *Coquette*, which called for cutting her curls and acquiring a new hairstyle and a new personality. But neither the film nor her persona convinced her fans. Pickford resented her public image, as she recorded in her memoirs: "Every now and then, as the years went by and I continued to play chil-dren's roles, it would worry me that I was becoming a personality instead of an actress. I would suddenly resent the fact that I had allowed myself to be hypnotized by the public into remaining a little girl. A wild impulse would seize me to reach for the nearest shears and remove that blonde chain around my neck."

Greer Garson also got tired of the image that MGM had created for her, the graciously noble, English-like lady, epitomized in *Mrs. Miniver*. A professional actress, Garson felt qualified to play a wider range of roles, hence her strong interest in getting the part of the bitter, adulterous wife in *From Here to Eternity*, a role played with great success by Deborah Kerr. Indeed, Kerr wanted this part for the same reason; she too was typically cast as the coolly elegant and reserved lady. Director Zinnemann's decision to cast against type became a turning point in Kerr's career. After this part, she was able to demand any role and the nomination for playing it enhanced her self-confidence as an actress.

Typecasting has characterized the careers of both leading and support-ing players. Specializing in plump, middle-aged matrons, Jane Darwell was cast in over sixty standardized roles modeled on her Oscar-winning role as Ma Dodd in *The Grapes of Wrath*. "Those mealy mouthed women, how I hated them," she once observed. "I played so many of them, those genial small-town wives, that I was getting awfully tired of them."

Rita Moreno, the first Latina to win an Oscar, became completely identified with her feisty Puerto Rican heroine in *West Side Story,* after which she received offers all in tune with her stereotypical image as a "Latin spitfire." Moreno decided not to "get stuck" with this kind of role for the rest of her career and subsequently went back to the theater. After a decade of stage work, Moreno was ready to begin a second chapter in Hollywood, with a more "neutral" screen image.

Glenn Close, too, was able to shake her screen image of earth mothers with the aid of one commercial hit, *Fatal Attraction,* and received an Oscar nomination for it. As she recalled: "I wanted to break out of the kinds of roles I used to do because I was boring myself." After that 1987 success, Close was cast in another juicy and villainous role in *Dangerous Liaisons,* for which she received her second Best Actress (and fifth) nomination.

Since acting involves role-playing and film is perceived as a "realistic" medium, some viewers fail to separate between actors' lives on-screen and offscreen. Ray Milland recalled that after the release of *The Lost Weekend,* he found himself being looked upon as an authority on alcoholism. Jack Lemmon, who also played a hard-drinking man in *Days of Wine and Roses,* shared the same experience, as he told the *New York Times:* "You don't know how many people think of me as a drunk and send me letters telling me of the glories of Alcoholics Anonymous."

The trap involved in sporting an established screen image was most acutely felt by Julie Andrews, who won an Oscar *(Mary Poppins)* and another nomination *(The Sound of Music)* for a similar role: the virtuous, wholesome heroine. This image stuck so deeply in audiences' collective memory that Andrews couldn't rid herself of it. In 1964, Andrews replaced Doris Day as America's top female star, playing good-natured, reliable, and maternal women who represented traditional values.

However, as critic Linda Gross observed, Andrews remained popular only as long as the status quo was maintained in American society; after four years, Andrews's image became outdated and out of step. Unfortunately, Andrews was unable "to shake this sugary image in a time when sugary [was] out of favor, its place taken by conflict and conscience." The zeitgeist was now represented by the next generation of female stars: Jane Fonda, Diane Keaton, Ellen Burstyn, and Meryl Streep. Andrews's clean-cut image was so solid that she couldn't change it even when she played vastly different roles, such as one in *S.O.B.,* in which she exposed her breasts.

"I hope I am not as square as some people might think," Andrews once observed, expressing mild resentment at her public image. "I hope I have many facets." Andrews was aware that her career suffered because her image crystallized quite early: "If you have a large success at something, you are inclined to get typed." Andrews further believes that "the lack of good roles for women and the bracketing" have made her a victim of type-casting. She wished to play more dramatic roles, comedies, and musicals, without being typed. Children's films still interested her, though she didn't want to do anything that would seem a copy of *Mary Poppins*. Hoping that at least critics would recognize her as a better actress than she was given credit for, Andrews went out of her way to break her mold. In the musical comedy *Victor/Victoria*, she played a passionate woman disguised as a man who impersonates women.

The effects of typecasting are severely felt by actors who played a pow-erful role that became their trademark. Gloria Swanson recalls that after her 1950 stunning performance, "more and more scripts arrived at my door that were awful imitations of *Sunset Boulevard*, all featuring a 'deranged super-star crashing toward tragedy.'" A strong woman, Swanson vowed: "I didn't want to spend the rest of my life, until I couldn't remember lines any longer or read cue cards, playing Norma Desmond over and over again." At the same time, she resented that "serious producers and directors were fool-ish enough to think that this was the only role I could play and get box-office returns."

Hollywood believes in repeating successful formulas, which means, among other things, recasting stars in similar roles. Sylvia Miles "special-ized" in playing tough but vulnerable floozies, earning a first nomination for *Midnight Cowboy* and a second for *Farewell, My Lovely*. Miles claims to have a drawer in her apartment with many similar parts, marked as "whores with hearts of gold, waitresses, tough broads." For her effective portrait of a prostitute in *Cinderella Liberty*, Marsha Mason received her first nomination. She later complained, "if you play down-and-out loser parts, they send you down-and-out loser parts."

Although women have been more confined by typecasting, men have been victims too. Bruce Dern played numerous villains, first in NBC's *Alfred Hitchcock Presents*, then in *The Cowboys*, in which he "dared" to kill John Wayne on-screen. Dern holds that his recognition as an actor came rather late because "I was sold wrong." "I would have been much further along if I had gotten a better agent earlier. Everyone in this business is sold, and I was sold as a cuckoo, a bad guy, a psychotic." The Academy legit-imized this typecasting when it nominated Dern for playing the demented-ly chauvinist captain who commits suicide in *Coming Home*.

The second kind of typecasting is most severely felt by supporting play-ers, doomed for the rest of their careers to function as second bananas. In some respects, the Academy itself is responsible for such typecasting, making the distinction between leading and character players official in the Academy Players Directory, the industry's chief casting tool. Until the late 1970s, players who won or were nominated for supporting awards tended to remain in this category.

A strong screen image, created in a first film and certified by an Oscar nomination, is that of Sidney Greenstreet, who made an auspicious debut as Kasper Guttman, the ruthless villain in *The Maltese Falcon*. This image suited his size, being a bulky man of three hundred pounds. Greenstreet went on to play so many master villains that he became Hollywood's classic screen villain. Offended that Warner relegated him to such limited range, Greenstreet was particularly sensitive to the critics' view that he was only capable of playing villains. Warner never trusted his ability to sell a movie on his own and thus never cast him in a leading role.

After making his stage debut in London at seventeen, Peter Ustinov suffered from similar typecasting in Hollywood, and played only older, often eccentric men. Ustinov never became a leading man and was always associated with screen actors older than those his own age. "It was a mistake," Ustinov later conceded. "For years I played nothing but old men."

The same fate was met by Lee J. Cobb, a leading man in the theater but mostly a character actor in film. Cobb played secondary roles, often tough racketeers and stern politicians, winning nominations for *On the Waterfront* and *The Brothers Karamazov*. Gig Young's lifelong dream was to be a leading man, but his Oscar *(They Shoot Horses, Don't They?)* and his two other nominations were all in the supporting league. Similarly, Angela Lansbury, Celeste Holm, Donna Reed, Shirley Jones, and Teresa Wright began and ended their screen careers as supporting actresses, especially after winning awards in this category.

Though typecasting is still a norm in Hollywood, it is not as rigid as it used to be, particularly for men. In the last two decades, several actors began their careers and won Academy recognition as supporting players, but later made smooth transition to leading roles. This group includes George C. Scott, Roy Scheider, Al Pacino, Robert Duvall, and Robert De Niro.

Gene Hackman began his career as a character actor, distinguishing himself in secondary parts in films such as *Bonnie and Clyde* (his first nomination). His part in *I Never Sang for My Father* brought, to his disappointment, a second supporting nomination—"I guess the Academy is trying to tell me something," he said. Even so, Hackman was proud to state: "I never approach a film as if I'm playing a supporting character. If I do, then I'm just a supporting character. I approach it as if it's the most important thing in my life."

In 1971, Hackman won Best Actor for *The French Connection,* after which he has played both leading and supporting roles—by choice. For his secondary role, as a sadistic sheriff in *Unforgiven,* Hackman won a second, supporting Oscar, in 1992. Hackman belongs to the new breed of star character actors who get lead roles without conforming to Hollywood's previous traditional typecasting, demanding that leading men be attractive and project a romantic image.

In recent years, lead actors have had to be neither attractive nor romantic to be cast in starring roles. Just look as Walter Matthau's career. In the 1950s, Matthau was typically cast in villainous roles, seeming to be destined to stay in the supporting league. But he rose to sudden stardom in Neil Simon's *The Odd Couple,* in a role specifically written for him. Matthau went on to star in a succession of comedies, earning a supporting Oscar for *The Fortune Cookie,* and two Best Actor nominations for *Kotch* and *The Sunshine Boys.* Interestingly, the same slouching posture, awkward walk, and unhandsome face, which had kept him from becoming a leading man in the 1950s and 1960s, were used to different effect in the 1970s, when he got to play romantic roles for the first time, beginning with *House Calls,* acting opposite Glenda Jackson.

Oscar Anxiety

The fierce competition, the desirability of the Oscar and its immense effects on the winners may explain the obsession with winning the award. And those who have won the Oscar are under tremendous pressure to prove that they are worthy of it. Perpetual professional anxiety might indeed be one of Oscar's most devastating consequences.

Producers, directors, and actors go out of their way to obtain the coveted award. Publishing tycoon William Randolph Hearst was so consumed with getting an Oscar for his mistress Marion Davies that his activities in the film industry were single-mindedly driven by this goal, first joining forces with MGM, then with Warner. Hearst succeeded in getting Davies some good roles, but failed to get her the award; she was never even nominated. David O. Selznick also worked hard to get a second Oscar for his wife, Jennifer Jones, and, though failing to achieve that, his power and publicity campaigns had some influence in getting Jones nominations for unworthy performances like hers in *Duel in the Sun.*

The award may have damaging effects on the winner's interactions with peers, friends, and family. "A picture taken after the Oscar banquet of Brian (Aherne) sitting alone in an empty room," Joan Fontaine observes, "feet up on a chair, my fur coat over his arm, waiting patiently for the photographers to finish with the winners, graphically illustrates the plight of marriage when the wife is more successful than the husband." Furthermore, after winning, "there was many a doubter, many a detractor, many an ill-wisher. It's an uneasy head that wears the crown."

Mercedes McCambridge also believes that "there is a price tag and mischief in the lovely statue with my name on it." "I mustn't think that taking bows was all that would be expected of me," she writes. "Oscar was calling the tune now, and it gave me a funny feeling: Did the Oscar belong to me, or did I belong to it? Which one of us would always be in debt to the other?"

Pressure to live up to the critics' expectations might make the award a burden for the winners. "The way to survive an Oscar," Humphrey Bogart said after winning his, "is to never try to win another one. You've seen what happens to some Oscar winners. They spent the rest of their lives turning down scripts while searching for the great role to win another one. Hell, I hope I'm never even nominated again. It's meat-and-potatoes roles for me from now on."

A generation later, Meryl Streep reiterated Bogart's fears more succinctly: "I'm freaked out. It's like a mantel visited on me that has no relation to what I do or who I am." Some of Streep's friends didn't speak to her after she was hailed as "America's Best Actress" on the cover of *Time* magazine. It was a traumatic experience, as she noted: "Hype like that is very destructive. It takes a piece out of every other actress." Baffled by her meteoric rise to stardom, Streep has no explanation as to exactly how it happened. "It's very difficult. You get a big buildup and it's almost like nothing can live up to it."

The anxiety involved in winning the Oscar and then living up to it reflects the inherent character of show business in general. Acting is one of the most precarious professions: the rise to stardom may be sudden, but the decline can be just as dramatic. One of Hollywood's sad realities is the dictum, "You are as good as your last picture." Two failures at the box office are enough to destroy careers of multiple achievements. Under these circumstances, no wonder film artists can be insecure—they need to prove themselves with the financial, not just artistic, reception of each of their movies. Unlike other professions, in which practitioners achieve security at some point in their careers, filmmakers must constantly struggle to maintain their status, over which they have less control than other professionals.

"Looking back on Hollywood," Joan Fontaine observes, "I realize that one outstanding quality it possesses is not lavishness, the perpetual sunshine, the golden opportunities, but *fear*. Fear stalks the sound stage, the publicity departments, the executive offices. Since careers often begin by chance, by the hunch of a producer or casting director, a casual meeting with an agent of publicist, they can evaporate just as quixotically."

Hollywood has always been characterized by a here-and-now orientation. What counts, ultimately, is the commercial standing of films and the *current* popularity of directors and actors. Oscar-winners of previous years are quickly forgotten, not just by the public, but by the Academy and the industry. Former winners are resentful that they are never invited to the ceremonies as guests of honor. Winners quickly become members of a "forgotten legion," unless they win another Oscar and remain active in the industry. Frank Capra, a three-time Oscar-winner and one of the most popular American directors, observed after spending decades in Hollywood: "Show business is brutal to has-beens. Those pushed off the top are rolled into the valley of oblivion; often they are mired in degradation. I saw it all around me: D. W. Griffith—a forgotten man; Mack Sennett—walking unnoticed in the city he had once ruled as a King of Comedy; old stars pleading for jobs as extras."

Most artists are aware that success in show business, which the Oscar symbolizes, can be fleeting. Yet the Oscar exerts such a pervasive influence that the artists continue to regard it as the ultimate achievement of their lives. And so long as they do, the Oscar's mythologies—and anxieties—continue to thrive.

CHAPTER 14

Can the Oscar Be Bought?

As is clear, movies do not operate in a social or political void. And as the prime award in the international film world, the Oscar is not immune to political pressures and forces operating within and without the movie industry. Political factors have always influenced the types of movies and performances nominated for, and winning, Oscars.

Studio Politics

In the first year, Academy voters were asked to display "rare discrimination and honest judgment" in their choices. Members were advised "to evince equal discrimination so that the final awards may be fairly representative of the industry's opinion of its best achievements." After the second ceremonies, the Academy Board was proud to report that "so far, there has been no evidence of studio politics," and that producers have "freely nominated pictures from studios other than their own." However, as David O. Selznick once noted, the Academy was always "influenced unduly by transient tastes, by commercial success, by studio log-rolling and by personal popularity in the community of Hollywood."

Both nominations and final selections have been prejudiced by the studios' ad campaigns, even though there was always ambivalence toward outright politicking for a particular studio's movies and contract artists. Back in the studio system, ads were considered to be clear violations of fair and dispassionate selection procedures. However, those in favor of using ad campaigns suggest that politicking is not unique or confined to the Oscar, that even the more esoteric and prestigious Nobel Prize is subject to extensive campaigning by scientists, both formal and informal. Still, the difference is that campaigns for the Nobel Prize are conducted by peers, whereas campaigns for Oscars are guided by the studios and the individual artists themselves.

Filmmakers campaign for their movies because they attribute tremendous importance to winning an Oscar, or even receiving a nomination. The Oscar has become a legitimate measure of evaluating screen careers. Studios, directors, and actors gauge their careers in terms of the number of Oscar nominations and awards they have received. Hence, independent producer David O. Selznick was proud to proclaim that his films had received collectively thirty-six nominations and that two, *Gone With the Wind* and *Rebecca,* won Best Picture.

The major studios always had the resources and facilities to carry out sophisticated and effective campaigns on behalf of their movies. The studios' publicity departments could make stars out of their contract players, sell their movies to the public, and persuade members to vote for their pictures. Not to be forgotten is that the Academy began its existence as a guild-busting company union manipulated by the biggest studio, MGM. Louis B. Mayer, who ruled MGM for two decades, was one of the Academy's charter founders and, thus, was instrumental in drafting its goals.

During his reign, MGM received more than its fair share of nominations and awards. In the first decade, MGM earned a total of 153 nominations and 33 awards, a record surpassing that of other studios. Paramount ranked a distant second, with 102 nominations and 18 awards, followed by Warner with 71 nominations and 15 awards. In contrast, Fox and Columbia featured poorly, the former with 54 nominations and 13 awards, the latter with 43 nominations and 10 awards.

In Oscar's first twelve years (from 1927/28 to 1939), of the 102 Best Picture nominees, 28 were produced by MGM, 17 by Paramount, 10 by Twentieth Century-Fox, 15 by Warner, 8 by Columbia, 7 by RKO, and 4 each by United Artists and Universal. Only three of the nominees were produced outside Hollywood, the British-made *The Private Life of Henry VIII* and *Pygmalion,* and the French *Grand Illusion.* Independent producers justifiably complained that their movies stood little chance of being nominated. Samuel Goldwyn had only four films *(Arrowsmith, Dodsworth, Dead End,* and *Wuthering Heights),* and Selznick two *(A Star Is Born* and *Gone With the Wind).*

MGM's defenders claim that in the 1930s the studio produced *more* films than any other studio, and that MGM made *better* films. What they mean is that MGM actually made films that were more suitable for winning Oscars. Of the first twelve Best Pictures, MGM made four: *The Broadway Melody* (1928/29), *Grand Hotel* (1931/32), *Mutiny on the Bounty* (1935), and *The Great Ziegfeld* (1936); *Gone With the Wind* (1939) was released by MGM but was a Selznick production.

In the early 1930s, MGM had at least two films nominated for Best Picture every year, and later in the decade even more. In 1936, no fewer than five MGM films competed for Best Picture: *The Great Ziegfeld*, which won, *Libeled Lady*, *Romeo and Juliet*, *San Francisco*, and *A Tale of Two Cities*.

MGM also dominated the 1930s' acting Oscars: ten out of the twenty Best Actors and Best Actresses were given to MGM players, including Norma Shearer, Marie Dressler, Helen Hayes, and Luise Rainer (in 1936 and 1937) among the women, and Lionel Barrymore, Wallace Beery, Spencer Tracy (in 1937 and 1938), and Robert Donat among the men.

Smaller studios had more limited opportunities in getting their products nominated. Rising director Frank Capra assured his Columbia boss, Harry Cohn, that he would get nominations for his 1930 Barbara Stanwyck comedy, *Ladies of Leisure*; he was therefore vastly disappointed when the film was ignored by the Academy. Quickly realizing the "disadvantage of working at Columbia," Capra learned that "the major studios had the votes. I had my freedom, but all the honors went to those who worked for the Establishment." The first Columbia movie to be nominated was Capra's 1933 comedy, *Lady for a Day*, and the first Columbia film to win the Best Picture Oscar was Capra's *It Happened One Night*, a year later.

For two decades, the Academy was controlled by the big studios, with nominations dominated by a few powerful cliques within the studios. "The trick," as Capra observed, "was to get nominated by the clique of major studio directors who had achieved membership—and those Brahmins were not about to doff their caps to the 'untouchables' of Poverty Row," as the small studios were then labeled. "Making good pictures was not enough," Capra quickly learned. "I would have to gain status with big name directors to get them to nominate me."

Under the leadership of Adolph Zukor, Paramount was also strongly represented in the Best Picture category during the Depression. In the first year, four of the five nominated films were produced by Paramount, including the winner, *Wings*. A large number of these movies were produced and/or directed by Paramount's prestige filmmaker, Ernst Lubitsch.

Columbia's participation in the Oscar race in the 1930s can also be described in terms of the output of its star director, Frank Capra: six out of Columbia's eight nominated films were directed by Capra, who won three directorial Oscars (in 1934, 1936, and 1938) over a period of four years. By contrast, the few RKO nominees were based on the strength of their performers: three of Katharine Hepburn's vehicles were nominated—*Little Women*, *Alice Adams*, and *Stage Door*—and two with the team of Fred

Astaire and Ginger Rogers, *The Gay Divorcee* and *Top Hat*. Similarly, two of Universal's four nominated films featured their star, Deanna Durbin, who helped save the studio from bankruptcy.

In the 1940s, MGM's domination of the Best Picture category declined: it produced only ten of the seventy nominated films, mostly the Greer Garson vehicles. RKO and Paramount followed, each with seven nominated films. RKO gained prestige from the Orson Welles films, two of which were nominated, *Citizen Kane* in 1941 and *The Magnificent Ambersons* in 1942. Paramount also benefited from the work of one writer-director, Billy Wilder. Three of Wilder's movies received nomination: *Hold Back the Dawn* in 1941, which he didn't direct but co-wrote with Charles Brackett; *Double Indemnity*, which he wrote and directed, and *The Lost Weekend*, which won Best Picture.

Up until the late 1940s, nominations and awards were restricted to the big studios. In 1948, seventy-two out of the 102 nominees contending for awards were featured in movies released by the major studios: MGM, Warner, Twentieth-Century Fox, Paramount, and RKO. The rest were in movies distributed by smaller companies, such as Universal, Columbia, and Republic; most of Universal's nominations were for the British-made *Hamlet*, which it distributed in America.

The studio that gained unexpected power in the 1940s was Twentieth-Century Fox, producing thirteen of the seventy nominated films, two of which won: *How Green Was My Valley* in 1941, and *Gentleman's Agreement* in 1947. By comparison, the best decade for Columbia was in the 1950s, in which three of its movies won Best Picture: *From Here to Eternity* in 1953, *On the Waterfront* in 1954, and *The Bridge on the River Kwai* in 1957.

United Artists was fairly represented in the first two decades, though it distributed only one winner, Selznick's *Rebecca*. However, from 1960 to 1990, no fewer than nine of the winners were distributed by UA, including: *The Apartment* in 1960, *West Side Story* in 1961, and *Tom Jones* in 1963. UA also holds the record for being the only studio to win three Best Pictures in a row: *One Flew Over the Cuckoo's Nest* in 1975, *Rocky* in 1976, and *Annie Hall* in 1977.

Overall, a peculiar kind of balance prevailed among the major studios in the Best Picture category during its first six decades. UA, Columbia, MGM, and Paramount each received about eight to ten Oscars, while Fox, Universal, and Warner were slightly underrepresented. Two films were British-produced, and several were made by a new studio, Orion, which, ironically, went bankrupt after winning two successive Best Pictures: *Dances With Wolves* in 1990 and *The Silence of the Lambs* in 1991.

In the studio era, film workers were expected to be loyal to their home studios, upon which their livelihood depended. As Joan Crawford noted:

"You'd have to be a ninny to vote against the studio that has your contract and produces your pictures." This meant that workers placed in the nomination and final ballots films and performers of their own studios. To assure nominations for their colleagues, their names were listed as first choice, followed by unlikely candidates from other studios, thus guaranteeing that there would be no serious competition.

Other dilemmas prevail today, when studios no longer exist in the same way. As Peter Bart wrote in a *Variety*'s Special Oscar Issue: "If you were an Academy member, do you vote for what you really believe represents the best work in each category, even if it's an Australian or Italian movie, and, as such, a blunt indictment of Hollywood—and your employer?"

A more significant change in the Oscar operations is the increased visibility of new players. Over the last fifteen years, smaller, independent companies—indies, as they are known in the industry—have become an important force in the American cinema with a strong presence in the Oscar contest.

Indies Grabbing Oscars

When independent producer Samuel Goldwyn's *The Best Years of Our Lives* swept most of the 1946 Oscars, it created shock waves, and the beginning of the decline in the studios' dominance. Then, three Best Picture winners in the 1950s—*Marty, Around the World in 80 Days,* and *The Bridge on the River Kwai*—were made outside Hollywood.

The flowering of the independents became most visible in 1985, when *Kiss of the Spider Woman,* a small-budget film financed by a new company, Island Alive, was surprisingly nominated for Best Picture. William Hurt won Best Actor for his performance in that film and Geraldine Page won Best Actress for *The Trip to Bountiful,* also produced by a small, non-Hollywood company.

Then, in 1986, all five Oscar nominees were made outside of the Hollywood establishment: Oliver Stone's *Platoon,* which won, Ismail Merchant and James Ivory's *A Room With A View,* Roland Joffe's *The Mission,* Woody Allen's *Hannah and Her Sisters,* and Randa Haines's *Children of a Lesser God.* The blockbuster success of the Vietnam epic *Platoon,* which sold over a hundred million dollars worth of tickets even before winning Best Picture, and the solid box-office receipts of *A Room With a View* proved that there is money to be made out of specialized quality films. These movies also showed that Hollywood was opening up its gates to offbeat, unusual work. The message was loud and clear: The indies are marching into the mainstream.

The box-office success of Steven Soderbergh's *sex, lies and videotape* in 1989 was yet another piece of evidence that there was vibrant life outside the system. *sex, lies and videotape* was not an avant-garde film, but it was also not the result of consensus movie-making. Soderbergh's first film showcased a talented, self-assured director who came (in Hollywood terms) out of nowhere to win the Palme d'Or at the Cannes Film Festival. With production costs of $1 million and grosses of $25 million, *sex, lies and videotape* boasted a better input-output ratio than the hugely successful *Batman* (which cost over $50 million and earned $245 million). This intimate film, which was nominated for the original screenplay Oscar, may well have been the most profitable movie of the entire decade.

In 1992, *Howards End, The Crying Game,* and *The Player* were not only box-office smashes, they also garnered more Oscar nominations than the big studio releases. This led mainstream Hollywood to seek more extensive inroads into the independent community. Hollywood began to understand that indies are the soul of the medium in a way that the potboilers of Macaulay Culkin (of the *Home Alone* movies), Arnold Schwarzenegger (the *Terminator* pictures), Sylvester Stallone *(Cliffhanger, Demolition Man)* never can be.

In 1995, Tim Robbins's *Dead Man Walking* featured prominently in the Oscar contest, with Best Picture and Best Director nominations, and the Best Actress Oscar to Susan Sarandon. In 1996, four of the five Best Picture nominees were indies, films financed and made outside the Hollywood studio system: *The English Patient, Fargo, Secrets & Lies,* and *Shine.*

The Oscar nominations and awards for the indies would seem to express the disgust of the Hollywood Establishment for its own bloated and empty product. Indeed, while Hollywood was spending time, energy, and big bucks churning out and marketing big-budget, over-produced, special-effects and star-studded formulas *(Independence Day, Volcano, Speed 2, Batman and Robin),* something significant was happening out on the fringe, Off-Off Hollywood: The American indie cinema was enjoying exhilarating years with young, bold filmmakers, critical support, receptive audiences, and the promise of an even better future.

The emergence of a viable alternative cinema, a second Hollywood with its own institutional structure and talent, is one of the most exciting developments in American culture of the last two decades. The Oscars have reflected it, with many of the decade's winners of the best original screenplay given to indies: Neil Jordan's *The Crying Game* in 1992, Quentin Tarantino's *Pulp Fiction* in 1994, Christopher McQuarrie's *The Usual Suspects* (directed by Bryan Singer) in 1995, Billy Bob Thornton's *Sling Blade* in 1996. Paul Thomas Anderson, the new genius on the block, has received two writing nominations, for *Boogie Nights* in 1997 and for *Magnolia* in 1999, both made by New Line.

In fact, one studio that began independent and is now considered mini-major has dominated the Oscar contest in the 1990s: Miramax, owned by Disney since 1993. As run by its co-presidents, Harvey and Bob Weinstein, Miramax has been the most influential studio in town for a whole decade. In every year since 1992, Miramax has been represented in the Best Picture category with such innovative, envelope-pushing movies as *The Crying Game.* Since then, *The Piano* was nominated in 1993, *Pulp Fiction* in 1994, *Il Postino (The Postman)* in 1995, *The English Patient* in 1996, *Good Will Hunting* in 1997, *Life Is Beautiful* and *Shakespeare in Love* in 1998, and *Cider House Rules* in 1999.

In 1998, Miramax outdid itself with two Best Picture nominees, *Shakespeare in Love* and *Life Is Beautiful,* which together garnered twenty-three nominations, winning ten: seven for *Shakespeare in Love,* including Best Picture and Best Actress to Gwyneth Paltrow, and three for *Life Is Beautiful,* including Best Actor to Roberto Benigni. *Shakespeare in Love* marked the distributor's seventh consecutive year with a Best Picture nominee, a record unmatched by any other studio in town. Miramax has won the Best Screenplay Oscar in six of the past seven years: *The Crying Game, The Piano, Pulp Fiction, Sling Blade, Good Will Hunting, Shakespeare in Love,* and *Cider House Rules.*

Ad Campaigns

Ad campaigns are used by both studios and filmmakers to call the Academy's attention to "worthy" achievements. These campaigns have become extremely elaborate over the years, reaching their zenith in the 1990s. But it would be a mistake to believe that advertising is a recent phenomenon. There have always been efforts to persuade members to vote for a particular film, though they were not as explicit or expensive.

The studio for which artists worked and their position within its power structure played a role. There was a clear link between Mary Pickford's win for *Coquette* and the fact that her husband, Douglas Fairbanks Sr. was then the Academy president. It is doubtful that Norma Shearer would have received five nominations and one Oscar had she not been married to Wunderkind Irving G. Thalberg, MGM's head of production.

Despite respect for her recognized talent, Greta Garbo was a victim of MGM's inner politics. On her first nomination, for *Anna Christie,* advertised as "Garbo Talks!" she lost out to Norma Shearer, who won for *The Divorcee,* another MGM movie. At her second nomination, for *Camille,* Garbo lost out to another lesser actress, Luise Rainer, in *The Good Earth.* Rainer was then supported by Louis B. Mayer, though three years later he would drop her and her career would terminate. In 1939, when Garbo received her third nomination for *Ninotchka,* she lost because *Gone With the Wind* swept all the major awards, including Best Actress which went to Vivien Leigh. Unlike Garbo's previous competitors, Leigh at least gave a good performance.

Studio politics also deprived Bette Davis of a nomination, and possibly an award, for her performance in *Of Human Bondage.* Davis was then under contract to Warner, which loaned her out to RKO for that film. Conceivably, neither Warner's nor RKO's members voted for Davis, whose name was added to the nominees list as a write-in. RKO knew that if she won, the rewards would be reaped by Warner, and Davis was not very popular at Warner.

Clark Gable believed that he was outvoted for what he considered to be the best work of his career, Rhett Butler in *Gone With the Wind,* because of strained relations with producer David O. Selznick, and because MGM's publicity machine was not behind him; the winner was Robert Donat for *Goodbye, Mr. Chips,* which was made by MGM.

In 1953, Columbia Pictures made no secret that it backed Burt Lancaster, and not Montgomery Clift, in *From Here to Eternity.* Both were nominated for Best Actor, though neither won; the winner was William Holden in *Stalag 17.* Clift was not supported because he was an outsider in Hollywood, "suffering" from his reputation as a New York stage actor. Performers who came from New York and continued to appear in both films and plays, like Geraldine Page and Julie Harris, were regarded as suspects in the movie colony at that time. In the same year, Van Heflin and Jean Arthur failed to get nominations for *Shane,* because neither was under contract to Paramount. Instead, the studio campaigned for William Holden, who had been with Paramount for years, and for Audrey Hepburn *(Roman Holiday);* both won.

In 1954, the odds were against Judy Garland, despite an impressive performance in *A Star Is Born.* For one thing, Warner, which produced the movie, was then in conflict with the Academy, and for another, Garland was not supported by the studio. By contrast Grace Kelly, who won that year for *The Country Girl,* was supported by MGM, her studio, and by Paramount, which produced the film.

Studio affiliations often explain the factors responsible for actors winning—or losing—the Oscar. In 1958, when Shirley MacLaine was first nominated for *Some Came Running,* MGM supported its veteran performer, Elizabeth Taylor, in the prestige blockbuster *Cat on a Hot Tin*

Roof; the winner was Susan Hayward in *I Want to Live!* In 1960, MacLaine gave the best performance of her career to date in *The Apartment,* but once again MGM launched a massive campaign in the trades supporting the ailing Taylor in *Butterfield 8.* As discussed the Academy's sympathy was for Taylor, whose bout with death was more responsible for her ultimate win than her acting.

How effective have these ad campaigns been? In 1945, Joan Crawford and her press agent, Henry Rogers, conducted one of the biggest campaigns in Hollywood's history. According to biographer Bob Thomas, during the filming of *Mildred Pierce,* producer Jerry Wald sensed that something extraordinary was happening, upon which he called Rogers and suggested:

> "Why don't you start a campaign for Joan to win the Oscar?"

> "But Jerry, the picture is just starting," noted Rogers.

> "So?

> "So how would I go about it?"

> "It's simple. Call up Hedda Hopper and tell her, 'Joan Crawford is giving such a strong performance in Mildred Pierce that her fellow-workers are already predicting she'll win the Oscar for it.'"

> "Jerry, you're full of shit."

> "Possibly. But it might work. What have you got to lose?"

Indeed, in his daily reports to the famous gossip columnist Rogers delivered some "confidential" reports. A few days later, Hopper wrote: "Insiders say that Joan Crawford is delivering such a terrific performance in *Mildred Pierce* that she's a cinch for the Academy Awards." Other columnists followed Hopper, all predicting an Oscar for Crawford. One night, Wald called Rogers, triumphantly announcing, "I think we've got it made." Wald had just heard from producer Hal Wallis that "it looks like Joan Crawford has a good chance to win the Oscar." "I don't know where I heard it," Wallis said. "I may have read it somewhere." That's exactly what Rogers and Warner wanted—to create a favorable climate for Crawford. It helped, of course, that *Mildred Pierce* opened to quite good reviews and that it was nominated for Best Picture.

How crucial was the campaign for Crawford's win? Wouldn't she have won Best Actress without it? In 1945, Crawford competed against three stars, Ingrid Bergman in *The Bells of St. Mary's,* Greer Garson in *The Valley of Decision,* and Jennifer Jones in *Love Letters.* All three had recently won Oscars: Garson in 1942, Jones in 1943, and Bergman in 1944. The fifth nominee, novice Gene Tierney for *Leave Her to Heaven,* was unlikely to win. A veteran of twenty years in Hollywood, Crawford enjoyed the sympathy of the press, which resented the way she was mistreated—and fired—by Louis B. Mayer. Furthermore, Mayer himself said in public that he would vote for Crawford, and not for his favorite star, Greer Garson, because "Crawford deserved it." Under these circumstances, Crawford would have won the Oscar without this massive campaign.

Campaigning by individual performers made a point in 1943, when Teresa Wright called attention through "discreet" ads for her performances in *Mrs. Miniver* and *The Pride of the Yankees.* Wright received a supporting nomination in the former and a lead one in the latter, winning for *Mrs. Miniver.* Wright would probably have won even without all the publicity since *Mrs. Miniver* swept the 1942 awards.

A much bigger and expensive campaign by an actress for herself was carried out by Rosalind Russell, who spent over ten thousand dollars in 1948 to get a Best Actress nomination for *Mourning Becomes Electra.* Additionally, RKO spent a huge (undisclosed) amount of money on her and the movie. Russell received a nomination, but lost the award, which some attributed to oversaturating the voters.

In 1961, Shirley Jones was advised to invest the five thousand dollars she had intended to put toward building a new wing on her home into publicizing her work in *Elmer Gantry;* she won the supporting award, though it is unclear how determining a factor the campaign was.

Even if campaigns by players do not result in winning, they still pay off in other important ways. Peter Falk campaigned for his performance in *Murder, Inc.,* which cost him five thousand dollars. It was his third picture, but the first made in Hollywood. Falk considered the campaign worthwhile, because, as he said, "I'm a newcomer out here, thought of as a New York actor with some reputation, but they couldn't place me." *Murder, Inc.* was a small crime film, "the kind that usually gets passed by in the midst of all the big pictures." Falk's motive was "to stir up talk," so that "the talk itself will help the career." "Whether I get the nomination or not, I consider it the best investment I've ever made, and I don't have much money." It was a worthwhile investment: Falk earned his first supporting nomination, which established his reputation in Hollywood, and received other important roles, including one in Frank Capra's 1961 *Pocketful of Miracles,* which got him a second supporting nomination.

However, personal campaigns can be shameless. Take Richard Harris, who received a second Best Actor nomination for *The Field,* a film no one saw. The feeling in Hollywood was Harris should win, not for his performance in the picture, but for his performance in getting nominated. As one journalist put it, "Harris worked the town better than Ronald Reagan worked a room—there wasn't a voter's cheek he didn't kiss."

Times have indeed changed. Those embarrassed by the current, aggressive campaigning look back with nostalgia at Oscar's more dignified players. Two of Hollywood's most respected and most nominated players, Spencer Tracy and Katharine Hepburn, never campaigned for themselves and never pressured their studios to do so for them.

Politicking and excessive advertising can have a boomerang effect, as John Wayne's patriotic campaign for *The Alamo* showed. One ad compared the Alamo's fighters with contemporary politicians, stating: "There were no ghostwriters at the Alamo, only men." The publicity cashed in on the fact that 1960 was an election year: *The Alamo* was released in July, about three months before the presidential elections. "Remember the Alamo," said Wayne on-screen as Davy Crockett, and offscreen as a political figure. Another full-page ad read: "What will Oscar say this year to the world?" with a picture of the Alamo's battered fortress.

According to *Newsweek,* publicist Russell Bidwell received the highest amount of money ever paid to a publicist to promote a movie, $125,000, all costs and salaries of his New York and Hollywood offices for a year, plus a huge operating budget. With a high emotional and financial drive, Bidwell managed to get *The Alamo* seven nominations, including Best Picture, but no acting or directorial nominations for Wayne.

Much more criticized than Wayne was Chill Wills, who played Beekeeper, Crockett's whiskey-drinking humorous sidekick. Wills was charged with using deplorable means to seek for himself a supporting nomination. At fifty-eight, after half a century in film, Wills realized that it was his only chance to win the award. Thus, he didn't hesitate to print ads on the order of: WE OF THE ALAMO CAST ARE PRAYING HARDER THAN THE REAL TEXANS PRAYED FOR THEIR LIVES AT THE ALAMO FOR CHILL WILLS TO WIN THE OSCAR. COUSIN CHILL'S ACTING WAS GREAT, he wrote, signing, YOUR ALAMO COUSIN. Another ad read: WIN, LOSE, OR DRAW. YOU'RE STILL MY COUSINS AND I LOVE YOU ALL.

Comedian Groucho Marx, appalled by Wills's methods, wrote back: "Dear Mr. Wills. I am delighted to be your cousin. But I'm voting for Sal Mineo" (nominated for *Exodus)*. Wayne himself didn't approve of Wills's campaign and reproached him in the press, which prompted Groucho Marx's comment, "for John Wayne to impugn Chill Wills's taste is tantamount to Jayne Mansfield criticizing Sabrina for too much exposure." At the end of the day, neither Wills nor Mineo won; the winner was Peter Ustinov in *Spartacus.*

The Alamo's campaigns led to heated controversies over the professional and moral ethics involved in promoting movies. When considering whether advertising for Oscar nominations paid off, critic Dick Williams saw "nothing reprehensible in artists or productions blowing their own horns, because it is done in almost every other phase of American life." Nonetheless, Williams objected to the fact that "Oscar voters are being appealed to on a patriotic basis," and resented the implication that "one's proud sense of Americanism may be suspected if one does not vote for *The Alamo*." At Wayne's request, Bidwell responded to the charge: "Along with the *Los Angeles Times*, you suggest very emphatically that we have conducted a campaign that to vote against *The Alamo* is un-American. This is a gratuitous and erroneous conclusion on your part."

Campaigns on behalf *The Alamo* might have helped getting nominations but no awards. The picture lost in every category but sound. *The Alamo* wasn't a bad film, but it was up against competition from Billy Wilder's *The Apartment*, which won; Richard Brooks's *Elmer Gantry*, the British *Sons and Lovers*, and Fred Zinnemann's *The Sundowners*.

A year later, in 1961, George C. Scott declined his nomination in *The Hustler*, deploring the demeaning effects of the Oscar race, particularly the explicit campaigning by press agents for award-conscious players. However, Burt Lancaster, nominated that year for *Elmer Gantry*, felt that "ads in the trade papers serve a purposeful function as part of the public relations of our business," akin to saying, "See my pictures before you vote." In response to Scott's accusations, Lancaster said, "No one's putting a gun to his head to buy any ads. His attitude really doesn't make any sense. He's under no pressure to take out any ads."

The controversies over *The Alamo* and Scott's protests motivated the Academy's Board to take a public stance that called the attention of all potential nominees "for the importance of maintaining a standard of dignity in any and all media of advertising." Always sensitive to public opinion outside the industry, the Board stated that "regrettably, in past years a few resorted to outright, excessive and vulgar solicitation of votes," which became "a serious embarrassment to the Academy and our industry." It therefore suggested "to eliminate those advertising practices which are irrelevant to the honest evaluation of artistic and technical accomplishments and violate the principles under which the Academy was established."

But, ultimately, the Academy left the issue "to the good conscience of the nominees, confident that they are well aware of the difference between that which enhances and that which lessens the status of the Academy." "The Academy can command respect," the statement concluded, "only as long as its members and the nominees take onto themselves the responsibility of dignified conduct." This request, as Murray Schumach noted in the *New York Times,* was "like asking Pavlov's dogs to ignore their conditioned reflexes."

Needless to say, the warnings didn't change the situation at all. On the contrary, in the 1960s, advertising campaigns for less than worthy films reached their peak, resulting in a severe decline in the Academy's public credibility. Fox outdid the other studios after its successful campaign for *The Sound of Music,* which was referred to in the industry as "The Sound of Money."

In the next four years, Fox was determined to win nominations and awards at all costs for such clinkers as *The Sand Pebbles* in 1966, *Doctor Dolittle* in 1967, and *Hello, Dolly!* in 1969. Through special screenings, fancy banquets with wonderful menus, and letters to each member, Fox managed to get multiple nomination for each of the aforementioned movies, which was enough to repudiate the Oscar's prestige in the public eye. Further, it showed that the most dismal films can get nominations, if they are sold and marketed by the right campaigns. Many began to suspect that Oscar's official function has changed from honoring the best films to rescuing faltering films at the box office. Oscar's rescue mission soon became a public joke.

To be sure, the Oscars have always had effects on the commercial status of the winning films, and the ceremonies' ability to promote movies has always been known as a public fact. Nonetheless, it is one thing to honor decent films such as *Chariots of Fire,* which was critically acclaimed but commercially unsuccessful initially, and quite another to nominate mediocre films, like *Cleopatra,* as a compensation for its immense budget. To honor a downright artistic failure, like *Doctor Dolittle,* in order to help recoup its mammoth costs, was both ridiculous and embarrassing.

At the same time, ad campaigns have helped small, specialized independent films that otherwise would have withstood no chance of getting nominated. In 1968, *Rachel, Rachel,* directed by Paul Newman and starring Joanne Woodward, received four nominations, including Best Picture, due to the efforts of Warren Cowan, a leading press agent. Conventional strategies were used to get free exposure for the artists in newspapers and talk shows and, of course, ads in the trades. But Cowan also set up private screenings for small cliques of opinion-makers columnists, public relations specialists, and people who would get the word-of-mouth going.

A grand premiere for *Rachel, Rachel* was arranged in New York, with Newman and Woodward making appearances on all the TV shows. The two stars spent Labor Day posing for the cover of *Life,* which was not in their nature, but this movie was special to them. The campaign would not have been effective if *Rachel, Rachel* were not a good movie; the New York Film Critics cited Woodward as Best Actress and Newman as Best Director. Ultimately, the campaign proved more effective in the nomination process, for *Rachel, Rachel* did not win any award.

Over the years, budgets for ad campaigns grew steadily. In 1982, the major studios spent about four million dollars between mid–December and mid–March on screenings, advertising, and promotion, a modest amount by today's standards. These ads appear in the two trades, *Hollywood Reporter* and *Daily Variety*, where a color page costs thousands of dollars. The trade ads have become a sticking point for both studios and the Academy. "It's a concern—anything that suggests that Oscar can be bought is damaging," said Rick Robertson, AMPAS's administrator.

An extensive campaign doesn't ensure major nominations. Eighteen pages were bought for Bob Fosse's *Star 80* in *Daily Variety*, but the film did not get a single nomination. And 20th Century-Fox bought many ads for *Heart Like a Wheel* and its star, Bonnie Bedelia, but got only one nomination, for costume design. In 1984, *Silkwood* benefited from fifty pages in *Variety*, *Yentl* from thirty-one, and *Terms of Endearment* from twenty-eight. *Terms of Endearment*, which won, did not need as much publicity as *Yentl* or *Silkwood*, because it opened to rave reviews and immediately became a box-office hit. It was also a much easier film to sell than either *Yentl* or *Silkwood*.

Advertising ensures that a movie will not be accidentally overlooked, which was crucial to *Yentl*, since it divided critics and opened to lukewarm reviews—it received five nominations. It's hard to tell whether *Silkwood*'s five nominations were attributable to the ad campaign. Meryl Streep would have been nominated for Best Actress and Mike Nichols for Best Director without the campaign; but Cher, nominated for supporting award, certainly benefited from the ads.

New rules govern the industry, which has changed a lot in the 1990s. The current, free-lance system, with no contract players or studio stars, and the changing structure of the Academy membership, have resulted in the unanticipated nominations of films and artists that in the studio era would not have been nominated. Pictures enjoying neither critical acclaim nor commercial popularity still have a chance to get nominated.

Martin Ritt's 1983 drama, *Cross Creek*, was panned by most reviewers and died quickly at the box office. Universal, which distributed the film, refused to share the costs, and thus it couldn't be seen during the crucial time of the nominations. Unfazed, producer Robert Radnitz booked *Cross Creek* at a Malibu theater and made up handbills for the members. With only six pages in *Daily Variety*, *Cross Creek* garnered four nominations, two of them for Rip Torn and Alfre Woodard as supporting players.

The key to Academy nominations is getting a picture seen by as many voters as possible before the nomination season—that's the only justification for the ad campaigns. All the studios schedule free screenings for films that have Oscar potential, and there are also free screenings arranged by the various guilds.

The studios try to boost the profile of their prestigious pictures. The common practice now is to send out video cassettes, making it convenient for Academy members who otherwise might not opt to attend special Oscar screenings. The Academy's official line is that there is no substitute for seeing a movie in the theater, though everyone realizes how important videos are nowadays.

William Goldman has observed that if videocassettes had existed before, movies that had been overlooked would have been honored. Peckinpah's *Ride the High Country,* Scorsese's *Mean Streets,* Lawrence Kasdan's *Body Heat* would have likely garnered Best Director and acting nominations, if not Best Picture. In recent years, Edward Norton in *American History X,* Nick Nolte in *Affliction,* and Ian McKellen in *Gods and Monsters,* to mention just a few, would not have been nominated for Best Actor without the benefit of videocassettes. How else would Julie Christie be nominated for a tiny picture like *Afterglow,* which opened in December and barely grossed two million dollars? Academy members are not youths brimming with vitality—they don't venture out of their houses to see small pictures.

It is never too early to launch an Oscar campaign. Samuel Goldwyn Company mailed out six thousand postcards in September 1993, touting its art house hit, *Much Ado About Nothing,* which starred Kenneth Branagh and Emma Thompson. Below the laudatory blurbs was the phrase: "For your consideration—all categories." They also sent the soundtrack CD to call attention to Patrick Doyle's score and paperback books that included the script. *Much Ado* had opened in May to glowing reviews, grossing more than twenty-two million dollars, but their are eight months between May and January, and members tend to forget good movies. It's conventional wisdom in Hollywood that movies that open early in the year get overlooked at Oscar time.

Similarly, Sony Pictures Classics mailed out paperback copies of Virginia Woolf's novel, *Orlando,* to promote their film, which starred Tilda Swinton. Books, screenplays, and even trailers for the videotapes are now customarily sent for major movies by every studio.

Miramax, which boasts one of the industry's largest and most savvy public-relations departments, enlists outside consultants to handle various aspects of Oscar campaigns, screenings, and gossip-column items.

Miramax learned how to put on an effective campaign when they brought the unlikely *The Crying Game* into Oscar prominence.

In 1993, Miramax engineered an amazingly overblown ad campaign for *The Piano* in the trades, mailing out elegant booklets printed on expensive parchment. One of the unusual aspects of *The Piano*'s campaign was its emphasis on the achievements of the women involved in the production. The picture garnered nominations for women in seven categories, including Director and screenplay to Jane Campion, who won the latter. Harvey Weinstein claimed that the costs of the campaign were $250,000 for ads; his competitors said $750,000. One sarcastic commentator said it cost almost as much to promote the movie as to make it. Even so, by today's standards these figures are minuscule.

While the race to win Oscars goes on for months, the five-week window between the nominations and the March 23 ballot deadline is crunch time for those who manage Oscar campaigns. The goal is to campaign aggressively without appearing desperate. According to Amy Wallace of the *Los Angeles Times,* the studios purchased airtime for advertising in New York and Los Angeles, where most of the Academy voters live, to campaign for their nominees. A recap of Annette Bening's vacuuming scene from *American Beauty* ran during NBC's *Friends,* and nominated actor Michael Caine and *Cider House Rules* director, Lasse Hallström, took time during *NYPD Blue* to promote their film as an American classic.

The campaigns evoke more public appearances from those who are usually low-key performers. Kevin Spacey attended a number of high-profile evenings for *American Beauty,* and co-star Bening, days away from delivering her fourth baby, made an appearance with Jay Leno. Several other nominees appeared on award shows like the Golden Globes, banking on recognition from the television audience for a boost.

Nothing happens in a vacuum, according to Dawn Taubin, Warner's marketing executive. Warner aired a new TV ad in New York and Los Angeles that didn't even mention *The Green Mile*'s star (Tom Hanks) by name, instead opting to promote the Oscar-nominated screenwriter Frank Darabont. There is no magic formula, but shrewd Academy campaigns go for what Taubin called the cumulative effect of campaign: trade publications, publicity appearances, the inclusion of movies and stars in articles about these events.

While the studios do not reveal the costs of these campaigns, a four-week analysis by the *Los Angeles Times'* Wallace, using the trade papers (*Variety* and *Hollywood Reporter*) showed how aggressive these campaigns are. The Best Picture front-runners were DreamWorks' *American Beauty* and Miramax's *The Cider House Rules,* and those projections were consistent with the ads tally from *Daily Variety* since the nominations were announced.

Of the four studios with Best Picture contenders, Disney spent the least on advertising, about $141,000 on *The Sixth Sense,* and $198,000 on *The Insider.* Warner spent about $313,000 to promote *The Green Mile,* while Miramax paid about $350,000 for *Cider House.* DreamWorks spent by far the most on post-nominations ads, more than $774,000 on *Variety's* most premium advertising (six fill-page front cover ads at $29,100 a piece) for *American Beauty.* By contrast, Warner bought three full-page covers, and Disney bought two. Some of DreamWorks' spending was necessitated by congratulatory ad-buying that's considered de rigueur after wins. *American Beauty* won the Directors, Writers and Actors Screen Guild prizes.

There is no ceiling on how much money the studios will spend to promote their nominees. When a postal service mishap caused the Academy to postpone the ballot deadline by two days (March 23, rather than the 21), the studios rallied to book ad space for the extra two days. More extensive advertising was placed for films that were still in wide release, such as *American Beauty* and *Cider House.* For those films, Oscar wins means more than a 15 percent increase at the box office. Even before the Oscar show, heavy advertising motivates moviegoers to see the nominees; by contrast, films that are gone or are in limited release tend to spend less.

But a lesser campaign does not necessarily mean that the film will lose in its nominated categories. *The Silence of the Lambs* was released in February 1991, and was available on video before it was nominated for important Oscars. Orion didn't spend a lot on pre-Oscar buzz, but *The Silence of the Lambs* still won Best Picture, Actor, Actress, Director, and Adapted Screenplay.

Although ad bombardments may appear nonsensical, they are predicated on solid business decisions—-relationships that need to be nurtured. As Wallace pointed out, the relative lack of ads for *The Sixth Sense* didn't mean that Disney was more tasteful than the other studios. But Disney already had a first-look deal with *Sixth Sense*'s Oscar-nominated director, M. Night Shyamalan, and committed to backing his next film, *Unbreakable.*

Miramax gave *Music of the Heart*'s Best Actress nominee, Meryl Streep, a restrained bravado, based on the belief that "You don't have to prove anything to her with a bells-and-whistles campaign." But Streep may be the exception—many stars and directors pay close attention to how much money the studios spend to promote their films; both egos and reputations are at stake.

American Beauty's Best Picture represented, as Dana Harris wrote in *Variety,* a coming-of-age for DreamWorks, an upstart studio. The film's five

Oscars, including Best Director and Actor, were a sweet victory after the disappointment the company had faced the year prior, when *Saving Private Ryan* earned Best Director for Spielberg but lost Best Picture to Miramax's *Shakespeare in Love*. DreamWorks' shrewd marketing, orchestrated by the gifted Terry Press, helped achieve the landslide victory. Some saw the 2000 battle between Miramax and DreamWorks as a repeat of the last year's skirmish. In March, DreamWorks bought 38 percent more *Variety* pages for *American Beauty* than Miramax did for *Cider House*. Even so, the feeling was that Miramax got what they wanted out of the nominations for *Cider House*, doubling the movie's grosses to over $50 million.

Press's marketing campaign for *American Beauty* began in September after the buzz from the Toronto Film Festival, where the movie world-premiered. Despite word that the movie was too dark, that it engaged too many controversial issues—drugs, murder, adultery—for the Academy's older voters, the campaign stressed that the film was fresh and ultimately positive and humane. This was followed by a Christmas card from *American Beauty*'s Burnham family, inviting guests to an open house. At a La Cienega restaurant, screenwriter Ball, director Mendes, and actors Spacey and Bening mingled with guests as soundtrack artist Elliot Smith performed. The strategy obviously worked—*American Beauty* emerged triumphant at Oscar time.

CHAPTER 15

The Politics of Oscar

Historical and political factors have always influenced the types of films nominated for and winning the Oscars. Filmmakers are continuously subjected to stimulating—and disruptive—forces of the sociocultural contexts in which they work.

World War II disrupted the careers of many actors and directors who were mobilized into the war, with some losing the popularity which they had previously enjoyed. Clark Gable, "The King," joined the Air Force in 1942, rising in rank from lieutenant to major, and receiving the Distinguished Flying Cross and Air Medal for his bombing missions over Germany. Gable's first film after being absent from the screen for four years, *Adventure,* was trumpeted by MGM as "Gable's Back and Garson's Got Him." But this, as well as other Gable postwar films, failed and his popularity began to decline.

The career momentum of Mickey Rooney, who had been America's biggest box-office draw with the Andy Hardy series, was also interrupted by his military service, after which his popularity plummeted.

At the same time, other careers benefited from the war. Humphrey Bogart became a major star in the 1940s, after his appearances in *The Maltese Falcon* and *Casablanca,* the film that established him as a major screen hero. In other cases, the war delayed recognition that would have been received earlier. William Holden became a star with his very first film, playing the boxer-violinist in *Golden Boy* (1939). Then, mobilized to the Army, Holden did not make a single movie for three years. But after the war, Holden's screen image ripened and his popularity rose, reaching a climax in 1950 with two films, *Born Yesterday* and *Sunset Boulevard,* both nominated for Best Picture. Holden won Best Actor for *Stalag 17* in 1953.

World War II had quantitative as well as qualitative impact on the film industry, influencing the subject matter and style of the films produced. About one-third of Hollywood's output (five hundred out of seventeen hundred films) between 1942 and 1945 dealt with the war, directly or indirectly. Ultimately, most of these movies were more important historically than artistically, fulfilling, as Ken Jones and Arthur McLure have observed, a twofold goal: "to give unity of purpose for the war itself, and to give strength of purpose to the people on the home front." Heavily propagandistic, these movies served as morale boosters, dealing with timely issues that were of interest to most Americans at the time. Viewers often perceived and enjoyed these films as flag-wavers, without applying to them the usual critical yardsticks.

All the Oscar categories were influenced by the war, but especially the major ones: Best Picture, Best Director, the acting, and the writing awards. The male acting Oscars, as could be expected, were more determined by the war experience—the war film is a typically "masculine" genre. Four of the Best Actors in the 1940s were chosen for a role in a war-themed movie: Gary Cooper in *Sergeant York,* James Cagney in *Yankee Doodle Dandy,* Paul Lukas in *Watch on the Rhine,* and Fredric March in *The Best Years of Our Lives.*

By contrast, only one Best Actress, Greer Garson in *Mrs. Miniver,* won for a film about the war. In fact, some of the female winners during the war were honored for stereotypical roles, such as the victimized wife, played by Joan Fontaine in *Suspicion* and Ingrid Bergman in *Gaslight.* Seen historically, these roles were too traditional, since women during the war participated actively in the economy for the first time. The only Oscar role that reflected the conflict between career and domesticity that many American women must have faced at the end of the war, was Joan Crawford's in *Mildred Pierce,* though, as mentioned, at the end of the movie, the protagonist is punished for having stepped into a male world and is relegated to her traditional role of housewife-mother.

Many films during the war were lavishly praised by the critics and seen by the masses for their patriotic rather than artistic values. Three films about the war won Best Picture: *Mrs. Miniver* in 1942, *Casablanca* in 1943, and *The Best Years of Our Lives* in 1946. *Mrs. Miniver,* the least distinguished of the three, at once reflected and reinforced the mood of the homefront through its description of a "typical" British family during the Blitz. Reviewers pointed out that it was actually the war, not the film, which earned the Academy votes. Released in July 1942, *Mrs. Miniver* became a blockbuster, and winning six Oscars made it the most talked about film of the year.

The timeliness of these films suited the zeitgeist. Howard Hawks's *Sergeant York* reflected America's dominant ideology of July 1941, just months prior to the country's entry into the war. Its hero, Alvin York, starts as a conscientious objector and ends up totally committed to the war's cause, a transformation that articulated the feelings of millions of Americans who initially were reluctant to join the fighting. Celebrating George M. Cohan's life, *Yankee Doodle Dandy* was released in May 1942, just as American soldiers departed to fight in Europe. "What could be more timely," wrote critic Patrick McGilligan, "than to have recalled for us the career of America's lustiest flag-waver."

Casablanca, the 1943 Oscar winner, was even timelier: it was released after the city of Casablanca had been chosen as the site of the Allied Forces Conference. The movie boasted a glorious cast headed by Humphrey Bogart, Ingrid Bergman, Claude Rains, and Paul Henreid. It is the movie that made Bogart an international star, crystallizing his immortal screen image as Rick Blain, the most famous cafe owner in film history. *Casablanca* was not a major box-office hit in its initial release, but over the years it has become a classic. In a recent American Film Institute (AFI) poll, *Casablanca* was chosen as one of the ten Best American films of all time.

Wyler's *The Best Years of Our Lives* would have won Oscars in any year. However, released in 1946, it, too, cashed in on its timely issues: the adjustment problems of war veterans to civilian life. As shown, the inspiration for this movie came from an article in *Time* magazine.

The nominations and awards given to films about the war reflected changes in public opinion. In 1941, only one of the six major Oscars went to a war film: Gary Cooper in *Sergeant York.* In 1942, five out of the six awards; the exception was Supporting Actor Van Heflin, in the crime melodrama *Johnny Eager.* In 1943 again, five of the six major Oscars were for such films; the exception was Ingrid Bergman in *Gaslight.* In 1944, two of the Best Picture nominees were socially relevant: David O. Selznick's *Since You Went Away* and Fox's political biopicture *Wilson.*

Most of the writing awards in the 1940s also honored war movies: Emeric Pressburger for his original story, *The Invaders;* the four screenwriters of *Mrs. Miniver;* William Saroyan for his original story *The Human Comedy;* the three screenwriters of *Casablanca;* Lamar Trotti for his original screenplay *Wilson;* and Charles G. Booth, for the original script of Henry Hathaway's *The House on 92nd Street* (1945), which depicted an FBI's successful destruction of a spy ring in America.

After *The Best Years of Our Lives,* the war was quickly forgotten by Hollywood and by the Academy. In 1946, the Best Picture nominees included Olivier's *Henry V* and the melodrama *The Razor's Edge,* based on Somerset Maugham's book. In 1947, two spiritual comedies—*The Bishop's Wife* and *Miracle on 34th Street*—and a literary adaptation, David Lean's *Great Expectations,* were nominated. Olivier's *Hamlet,* Jean

Negulesco's *Johnny Belinda,* and the ballet melodrama *The Red Shoes* competed for the top prize in 1948.

The second era in which politics impinged directly on the Oscar Awards was in the early 1950s, during Senator Joseph McCarthy's second round of Hollywood investigations; the first was in 1947. Most of the winning films in those years could be described as light, escapist fare. In sharp contrast to the 1940s, in which the Oscar honored timely films, just a few years later, Hollywood was so fearful of McCarthy that it went to the other extreme, honoring films that had little to do with the surrounding political reality. The 1950 Best Picture nominees included tales about Hollywood *(Sunset Boulevard),* the New York theater *(All About Eve),* a witty comedy *(Born Yesterday),* a family comedy about marriage and suburbia *(Father of the Bride),* and an adventure set in the African jungles *(King Solomon's Mines).*

The Oscar winners of 1951 and 1952 were also nonpolitical, escapist entertainment, showing again the Academy's fear of voting for films that were critical of the American Way of Life. MGM's musical, *An American in Paris,* featuring George Gershwin's celebrated score, won the 1951 Best Picture, competing against serious films, such as George Stevens's *A Place in the Sun,* based on Theodore Dreiser's novel *An American Tragedy,* and Elia Kazan's powerful version of *A Streetcar Named Desire.* The win must have surprised MGM itself, for the next day it took out ads in the trades that showed Leo the Lion smirking coyly at the Oscar statuette. The caption read: "Honestly, I was just standing in the sun waiting for a streetcar."

The 1952 Best Picture, Cecil B. DeMille's circus adventure-melodrama, *The Greatest Show on Earth,* unaccountably won over Fred Zinnemann's psychological Western, *High Noon,* and John Ford's picturesque romance, *The Quiet Man. High Noon* earned the largest number of nominations, seven, and was earlier cited by the New York Film Critics—it probably lost for political rather than artistic reasons. More than a few critics perceive *High Noon* as an allegory of American foreign policy during the Korean war. Marshal Kane (Cooper) is eager to achieve peace after cleaning up the town five years earlier (World War II), but reluctantly, he's forced to face a new aggression (the Korean war). According to this ideological reading, the Quaker wife (played by Grace Kelly) stands in for the American pacifists and isolationists, though she too later changes her mind and ends up supporting her husband's cause, and even kills. *High Noon* propagated the widely acceptable idea that "war in certain circumstances may be both moral and inevitable."

Critic Philip French regards *High Noon* as a liberal statement, the archetypal Kennedy Western, standing in sharp contrast to *Rio Bravo,* which he considers the archetypal Barry Goldwater Western. Considered in this light,

High Noon is seen as an existential parable about a man, Marshal Kane, who stands alone to defend his moral principles in the McCarthy era. The town-folk, who refuse to help the marshal, desert him one by one, and are viewed as the American masses afraid to stand up and fight for civil rights.

These particular readings may or may not be valid, but most would agree that *High Noon* deals with civic responsibility, passive versus active involvement in public life, and heroic behavior in political crises—all issues with explicitly political overtones in the 1950s. The filmmakers responsible for *High Noon*, producer Stanley Kramer, direc-tor Fred Zinnemann, and screenwriter Carl Foreman, were known for their liberal politics. This was Foreman's last film: he was forced into exile to England. Cooper, known for his Republican leanings, claimed to be unaware of the political message of his role. But some of his col-leagues, like John Wayne, objected to the film's message, claiming that the rugged men of the West, who fought nature and the Indians would unite—not cower—in the face of four villains. In a 1971 interview, Wayne described *High Noon* as "the most un-American thing I've ever seen in my whole life," referring to "ole Coop putting the marshal's badge under his foot and stepping on it. I'll never regret having helped run Foreman out of this country."

The downbeat mood of Sydney Pollack's *They Shoot Horses, Don't They?* must have also worked against its inclusion in the 1969 Best Picture contest, despite the fact that it was critically acclaimed and nominated for nine awards. Its omission among the five top contenders was conspicuous, due to the fact that the film was nominated for many important categories: Jane Fonda for the lead, and Susannah York and Gig Young for the sup-porting categories. Based on Horace McCoy's Depression-era novel, the narrative depicts a harrowing six-day marathon dance contest, stressing the fantasies, illusions, and madness of young people in Los Angeles of the early 1930s. The shabby locale and despair of the characters, most notably of Gloria (Jane Fonda), a suicidal would-be actress, and another starlet (Susannah York), whose fantasy is to be the next Jean Harlow, must have also depressed the Academy, for it favored the lighthearted fare of *Hello, Dolly!* and *Butch Cassidy and the Sundance Kid* for Best Picture nominees over Pollack's disturbing parable.

That Academy members, like ordinary moviegoers, tend to judge a film by the importance of its subject and relevance of its issues was also clear in 1982, when *Gandhi* swept most of Oscars. Cinematically, it was a rather conventional, solemn biography of the noble political figure, lacking epic scope and visual imagination. *Gandhi* could have been a better movie had it been directed by a more subtle and inventive filmmaker like David Lean.

However, Gandhi's figure was so inspirational and his preaching for anti-violence so timely a message in the context of the 1980s that Academy voters favored the movie over Spielberg's *E.T.* and Sidney Lumet's *The Verdict.*

Once again, Sydney Pollack lost the Oscar for the wrong reasons. His comedy, *Tootsie,* was accomplished on every level, but it lacked the noble intent and "important" theme that *Gandhi* possessed. The *New York Times* critic Vincent Canby described *Gandhi* as having "the air of an important news event, something that is required reading." Faulting it for its earnestness, Canby wrote: "All films about saintly men tend to look alike, even though the men themselves may be radically different." But Canby understood the Academy's motivation: "To honor a film like *Gandhi,* a perfectly reverent if unexceptional film about an exceptional man, they are paying their dues to the race (human), certifying their instincts (good)," and also the belief that movies about worthy subjects can make money.

Variety's editor, Peter Bart, recalled: "Frankly, I was aghast in 1982, when *Gandhi* beat out *E.T.* and *Tootsie.* I felt my colleagues in the Academy were so eager to vote with their heads they abandoned their hearts." It is worth noting that the Academy's taste didn't differ much from the critics'. *Gandhi* opened to almost unanimously favorable review; the only dissenting voices among the major critics were Andrew Sarris and Pauline Kael. And it won the New York Film Critics, the National Board of Review, and the Golden Globe awards. However, there was no consensus among critics that year: the Los Angeles Film Critics cited *E.T.* as Best Picture, and the National Society cited *Tootsie.*

The reception of Orson Welles's 1941 masterpiece, *Citizen Kane,* by the Academy, film critics, and the public at large illuminates once more the complex interplay between movies, studio intrigues, and the politics of society at large. Contrary to popular belief, the merits of *Citizen Kane* were recognized at the time, though not as fully as they should have been. It was gossip columnist Louella Parsons who began spreading the rumor, after seeing an advance preview, that its narrative was "a repulsive biography" of her employer, William Randolph Hearst (played by Orson Welles). Hearst accepted her view at face value, without even seeing the movie, but because there was nothing libelous about it, all he could do was to demand that RKO shelve the movie and threaten to withdraw the support of his press empire from Hollywood. There was some talk to can *Citizen Kane,* and its release was postponed a number of times until it finally opened in May 1941. RKO had problems convincing theaters to book the movie, and Hearst's newspapers' boycotting the ads didn't help either.

Citizen Kane received mostly good reviews, though it failed commercially across the nation. At Oscar nomination time, in January 1942, shortly after the United States declared war, *Citizen Kane* was not exactly overlooked by the industry. The film was nominated for nine Oscars, including Best Picture, and Orson Welles himself received three nominations, as co-screenwriter (with Joseph L. Mankiewicz), Director, and Actor. The cinematography, editing, music, sound, and art direction also received nominations. But the competition for Best Picture in 1941 was extremely intense: *Citizen Kane* was in contest with no fewer than nine other pictures: *Blossoms in the Dust* (four nominations), *Here Comes Mr. Jordan* (seven), *Hold Back the Dawn* (six), *How Green Was My Valley* (ten), *The Little Foxes* (nine), *The Maltese Falcon* (three), *One Foot in Heaven* (one), *Sergeant York* (eleven), and *Suspicion* (three). With so many good films in the race, it was inevitable that the Oscars would be spread among several films and that some excellent films would not win any awards.

To the Academy's credit, the winning film, John Ford's *How Green Was My Valley,* sweeping five awards, might not have been a landmark in American film history, but it was an exquisitely executed movie with a strong visual component, in addition to having more acceptable values and a more traditional morality than *Citizen Kane.* Ford's movie was chosen for a variety of reasons: its popular ideology and its cherishing of the sacredness of the family (after all, the country was at war), but also for its aesthetic merits and high-quality acting.

Citizen Kane, by contrast, was dumped because of its downbeat, pessimistic message, Hearst's power in Hollywood, and Welles's status as an outsider. There is no doubt that *Citizen Kane*'s cinematic merits were not sufficiently recognized at the time, not just because of the dispute with Hearst, but also because its innovations were revolutionary, well ahead of their time. Furthermore, Welles was young, twenty-six, and a newcomer in Hollywood; *Citizen Kane* was his very first movie. Ironically, the film's most controversial aspect, its screenplay, was the only category honored by the Academy. At the same time, William Wyler's *The Little Foxes* was another distinguished movie that lost in each of its nine nominated categories. And John Huston's directorial debut, *The Maltese Falcon,* another classic of its kind, also failed to receive a single award.

The Academy's tendency to choose earnest movies that deal with "important" or "noble" issues over audacious movies that are more artistically innovative or politically charged is easily documented. Preference is always for safe, noncontroversial films with messages that are broadly acceptable:

In 1941, *How Green Was My Valley* over *Citizen Kane*
In 1951, *An American in Paris* over *A Place in the Sun*

In 1952, *The Greatest Show on Earth* over *High Noon*
In 1956, *Around the World in 80 Days* over *Giant*
In 1964, *My Fair Lady* over *Dr. Strangelove*
In 1967, *In the Heat of the Night* over *Bonnie and Clyde*
In 1971, *The French Connection* over *A Clockwork Orange*
In 1976, *Rocky* over *Network* and *All the President's Men*
In 1980, *Ordinary People* over *Raging Bull*
In 1981, *Chariots of Fire* over *Reds*
In 1982, *Gandhi* over *Tootsie* and *E.T.*
In 1990, *Dances With Wolves* over *GoodFellas*
In 1994, *Forrest Gump* over *Pulp Fiction*
In 1997, *Titanic* over *L.A. Confidential*
In 1998, *Shakespeare in Love* over *Saving Private Ryan*

Politics and Film Artists' Careers

The public exposure of film artists, on-screen and off, has often made them the first to be affected by changes in the political climate. Film's strategic position as a powerful medium has always been recognized by the ruling elite. Arguably the worst years for American film artists were during Senator Joseph McCarthy's political witch-hunt, when the careers of many Hollywood artists were destroyed.

Gale Sondergaard, the first supporting winner *(Anthony Adverse)*, became one of the earliest political casualties due to her marriage to director Herbert Biberman, who was suspected of Communist leanings and later became one of the "Hollywood Ten." Blacklisted at the peak of her career, Sondergaard couldn't work for decades. Her appeal to the Screen Actors Guild for protection was rejected on the grounds that "all participants in the International Communist Party conspiracy against our nation should be exposed for what they are—enemies of our country and our form of government." Sondergaard emerged out of forced retirement in 1965 in a one-woman show Off-Broadway, and later made several comebacks, none too successful. In 1978, as a gesture of reconciliation, the Academy asked her to be a presenter at Oscar's fiftieth anniversary.

Another supporting winner, Anne Revere, for *National Velvet,* was also at the peak of her craft when she was blacklisted for taking the Fifth Amendment before the HUAC, on April 17, 1951. By that time, Revere had thirty-five films to her credit. Her part in *A Place in the Sun,* in which she played Montgomery Clift's mother, was severely cut, leaving only a few of her scenes. Rumor has it that actor Larry Parks named Revere (along with others) as a member of the Communist Party. Revere was out of work for close to a decade, but, like many others, she found rescue in the Broadway theater, winning a Tony Award for Lillian Hellman's *Toys in the Attic*. Audacious director Otto Preminger, who helped restore the careers of many blacklisted artists, facilitated Revere's comeback in his movie *Tell Me That You Love Me, Junie Moon* (1970), but at sixty-seven, she was too old to resume an active screen career.

Kim Hunter made a spectacular debut in *A Streetcar Named Desire*, for which she won a supporting Oscar. However, shortly after her career was ruined when her name appeared in Red Channels, a Red-scare pamphlet. Hunter, too, was unable to get any work in Hollywood or New York and was finally rescued by the producers of the television series *Omnibus*.

Lee Grant had an auspicious Hollywood beginning, winning a supporting nomination for her very first film, *Detective Story*, in which she played a shoplifter. She was married at the time to writer Arnold Manoff and was a close friend of actor J. Edward Bromberg, both of whom were suspected Communists. Grant did not get any work for ten years because she refused to cite her husband before the Committee. "The Committee wanted me to turn Arnold in," she later recalled. "I simply wouldn't do it. No work was ever important enough to make me turn in my husband!"

Fortunately, Grant was still able to work in the theater—"movies and TV were closed to us, but not the theatre." But "doing a play a year wouldn't support me, so I went to Herbert Berghof and he set me up in a class." Grant taught drama for many years, during which her attorney worked hard to prove her innocence. Her name was indeed taken off a list with a mild apology from Washington, D.C., Despite this experience, Grant never became bitter, as she told the *Daily News:* "I was lucky, I was only 32 when it was over, I still feel I have time to make up for. It was a fascinating war which fulfilled part of my life. I never would have believed it if I hadn't been part of it."

Grant returned to films in an impressive role in *The Balcony* (1966), and has not stopped working since, both as an actress and as director. In the 1970s, Grant won two more nominations, and a supporting Oscar for *Shampoo* in 1975. In her acceptance speech, Grant said: "I would like to thank the artistic community for sustaining me in my wins and losses, and sitting on the curb, whatever it was." Her remarks were greeted with a huge applause.

Larry Parks's career reached its zenith with a nomination for the title role in *The Jolson Story* (1946). But his career plumetted when he was forced to admit to past membership in the Communist Party. Officially,

Parks was never blacklisted, but Columbia did not renew his contract and other studios wouldn't hire him either.

Few actors have arrived in Hollywood with the reputation of John Garfield, of the Group Theater's fame. For his very first film, *Four Daughters,* Garfield received a supporting nomination, and a few years later, a lead nomination for *Body and Soul.* However, in 1952, Garfield's career ended abruptly when he died of a heart attack the night before he was supposed to appear before the Committee. Garfield wasn't accused of any particular thing, but he was suspected of left-wing politics because of his membership in The Group Theater.

McCarthyism damaged foreign artists as well. Maurice Chevalier, who was popular in the United States in the 1930s, was refused reentry in 1951, for having signed a Communist-inspired decision, "the Stockholm Appeal," which called for banning all nuclear weapons.

French actress Simone Signoret also encountered difficulties in getting offers from Hollywood, despite promises. As she recalled in her memoirs: "Each time there had been a vague offer of my participation in an American production made in France, negotiations had rapidly broken off." In the late 1950s, despite assurance from American directors that times had changed, Signoret held onto her belief that "McCarthy was not dead, even if the citizens of this country thought they had buried him." Several offers fell through for what she describes as "Washingtonian reasons."

When Signoret was offered the lead in *Room at the Top,* her feeling was "if I was going to lose Alice, I wanted to know immediately." She feared that, if Americans were involved, "there was no point in beginning to negotiate." But it was a British production, and Signoret not only got the part but also won Best Actress for it.

Producers and directors also suffered from McCarthyism. The Hollywood Ten, a group of directors and screenwriters subpoenaed to appear before the HUAC in 1947 and cited for contempt of Congress because they refused to disclose their political affiliations, included: producer-director Herbert Biberman, director Edward Dmytryk, producer-writer Adrian Scott, and screenwriters Alvah Bessie, Lester Cole, Ring Lardner Jr., John Howard Lawson, Albert Matz, Samuel Ornitz, and Dalton Trumbo. Tried at a Federal Court in Washington, D.C., in April 1948, they were given the maximum sentence of a year in jail and a fine of one thousand dollars. Blacklisted, some went abroad, others were forced into retirement, and still others wrote scripts while using pseudonyms.

Most of the Hollywood Ten were prominent artists with Oscar Awards and nominations to their credit. Edward Dmytryk was nominated for Best Director for *Crossfire,* which was also nominated for Best Picture. After his release from jail, he went into self-imposed exile in Europe. However, in 1951, Dmytryk cooperated with the Committee and even became a "star witness" in its second round of hearings. His testimony incriminated several colleagues, but he was able to work. In 1954, Dmytryk's version of Herman Wouk's *The Caine Mutiny* received a Best Picture nomination.

Oscar-nominated director Robert Rossen was also blacklisted. In 1947, he was subpoenaed to appear before the Committee, but the hearings were suspended. Rossen continued to work and his picture *All the King's Men* won the 1949 Oscar, though he failed to win the directing award, probably because of politics. There is usually a strong correlation between the two categories, but the 1949 winner was Joseph L. Mankiewicz for *A Letter to Three Wives*.

In the second round of hearings, Rossen was identified as a Communist, and his refusal to testify resulted in blacklisting. Like Dmytryk, two years later, he requested a second hearing in which he admitted membership in the Communist Party and was subsequently able to work, though he decided never again to return to Hollywood. In 1961, Rossen scored his greatest success with *The Hustler*, nominated for nine awards, including Best Picture and Director, winning two technical awards.

Jules Dassin was identified as a Communist by Edward Dmytryk, which forced him into European exile. He became one of the few American directors to have made good films abroad, including *Night and the City* in England, and *Rififi* in France. Even so, a major American company agreed to distribute *Rififi* on one of two conditions: that Dassin sign a declaration renouncing his past and stating he was duped into subversive associations, or that his name be removed from the film as writer-director. When Dassin refused, the film was dropped and a small distributor released it; earlier negotiations with United Artists failed because of "hostile" public opinion.

Dassin's *He Who Must Die* also failed to get a major American distributor, and when the film was finally shown, only a few Hollywood figures came to see it, among them, Richard Brooks, Gene Kelly, and Walter Wanger. It took over a decade for Dassin's reputation to be restored with the release of *Never on Sunday* in 1960, his greatest commercial success, which won him his first and only directorial nomination.

Among the blacklisted writers was Carl Foreman, whose script for *High Noon* was nominated. Under pressure, Foreman left for England, working there for years underground, using the pseudonym Derek Frey for his script for Joseph Losey's *The Sleeping Tiger*. Foreman was given no credit for *The Bridge on the River Kwai*, which won all the major awards, including best screenplay to Pierre Boule, the author of the book, who had nothing to do with the script.

The Academy itself became a victim of McCarthy's political hysteria, when, on February 6, 1957, it decided to enact the following rule: "Any person who, before any duly constituted federal legislative committee or body, shall have admitted that he is a member of the Communist party (and has not since publicly renounced the Party) or who shall have refused to answer whether or not he is or was a member of the Communist Party or shall have refused to respond to a subpoena to appear before such a committee or body, shall be ineligible for any Academy Award so long as he persists in such a refusal."

More than any other talent group, writers suffered from this rule. Michael Wilson won the writing Oscar with Harry Brown for *A Place in the Sun,* but, refusing to answer charges of Communist affiliation, he found himself out of work. In 1956, William Wyler's *Friendly Persuasion,* nominated for many awards, was released without giving credit to Wilson's script, which he had written a decade before; the only credit mentioned onscreen was "from the book by Jessamyn West."

In the 1957 ceremonies, an interesting incident occurred when the Best Story went to Robert Rich for *The Brave One,* but no writer claimed the award. The Writers Guild acknowledged that "it knew nothing about the man, who's as much of a mystery to us as he is to everybody else." Producer Frank King told the *New York Times* that he had no idea of his writer's whereabouts, but added that he was a brilliant young writer whom he had met in Germany, where he served as an American Army man. To the Academy's embarrassment, it turned out that Rich was the pseudonym for blacklisted writer Dalton Trumbo, one of the Hollywood Ten. Trumbo received his long overdue Oscar in 1975, when producers Frank and Maurice King sent the Academy an affidavit verifying his identity.

One of 1958's most acclaimed films, *The Defiant Ones* earned nominations in most categories, including story and screenplay to Nathan E. Douglas and Harold Jacob Smith. But Douglas was the pseudonym of Ned Young, a blacklisted writer. The Academy, embarrassed for having to declare a member of a team ineligible, revoked its rule in January 1958. The Board of Directors denied that the motive for revoking the 1957 rule was linked to *The Defiant Ones.* But it issued a statement calling the previous rule "unworkable and impractical to administer and enforce." According to the new regulations, the Academy would simply "honor achievements as presented." Dalton Trumbo hailed that decision as the official end of the blacklist, though he continued to wonder how the industry could officially rescind a blacklist that it had never acknowledged existed in the first place.

Using the Oscar Show for Propaganda

Most artists believe that politics should be kept entirely out of the Oscars. In practice, however, this separation is impossible to achieve, because film is an inherently political medium. Moreover, a dilemma occurs between artists' freedom to express themselves honestly and candidly, and the Academy's desire to neutralize the Oscar show politically.

Speeches with explicit political overtones are the most outrageous aspects of the ceremonies because they are the least predictable; it is the only part of the show that cannot be rehearsed in advance. The show's live audiences and television viewers have come to expect such explosive incidents. That John Wayne and Jane Fonda, two of the most overtly political actors, did *not* use the Oscar platform for political speeches was held in high regard by some but disappointed those who expected them to take advantage of the unique opportunity.

The explicit use of the Oscar show for advocating social causes was mostly a phenomenon of the 1970s. Jane Fonda was praised for her performance in *They Shoot Horses, Don't They?* for which she won the New York Film Critics Award. However, many believed that Fonda's chances to win were spoiled by her radical politics: she supported the Black Panther Movement, and conducted fund-raisers for reluctant G.I. and U.S. Servicemen's Fund. There were other good performances in 1969, such as Liza Minnelli's in *The Sterile Cuckoo,* but majority opinion held that Fonda deserved the Oscar; the winner, however, was Maggie Smith for *The Prime of Miss Jean Brodie.*

Two years later, when Fonda received her second nomination for *Klute,* the industry speculated that she would either renounce her nomination or use the occasion to promote her politics. Earlier she had sent a Vietnam vet to accept the Golden Globe from the Hollywood Foreign Press. For a while, Fonda considered declining the prize, if she won, but on second thought, she decided to attend the ceremonies. Fonda explained: "A woman who is much wiser than I am said to me: 'You're a very subjective individual, an elite individual. The Oscar is what the working class relates to when it thinks of people in the movies. It's important for those of us who speak out for social change to get that kind of acclaim.'" At Oscar night, when her name was announced, there was a mixture of cheers and boos, but, contrary to expectations, Fonda gave a restrained speech: "Thank you. And thanks to those of you who applauded. There's a lot I could say tonight. But this isn't the time or the place. So I'll just say thank you."

Shortly after, Fonda was informally blacklisted and didn't work for several years in America. Earlier, she had formed with actor Donald

Sutherland, as part of her anti-Vietnam battle, "the Anti-War Troupe," which toured military camps in defiance of the Pentagon. In July 1972, Fonda went to North Vietnam, a move which put her career—and life—on the line. When she got back, she was labeled by her opponents "a Commie slut" and "Hanoi Jane."

Undaunted, Fonda co-produced *F.T.A. (Free the Army)*, a filmed version of the tour. She also campaigned with other actors for the Presidential Election of Senator George McGovern. In 1973, she married Tom Hayden, the antiwar militant. Joining forces with cinematographer Haskell Wexler, the three co-directed *Introduction to the Enemy*, which documented her visit to Vietnam.

For a decade, Fonda's record as a screen actress was rather poor. She appeared in Jean-Luc Godard's *Tout va bien (Everything's All Right)*, a film about the 1968 student revolutions and strikes. She showed her commitment to socially relevant films in playing Nora, Ibsen's feminist heroine, in Joseph Losey's 1973 *A Doll's House*. But a cameo role in the American-Soviet production *The Blue Bird* in 1975 was downright embarrassing.

For her American comeback, Fonda chose a comedy, *Fun With Dick and Jane* (1977), co-starring George Segal. But the turning point of her career was *Julia*, in which she was cast as playwright Lillian Hellmann, a part that "means more to me than any movie I've ever made." When Fonda was asked to co-host the 1977 Oscar show, it was interpreted as a sign of Hollywood's "forgiveness." In 1978, Fonda's second Oscar for *Coming Home* proved that she emerged triumphantly from her aborted career. Her comeback was compared to Ingrid Bergman's, whose second 1956 Oscar for *Anastasia* also represented a kind of reconciliation. Both Fonda and Bergman were restored to "respectability" while still young—in contrast to many blacklisted artists who had lost the most creative years of their lives.

In the 1980s, Fonda's politics have mellowed and she has become accepted as a mainstream actress. Her new causes were the ERA (now defunct), opposition to nuclear weapons, rent control, and issues that were more accessible to the public. Fonda supported her then husband's grassroots organization, CED (Campaign for Economic Democracy), whose goal was to curb the power of large corporations. Maturity and a second motherhood changed Fonda, though she was still committed to films with strong political convictions.

Looking back on her past, Fonda concedes to have been "a bit shrill." But she also reached the conclusion that "rallies and speeches aren't necessarily as effective as making one hell of a good movie." In the 1980s, Fonda became a media star due to the popularity of her books and videos, "The

Jane Fonda Workout." Watching her co-host the 1986 Oscar show, in which she introduced Kermit the Frog, was an ironic commentary on the fate of a once-radical actress.

Charlie Chaplin, another political victim, was also "pardoned" by the industry and restored to legitimacy with an Honorary Oscar in 1972. Chaplin failed to win a single award for *The Great Dictator* (1940), despite a brilliant performance. Politics had something to do with it: Chaplin was suspected of a leftist bent during World War II. He had declared that he was in favor of launching a second front in Europe to help the Russians. The subjects of *Modern Times* (1936), a satire on individual impotence in the technological age, and *The Great Dictator,* a satire of Hitler and fascism, also made him a suspect. At the end of this film, shot before the United States joined the war, Chaplin stepped out of character and made an impassioned speech for freedom. There was also malicious gossip over his reluctance to apply for an American citizenship, which made him even more suspect. Public opinion turned against Chaplin after *The Great Dictator,* which was his last commercial American hit. Chaplin's subsequent films, *Monsieur Verdoux* (1947) and *Limelight* (1957), were both failures.

Chaplin was plagued because he refused to go on record that he was uninterested in the Soviet Union, which, ironically, he had never visited. Threatened with a subpoena to testify before the HUAC, Chaplin sent a telegram: "I am not a Communist, neither have I ever joined any political party or organization in my life." In 1952, when the Attorney General instructed the Immigration Authorities to deny Chaplin a reentry visa, he vowed never again to return to the United States. Chaplin's friends found it ironic that he was suspected of leftist politics, as in his personal lifestyle he represented "the height of wealthy conservatism."

Twenty years after he left, Chaplin returned to the United States on a reconciliation tour. He was first honored by the Lincoln Center Film Society, where he received a standing ovation from his fans. It was just the beginning of what he described as a "renaissance." The Honorary Oscar was given "for the incalculable effect Chaplin has had on making motion pictures, the art form of this century." These gestures proved that the New Hollywood had finally taken over the old guard.

A year later, in 1973, a major controversy erupted when Marlon Brando was named Best Actor for *The Godfather.* Brando's contempt for Hollywood had been a known fact for a long time. Arriving for his first film, *The Men,* Brando shocked the press when he stated that his only motive for being in Hollywood was his lack of courage to reject the tremendous amounts of money he was offered to make films. But somehow, people got used to his eccentricities, viewing them as part of his personality.

Besides, Brando was such a brilliant actor that he could get away with such outrageous statements. Brando's derisive attitudes did not damage his career at all; they made him even more alluringly mysterious.

Prior to *The Godfather*, Brando was nominated five times for Best Actor, the last time for *Sayonara*, which he made because he identified with its plea for racial understanding. In the 1960s, looking for interesting vehicles, Brando appeared in *Candy*, in which he played a guru; *Reflections in a Golden Eye*, playing a gay serviceman; and *The Countess from Hong Kong* (directed by Charlie Chaplin), as an American diplomat. Most of these films failed. Just when filmmakers declared him a has-been, Brando delivered a brilliant comeback performance, as Don Corleone in *The Godfather*, for which he was forced to take a screen test for the first time in his career. Paramount was at first reluctant to cast Brando, holding that he had lost his box-office power, but his test was convincing—he could hardly be recognized.

Brando's performance got rave reviews and numerous awards. However, he turned down his sixth Oscar nomination with a short telegram: "There is singular lack of honor in this country today." The Oscar, according to columnist Bob Thomas, was an emotional gesture, "a sense of reaffirmation of an admittedly great, but wayward actor who had become alienated by or with Hollywood." It was a strange gesture, a welcome home extended to an actor who in no way wished to be welcomed home.

At the ceremonies, applause followed when Brando was announced the winner. Thereupon as noted earlier, Native American Sacheen Littlefeather walked to the podium and read a statement from him. Brando voiced his protest against the treatment of Indians, on and offscreen, through an Apache member of the Native American Affirmative Image Committee. He wrote: "I, as a member of this profession, do not feel that I can as a citizen of the United States accept an award here tonight. I think awards in this country at this time are inappropriate to be received or given until the condition of the American Indian is drastically altered." And he concluded, "If we are not our brother's keeper, at least let us not be his executioner."

Brando was criticized by those who felt he should have at least refused the award in person; Brando later explained that he was on his way to Wounded Knee to support the Oglala Sioux's protest against discrimination. At the same time, Brando's rejection of the Oscar did not surprise those who knew him—and didn't meet with unanimous criticism.

The next explosive incident occurred in the 1975 show, when Burt Schneider and Peter Davis were cited for their anti–Vietnam documentary, *Hearts and Minds*. In his acceptance speech, Schneider read a wire from a Vietcong leader: "Please transmit to all our friends in America our recognition of all they have done on behalf of peace for the application of the Paris Accords on Vietnam." This blatant propaganda outraged many viewers, who called NBC in anger. Consequently, Frank Sinatra, one of the emcees of the show, was asked by the Academy to make the following statement: "We are not responsible for any political references made on this program tonight, and we are sorry that they are made." It was the first time that the Academy has taken an explicit stand as an organization against propaganda voiced on its platform.

After several controversies, the 1976 Oscar show was quiet and smooth. *Films in Review* described it as "negatively notable, no protests, no winners refusing awards, no political speeches, no surprises." But the following year saw another casualty, playwright Lillian Hellman, restored to legitimacy. Hellman's career was damaged in the 1950s, after a successful decade in Hollywood as a screenwriter, adapting some of her Broadway plays, including *The Little Foxes* to the screen. Hellman was declared an uncooperative witness when she refused to testify before the Committee, sending the now-famous, often-quoted letter.

The invitation to participate in the show, as presenter of the writing awards, was yet another attempt by the New Hollywood to reconcile with victims of the McCarthy era. Following an emotional standing ovation, which caught her by surprise, Hellman said: "My second reason for being here is perhaps only important to me. I was once upon a time a respectable member of this community. Respectable didn't necessarily mean more than I took a daily bath when I was sober, didn't spit except when I meant to, and mispronounced a few words of fancy French. Then suddenly, even before Senator Joseph McCarthy reached for that rusty, poisoned ax, I and many others were no longer acceptable to the owners of this industry. They confronted the wild charges of Joe McCarthy with a force and courage of a bowl of mashed potatoes." She then concluded: "But I have a mischievous pleasure in being restored to respectability, understanding full well that the younger generation who asked me here tonight meant more by that invitation than my name or my history."

Warren Beatty, one of the show's co-hosts, remarked: "When I saw who was on this show tonight, Lillian Hellman, Norman Mailer, Jane Fonda, Donald Sutherland, I thought maybe the nicest thing to do was to say a few nice things about Reagan and Goldwater." Beatty, of course, could not know then that in two years Ronald Reagan would be elected President.

A scandalous incident took place in the 1978 ceremonies, when Vanessa Redgrave won the supporting Oscar for *Julia*. Before the show began, members of the Jewish Defense League (JDL) picketed outside the Music Center, protesting her involvement in *The Palestinians,* an anti-Zionist documentary. Redgrave had taken an anti-Israeli stand when she became an outspoken proponent of the Palestine Liberation Organization

(PLO). Neither the JDL signs, stating REDGRAVE AND ARAFAT: A PERFECT LOVE AFFAIR, and HELL NO TO VANESSA REDGRAVE AND THE PLO, nor the PLO signs, VANESSA: A WOMAN OF CONSCIENCE AND COURAGE, were seen by the TV viewers. The police and special security managed to keep the two groups apart.

Redgrave's views sharply divided the industry. Jewish producers, heavily represented in Hollywood, supported artists' rights to express freely their opinions offscreen. JDL's demand from Fox, which produced *Julia,* never to hire Redgrave again and to repudiate her support of the PLO, were dismissed by the studio and the Screen Actors Guild. The studio's reaction was: "While Fox as a company and the individuals who work there do not agree with Redgrave's political philosophy, we totally reject and we will not be blackmailed into supporting any policy of refusing to employ any person because of their political beliefs."

Redgrave's performance in *Julia* was brilliant, and it followed three previously nominated roles, in *Morgan, Isadora,* and *Mary, Queen of Scots.* Moreover, the competition in the supporting category was weak in 1977: Leslie Brown in *The Turning Point,* Quinn Cummings in *The Goodbye Girl,* Melinda Dillon in *Close Encounters of the Third Kind,* and Tuesday Weld in *Looking for Mr. Goodbar.*

Academy officials expected Redgrave to make a political speech if she won, and they did not mind when she spoke about the meaning of *Julia* to her: "I think Jane Fonda and I have done the best work of our lives and I think this was in part due to our director, Fred Zinnemann. I also think it is in part because we believed in what we were expressing: two out of millions who gave their lives and were prepared to sacrifice everything in the fight against fascist racist Nazi Germany." But then Redgrave proceeded with an impassioned propagandistic speech: "You should be very proud that in the last few weeks you stood firm and you refused to be intimidated by the threats of a small bunch of Zionist hoodlums whose behavior is an insult to the stature of Jews all over the world and to their great and heroic record against fascism and oppression. I salute that record and I salute all of you for having stood firm and dealt the final blow against that period when Nixon and McCarthy launched a worldwide witch-hunt against those who tried to express in their lives and their work the truths that they believed in." And she concluded: "I salute you and I thank you, and I pledge to you that I'll continue to fight against anti-Semitism and fascism."

Paddy Chayefsky, who presented the writing awards, chastised Redgrave: "I'm sick and tired of people exploiting the occasion of the Academy Awards for the propagation of their own political propaganda. Redgrave's win is not a pivotal moment in history, and doesn't require a proclamation." Charlton Heston, who had voted for Redgrave, reflected many people's opinion when he said, "I thought it as much an error to interject what amounted to political commentary into her acceptance remarks as it was an error for people to oppose her nomination on political grounds." But Redgrave's win was interpreted as yet another sign of the New Hollywood's "maturity"—it is unlikely that Redgrave would have won the Oscar in the 1950s.

Redgrave's politics were at the center of another controversy a few months later when she was cast as an Auschwitz concentration camp survivor in *Playing for Time,* Arthur Miller's television drama based on Fania Fenelon's memoirs. This time, her casting drew sharp protests from the Jewish community and the entertainment industry. Rabbi Marvin Hier said it was like "selecting Edgar Hoover to portray Martin Luther King," and Sammy Davis Jr. felt "It would be like me playing the head of the Ku Klux Klan." Dore Schary, MGM's former chief and honorary chairman of the Anti-Defamation League, issued a statement that charged CBS with "a profound lack of sensitivity and understanding," calling the casting "a trick" and "a stunt."

In their defensive response, the producers said other actresses, such as Barbra Streisand and Jane Fonda, were considered for the part, and that Redgrave was the best actress available; some actresses refused to shave their heads, as was required by the role. The producers reiterated their philosophy that performers should not be penalized for their views, and that it was a matter of principle to remove politics from artistic decisions. Once again, Redgrave's performance was nothing short of brilliance, earning her a well-deserved Emmy Award.

In 1982, following a storm of protests from subscribers and musicians, the Boston Symphony Orchestra cancelled its performances of Stravinsky's *Oedipus Rex,* which were to feature Vanessa Redgrave. Other than that, Redgrave's politics have not damaged her getting work. She was later cast in some desirable roles, including *The Bostonians,* as Olive Chancellor, a wealthy suffragette, for which she received a fifth Oscar nomination and the National Society of Film Critics Award; and in David Hare's *Wetherby,* as the emotionally stifled teacher, for which she won another National Society Award. Critic Andrew Sarris noted, "I would have given the Oscar to Vanessa Redgrave for *Wetherby,* but I don't know if I would have waited around for her acceptance speech."

The uproar surrounding *Julia* was barely forgotten, when another dispute erupted in the 1979 ceremonies, caused by the nomination of two Vietnam War films for Best Picture: Michael Cimino's *The Deer Hunter* and Hal Ashby's *Coming Home,* each garnering a large number of nominations. Unlike World War II, which saw the immediate production of war films, it took almost a decade for Hollywood to make movies about Vietnam. The only exception was John Wayne's *The Green Berets* in 1968, the first major film in favor of the American involvement in Vietnam. Both studios, Universal in the case of *The Deer Hunter* and UA in *Coming Home,* had fears that the public would not support them, though they were proud of their quality: *The Deer Hunter* opened to rave reviews, and *Coming Home* to mixed-to-positive reviews.

The Academy voters split the major awards between the two movies. *The Deer Hunter* won five: Best Picture, Director (Cimino), Supporting Actor (Christopher Walken), sound, and editing; and *Coming Home* won the two lead acting awards (Jane Fonda and Jon Voight), and original screenplay (Waldo Salt and Robert C. Jones, using Nancy Dowd's story). Ironically, John Wayne was chosen as the Best Picture presenter, though one could only speculate how he felt about handing it in to *The Deer Hunter;* this time, the Duke kept his mouth shut!

During the ceremonies, there were mass demonstrations outside the auditorium, mostly against *The Deer Hunter,* and some in favor of *Coming Home*. Director Cimino was accused of violating historical truth and artistic responsibility, though he claimed that his aim was to make a surrealist, not a realistic, picture. "My film has nothing to do with whether the war should or should not have been," he later said. "This film addresses itself to the question of ordinary people of this country, who journeyed from their homes to the darkness and back. How do you survive that?" *The Deer Hunter* is a movie," Cimino explained, "It is not a newsreel. I was not trying to re-create reality."

But Cimino's rationale didn't pacify his critics. On the night of the awards, the police arrested members of "Vietnam Veterans Against the War," who protested against the movie's "misinterpretation of reality." Another dissenting group, "Hell No, We Won't Go Away Committee," denounced the film as "a racist attack on the Vietnamese people," citing the vicious violence, particularly Russian Roulette, used by the Vietnamese. "We didn't want the film to be honored blindly," said Linda Garrett, who formed the Committee. "Even my progressive friends seemed blinded by the power of the film, its emotional impact. They felt it was a great film despite its racism, despite its misinterpretation of history." Other critics charged that Americans were portrayed as innocent victims, which eliminated any discussion of the war's issues. A shocked Cimino claimed that his intention was to make an antiwar statement.

Furthermore, the winners' speeches and off-camera remarks were seen as violations of collegial professional ethics. Jane Fonda charged that *The*

Deer Hunter was a racist film that represented the Pentagon's view of Vietnam. Referring to the demonstrators as "my friends," she said *Coming Home* was a "better picture." And winning the Oscar for playing a sensitive paraplegic war veteran, Jon Voight said, "I accept this for every guy in a wheelchair."

Global politics have also entered the Oscar ceremonies through the nomination of foreign artists. In 1981, the Hungarian producer of the Best Animated Short, *The Fly,* was unable to obtain a visa to attend the show. Instead, an official of the Hungarian Embassy in the United States was authorized to represent him, showing again how intricate the connection between politics and film is.

Foreign cinemas are more explicitly political than American movies. Additionally, the nomination of foreign films that are political in nature stems from the particular regulations of this category. Films are sent for consideration by the equivalent academies of foreign countries before a committee narrows them down to five. Academy members are required to prove that they have seen all five nominees before voting, which means that a small number of the electorate participates in the selection of foreign films.

Hence the Foreign-Language Picture category is particularly vulnerable to political pressures. Four of the five nominees of the 1985 Best Foreign-Language Picture were political works with strong ideological messages. The winner, the Argentinean *The Official Story,* is a disturbingly emotional drama about an upper-middle class high-school history teacher, who begins to suspect that her adopted daughter is a child of one of the desaparecidos, the Argentineans abducted during the junta's counterinsurgency. In his speech, producer Luis Perenzo said: "On another March 24, 10 years ago, we suffered the last military coup in my country. We will never forget this nightmare, but we are certain now to begin with our new dreams."

The Official Story competed against the Yugoslavian *When Father Was Away on Business,* a family tale set in Sarajevo in the 1950s, when the country was torn between Marshal Tito's policies and the Stalinist Soviet Union. The other nominees were the Hungarian *Colonel Redl,* about Alfred Redl, the powerful intelligence officer of the Austro-Hungarian Empire who, according to the movie, when threatened by the Russians with public revelation of his homosexuality, agreed to become their agent, then committed suicide. *Angry Harvest* was a psychological World War II drama about the relationship between a Jewish woman escaping the Nazis and a devout Polish farmer. The fifth contender was the French comedy *Three Men and a Cradle,* which dealt with changing definitions of gender, particularly male roles.

Almost every year, explicitly political remarks appear in the presenters' or winners' speeches. Hence presenter Richard Gere made a plea, asking viewers to gather their vibes and drive the Chinese out of Tibet. And politically oriented actor-companions Tim Robbins and Susan Sarandon interrupted the scheduled programming to urge the United States to allow HIV-positive Haitians into the country.

In March 1992, demonstrators outside the Oscar show waved signs that read STOP HOLLYWOOD'S HOMOPHOBIA, and MAKE QUEER FILMS. Protesters complained about the negative portrayal of gays in *The Silence of the Lambs* and *JFK* (both nominated for Best Picture), and *Basic Instinct,* which had just opened theatrically, a movie in which a bisexual killer uses an ice pick to slay her male lovers. Inside the auditorium, the ceremony was disrupted briefly during a commercial, when a tuxedoed man shouted statistics about Hollywood's neglect of the AIDS epidemic. Security guards pulled him from the auditorium, and the TV viewers did not see it.

Many people think that turning the annual Oscar ceremonies into a political platform diminishes the prestige of the award and spoils the fun of the show itself. However, it would be a mistake to think that there will be no more controversies in the future. Whether the Academy likes it or not, the Oscar ceremonies are bound to have explosive political occurrences due to film's inherent nature as a political medium and due to the event's extraordinary exposure. After all, what other public occasion provides a captive and attentive audience of one billion viewers?

Conclusion:
Oscar, Hollywood,
and American Culture

The Oscars dominate the Hollywood industry's activities for the entire year. Except for the two months after the show, Oscar-related activities prevail all year round. In June 2000, barely two months after the ceremonies, the Academy issued a call for Scientific-Technical Achievements for the 2001 Oscars. The first public announcement related to the seventy-third Oscars, to take place in March 2001, officially began the Oscar race. Entry forms for these awards were mailed to eight hundred companies and individuals in the film-related scientific community around the world, as well as to all past winners. Scientific and Technical Awards are considered for advances which have proved significant to the film industry through successful use, according to Awards Administration Director Richard Miller; they don't have to be invented during the current year. Entry applications, which must be submitted to the Academy no later than August 1, 2000, are brought to the attention of the Scientific and Technical Awards Committee and are evaluated by sub-committees of engineers and scientists before being voted upon by the Academy's Board of Governors.

The Oscars have changed the entire operation of the film industry through their pervasive influence on every aspect of filmmaking: the studios, individual filmmakers, film critics, and moviegoers.

To begin with, the studios release their most prestigious and important pictures in the late fall and early winter, particularly in the month of December. The thinking behind this is that these movies will be fresh in the members' minds by the time they receive the nomination ballots in January.

Indeed, all things being equal, films released in December have better chances to get nominated than those released in any other month. Of the fifty films nominated for Best Picture in the 1980s, eighteen (40 percent) were released in December, and thirty-four films between September and December. By contrast, only six of the fifty films opened between January and April: *Missing, Witness,* and *Hannah and Her Sisters* in February; and *Coal Miner's Daughter, Tender Mercies,* and *A Room With a View* in March. These pictures were released in the winter because their producers didn't consider them to be "Oscar stuff" or serious contenders for Academy nominations.

In some years, as in 1988, all five Best Picture nominees were released in December. *(The Accidental Tourist, Dangerous Liaisons, Mississippi Burning, Rain Man,* and *Working Girl).* By contrast, many films would have stood better chances of getting nominations had they been released at more strategically fortuitous times. For example, Martin Scorsese's *The King of Comedy* and David Jones's *Betrayal,* both released in January 1983, would have featured more prominently in the nominations had they been released in the fall. It is doubtful that *The King of Comedy* would have been more successful at the box office—it was a fiasco—or that it would have garnered a Best Picture nomination, but its three superb performances by Robert De Niro, Jerry Lewis, and Sandra Bernhardt would have received a more serious consideration for acting nominations. Similarly, the British film *Betrayal,* with a screenplay by Harold Pinter from his play, also contained three superlative performances by Ben Kingsley, Jeremy Irons, and Patricia Hodge, each of whom wasn't nominated but deserved to be.

The release date has not always been a crucial variable. In the 1930s, only seven of the ninety-two nominated films (7.6 percent), and in the 1940s, ten (14 percent) of the seventy films premiered in December. The specific month began to play strategic role in the 1950s, when ten (20 percent) of the nominated films opened in December. And it became even more important in the 1960s, when sixteen (32 percent) of the nominated films were released in December, many around Christmas time. The "Awards Year" rule stipulates that films must play at least one week in Los Angeles prior to December 31.

However, one should not come to the conclusion that the film's release date counts more than its artistic merits, though a strategic release certainly contributes to a film's visibility. Woody Allen, highly respected for his many talents, has shown complete disregard for the timing of his films' release. All of Allen's 1980s' pictures were released in February or March—the worst season as far as Oscars are concerned—including *Hannah and Her Sisters* (1986), which nevertheless received rave reviews and major nominations and Oscars.

The Oscar's effect on the release date is an example of an unanticipated consequence. Another displacement of goals in the award's operation has been its gradual acceptance as an institutionalized yardstick of artistic quality. The Oscar has become such an integral part of the film world that critics are evaluating a film's merits (acting, writing, direction) in terms of Oscars. For better or for worse, the Oscar has become a legitimized measure of cinematic excellence.

For instance, in 1958, critic Anthony Carthew wrote about David Niven's performance in *Separate Tables:* "I knew I was seeing a piece of acting worth an Oscar." Niven did win Best Actor for this film. And the National Observer's Clifford A. Ridley was so smitten with Liza Minnelli in *The Sterile Cuckoo* that he commented: "She does not play nineteen-year-old Pookie Adams, she is Pookie Adams, and you may mark your Oscar ballots right now"; Minnelli received her first Best Actress nomination for this role. *Variety,* the popular trade magazine, is known for using "inside Hollywood" terms in its reviews. Reviewing *Arthur,* its critic noted that "John Gielgud gives a priceless performance, truly the kind that wins supporting Oscars." Gielgud won.

But critics use the Oscar not only for praise. Pauline Kael did not like Gena Rowlands's performance in *A Woman Under the Influence,* noting that Rowlands was doing too much, "enough for half a dozen tours de force, a whole row of Oscars." The Oscar is often used as a tool for derogation, as in David Denby's review of *Places in the Heart,* a film he didn't like because it was "too pious." "Parched and academic," wrote Denby, "the movie is too square for art—though it's perfectly designed for Oscars." Denby was right, at least as far as prediction of Oscars was concerned—*Places of the Heart* received seven nominations, including Best Picture.

Film critics and audiences have incorporated the Oscar into their lingo, making value judgments in terms of "Oscar caliber" movies and performances. In fact, shortly after a films' release, many try to predict their chances of getting nominations and awards. In 1983, *The Big Chill* opened to rave reviews, with Richard Corliss writing in *Time,* "the eight star actors deserve one big Oscar." And Andrew Sarris stated in his review of *Twice in a Lifetime* (1985) that Amy Madigan "deserves an Oscar." Madigan was indeed nominated. That critics are able to predict the Oscar nominees and winners only shows that the parameters of what is a so-called "Oscar caliber" film or performance are quite established.

That the Oscar has been institutionalized as a legitimate symbol of success is also reflected in its portrayal in movies about Hollywood. *The Bad and the Beautiful* (1952), Vincente Minnelli's glossy melodrama, was one of the more successful "Hollywood on Hollywood" films. Using flashbacks as a device, its narrative consists of a series of recollections by a director (Barry Sullivan), a glamorous star (Lana Turner), a screenwriter (Dick Powell), and a studio executive (Walter Pidgeon) about their encounters with a ruthless Oscar-winning producer (Kirk Douglas). Offering an inside view of Hollywood, *The Bad and the Beautiful* received special attention from the Academy, with five nominations and two awards, screenplay to Charles Schnee and supporting actress to Gloria Grahame.

Curiously, most of the "self-examination" movies have provided an unflattering view of Hollywood and a disparaging attitude toward the Oscar. Joseph Levine's *The Oscar* (1966), based on Richard Sale's book, was a vulgar soap opera on the informal operations of the award. The story centers on a selfish actor, Frankie Fan (Stephen Boyd), who, waiting impatiently to be announced winner, recalls in flashback abuse from the drama coach (Eleanor Parker) who launched his career, marriage to a glamorous star (Elke Sommer) for publicity, betrayal of an old friend (Milton Berle), and aggressive Oscar campaigns. Frankie's illusions are shattered when, much to his shock, another actor wins the Oscar.

The Oscar was the worst publicity Hollywood could have devised for itself. Panned by all critics, it was also a fiasco at the box office. "Obviously the community doesn't need enemies so long as it has itself," wrote the *New York Times*'s Bosley Crowther. Other critics noted that "discriminating moviegoers prefer to watch the real thing—the Oscarcast—on television and hypothecate to themselves as to the behind-the-scenes chaos involved."

The Oscar has also been used on-screen in humorous and cynical ways. With a good sense of irony, Billy Wilder cast Henry Fonda in 1979's *Fedora* as an Academy President sent to a remote island to present an honorary Oscar to an aging but legendary star (Martha Keller), possibly standing in for Greta Garbo or Gloria Swanson. Fonda himself had not won an Oscar by 1979; he won in 1981. Blake Edwards also played a joke on Hollywood, casting his wife-actress Julie Andrews in *S.O.B.* (1980) as an actress who has won an Oscar for *Peter Pan* (i.e., *Mary Poppins)* and is now going out of her way to change her wholesome screen image by exposing her breasts.

There's always been ambivalence by at least some filmmakers toward the Oscar. Pioneer D. W. Griffith is reported to have said at the mention of the Academy of Motion Picture Arts and Sciences, "What art? What science?" And Hitchcock, who never won a competitive Oscar, described it as "a coveted annual prize whose previous year's winners nobody can ever remember." Still, the fact remains that the Oscar has become, as producer Walter Mirisch said, "movies' most effective ambassador throughout the world." "The nickname stuck," Mirisch elaborated, "and I have never been in any country in the world where the word *Oscar* has not entered the language." Indeed, what better proof of legitimization than the Oscar's entrance into the most respectable dictionaries?

At present, the Oscar is more acceptable than ever before as the ultimate symbol of achievement. Asked for his attitude toward the Oscar, William Hurt, the 1985 winner, said, "If this was the way they chose to tell me that they liked my work, then I was going to accept it. There are enough people that I now know and trust and admire and respect, who are members of that institution, that I can't piss on it." The acceptance of the Oscar is universal, as Simone Signoret observed: "In the French industry, there's always a smart guy who says before the umpteenth take of the same shot: 'Come on, let's do it again and we'll get the Oscar.'"

Oscar's Preeminence

As noted, the Oscar show is watched by one billion people, in and outside America, many of whom are not moviegoers. This extends the Oscar's visibility way beyond the borders of the film world and the borders of the United States. The Oscar has become a preeminent symbol of mainstream American culture. Watching the show, international viewers get a microcosm of American films, American television, and American culture. This function contributes explicitly and implicitly to American cultural imperialism all over the world. The Oscar show serves as propaganda not just for American movies but also for the American Way of Life.

Watching the annual ceremonies has become an obligatory ritual for most Americans. The Oscar functions as a secular ritual in American culture. Like religious rituals, the Oscar ceremonies are prescheduled, occurring every year at the same time. They are highly organized, following a strict set of rules; there are hundreds of "Academy Commandments." The ceremonies are collective, requiring the participation of a large public, live and via television. And most important of all, the Oscar reaffirms the central values of mainstream American culture.

The Oscar embodies such basic American values as democracy, equality, individualism, competitiveness, upward mobility, hard work, occupational achievement, and monetary success. The award highlights the inherent contradictions in achieving these values, the dilemmas between cultural myths and their corresponding reality. Each value exemplified by the Oscar can be stated as a dichotomy of opposite orientations: democracy versus elitism, equality versus discrimination, universalism versus particularism, individualism versus collectivism, competition versus collaboration, hard work versus luck, success versus failure.

More than any other category, it is the acting awards that express the cultural contradictions inherent in American values. In no other profession is the conflict between the ideal of democracy and the reality of elitism more apparent. Acting is one of the most democratic professions, with a broader social class base than other occupations. The choice of acting as a career has provided a channel for upward mobility to over half of the Oscar-nominated players, many of whom came from poor, uneducated families and from ethnic minorities. Acting is one of the most accessible professions, easily entered but also easily left. Entry requires less formal education or training than other professions; experience and "on the job" training are far more important than schooling.

Actors' biographies are replete with rags to riches and overnight success stories, myths that are still powerful in attracting new members into acting. One of the most startling success stories is exemplified by Sylvester Stallone. A product of a broken home, Stallone grew up in New York's Hell's Kitchen, then in Silver Springs, Maryland, and then in Philadelphia. After spending years homes of foster parents, he was booted out of fourteen schools in eleven years. Stallone attended the drama department of the University of Miami for a while, where his instructors discouraged him from pursuing acting. He then tried his hand at various jobs, the most glamorous of which was as an usher at the Baronet Theater in New York City.

Determined to become an actor, however, Stallone managed to get some bit roles in films such as *Bananas* and *The Prisoner of Second Avenue*. When his career seemed to have reached a dead end, Stallone decided to create his own opportunity and to write a screenplay. The result was *Rocky,* whose script he reportedly completed in three days, with a narrative that is similar to his own story: a down-and-out prizefighter rises to stardom against great odds. The rest is film history: *Rocky* won the 1976 Best Picture and established Stallone as the preeminent male star of his generation.

As well as being accessible and democratic, acting is also one of the most stratified professions. The Oscar winners and nominees constitute a small elite composed of the most accomplished actors occupying the top positions of money, prestige, and power in the film world. The gap in rewards between the elite and rank-and-file members is immense. The supply of film artists has always surpassed the demand for them, which means that most actors are unemployed most of the time. By contrast, most Oscar-winners go from one film project to another, and from the screen to the stage and television. As was mentioned, accumulative advantage is in operation: the rich players become richer and the famous more famous, while the unsuccessful become progressively less so.

The contradiction between hard work and luck as determinants for successful careers is also exemplified by the Oscar winners' careers. The Protestant ethic of hard work is still a legitimate avenue for achieving success. In acting, there is strong emphasis on motivation, ambition, self-discipline, and energy as crucial requirements for success. Veteran actors like John Wayne rationalized their success by stressing the hard work involved in making movies, the physical rigor, the irregular time schedules, the long hours, and the grim working conditions. Walter Matthau was not joking when he once described acting as "the hardest job known to mankind."

But despite the emphasis on hard work, actors also realize that they have little or no control over their opportunities, that luck, fate, and other circumstances play important roles in shaping their careers. Gary Cooper, a two-time Oscar-winner, regarded acting as "just a job," which made him successful, because he was "the right man at the right time." Cooper also differed from his colleagues in considering movie acting as "a pretty silly business for a man because it takes less training, less ability, and less brains to be successful at it than any other business I can think of." Attitudes toward acting among men range from Jack Lemmon's, "I have never lost a total passion to my work," and William Hurt's, "I am proud to be an actor," to Marlon Brando's "acting has never been the dominant force in my life."

Nonetheless, most artists acknowledge the role of luck and accidental contingencies in their screen careers. Some became actors by accident, without ever making a conscious or deliberate decision to pursue acting. Jimmy Stewart, who majored in architecture at Princeton but never practiced, once summed up his career: "If I hadn't been at some particular place at some particular time and some man hadn't happened to say so-and-so, and I hadn't answered this-and-that, I'd still be hunting for a job in an architect's office."

Another star, Bing Crosby, viewed his popularity as a series of lucky accidents, naming his autobiography *Call Me Lucky.* "I'm not really an actor. I was just lucky." Clark Gable used to say, "If it hadn't been for people like Howard Strickling (MGM publicity man), I'd probably have ended up a truck driver."

Luck also plays a considerable part in getting the Oscar-winning role. The Academy's history is replete with Oscar-winning roles played by actors neither intended nor originally cast in them. What would have happened to Jack Nicholson if Rip Torn hadn't turned down the part of the dropout lawyer in *Easy Rider,* Nicholson's film break after ten long years in Hollywood? Would this part have made Rip Torn a star had *he* played it?

The conflict between individualism and collaboration is also demonstrated by the Oscar. Rugged, romantic individualism is most fully expressed in competitive achievement, and thousands of films have portrayed it on-screen. But romantic individualism also means rewarding artists for individual contributions in their respective expertise. At the same time, film is a collaborative art, though it is often hard to single out the relative contribution of each element (writing, direction, acting, cinematography, editing) to the overall success or failure of the final product, because each element is interdependent. However, the Oscar follows the primacy of individualism in American culture by honoring *individual* achievements.

It is almost impossible to define the elements of an effective screen performance, though one knows a good performance when one sees it. Not to mention talent, individual performances depend on the support from other players, on the way they are photographed, the manner in which they are edited. Not surprisingly, screen players resent their lack of control over the final shape of their work—often opting to work in the theater where they feel more directly responsible.

But, ironically, more than other elements, the acting is often blamed for the overall low quality of a film—and actors are undeservedly praised when they appear in good or commercial films. When a film is powerful, every aspect of its seems to be good. Good films tend to overcome mediocre performances, but effective individual acting has a harder time overcoming a bad movie. This is one of the inherent problems in evaluating films—the ability to distinguish the contribution of each element to the overall quality. Good films get nominations and awards in most categories, even in those which do not merit a nomination. By contrast, excellent individual contributions are ignored if they are contained in average or bad pictures.

Moreover, the structure of many films depends on ensemble acting, with a group of players complementing each other. As was mentioned, only Sam Shepard was nominated in *The Right Stuff,* Glenn Close in *The Big Chill,* Julianne Moore and Burt Reynolds in *Boogie Nights,* and Tom Cruise in *Magnolia,* four films that rely heavily on large casts and ensemble acting. It is in such cases that other, less relevant factors, such as actors' former work, previous number of nominations, and popularity in Hollywood begin to play a role in determining their chances to win the Oscar.

Some critics have proposed to establish a supplementary category, for the best ensemble acting, honoring the *collective* achievements of a team of players. However, this is unlikely to happen. It not only runs against the individualistic nature of the awards, but also against individual competitiveness and achievement, values that are highly cherished in American culture. "The comparatively striking feature of American culture," sociologist Philip Slater once observed, "is its tendency to identify standards of excellence with competitive occupational achievement." Yet competition also has negative effects, as Slater noted: "The competitive life is a lonely one and its satisfactions are very short-lived, for each race leads only to a new one."

Finally, the Oscar also functions as an arena for conflict between universalism and particularism. Had the Oscar operated on completely matter-of-fact and rational principles, quality of work would have been the sole criterion upon which artists would be evaluated. A universalistic ethos requires that artists producing high-quality work would be rewarded regardless of ascribed statuses such as age, gender, race, religion, or nationality. However, such a reward system is utopian and does not exist, even in the science world. Indeed, one of Oscar's effects is to call attention to the operation of multiple of yardsticks in evaluating film art. Hence, the more disagreement there is about the Oscars, the more critically aware the public becomes of the problems involved in judging film art.

What is amazing about the Oscar is its *public* and *immediate* manifestation of these cultural values. Through the Oscar show, audiences get to participate in the making or breaking of careers, in the rise and fall of artists, and in perpetuating overnight-success stories, all of which happen on their own television sets before their eyes.

Table 1: *Awards in Six Categories by Year; 1927/28–2000*

Year	Picture	Director	Actor	Actress	Supporting Actor	Supporting Actress
1927/8	*Wings*	Frank Borzage (*Seventh Heaven*) Lewis Milestone (*Two Arabian Nights*)	Emil Jannings (*The Way of All Flesh; The Last Command*)	Janet Gaynor (*Seventh Heaven; Street Angel; Sunrise*)		
1928/9	*The Broadway Melody*	Frank Lloyd (*The Divine Lady*)	Warner Baxter (*In Old Arizona*)	Mary Pickford (*Coquette*)		
1929/30	*All Quiet on the Western Front*	Lewis Milestone	George Arliss (*Disraeli*)	Norma Shearer (*The Divorcee*)		
1930/1	*Cimarron*	Norman Taurog (*Skippy*)	Lionel Barrymore (*A Free Soul*)	Marie Dressler (*Min and Bill*)		
1931/2	*Grand Hotel*	Frank Borzage (*Bad Girl*)	Fredric March (*Dr. Jekyll and Mr. Hyde*); Wallace Beery (*The Champ*)	Helen Hayes (*The Sin of Madelon Claudet*)		
1932/3	*Cavalcade*	Frank Lloyd	Charles Laughton (*The Private Life of Henry VIII*)	Katharine Hepburn (*Morning Glory*)		
1934	*It Happened One Night*	Frank Capra	Clark Gable	Claudette Colbert		

347

Table 1 (Continued)

Year	Picture	Director	Actor	Actress	Supporting Actor	Supporting Actress
1935	Mutiny on the Bounty	John Ford (The Informer)	Victor McLaglen (The Informer)	Bette Davis (Dangerous)	Walter Brennan (Come and Get It)	Gale Sondergaard (Anthony Adverse)
1936	The Great Ziegfeld	Frank Capra (Mr. Deeds Goes to Town)	Paul Muni (The Story of Louis Pasteur)	Luise Rainer		
1937	The Life of Emil Zola	Leo McCarey (The Awful Truth)	Spencer Tracy (Captains Courageous)	Luise Rainer (The Good Earth)	Joseph Schildkraut (The Life of Emil Zola)	Alice Brady (In Old Chicago)
1938	You Can't Take It With You	Frank Capra	Spencer Tracy (Boys Town)	Bette Davis (Jezebel)	Walter Brennan (Kentucky)	Fay Bainter (Jezebel)
1939	Gone with the Wind	Victor Fleming	Robert Donat (Goodbye Mr. Chips)	Vivien Leigh	Thomas Mitchell (Stagecoach)	Hattie McDaniel
1940	Rebecca	John Ford (The Grapes of Wrath)	James Stewart (The Philadelphia Story)	Ginger Rogers (Kitty Foyle)	Walter Brennan (The Westerner)	Jane Darwell (The Grapes of Wrath)
1941	How Green Was My Valley	John Ford	Gary Cooper (Sergeant York)	Joan Fontaine (Suspicion)	Donald Crisp	Mary Astor (The Great Lie)
1942	Mrs. Miniver	William Wyler	James Cagney (Yankee Doodle Dandy)	Greer Garson	Van Heflin (Johnny Eager)	Teresa Wright

348

Year	Film	Director	Actor	Actress	Supporting Actor	Supporting Actress
1943	*Casablanca*	Michael Curtiz	Paul Lukas (*Watch on the Rhine*)	Jennifer Jones (*The Song of Bernadette*)	Charles Coburn (*The More the Merrier*)	Katina Paxinou (*For Whom the Bell Tolls*)
1944	*Going My Way*	Leo McCarey	Bing Crosby	Ingrid Bergman (*Gaslight*)	Barry Fitzgerald	Ethel Barrymore (*None But the Lonely Heart*)
1945	*The Lost Weekend*	Billy Wilder	Ray Milland	Joan Crawford (*Mildred Pierce*)	James Dunn (*A Tree Grows in Brooklyn*)	Anne Revere (*National Velvet*)
1946	*The Best Years of Our Lives*	William Wyler	Fredric March	Olivia De Havilland (*To Each His Own*)	Harold Russell	Anne Baxter (*The Razor's Edge*)
1947	*Gentleman's Agreement*	Elia Kazan	Ronald Colman (*A Double Life*)	Loretta Young (*The Farmer's Daughter*)	Edmund Gwenn (*Miracle on 34th Street*)	Celeste Holme
1948	*Hamlet*	John Huston (*The Treasure of the Sierra Madre*)	Laurence Olivier	Jane Wyman (*Johnny Belinda*)	Walter Huston (*The Treasure of the Sierra Madre*)	Claire Trevor (*Key Largo*)
1949	*All the King's Men*	Joseph L. Mankiewicz (*A Letter to Three Wives*)	Broderick Crawford	Olivia De Havilland (*The Heiress*)	Dean Jagger (*Twelve O'Clock High*)	Mercedes McCambridge
1950	*All About Eve*	Joseph L. Mankiewicz	Jose Ferrer (*Cyrano de Bergerac*)	Judy Holliday (*Born Yesterday*)	George Sanders	Josephine Hall (*Harvey*)

Table 1 *(Continued)*

Year	Picture	Director	Actor	Actress	Supporting Actor	Supporting Actress
1951	*An American in Paris*	George Stevens *(A Place in the Sun)*	Humphrey Bogart *(The African Queen)*	Vivien Leigh *(A Streetcar Named Desire)*	Karl Malden *(Streetcar)*	Kim Hunter *(Streetcar)*
1952	*The Greatest Show on Earth*	John Ford *(The Quiet Man)*	Gary Cooper *(High Noon)*	Shirley Booth *(Come Back Little Sheba)*	Anthony Quinn *(Viva Zapata!)*	Gloria Grahame *(The Bad and the Beautiful)*
1953	*From Here to Eternity*	Fred Zinnemann	William Holden *(Stalag 17)*	Audrey Hepburn *(Roman Holiday)*	Frank Sinatra	Donna Reed
1954	*On the Waterfront*	Elia Kazan	Marlon Brando	Grace Kelly *(The Country Girl)*	Edmond O'Brien *(The Barefoot Contessa)*	Eva Marie Saint
1955	*Marty*	Delbert Mann	Ernest Borgnine	Anna Magnani *(The Rose Tattoo)*	Jack Lemmon *(Mister Roberts)*	Jo Van Fleet *(East of Eden)*
1956	*Around the World in 80 Days*	George Stevens *(Giant)*	Yul Brynner *(The King and I)*	Ingrid Bergman *(Anastasia)*	Anthony Quinn *(Lust for Life)*	Dorothy Malone *(Written on the Wind)*
1957	*The Bridge on the River Kwai*	David Lean	Alec Guinness	Joanne Woodward *(The Three Faces of Eve)*	Red Buttons *(Sayonara)*	Miyoshi Umekil *(Sayonara)*
1958	*Gigi*	Vincente Minnelli	David Niven *(Separate Tables)*	Susan Hayward *(I Want to Live!)*	Burl Ives *(The Big Country)*	Wendy Hiller *(Separate Tables)*

350

Year	Picture	Director	Best Actor	Best Actress	Best Supporting Actor	Best Supporting Actress
1959	*Ben-Hur*	William Wyler	Charlton Heston	Simone Signoret (*Room at the Top*)	Hugh Griffith	Shelley Winters (*The Diary of Anne Frank*)
1960	*The Apartment*	Billy Wilder	Burt Lancaster (*Elmer Gantry*)	Elizabeth Taylor (*Butterfield 8*)	Peter Ustinov (*Spartacus*)	Shirley Jones (*Elmer Gantry*)
1961	*West Side Story*	Robert Wise; Jerome Robbins	Maximilian Schell (*Judgment at Nuremberg*)	Sophia Loren (*Two Women*)	George Chakiris	Rita Moreno
1962	*Lawrence of Arabia*	David Lean	Gregory Peck (*To Kill a Mockingbird*)	Anne Bancroft (*The Miracle Worker*)	Ed Begley (*Sweet Bird of Youth*)	Patty Duke (*The Miracle Worker*)
1963	*Tom Jones*	Tony Richardson	Sidney Poitier (*Lilies of the Field*)	Patricia Neal (*Hud*)	Melvyn Douglas (*Hud*)	Margaret Rutherford (*The V.I.P.s*)
1964	*My Fair Lady*	George Cukor	Rex Harrison	Julie Andrews (*Mary Poppins*)	Peter Ustinov (*Topkapi*)	Lila Kedrova (*Zorba the Greek*)
1965	*The Sound of Music*	Robert Wise	Lee Marvin (*Cat Ballou*)	Julie Christie (*Darling*)	Martin Balsam (*A Thousand Clowns*)	Shelley Winters (*A Patch of Blue*)
1966	*A Man for All Seasons*	Fred Zinnemann	Paul Scofield	Elizabeth Taylor (*Who's Afraid of Virginia Woolf?*)	Walter Matthau (*The Fortune Cookie*)	Sandy Dennis (*Who's Afraid of Virginia Woolf?*)
1967	*In the Heat of the Night*	Mike Nichols (*The Graduate*)	Rod Steiger	Katharine Hepburn (*Guess Who's Coming to Dinner?*)	George Kennedy (*Cool Hand Luke*)	Estelle Parsons (*Bonnie and Clyde*)

Table 1 (Continued)

Year	Picture	Director	Actor	Actress	Supporting Actor	Supporting Actress
1968	Oliver!	Carol Reed	Cliff Robertson (Charly)	Katharine Hepburn (The Lion in Winter)	Jack Albertson (The Subject Was Roses)	Ruth Gordon (Rosemary's Baby)
1969	Midnight Cowboy	John Schlesinger	John Wayne (True Grit)	Maggie Smith (The Prime of Miss Jean Brodie)	Gig Young (They Shoot Horses, Don't They?)	Goldie Hawn (Cactus Flower)
1970	Patton	Franklin J. Schaffner	George C. Scott	Glenda Jackson (Women in Love)	John Mills (Ryan's Daughter)	Helen Hayes (Airport)
1971	The French Connection	William Friedkin	Gene Hackman	Jane Fonda (Klute)	Ben Johnson (The Last Picture Show)	Cloris Leachman (The Last Picture Show)
1972	The Godfather	Bob Fosse (Cabaret)	Marlon Brando	Liza Minnelli (Cabaret)	Joel Grey (Cabaret)	Eileen Heckart (Butterflies Are Free)
1973	The Sting	George Roy Hill	Jack Lemmon (Save the Tiger)	Glenda Jackson (A Touch of Class)	John Houseman (The Paper Chase)	Tatum O'Neal (Paper Moon)
1974	The Godfather, Part Two	Francis F. Coppola	Art Carney (Harry and Tonto)	Ellen Burstyn (Alice Doesn't Live Here Anymore)	Robert De Niro	Ingrid Bergman (Murder on the Orient Express)
1975	One Flew Over the Cuckoo's Nest	Milos Forman	Jack Nicholson	Louise Fletcher	George Burns (The Sunshine Boys)	Lee Grant (Shampoo)

352

Year	Film	Director			
1976	Rocky	John Avildsen	Peter Finch (Network)	Faye Dunaway (Network)	Jason Robards (All the President's Men)	Beatrice Straight (Network)
1977	Annie Hall	Woody Allen	Richard Dreyfuss (The Goodbye Girl)	Diane Keaton	Jason Robards (Julia)	Vanessa Redgrave (Julia)
1978	The Deer Hunter	Michael Cimino	Jon Voight (Coming Home)	Jane Fonda (Coming Home)	Christopher Walken	Maggie Smith (California Suite)
1979	Kramer Vs. Kramer	Robert Benton	Dustin Hoffman	Sally Field (Norma Rae)	Melvyn Douglas (Being There)	Meryl Streep
1980	Ordinary People	Robert Redford	Robert De Niro (Raging Bull)	Sissy Spacek (Coal Miner's Daughter)	Timothy Hutton	Mary Steenburgen (Melvin and Howard)
1981	Chariots of Fire	Warren Beatty (Reds)	Henry Fonda (On Golden Pond)	Katharine Hepburn (On Golden Pond)	John Gielgud (Arthur)	Maureen Stapleton (Reds)
1982	Gandhi	Richard Attenborough	Ben Kingsley	Meryl Streep (Sophie's Choice)	Louis Gossett (An Officer and a Gentleman)	Jessica Lange (Tootsie)
1983	Terms of Endearment	Richard Brooks	Robert Duvall (Tender Mercies)	Shirley MacLaine	Jack Nicholson	Linda Hunt (The Year of Living Dangerously)
1984	Amadeus	Milos Forman	F. Murray Abraham	Sally Field (Places in the Heart)	Hang S. Ngor (The Killing Fields)	Peggy Ashcroft (A Passage to India)
1985	Out of Africa	Sydney Pollack	William Hurt (Kiss of the Spider Woman)	Geraldine Page (The Trip to Bountiful)	Don Ameche (Cocoon)	Anjelica Huston (Prizzi's Honor)

Table 1 (Continued)

Year	Picture	Director	Actor	Actress	Supporting Actor	Supporting Actress
1986	Platoon	Oliver Stone	Paul Newman (The Color of Money)	Marlee Matlin (Children of a Lesser God)	Michael Caine (Hannah and Her Sisters)	Dianne Wiest (Hannah and Her Sisters)
1987	The Last Emperor	Bernardo Bertolucci	Michael Douglas (Wall Street)	Cher (Moonstruck)	Sean Connery (The Untouchables)	Olympia Dukakis (Moonstruck)
1988	Rain Man	Barry Levinson	Dustin Hoffman (Rain Man)	Jodie Foster (The Accused)	Kevin Kline (A Fish Called Wanda)	Geena Davis (The Accidental Tourist)
1989	Driving Miss Daisy	Oliver Stone (Born on the Fourth of July)	Daniel Day-Lewis (My Left Foot)	Jessica Tandy	Denzel Washington (Glory)	Brenda Fricker (My Left Foot)
1990	Dances With Wolves	Kevin Costner	Jeremy Irons (Reversal of Fortune)	Kathy Bates (Misery)	Joe Pesci (GoodFellas)	Whoopi Goldberg (Ghost)
1991	The Silence of the Lambs	Jonathan Demme	Anthony Hopkins	Jodie Foster	Jack Palance (City Slickers)	Mercedes Ruehl (The Fisher King)
1992	Unforgiven	Clint Eastwood	Al Pacino (Scent of a Woman)	Emma Thompson (Howards End)	Gene Hackman	Marisa Tomei (My Cousin Vinny)

Year	Picture	Director	Actor	Actress	*Supporting* Actor	*Supporting* Actress
1993	*Schindler's List*	Steven Spielberg	Tom Hanks (*Philadelphia*)	Holly Hunter (*The Piano*)	Tommy Lee Jones (*The Fugitive*)	Anna Paquin (*The Piano*)
1994	*Forrest Gump*	Robert Zemeckis	Tom Hanks	Jessica Lange (*Blue Sky*)	Martin Landau (*Ed Wood*)	Dianne Wiest (*Bullets over Broadway*)
1995	*Braveheart*	Mel Gibson	Nicolas Cage (*Leaving Los Vegas*)	Susan Sarandon (*Dead Man Walking*)	Kevin Spacey (*The Usual Suspects*)	Mira Sorvino (*Mighty Aphrodite*)
1996	*The English Patient*	Anthony Minghella	Geoffrey Rush (*Shine*)	Frances McDormand (*Fargo*)	Cuba Gooding Jr. (*Jerry Maguire*)	Juliette Binoche
1997	*Titanic*	James Cameron	Jack Nicholson (*As Good As It Gets*)	Helen Hunt (*As Good As It Gets*)	Robin Williams (*Good Will Hunting*)	Kim Basinger (*L.A. Confidential*)
1998	*Shakespeare in Love*	Steven Spielberg (*Saving Private Ryan*)	Roberto Benigni (*Life Is Beautiful*)	Gwyneth Paltrow	James Coburn (*Affliction*	Judi Dench
1999	*American Beauty*	Sam Mendes	Kevin Spacey	Hilary Swank (*Boys Don't Cry*)	Michael Caine (*Cider House Rules*)	Angelina Jolie (*Girl, Interrupted*)

Table 2: *Best Picture Nominees by Genre (in percentage)*

Genre	Nominees	Winners	All
Drama	48.9	38.9	47.1
Comedy	18.0	13.9	17.3
Historical	9.4	15.3	10.4
Musical	7.7	11.1	8.3
Action-Adventure	6.3	5.5	6.2
War	4.6	8.3	5.2
Suspense	3.1	2.8	3.1
Western	2.0	4.2	2.4
Total	100.0	100.0	100.0
	(350)	(72)	(422)

Table 3: *The Oscar Winning Films by Number of Nominations and Commercial Appeal*

Year	Film	Nominations	Awards	Domestic Rentals*
1927/8	Wings	2	2	†
1928/9	Broadway Melody	3	1	3.00
1929/30	All Quiet On The Western Front	4	2	1.50
1930/1	Cimarron	6	3	2.00
1931/2	Grand Hotel	1	1	2.20
1932/3	Cavalcade	4	3	3.50
1934	It Happened One Night	5	5	†
1935	Mutiny on the Bounty	7	1	†
1936	The Great Ziegfeld	7	3	†
1937	The Life of Emil Zola	10	3	†
1938	You Can't Take It With You	7	2	†
1939	Gone with the Wind	11	8	76.70
1940	Rebecca	10	2	1.50
1941	How Green Was My Valley	10	5	2.80
1942	Mrs. Miniver	12	6	5.50
1943	Casablanca	8	3	3.70
1944	Going My Way	9	7	6.50
1945	The Lost Weekend	6	4	4.30
1946	Best Years of Our Lives	9	7	11.30
1947	A Gentleman's Agreement	8	3	3.90
1948	Hamlet	7	4	3.25
1949	All the King's Men	7	4	2.40

* in millions of dollars
† no data

Year	Film	Nominations	Awards	Domestic Rentals
1950	All About Eve	14	6	2.90
1951	An American in Paris	8	6	4.50
1952	The Greatest Show on Earth	5	2	14.00
1953	From Here To Eternity	13	8	12.20
1954	On the Waterfront	11	8	4.50
1955	Marty	8	4	2.00
1956	Around the World in 80 Days	8	5	23.12
1957	The Bridge on the River Kwai	8	7	17.19
1958	Gigi	9	9	7.30
1959	Ben Hur	12	11	36.65
1960	The Apartment	10	5	6.65
1961	West Side Story	11	10	19.45
1962	Lawrence of Arabia	10	7	16.70
1963	Tom Jones	10	4	16.95
1964	My Fair Lady	12	8	12.00
1965	The Sound of Music	10	5	79.75
1966	A Man For All Seasons	8	6	12.75
1967	In the Heat of the Night	7	5	10.91
1968	Oliver!	11	6	16.80
1969	Midnight Cowboy	7	3	20.32
1970	Patton	10	7	28.10
1971	The French Connection	8	5	26.31
1972	The Godfather	10	3	86.27
1973	The Sting	10	7	78.20
1974	The Godfather, Part Two	11	6	30.67
1975	One Flew Over the Cuckoo's Nest	9	5	59.24
1976	Rocky	10	3	55.92
1977	Annie Hall	5	4	18.09
1978	The Deer Hunter	9	5	27.53
1979	Kramer vs. Kramer	9	5	60.00
1980	Ordinary People	6	4	23.12
1981	Chariots of Fire	7	4	30.60
1982	Gandhi	11	8	24.75
1983	Terms of Endearment	11	5	50.25
1984	Amadeus	11	8	22.82
1985	Out of Africa	11	7	43.10
1986	Platoon	8	4	69.74
1987	The Last Emperor	9	9	18.82
1988	Rain Man	8	4	43.60*

Year	Film	Nominations	Awards	Domestic Rentals
1988	*Rain Man*	8	4	86.81
1989	*Driving Miss Daisy*	9	4	50.50
1990	*Dances With Wolves*	12	7	91.53
1991	*The Silence of the Lambs*	7	5	9.88
1992	*Unforgiven*	9	4	44.40
1993	*Schindler's List*	12	7	44.16
1994	*Forrest Gump*	13	6	156.00
1995	*Braveheart*	10	5	31.81
1996	*The English Patient*	12	9	32.76
1997	*Titanic*	14	11	
1998	*Shakespeare in Love*	13	7	
1999	*American Beauty*	8	5	66.62*

*Still in release

Table 4: *The Most Nominated Films, 1927–2000*

10 nominations: 29 movies

Year	Film	Nom.	Oscars
1937	*The Life of Emil Zola*	10	3
1939	*Mr. Smith Goes to Washington*	10	1
1940	*Rebecca*	10	2
1941	*How Green Was My Valley*	10	5
1943	*The Song of Bernadette*	10	4
1953	*Roman Holiday*	10	3
1956	*Giant*	10	1
1957	*Sayonara*	10	4
1960	*The Apartment*	10	5
1962	*Lawrence of Arabia*	10	7
1963	*Tom Jones*	10	4
1965	*Dr. Zhivago*	10	5
	The Sound of Music	10	5
1967	*Bonnie and Clyde*	10	2
	Guess Who's Coming to Dinner	10	2
1969	*Anne of the Thousand Days*	10	1
1970	*Airport*	10	1
	Patton	10	7

Year	Film	Nom.	Oscars
1972	*Cabaret*	10	8
	The Godfather	10	3
1973	*The Exorcist*	10	2
	The Sting	10	7
1976	*Network*	10	4
	Rocky	10	3
1978	*Heaven Can Wait*	10	1
1981	*On Golden Pond*	10	3
1982	*Tootsie*	10	1
1991	*Bugsy*	10	2
1995	*Braveheart*	10	5

11 nominations: 19 movies

Year	Film	Nom.	Oscars
1939	*Gone with the Wind*	11	8
1941	*Sergeant York*	11	2
1942	*The Pride of the Yankees*	11	1
1950	*Sunset Boulevard*	11	3
1954	*On the Waterfront*	11	8
1961	*West Side Story*	11	10
1968	*Oliver!*	11	5
1974	*Chinatown*	11	1
	The Godfather, Part II	11	6
1977	*Julia*	11	3
	Star Wars	11	7
	The Turning Point	11	0
1982	*Gandhi*	11	8
1983	*Terms of Endearment*	11	5
1984	*Amadeus*	11	8
	A Passage to India	11	2
1985	*The Color Purple*	11	0
	Out of Africa	11	7
1998	*Saving Private Ryan*	11	5

12 nominations: 9 movies

Year	Film	Nom.	Oscars
1942	*Mrs. Miniver*	12	6
1948	*Johnny Belinda*	12	1

Year	Film	Nom.	Oscars
1951	*A Streetcar Named Desire*	12	4
1959	*Ben-Hur*	12	11
1964	*My Fair Lady*	12	8
1981	*Reds*	12	3
1990	*Dances With Wolves*	12	7
1993	*Schindler's List*	12	7
1996	*The English Patient*	12	9

13 nominations: 5 movies

1953	*From Here to Eternity*	13	8
1961	*Judgment at Nuremberg*	13	2
1964	*Mary Poppins*	13	5
1994	*Forrest Gump*	13	6
1998	*Shakespeare in Love*	13	7

14 nominations: 2 movies

1950	*All About Eve*	14	6
1997	*Titanic*	14	11

Index

362

365

366

369